Feminist Film Studies

Feminist Film Studies is a readable, yet comprehensive textbook for introductory classes in feminist film theory and criticism.

Karen Hollinger provides an accessible overview of women's representation and involvement in film, complemented by analyses of key texts that illustrate major topics in the field. Key areas include:

- a brief history of the development of feminist film theory
- the theorization of the male gaze and the female spectator
- women in genre films and literary adaptations
- the female biopic
- feminism and avant-garde and documentary film
- women as auteurs
- Black women in film
- lesbian representation
- women in Third Cinema.

Each chapter includes a "Films in Focus" section, which analyzes key texts related to the chapter's major topic, including examples from classical Hollywood, world cinema, and the contemporary period.

This book provides students in both film and gender/women's studies with a clear introduction to the field of feminist film theory and criticism.

Karen Hollinger is Professor of English in the Department of Languages, Literature, and Philosophy at Armstrong Atlantic State University, where she teaches courses on Film Studies, Gender and Women's Studies, Literary and Film Theory, American Literature, Television Studies and Popular Culture Studies.

Feminist Film Studies

Karen Hollinger

 Routledge
Taylor & Francis Group

LONDON AND NEW YORK

First published 2012
by Routledge
2 Park Square, Milton Park, Abingdon, Oxon OX14 4RN

Simultaneously published in the USA and Canada
by Routledge
711 Third Avenue, New York, NY 10017

Routledge is an imprint of the Taylor & Francis Group, an informa business

British Library Cataloguing in Publication Data
A catalogue record for this book is available from the British Library

Library of Congress Cataloging in Publication Data
Hollinger, Karen.
Feminist film studies / by Karen Hollinger.
p. cm.
Includes bibliographical references and index.
1. Feminist film criticism. 2. Feminism and motion pictures. 3. Motion pictures and women. 4. Women in motion pictures. 5. Feminist films--History and criticism. I. Title.
PN1995.9.W6H65 2012
791.43'6552--dc23
2012000723

ISBN: 978-0-415-57526-3 (hbk)
ISBN: 978-0-415-57528-7 (pbk)
ISBN: 978-0-203-14680-4 (ebk)

Typeset in Garamond
by Taylor & Francis Books

Contents

List of Illustrations

Acknowledgments

First of all, I want to thank Natalie Foster, who encouraged me to undertake this project in the first place and then offered her judicious advice and unfailing support throughout the writing process. I would also like to thank everyone at Taylor and Francis, especially Eileen Srebernik, for guiding the book so smoothly through the production process. Thanks also go to Armstrong Atlantic State University for providing several research and scholarship grants that afforded me the time to work on the book and the money for a summer research assistant. To that summer research assistant, Heather Benton, I also offer my gratitude for her careful contributions to the book's documentation and bibliography. The students in my Women and Film classes also deserve recognition for providing me with stimulating discussions of the material contained here and for encouraging me to undertake a project such as this. Without them, this book would never have been conceived, and it is intended to help other students like them to become acquainted with the important and fascinating field of feminist film studies.

Several chapters are extensions and revisions of material published in substantially different form elsewhere. A number of the ideas in the chapters on the woman's film, *Desert Hearts*, and *Thelma & Louise* were first discussed in *In the Company of Women: Contemporary Female Friendship Films* (Minneapolis: University of Minnesota Press, 1998) and those on the star-actress and Susan Sarandon's career found original expression in *The Actress: Hollywood Acting and the Female Star* (London and New York: Routledge, 2006). The psychoanalytic reading of *Vertigo* in Chapter 1 was first presented in "'The Look,' Narrativity, and The Female Spectator in *Vertigo*." *Journal of Film and Video* 39.4 (Fall 1987, 18–27): 18–27, the ideas on lesbian films were initially expressed in "Theorizing Mainstream Female Spectatorship: The Case of the Popular Lesbian Film" in *Cinema Journal* 37.2 (1998): 3–17, and an earlier consideration of the work of Margarethe von Trotta's cinematic presentation of relationships between women can be found in "Margarethe von Trotta and Films of Women's Friendship" in *Freundschaft: Motive und Bedeutungen* edited by Esther Wipfler (Munich: Scaneg Verlag, 2006).

The photos are from the Kobal Collection and were provided by The Picture Desk.

Finally, I would like to dedicate this book to my grandson Zachary, who is quite simply the best inspiration anyone could have. I would also like to thank my family Zach, Michael, Cathy, Geoff, and Walt for their support and for always being there to provide enjoyable companionship.

Introduction

In a period that many are calling postfeminist, even anti-feminist, or more positively neofemininist, it seems imperative that we look back at some of the ideas that feminist film theory and criticism have contributed to the study of film. Perhaps looking at feminism's contributions to film studies will make it less likely that feminism will so easily be chucked away as a movement of the past supplanted by a new wave of neo- or postfeminism that fashions itself more in touch with traditional femininity, and maybe the desire to reject traditional feminism will be seen as less appealing. Whatever conclusion the reader draws from this volume, it offers an admittedly eclectic consideration of some of the ways feminist criticism has shed a unique and enduring light on the representation of women in film and has elucidated the contributions of women filmmakers to the cinematic medium. It does not attempt to be exhaustive or comprehensive because such an endeavor would require a multi-volume encyclopedic study. Each of the book's chapters could easily be separate volumes in themselves because feminist film theory and criticism have expanded so widely that they have come to consider not just mainstream Hollywood cinema and its various genres, but also avant-garde and documentary film, women auteurs, the filmic representation of African American women, global cinema, lesbian films, and female stars, to name just some of major areas of analysis. *Feminist Film Studies* represents an attempt to look at some of the ideas of feminist film theory and criticism as they relate to various different types of film study. The book admittedly focuses on white, Western, heterosexual films, as feminist criticism itself has done until quite recently, but it also looks at lesbian, postcolonial, and African American cinema. Because feminist theory and criticism has had a white, Western, heterosexual focus, it is crucial not to minimize the importance of the study of lesbian, African American and postcolonial issues to feminist film study.

The book is organized into eight chapters, each of which focuses on a single area of feminist film study. Again, the selection of areas to be considered is eclectic as is the focus within the chapters. Because feminist film studies is such a broad and wide-ranging field and has made such extensive contributions to thinking about cinematic representations of women and the work of women involved in the film industry, one might focus on any number of areas or issues. I tried to zero in on some topics that I found particularly prominent, germinal, or, on the other hand, critically neglected. Additionally, each chapter contains a section entitled Films in Focus, which applies some of the ideas and concepts from the area of feminist film study under consideration to a particular film or films. The films were selected to illustrate important concepts prominent in the theoretical area under consideration and to serve as examples of possible ways specific areas of feminist film theory and criticism might inspire in-depth analysis of individual films.

The first chapter offers an overview of feminist film theory as it developed from its inception in the 1970s to the present time. It looks at some of the theoretical tools feminist critics have used to investigate films beginning with the images of women approach, moving to cinefeminism and psychoanalysis, and finally to the more recent emphasis on cultural studies. It examines the work of important feminist theorists like Molly Haskell, Claire Johnston, Laura Mulvey, and Christine Gledhill and considers their major ideas such as the male gaze, to-be-looked-at-ness, gendered spectatorship, and negotiation. The film in focus for this chapter is the Alfred Hitchcock classic *Vertigo*, a work of mainstream Hollywood cinema that feminist critics have given considerable attention and have seen in divergent ways as a particularly egregious example of Hollywood's employment of the misogynist male gaze or as a multifaceted work that does not merely utilize the male gaze but interrogates and critiques it. However one sees *Vertigo* in terms of its treatment of its female characters, it offers an excellent example of how a single film might be approached from different feminist perspectives.

The second chapter continues the focus on mainstream Hollywood and examines feminist analyses of Hollywood genre films. Here, the field from which one might choose is again wide. For instance, feminist critics have examined representations of women as femme fatales in film noir, objects of the male gaze in the musical, victims of male aggression in the horror film, and butt-kicking female heroes in action cinema, but the films that really seem to stand out are two interrelated genres that I argue actually represent two generations of a single women-oriented cinematic category. This category found its early incarnation in the woman's film or woman's picture of the 1930s–1950s and has been revived in the chick flicks of today. The chapter outlines the progression of Hollywood women's cinema from studio era woman's films through cycles of new woman's films, female friendship films, and literary adaptations to contemporary chick flicks. The focus for this chapter is the potential progressivity of these films and their relationship to their intended female audience. In the Films in Focus section, we examine the classic maternal melodrama *Stella Dallas*, a woman's film that inspired some heated feminist debate in regard to its effect on the female spectator. The chapter then looks at a prominent representative of the current wave of chick flicks, *The Devil Wears Prada*. The focus here is not only on these films as particular generational incarnations of Hollywood female-oriented cinema, but also on whether the woman's film and the chick flick really do form a continuum or whether they represent very different directions in terms of their representation of women. Does the chick flick embody a progressive move away from antiquated woman's film themes, or is it merely a reworking of these same ideas in a more contemporary guise?

Chapter 3 considers avant-garde and documentary filmmaking, areas that many feminist critics and filmmakers turned to as potentially progressive alternatives to mainstream filmmaking. The chapter examines the attractions and problems for women filmmakers involved in avant-garde filmmaking as well as the rise of the feminist avant-garde and its relation to the larger context of experimental cinema. It also delineates the major characteristics of feminist avant-garde cinema with particular attention to the development of feminist theory films, a group of films that arose in the 1960s and was directly influenced by feminist theoretical concepts. While some feminist filmmakers turned to experimental films as an alternative to Hollywood, others embraced the realist aesthetic of documentary filmmaking as a way to portray women's lives more authentically. The second part of Chapter 3 examines the development of the feminist documentary movement, its attractions for feminist filmmakers, and the question of the effectiveness of the documentary as a form of progressive cinema for women. The chapter also looks at feminist involvement in the realist versus anti-realist debate which is centered on the issue of directorial intervention or non-intervention in documentary films. The problems with documentary realism from a feminist perspective are discussed as are feminist suspicions that the realist aesthetic advocated by many documentary filmmakers covers over patriarchal biases in ways similar to the operation of illusionism in mainstream films. The Films in Focus section of this chapter analyzes three films: Maya Deren's classic avant-garde masterpiece *Meshes of the Afternoon*, Chantal Akerman's feminist theory film, *Je, tu, il, elle*, and Barbara Kopple's realist documentary *Shut Up & Sing*. In analyzing these films, focus is placed on the nature and effectiveness of their challenge to mainstream filmmaking practices.

Chapter 4 looks at some of the major aspects of lesbian film theory as they relate to the theorization of lesbian cinema. It examines a wide range of issues including the contributions of lesbian film criticism to feminist film studies, its recent hybrid identity and affiliation with queer studies, debates concerning the usefulness of psychoanalysis for lesbian film analysis, theoretical disagreements about the relationship between lesbian films and other categories of women's cinema, distinctions among different types of lesbian films, and finally the theorization of the lesbian spectator, the lesbian look, and the coupled lesbian subject position. The Films in Focus section for this chapter analyzes the controversy over the progressivity of the ground-breaking lesbian romance film *Desert Hearts*, which still remains one of the most popular lesbian films of all time.

The next chapter, Chapter 5, considers two types of Hollywood film with wide appeal to female audiences that have received limited attention from feminist critics: the literary adaptation and the biopic. The chapter examines in particular the films' relationship to feminism and their female viewers. Consideration of the literary adaptation begins with a discussion of the usefulness of the fidelity approach to adaptation study. Then, focus is placed on cinematic adaptations of nineteenth-century novels by or about women, most notably the cottage industry of Jane Austen adaptations that hit the screen beginning in the 1990s and continues to the present time. Explanations for the remarkable popularity of the Austen phenomenon are placed within the context of theorizations of literary adaptations in general and the heritage film in particular, a British genre that has stirred considerable controversy for its presentation of contemporary social, historical, and gender issues within period settings. The chapter also examines the women's biopic, yet another critically neglected cinematic form. It considers positive and negative evaluations of biopics of women and calls into question the characterization of women's biopics as dominated by female victimization. The Films in Focus section examines *Sense and Sensibility* as a germinal film in the contemporary cycle of Jane Austen adaptations and considers the effects the changes made from the novel had in increasing the film's popularity with female viewers. A second film analyzed in the Films in Focus section is *Frida*, an example of a female artist biopic that could easily be seen as following the victimology formula, but that actually offers a much more complex portrayal of its female subject than this characterization would suggest.

Chapter 6 examines two crucially important areas of film studies that have only recently been given sufficient attention: the representation of African American women in film and women of color in global cinema. It presents an overview of African American and postcoloinal feminist critical discussions of the racial marginalization and negative stereotyping that has existed and still exists not only within larger social structures but also within feminist critical circles as well. The chapter looks at attempts of feminist theorists to counteract these problems through the development of concepts such as the imperialist and oppositional gaze, transnationalism, hybridity, trauma theory, and post-Third Worldist feminism. Feminist film studies of race include not only looking at representations of women of color in films by male filmmakers, but also examining the works of female filmmakers of color. The Films in Focus section of this chapter examines two films by important feminist filmmakers whose works deal prominently with racial issues. First, it considers African American director Julie Dash's important feminist theory film *Illusions*, which uses a revision of the traditional passing narrative, an emphasis on Black female bonding, and a repudiation of the White male gaze to cast new light on the role of Black women both as they have been envisioned on screen and as they have been employed in the Hollywood film industry. The second work analyzed is diasporic Indian filmmaker

Deepa Mehta's *Fire*, a post-Third Worldist film that examines the role of women in postcolonial Indian society through a portrayal of two women's rejection of their traditional roles within the extended Indian family. Both films are examples of the groundbreaking films being made by women filmmakers of color, and they illustrate as well the attempts of feminist critics to call attention to this work.

Chapter 7 considers the place of auteurism in feminist film studies. Auteurist criticism, the examination of the work of prominent film directors and the artistic stamp they leave on their films, has since the early days of film studies always found a prominent place in critical and theoretical approaches to cinema. Determining a pantheon of great directors and analyzing their films in the context of their entire body of work remains a crucial part of film criticism even today. Feminist critics have had mixed reactions to this approach, regarding it, on the one hand, as a way that male critics have exercised a distinctly masculine bias in only recognizing the work of male auteurs and denying women recognition among the directorial greats. Other feminist critics have embraced auteurism as a useful method for calling attention to the work of neglected women directors by analyzing their films for their unique artistic stamp, a stamp that may or may not show decidedly feminist thematic content. Feminist auteurism has also been useful in promoting the study of contemporary women directors and advocating their elevation to the status of auteurs by showing how their films contain distinctly artistic qualities. The chapter discusses not only the attractions and disadvantages of feminist auteurism, but also looks at the importance of critical analyses of the work of Dorothy Arzner, the most accomplished female director of the Hollywood studio era. Critical work on Arzner's films has established her as a notable female auteur who managed to leave a definite feminist stamp on her films even though she remained within the mold of the Hollywood studio system. Her subversive narrative and stylistic strategies have been seen as models for contemporary feminist auteurism. The Films in Focus section of this chapter examines the work of the renowned German woman filmmaker, Margarethe von Trotta, who like Arzner was able to express a subversive feminist vision while remaining within the bounds of mainstream filmmaking. Because auteurism advocates examining not just a single film by a given director, but that director's whole body of work in order to extract a distinctive artistic stamp, the examination of von Trotta's work does not zero in on a single film, but rather looks at significant films within her oeuvre as they exemplify her artistic vision and its feminist dimensions.

The final chapter (Chapter 8) considers the often overlooked role of the actress as a major figure in the filmmaking process. Actresses have always been seen as important to the development of cinema, but their role in shaping the form and content of their films has largely been ignored. Auteurism has so strongly established the director as the artistic force behind a film that actors have been relegated to the level of pawns in the filmmaker's overall design. This chapter attempts to call much-needed attention to the role of the actress, especially the star actress, in shaping the final film text. It also examines critical and theoretical approaches to the cinematic presence of the actress, notably the emphasis on physical beauty rather than acting skill, the differences between considerations of male and female stars, film stardom as opposed to the status of television personalities, the association of certain actresses with various acting styles, and the prominence of critical studies of individual star actresses. The Films in Focus section examines the importance of the work of a major Hollywood star actress in shaping the final form of a particular film. We examine the career of Susan Sarandon and her crucial role in the creation of the mainstream feminist blockbuster *Thelma & Louise*.

It is hoped that this overview of feminist film studies will not lead its readers in any way to believe that they have now gotten the final or definitive word on feminist film analysis, but rather that it will serve as a stimulus to further investigation into this important and fascinating field of study. If I had only one thing to say to my reader, it would be not to stop with this book, but go on to explore a wide range of feminist approaches to film in greater depth. It has been my intention to stimulate in my reader a desire for an even more extensive exploration of feminist film theory and criticism than these pages are able to provide. If this book accomplishes that goal in any sense, it will have done its job.

Chapter 1

What is Feminist Film Theory?

The history of feminist film theory begins in the 1970s and parallels the development of film theory itself as an academic discipline. It stems from the woman's movement of the 1960s and was influenced by germinal feminist works like Simone De Beauvoir's *The Second Sex*, Betty Friedan's *The Feminine Mystique*, and Kate Millett's *Sexual Politics*. Providing the basis for feminist examinations of film were De Beauvoir's concept of women as "other," Friedan's discussion of the social mythology that works to bind women to a "natural" female role of passivity and maternal nurturing under a dominant patriarch, and especially Millett's examination of how the ideology of femininity is instilled in women through many forms of cultural texts from scientific theories to literary works (McCabe 2004: 3–5). From these sources and others, feminist film scholars began to shape their analyses of how film texts work to instill patriarchal ideology in female viewers, an approach known in literary scholarship as feminist critique. Yet the beginnings of feminist film theory were also influenced by the development in the 1970s of alternative feminist filmmaking by such prominent figures as Laura Mulvey and Sally Potter among others. So feminist film theory always had a dual composition: the critique of mainstream cinema and the advocacy of an alternate or counter-cinema.

Really, if there is one characteristic that dominates in the history of feminist film theory, it is this dualism, which takes many forms, including this split between the critical analysis of mainstream texts and a more activist agenda of promoting films by female filmmakers who offer alternate visions of a feminist women's cinema (Mayne 1994b: 50). Other dualisms exist as well, for example, between an emphasis on amassing more and more evidence of women's exclusion and distorted representation in mainstream cinema as opposed to uncovering ways in which these films deconstruct themselves by exhibiting contradictions, gaps and tensions within patriarchal ideology (Mayne 1994b: 51). Other critics set out to examine films that in spite of the overwhelmingly patriarchal dimensions of mainstream cinema still manage to speak to female audiences in various ways. Because feminist film theory was at its inception so tied to feminist film practice, there has also always been a questioning of what the relationship between theory and practice should actually involve. Should feminist theory devote itself to exposing the workings of mainstream film or to analyzing and thus promoting the work of alternative feminist filmmakers? Quickly, two theoretical strains developed to address these issues: the American quasi-sociological images of women approach and the British psychoanalytic and semiotic direction, strongly influenced by 1970s trends in film theory such as structuralism and poststructuralism.

The Images of Women Approach

The division between these two strands of 1970s feminist film theory represents the major structuring design of feminist film theory throughout the twentieth century, and it is a division which we will examine in some depth because it involves an essential disagreement about the critical methodology feminist theorists should employ. Beyond the general definition of feminist film theory as a mode of theoretical speculation that makes gender its investigative focus, the exact method of that investigation has been from the beginning disputed. The earliest critical stance came to be known as the images of women approach or reflection theory. It is a broadly sociological approach that sees film texts as simple reflections of social reality and critiques mainstream Hollywood films for presenting images of women that are, in fact, not reflections, but distortions of women's real lives which work to support patriarchal ideology. Its main representatives are Marjorie Rosen's *Popcorn Venus* (1973) and Molly Haskell's *From Reverence to Rape: The Treatment of Women in the Movies* (1974). Both Rosen and Haskell focus exclusively on Hollywood films and undertake survey analyses of movies from the silent period to the 1970s. Influenced by Kate Millett's conception of gender ideology as a conscious male conspiracy, Rosen takes a more condemnatory stance than Haskell. She sees the history of Hollywood representations of women as part of an overarching design to mold female audiences into docile, willing victims of male dominance through the presentation of negative female stereotypes (Thornham 1997: 14).

It is Haskell's somewhat more nuanced study that has attained a more prominent position in feminist theory. Although, like Rosen, Haskell traces a chronology of women's distorted representations in Hollywood films beginning in the silent period, she does not posit a conscious male conspiracy to use film images as a means of social control. She does, however, outline a trajectory from what she sees as the veneration of women in silent films to the misogynistic violence inflicted upon them in films of the 1960s and 1970s. Haskell argues that the latter film portrayals represent a backlash against women's gains in the real world; however, she also sees considerable resistance to distorted portrayals of women by prominent actresses and an expression of female concerns in certain films. Her most notable example of films that express women's concerns are the woman's films of the 1930s and 1940s, a major film genre that took as its subject issues felt to be important to women, focused on female protagonists, and targeted female audiences. For Haskell, actresses like Katherine Hepburn, Joan Crawford, and Barbara Stanwyck, working within the woman's film, created strong independent heroines who offered female moviegoers alternatives to negative female stereotypes. There were obvious problems with Haskell's rather simplistic and theoretically naive approach in which she consciously distances herself from feminism and looks back on the period of silent film as a utopia of male adoration for the pure, helpless and innocent woman, characterized most notably by Lillian Gish's roles in D.W. Griffith's films. Her survey approach is also problematic in that it seems to devolve into plot summaries of individual films. At the same time, however, Haskell's pioneering work is significant in a number of ways. First, she presents a then much needed critique of the violence being perpetrated against female characters in films of the 1960s and 1970s. Second, as we will see in our chapter on women and genre films, the attention she calls to the woman's film, a genre denigrated by the industry and almost universally ridiculed by male critics, began what came to be an extremely fruitful feminist examination of this important Hollywood genre (White 1998: 118). Third, her appreciation for the work of actresses and other women behind the scenes in the industry, especially screenwriters, also established directions later critics would follow (Kaplan 2008: 17).

As Diane Waldman pointed out as early as 1978, the really insurmountable problem with Haskell and Rosen's work and the images of women approach as a whole stems from its limited conception of representations of women onscreen as stereotypes and its simplistic advocacy of positive images. Both Rosen and Haskell suggest that Hollywood should be forced to change and present images that offer more positive role models for women, but they fail to explain what exactly these images would be. Do films really faithfully reflect outside reality? Wouldn't different social groups have different notions of what a positive image is? Isn't it too restrictive to expect filmmakers to construct films according to a checklist of positive characteristics for female characters? Even if this checklist could be constructed, do viewers really identify with film characters in such a way that they see them as role models? Does this concept of positive images help us to develop the critical tools needed to investigate film meanings? The myriad questions regarding the images of women approach opened it up almost immediately to devastating criticism from British feminists who turned to poststructuralism, semiotics, and psychoanalysis to fashion a more theoretically informed methodology for analyzing female representations on screen.

Cinefeminism

To a large extent, it was in reaction to the untheoretical nature of the images of women approach that cinefeminism developed. Whereas the major figures in the images of women approach were all American, major theorists of cinefeminism were all British: Claire Johnston, Pam Cook, and Laura Mulvey. Drawing on ideas drawn from contemporary philosophy and literary theory, these critics adopted a methodology that was still entirely textually based in that, like the images of women approach, it proposed close analysis of individual film texts, but it conceived of itself as moving beyond the simple enumeration of stereotypes of women presented in films to an analysis of how films work ideologically to construct women as signs in a complex textual system that supports and even naturalizes patriarchal ideology by defining women as other to men. Rather than seeing cinema as referring to reality, these critics saw it as a construction reflective of male fantasies and desires that are projected onto female figures on screen. By uncovering the work of these filmic fantasies through the use of deconstruction, semiotics, and psychoanalysis, cinefeminist critics believed they could expose the processes that underlie women's misrepresentation in film.

The most important theorist to launch an attack on the images of women approach from a cinefeminist perspective was Claire Johnston in her ground-breaking 1973 essay "Women's Cinema as Counter-Cinema." Johnston argues against the realist aesthetic employed by the images of women theorists, contending that female images in film do not reflect women's reality at all, but are instead myths constructed by patriarchal ideology and manipulated for the satisfaction of male desires. Johnston specifically looked at the films of John Ford and Howard Hawks, two major Hollywood auteurs of the studio era, and showed how women exist in their films as signs meaningful only within male fantasy and not as significant in themselves. For Ford, women represent home, culture, and civilization, and through them, he expresses male ambivalence to such things. For Hawks, women are intruders in male groups, who must either become one of the boys or be seen as traumatic presences that must be eliminated (Johnston 1990b: 27).

Johnston does not just enumerate instances of women's portrayal as male fantasy figures; she goes on to call for feminist action against these representations. To this end, she initiated the study of female filmmakers working within the Hollywood system, a direction that would have far-ranging influence on feminist criticism. She looks, for instance, at the work of Dorothy Arzner and Ida Lupino for feminist inspiration. According to Johnston, Arzner created internally self-critical films that on the surface seem to support patriarchal ideology but underneath contain moments of resistance. This is an important concept drawn from the work of French Marxist critics in the film journal *Cahiers du cinema*, and it would have great resonance with feminist critics. The *Cahiers* critics proposed that films can be divided into essentially two categories: ideologically innocuous films that totally support the dominant ideology and internally self-critical films that seem to support the dominant way of thinking but turn out to have gaps, fissures, and "structuring absences" that critique it from within (Cook and Johnstone 1990: 26). Johnston proposed that studying Hollywood films, both those by male and female directors, should lead feminist theorists to an activist position from which they would advocate new feminist filmmaking techniques operating on all levels, both within and outside of the male dominated film industry, to create revolutionary films that would demystify the workings of patriarchal ideology (1990b: 33).

Johnston's work was quickly followed by Laura Mulvey's ground-breaking 1975 essay "Visual Pleasure and Narrative Cinema." Mulvey moved feminist criticism firmly into the realm of cinepsychoanalysis, employing key Freudian and Lacanian psychoanalytic terms like the Oedipus Complex, the mirror stage, castration anxiety, fetishism, voyeurism, and scopophilia to describe the workings of mainstream film. In "Visual Pleasure," Mulvey articulates her now famous, or infamous, pronouncement that in Hollywood cinema the gaze is male. She argues for the deep-rooted nature of patriarchal ways of viewing narrative films and for the intimate connection among the male gaze, the patriarchal unconscious and spectatorial pleasure. For Mulvey, the spectator position offered by Hollywood cinema is masculine with female characters positioned merely as objects of male desire. From the perspective of male characters with whom the spectator is encouraged to identify, the sight of the female body represents two things: "to-be-looked-at-ness" (woman as spectacle) and beneath this surface glamour the horror of female lack, evoking castration anxiety (the male fear of his own possible lack of phallic power). To counteract this evocation, two means are employed, one visual and the other narrative. The first is fetishistic scopophilia, disavowal of castration by the substitution of a glamorized female form for the feared object through the reduction of the female star to pure spectacle. The second is sadistic voyeurism, the narrative investigation of the feared female object in order to reenact the original castration trauma, reassert control (usually by punishing her), and thereby disavow castration (Mulvey 1989d: 21). Mulvey's essay has been extremely influential on feminist film theory and on film theory in general because it not only confronts head-on the crucial questions of pleasure, spectatorship, and gender identity in mainstream cinema but draws these terms together into a relational whole. Her work has also been highly productive in that it stimulated the most hotly contested debates in feminist theory throughout the 1980s and 1990s. These debates center on three issues raised in Mulvey's essay: the male gaze, feminist counter-cinema, and the female spectator. Each of these issues has led to notable developments in feminist film theory, as well as considerable disagreement.

"Visual Pleasure and Narrative Cinema" almost immediately met with some serious objections to its radical notion that in Hollywood cinema the gaze is male. Mulvey's totalizing conception of the workings of the Hollywood system as dominated by male structures of seeing struck many as hopelessly pessimistic, leaving the female image, as well as the female spectator, in a position of silence, masochism, and complete absorption within male fantasy.

Mulvey seemed to hold out no hope of progressive change in regard to the representation of women within the mainstream. Her use of psychoanalytic concepts also was seriously challenged. For instance, David Rodowick claims her concept of the male gaze involves a misunderstanding of Freud, who, according to Rodowick, did not break down desire into active/male and passive/female binaries and would never pair voyeurism with fetishism as Mulvey does (2000: 195). More recently, Clifford T. Manlove argues that Mulvey's account of the visual drive in psychoanalysis overemphasizes the role of pleasure (2007: 84) and misinterprets Lacan, who never described the gaze as gendered. According to Manlove, Lacan proposed that everyone looks, not just men, and everyone fears castration (2007: 90). Mulvey's idea of the male gaze has also been attacked for reducing Hollywood cinema to a monstrous anti-female monolith, ignoring socio-historical changes that have influenced cinematic portrayals, and failing to explain why women would ever enjoy, or even watch, films that represent them only as male fantasy figures and castration threats. Many also quarried whether there might be a female gaze in Hollywood films, perhaps directed at handsome male stars, who are clearly coded for to-be-looked-at-ness, like their female counterparts. Others, like B. Ruby Rich, proposed as early as 1978 that feminist critics needed to move away from repeatedly showing how patriarchal cinema eliminates women from the screen and start looking for ways to "go beyond" this negativity (Citron et al. 1999: 116).

In spite of these serious objections, Mulvey's argument is still important at least as a polemical gesture that stimulated thinking about the gender division within Hollywood film. E. Ann Kaplan in *Women and Film: Both Sides of the Camera* was one of the staunchest defenders of Mulvey's ideas and of the use of psychoanalysis in feminist film studies. For Kaplan, psychoanalysis is an essential tool that feminists can use to understand the patriarchal underpinnings of Hollywood films and to show how they oppress women and even persuade them to take pleasure in their own objectification (1983: 124). Similarly and much more recently, Annette Kuhn argued that while the concept of the male gaze may be limiting, it still raises important questions about the encounter between films and their spectators and how sexual difference organizes this encounter (2004: 1227). The usefulness of the theory of the male gaze continues to be debated. Perhaps, Judith Mayne makes the most cogent point in characterizing psychoanalysis as both limiting and "enormously productive" for feminist film theory (2004: 1263). As she sees it, the real issue is not whether feminists should be for or against psychoanalysis but determining if they can bring a new perspective to its use in film scholarship (Mayne 1994b: 57).

At the end of "Visual Pleasure and Narrative Cinema," Mulvey goes so far in her rejection of Hollywood film as to call for a radical filmmaking practice that breaks down the structures of mainstream cinema, especially the voyeuristic-scopophilic look, and destroys cinematic pleasure as we know it.

This destruction would divorce the view of the camera and position of the spectator from identification with the look of the film's male characters and free them into a "passionate detachment" that would in turn allow for a more critical and thoughtful cinematic experience (Mulvey 1989a: 26). Mulvey goes far beyond Claire Johnston, who also called for a feminist counter-cinema that will disrupt mainstream film practice both on the narrative and formal levels by telling stories differently and presenting them visually in new ways. In contrast to Mulvey, Johnston argued that feminists could not just abandon mainstream filmmaking. While advocating a radical feminist counter-cinema, she believed feminist critics still need to investigate and feminist filmmakers still need to infiltrate mainstream filmmaking in order to combat women's objectification and introduce female desire and fantasy into Hollywood texts (Thornham 1997: 30). Mulvey went further and advocated the complete rejection of mainstream cinema and the sexist pleasures it offers, something many viewers both male and female are just not prepared to do. As Linda Williams has pointed out, Mulvey's argument, which sees Hollywood film as "all about staging the mastery of women," does not really get at the enormous appeal mainstream film has for men and women alike (2004: 1268). Not only does Mulvey fail to explain that appeal; she entirely rejects it.

We will discuss the issue of feminist counter-cinema more fully when we consider women filmmakers in avant-garde and documentary filmmaking, where a counter-cinema perspective has had great influence, but it will suffice to say here that the nature of oppositional feminist filmmaking has been much discussed and involves a consideration of what the exact nature of women's counter-cinema should be as well as the attitude women filmmakers should take to Hollywood films: Should they attempt to solve the problems of Hollywood cinema or develop an entirely new film practice that examines the structure of film language in a critical, self-reflexive way that is not simply a reaction to mainstream models (Mayne 1994b: 57)? This issue is one that Mulvey's article first raised, and like the question of the female gaze, it remains a subject of intense feminist debate.

It is the situation of the female spectator, however, that has been the most controversial issue to arise from "Visual Pleasure and Narrative Cinema." Mulvey's essay has given birth to a veritable cottage industry of essays on the positioning of the female spectator, whom Mulvey seems to regard as condemned to the unenviable position of absorption in male fantasy. What Mulvey offers the female spectator is really no position at all. If she wants to watch mainstream films, she must assume a male subject position because that is all that is offered to her. Where could feminist critics go from here, and who, in fact, was this female spectator that Mulvey introduced, then denied, and feminist critics have since been trying to theorize? As ideas about female spectatorship continued to be formulated, it became increasingly clear that the female spectator being discussed was not the actual viewer sitting in the audience (the empirical spectator) but the textually created spectator, what in literary studies would be called the implied reader. As Mary Ann Doane explains: "I have never thought of the female spectator as synonymous with the woman sitting in front of the screen, munching her popcorn. ... It is a concept which is totally foreign to the epistemological framework of the new ethnographic analysis of audiences. ... The female spectator is a concept, not a person ... " (1989: 142–43). Or as Guiliana Bruno suggests, the female spectator is "an effect of discourse, a position, a hypothetical site of address of the filmic discourse" (1989: 105). After Mulvey foregrounded the existence of this female spectator, or for Mulvey really her virtual non-existence, feminist critics attempted to theorize her textual construction more thoroughly.

This project was first undertaken by Mulvey herself in "Afterthoughts on 'Visual Pleasure and Narrative Cinema' Inspired by King Vidor's *Duel in the Sun* (1946)," her 1981 follow-up to "Visual Pleasure and Narrative Cinema." Rethinking the idea of Hollywood cinema as a monolithic apparatus uniformly producing male subject positions and excluding female ones, Mulvey proposed, instead, a theory of female spectatorship that involves an oscillation between masculine and feminine poles of spectator positioning. Based on the Freudian theory of the girl's movement through a masculine phallic phase to the acceptance of a feminine sexual identity, Mulvey posits a greater tendency for female spectators to adopt bisexual identifications. The female spectator is said to oscillate between identification with the female image and the male figure of active looking and desire. In other words, active female spectatorship involves masculinization, and while the female audience may be "restless in its transvestite clothes" (Mulvey 1989a: 129), as Mulvey suggests, they really have no alternative but passive identification with their own cinematic objectification, with to-be-looked-at-ness.

In "Film and the Masquerade" (originally published in 1982), Mary Ann Doane argued not for oscillation, but for over-identification. According to Doane, mainstream film offers a female spectator position that allows women only one alternative – a narcissistic over-identification with the image of their like projected on the screen. As Doane sees it, "the female look demands a becoming" and as a result does not possess the distance that characterizes the voyeuristic male gaze: "For the female spectator, there is a certain over-presence of the image – she is the image" (1990: 45). This lost distance, Doane argues, might be recoverable if women on screen were perceived differently. Drawing on Joan Riviere's concept of femininity as masquerade, Doane advocates a perception of cinematic femaleness as "excess." This filmic "flaunting" of femininity could be used to achieve the distance lacking in dominant cinematic constructions of the female image and might allow for the "denial of the production of femininity as closeness, as presence-to-itself, as precisely imagistic" (Doane 1990: 49).

In *Alice Doesn't: Feminism, Semiotics, Cinema*, Teresa de Lauretis transformed the concept of female spectatorship from oscillation to double identification, simultaneous alignment with an active masculine gaze and figure of narrative movement as well as with a passive feminine image and figure of narrative closure (1984: 144). This double identification does not make mainstream cinema any less patriarchal than it is in Mulvey's formulation because de Lauretis still insists that visual as well as narrative pleasure in Hollywood film is male. The traditional Hollywood film reactivates the male Oedipal scenario, which produces spectatorial pleasure through the working out of male desire. This Oedipal drama offers a situation in which the male spectator "creates and recreates *himself* out of an abstract or purely symbolic other" (de Lauretis 1984: 121). In order for this drama to take place, this other must itself be created. As de Lauretis proposes, filmic narratives act not only to resolve male Oedipal anxieties but also to work out the female Oedipal drama in a way beneficial to patriarchy. She explains: "In other words, women *must either* consent *or* be seduced into consenting to femininity. ... for women's consent may not be gotten easily, but is finally gotten, and has been for a long time, as much by rape and economic coercion as by the more subtle and lasting effects of ideology, representation, and identification" (emphasis de Lauretis 1984: 134).

In "'Something Else Besides a Mother': *Stella Dallas* and the maternal melodrama," Linda Williams, whose ideas, with Doane's, will be discussed more fully as we consider theorizations of the woman's film in Chapter 2, suggests that certain female-oriented Hollywood genres create a multiply identified female spectator. According to Williams, many woman's films engage their female audience by appealing to the multiplicity of psychological and social particularities that characterize women's subcultural experience under patriarchy. They have "reading positions structured into their texts that demand a female reading competence" based on women's traditional social roles as wives, mothers, daughters, housekeepers, and caretakers (Williams 1984: 8). The many and contradictory roles that women are expected to play in patriarchal society prepare them for the multiple identification that female-oriented genres demand. Williams believes that female spectators view woman's films dialectically from a variety of different, even contradictory, subject positions and as a result they come to identify with contradiction itself rather than with a single character's controlling viewpoint. The female spectator is able to "alternate between a number of conflicting points of view, none of which can be satisfactorily reconciled" (Williams 1984: 20).

In "Desperately Seeking Difference" (first published in 1987), Jackie Stacey proposes that the homosexual pleasures of female spectatorship have been overlooked in theories of female spectatorship, and films that focus on one woman's obsession with another woman, such as *All About Eve* (Joseph L. Mankiewicz, 1950) and *Desperately Seeking Susan* (Susan Seidelman, 1985), offer female viewers pleasures that go beyond the alternatives of masculinization, masochism and marginality outlined by other feminist theorists (1990: 368). For Stacey, these films offer the female spectator identification with different forms of otherness among women that are not reducible to sexual difference because they involve both a female subject and object of desire (1990: 379). Similarly, in "Pre-text and Text in *Gentlemen Prefer Blondes*," Lucie Arbuthnot and Gail Seneca, as early as 1982, argued that the Howard Hawks 1953 musical *Gentlemen Prefer Blondes* affords pleasures to female viewers that have gone unrecognized. These pleasures offer the female spectator identification with the Marilyn Monroe and Jane Russell characters' resistance to their objectification by men, as well as with the strength of their friendship with each other (Arbuthnot and Seneca 1990).

Some critics have called into question the very idea of gendered spectatorship as a useful concept in film studies. In *In the Realm of Pleasure: Von Sternberg, Deitrich, and the Masochistic Aesthetic* (1988), Gaylyn Studlar offered a masochistic model of spectatorship that involves a non-gendered desire to fuse and be dominated rather than to control and dominate. Other models of spectatorship suggested by Miriam Hansen in "Pleasure, Ambivalence, Identification: Valentino and female spectatorship" (1986) and David Rodowick in *The Difficulty of Difference* (1991) have moved toward a notion of bisexual vacillation between masculine and feminine positions taken up by spectators regardless of actual gender, and in her 1984 essay "Fantasia," Elizabeth Cowie argues for a flexibility of spectator positioning in film viewing based on film's similarity to fantasy. She proposes that film, like fantasy, offers, multiple subject positions of cross-gender identification that are available to viewers of both sexes. These models of non-gendered film spectatorship pose a significant problem for feminist criticism. If spectatorship is really a free-floating, autonomous smorgasbord of offered identifications, then sexual difference may not even be an issue of determining significance in the cinematic viewing experience.

Certainly, many aspects of the spectator–text relationship can be theorized without reference to the spectator's gender. For instance, Murray Smith in *Engaging Characters: fiction, emotion, and the cinema* proposes that a structure of sympathy operates within a text guiding all viewers, regardless of gender, in their engagement with characters. This structure of sympathy includes three distinct elements: recognition, alignment, and allegiance. Recognition involves the various ways in which a text allows viewers to recognize its characters by perceiving "a set of textual elements, in film typically cohering around the image of a body, as an individuated and continuous human agent" (Smith 1995: 82). Alignment situates the spectator in regard to characters and includes two interlocking functions: spatio-temporal attachment – the spectators' connection to a certain character or characters whose actions seem to lead the way through the narrative; and subjective access – the degree of knowledge the spectator has about what a character is thinking and feeling (Smith 1995: 143). Finally, allegiance involves the text's creation of its own moral system which influences the spectator's evaluation of a character's moral status (Smith 1995: 188).

Smith proposes that this structure of sympathy is supplemented by an interconnected structure of empathy. Sympathetic reactions to characters involve what Smith calls "acentral imagining," understanding the character and situation represented and reacting emotionally to the thought of that character in that situation. Empathy, on the other hand, he defines as "central imagining," actually adopting the point of view and mental state of a character (Smith 1995: 76–77). According to Smith, empathic responses are brought about by one of two functions: emotional simulation or motor and affective mimicry. Emotional simulation involves imaginatively projecting oneself into a character's situation and hypothesizing the emotions that character is experiencing. Smith believes it most commonly occurs when the audience is given limited information about a narrative situation and therefore must adopt a character's point of view in order to predict resulting behavior (1995: 97). While emotional simulation is voluntary, motor and affective mimicry are not. They rely on the spectator's reflexive simulation via facial and bodily cues of the emotions perceived as experienced by a character (Smith 1995: 99). These non-gender specific influences on spectatorial response are undoubtedly important in analyzing textual methods of audience engagement, yet they should not be regarded as completely invalidating the idea of gendered spectatorship. The very fact that certain types of films or stars attract gender specific audiences suggests that gender cannot be ignored in evaluating a film's appeal to its viewers. As we shall see in Chapter 2, in film genres such as the woman's film where the address is specifically to a female audience, the issue of gendered spectatorship seems particularly pertinent. In fact, feminist critics have seen the female-oriented genre of the woman's film as a privileged site for the interrogation and application of just such a concept.

The Move to Cultural Studies

In the 1990s, a number of dissatisfactions with cinepsychoanalysis emerged, and many feminists began to look to new theoretical methodologies. The inability of psychoanalytic theorists to resolve debates over the male gaze, women's counter-cinema, and female spectatorship contributed significantly to this dissatisfaction. Psychoanalysis also came under attack for the seeming hopelessness of its portrayal of mainstream cinema as irresolutely misogynist and immune to social change; its White, Eurocentric, heterosexual exclusivity that ignores lesbians, women of color, and marginalized women throughout the world; its ahistoricity; exclusive textual determinacy; and use of oblique difficult terminology. Feminist critics, like Annette Kuhn in *Women's Pictures: Feminism and Cinema* (1994) and Christine Gledhill in her 1999 essay "Pleasurable Negotiations," began to advocate an approach that combines textual analysis with a greater concern for the audience–text relationship and is more cognizant of audience diversity in terms of not only gender, but also race, sexual orientation, and nationality. Influences on this new approach to feminist theory did not entirely or even primarily stem from film criticism, but rather came from television studies, which always had a more audience-oriented perspective than film studies. The major theorist of the cultural studies perspective is Gledhill, who in "Pleasurable Negotiations" set out the central tenet of cultural studies – the idea of negotiation. Gledhill argues that theories of the textually constructed female spectator ignore the socio-historical context in which the text was produced as well as institutional issues of production, distribution, and exhibition. To take into account these various factors, Gledhill suggested the concept of negotiation as a way to recognize texts as shaped by the struggle to make meaning among institutions and audiences. For Gledhill and other cultural studies theorists, texts could never be entirely progressive or reactionary, ideologically innocuous or internally self-critical. In fact, they are all internally self-critical or, in cultural studies terms, polysemic, open to various types of readings depending on the socio-historical situation of the spectator. For cultural studies critics, spectators are no longer products of the text; instead, the text is a product of the struggle and resulting negotiation among various different components, including active viewers as shaped by their socio-historical context. Texts must be studied in the context of their production and reception, and it must be recognized that they can be viewed differently based not only on the viewer's gender, but also on determinants such as class, race, and nationality. Films should not be studied as inoculating meaning into passive hypothetical spectators, but rather meaning should be seen as emerging from the way real viewers interact with texts.

This cultural studies perspective has led feminist theorists to two directions. In spite of cultural studies' audience-orientation, the first direction is still essentially text-oriented and examines a film's polysemy, namely, the various types of meanings it offers its audience. The second approach is audience studies and reception theory, which move decidedly away from texts to the study of audiences and extra-textual material that shape the reception of a text. Feminist audience studies practitioners do interviews, conduct surveys and use other ethnographic techniques to investigate how real women read texts. For instance, Helen Taylor in *Scarlett's Women* (1989) employed a questionnaire to study how female fans from Britain and the U.S. responded to both the novel and film versions of *Gone with the Wind*, and Jackie Stacey in *Star Gazing: Hollywood Cinema and Female Spectatorship* (1994) used a questionnaire and letters to study British women's responses to female Hollywood stars during and after World War II. These two strands of the audience studies approach have given feminist film theory a distinctly new direction, and one that has become a major form of feminist criticism today.

Cultural studies has been criticized on a number of counts for being relativist (seeing any meaning that a viewer gives to a text is right), populist (regarding any text is good if it is enjoyed), and unduly optimistic (ignoring how progressive aspects of texts are recuperated and robbed of their subversive potential by the dominant ideology). Some have also argued that it promotes redemptive readings of texts and audiences (Thornham 1997: 90), as opposed to the recruitist readings done by cinepsychoanalytic critics. This is an interesting distinction that requires further explanation. Cinepsychoanalysis can be said to be recruitist because it celebrates texts and filmmakers it judges to be feminist and condemns those it labels patriarchal. Feminist cultural studies, on the other hand, does not study films to determine whether they inform, challenge or educate female audiences in a progressive feminist way; instead, it examines the pleasures female audiences get from texts of all kinds. While championed by some as admirable in its accepting attitude to the viewing habits of all female spectators, this perspective can also be criticized as validating texts that seem from a feminist perspective clearly bad for viewers. These objections have led some to see the cultural studies approach as just as flawed, although in different ways, as cinepsychoanalysis was before it.

What is the current state of twenty-first century feminist film theory? As postfeminists have said about feminism as a whole, there are those who would argue there is no current need for feminist film theory at all. Its battles have all been won, and it is a movement of the past. B. Ruby Rich announced as early as 1998 that feminist film theory died in the 1990s when it lost its connection to the political activism of the women's movement and was overrun by queer studies, multi-culturalism, and cultural studies (McCabe 2004: 110–11). On the other hand, I would argue that feminist film studies is not only still alive and well, but has, in fact, become much more heterogeneous, dynamic, and open in its scope, encompassing not just film analysis but also television and new media studies; responding to the need to include issues of race, ethnicity and class in its analyses; adopting a more global reach; and becoming more pluralistic and eclectic in its theoretical framework and critical praxis. The remainder of this book sets out to show the impressive range of that scope, but first we will look at how ideas drawn from the images of women approach, cinepsychoanalysis and cultural studies can be used to analyze a classic Hollywood text, Alfred Hitchcock's *Vertigo*.

Films in Focus: *Vertigo*

In "Allegory and Referentiality: *Vertigo* and feminist film criticism," Susan White characterized *Vertigo* (Alfred Hitchcock, 1958) as one of the most analyzed films in the history of feminist criticism, and perhaps in the history of film criticism itself (1991: 910). Certainly, the film has been approached from various different perspectives, but we might begin by applying the images of women approach to see what insights it affords. This approach would lead us to examine the female characters in the film, asking if they represent positive and/or realistic representations of women or are merely negative stereotypes. Just looking at Madeleine (Kim Novak), Midge (Barbara Bel Geddes), and Judy (Novak again) in *Vertigo* without taking into consideration the context of the narrative, one would have to say unequivocally that they are not positive images of women. Madeleine is a beautiful but suicidal woman who is married to a very wealthy man. She appears to have no real occupation, not even as a socialite, and she wanders around San Francisco, seemingly believing she is possessed by her dead ancestor Carlotta Valdes. Marked heavily with the badge of to-be-looked-at-ness, she is the female ideal of the film's protagonist Scottie (James Stewart), based solely, it would appear, on her looks. We certainly do not get much sense of her intellectual capabilities. In fact, her intelligence seems to be of no importance to Scottie, who simply falls in love with her by following her around San Francisco and gazing at her beauty. But then we have to wonder if we can really judge Madeleine as a woman at all because the film eventually reveals that she does not even exist, or at least not in the form that is offered to Scottie. She is the construction of her supposed husband, the evil Gavin Elster (Tom Helmore), who has fashioned her as an ideal female image to lure Scottie into Elster's plot to murder his wife, the real Madeleine Elster.

Figure 1   Kim Novak as Madeleine Elster exhibiting to-be-looked-at-ness in *Vertigo*.

Midge and Judy are perhaps more realistic representations of women. At least, they really exist in the film's world, but neither is what one might call a positive image. Midge is hopelessly in love with and hopelessly unattractive to Scottie, standing in contrast to the glamorous Madeleine, whom Scottie clearly believes is the perfect woman. A plain career woman who wears glasses, which certainly in 1958 were not intended as a signifier of female beauty, Midge is presented as an odd combination of too much boyishness and a too motherly attitude to Scottie. Her unrequited love for him renders her more a pathetic figure than a positive one. Similarly, Judy is an unsophisticated sales clerk whom Scottie meets on the street and recognizes as bearing a strong resemblance to what he believes to be the dead Madeleine. He sets out to transform her into his former love. Judy is remarkable both in her lack of sophistication, especially in comparison to Madeleine, and in her masochistic willingness to allow Scottie to remake her completely into another women, the object of his desire. She even seems willing to accept Scottie's suggestion that how she looks, dresses, and acts cannot really matter to her. What he implies should matter to her is only what *he* wants, and although she tries to fulfill his dream that she could look, act, and really be Madeleine, by the film's end she fails to attain this goal. She carelessly, foolishly, or deliberately – her motivation is unclear – wears a necklace that she had worn when she was pretending to be Madeleine and that she then claimed had belonged to Madeleine's dead ancestor Carlotta. Scottie recognizes the necklace, realizes that Judy impersonated Madeleine, and in a fit of anger leads Judy to her death in a fall from the same tower where Madeleine had supposedly committed suicide. I guess we would have to characterize pitiful and masochistic Judy, who loves Scottie so much she is willing to sacrifice her entire personality to become what he wants, as failing even more spectacularly than Midge as a positive figure of a woman.

To move from positive images to realistic ones, which are not really the same thing, one might ask if any of these women are realistic at all. There were probably in 1958, and I would think still are today, career women who wear glasses and are unrequitedly in love with their male friends, beautiful depressed wealthy women, and unsophisticated shop girls, but we do not really seem to be getting anywhere with this type of images of women analysis, do we? Why? It may be because film is neither an unmediated representation of reality, nor a medium dedicated to providing positive role models for its audience. The images of women approach shows itself to be deeply flawed when we try to apply it to an analysis of a given film. Advocates of cinepsychoanalysis suggested that their approach offers a methodology for constructing a much more insightful investigation of the mechanisms at work in film, and feminist critics, beginning with Laura Mulvey, have used this approach extensively in examining *Vertigo*. Let us, therefore, consider Mulvey's psychoanalytic reading of the film in "Visual Pleasure and Narrative Cinema."

Mulvey sees *Vertigo* as focused strongly on the scopophilic eroticism of Scottie, its central male character. The male gaze is central to the film and oscillates between fetishistic scopophilia and sadistic voyeurism. Scottie's point of view "backed by the certainty of legal right and the established guilt of the woman" becomes the spectator's through Hitchcock's skillful use of identification processes and subjective camera positioning from the point of view of the male hero (Mulvey 1989d: 23). Thus, viewers become totally implicated in Scottie's perspective as the major figure of spectatorial identification. In discussing the film's major female characters, Mulvey identifies Madeleine, as we have noted above, as "a perfect image of female beauty and mystery", and Judy as a woman whose exhibitionism and masochism "make her an ideal passive counterpart to Scottie's active sadistic voyeurism" (1989d: 24). According to Mulvey, Judy knows her part and recognizes that she can keep Scottie's interest only by repeatedly performing it. So she plays and replays the role of Madeleine until in the repetition Scottie finally is able to "break her down," expose her guilt, and engineer her punishment (1989d: 24). Mulvey's narrow focus on the male gaze and its scopophilic and voyeuristic components actually leads her to a very limited view of *Vertigo*'s significance for the female spectator. She seems to wedge the female spectator inevitably into the male subject position and see her as forced to participate in his sadistic victimization of the female characters. In this way, female spectators in a sense have their fascination with the film text and its characters turned against them (Mulvey 1989d: 23).

A close psychoanalytic reading of *Vertigo* that goes beyond Mulvey and views the film in terms of not only the male gaze but also its narrative development can reveal it to be a much more complex and variegated text than Mulvey suggests. As numerous critics have pointed out, the film begins with a somewhat curious scene in which Scottie Ferguson in his job as a police detective is involved in a rooftop chase in pursuit of a criminal. Jumping from one roof to another, he falls and finds himself dangling from a storm gutter, looking down between two buildings to the ground below, and experiencing an attack of vertigo. A uniformed policeman also involved in the chase tries to save him but instead falls to his own death as Scottie looks on helplessly. We never see how Scottie gets down. As Robin Wood has commented, Scottie seems to be left dangling over the abyss for the whole film (1983: 33). From a psychoanalytic perspective, Scottie can be said to have witnessed the death of the

Father (the policeman in uniform as representative of authority) and in this way has reactivated his incompletely resolved Oedipal trauma.

According to Lacanian psychoanalytic theory, the Oedipal trauma for the boy involves his progress from an original feeling of oneness with his mother in the realm of the Imaginary to an experience of lack that leads him to separate from his mother, identify with his father, enter the Symbolic realm of language, and search for a mature heterosexual love relationship. Scottie's failure to resolve these problems can be seen in the film's second scene which reveals his relationship with Midge, who is presented here as his best friend. The scene takes place in Midge's apartment, where Scottie seems to be very much at home. He relaxes in a chair, amuses himself by balancing his cane on his finger, and later even lies down on the sofa. While superficially at ease, he acts as if he is confined, anxious to move on, and waiting to find release. He complains of the uncomfortable corset that he has been forced to wear since his rooftop accident and anxiously anticipates its removal. He and Midge also discuss his plans to do nothing for a while now that his vertigo has forced him to retire from the police department. As suggested above in our attempt to apply the images of women approach to *Vertigo*, Midge is a female character who combines personality traits that might initially seem irreconcilable. She is a boyish figure who wears plain sweaters with masculine-type collars and dark skirts. As a commercial artist, she makes her own living as an independent, practical career woman, yet she is also a mother figure to Scottie. She sits at her drawing board through most of this early scene in her apartment, looks down at Scottie, who is usually positioned below her, and asks him questions concerning his future plans with an almost parental concern. When Scottie asks her about her sketch of a new style of brassiere, she answers, "You're a big boy. You know about those things." She even soothes and caresses him in a motherly fashion when he falls from a kitchen step ladder in an attempt to overcome his vertigo. Scottie cautions her at one point in their conversation, "Midge, don't be so motherly!"

The boyish, yet motherly Midge can be seen as an identification figure for the female spectator. Like Midge, we too are constantly watching Scottie, studying his every move, and later trying to understand his developing obsession with Madeleine. Midge's motherliness fixes her in the female position, while her boyish qualities suggest a male affiliation. Her sexual identity seems to be in a state of turmoil; she expresses the same discomfort that the female spectator might feel in oscillating, as Mulvey suggests she does, between the active male subject position and the passive female image. The film, however, does not allow the female spectator to identify comfortably with Midge, but rather leads her to desire to move away from identification with this conflicted character, who seems to oscillate between masculine and feminine personality traits and is shown to be permanently divorced from what the narrative suggests is appropriate femininity. This scene in Midge's apartment is significant not only for its exposition of Midge's character but also for what it tells us about Scottie. In psychoanalytic terms, Scottie's stay in the comfortable safety of Midge's flat represents his sojourn in the realm of the Imaginary, where the infant finds comfort in unity with the Mother. But Scottie's accident, by providing him with an opportunity to look down from the rooftop into the abyss below, has allowed him to see "the lack," and he can never again be entirely comfortable in this Imaginary realm. He must now go off, as he says, "to wander" and find himself; he must break away from Midge's motherly affection and seek the resolution of his Oedipal trauma in romantic love, a heterosexual attraction to a wholly feminine woman.

In this pursuit, Scottie moves directly from the influence of a maternal figure to the domination of a paternal one, for the next scene in the film occurs at the office of Gavin Elster, Scottie's old school chum who has gotten in touch with him after many years. In this scene, Elster is clearly established as a paternal figure. He is a man of considerable authority as the director of a large shipping company, the impressive operations of which are visible in the massive structures of the shipyard seen through the large picture window behind his desk. In an opulent office, sitting behind a huge desk and looking considerably older than Scottie, Elster dominates their conversation and imposes his will on his friend despite Scottie's objections. Elster's domination is shown visually as well as narratively. He either sits majestically behind his desk as Scottie nervously wanders about the office, stands over the seated Scottie looking down at him, or steps up to a higher level of the room. Elster's position as a father figure is also evident in narrative aspects of the scene. He connects himself definitively with the past, especially with old San Francisco, which in the course of the film also comes to be associated with Madeleine's ancestor Carlotta Valdes. Elster speaks nostalgically about those days of "color, excitement, power, and freedom" and expresses a desire to have lived then. In psychoanalytic terms, this powerful man of the past reaches out to bring the infantile Scottie, struggling with Oedipal woes, into the realm of the Symbolic, under the "Law of the Father," and to a recognition of the realities of patriarchal society. The method that Elster uses to orchestrate Scottie's resolution of his Oedipal difficulties and thus bring about his entrance into patriarchy is to hold before him society's ideal image of femininity, the beautiful and mysterious Madeleine. Unfortunately for Scottie, Madeleine does not really exist; she is only an image, a creation of Gavin Elster's imaginative powers and Scottie's Oedipal desires. Elster sets her up as the object of Scottie's gaze and then allows Scottie to create her for himself through the exercise of this gaze, through what Mulvey calls his fetishistic scopophilia.

What follows in the film is a 15-minute sequence during which the spectator participates through the liberal use of subjective point of view shots in Scottie's observations of Madeleine and his growing obsession with her. This obsessive process culminates in the rebirth ritual of Scottie saving Madeleine from drowning and trying to control her self-destructive tendencies. Unfortunately for Scottie, Madeleine is not subject entirely to his control because she is not solely his visual creation; Gavin Elster has fashioned her narratively. If Scottie has created her through his gaze as a strong visual presence for both himself and the spectator, Elster has given her a story, and one that is particularly in accord with Scottie's Oedipal drama. In fact, Madeleine's story is the female version of Scottie's own dilemma. Like him, she is stranded in the Imaginary, where she is unable to sever her connection with the figure of the Mother in the person of Carlotta Valdes. Carlotta's story is an important diegetic element for the female spectator, who with Scottie and the male spectator is being drawn through the use of subjective camera positioning and the compelling nature of the narrative arc into an acceptance of Madeleine as an ideal image of femininity, a perfect alternative to the less conventionally feminine Midge. Carlotta, however, is portrayed as a victim of patriarchy's oppression of women. Significantly, the spectator and Scottie are led to her story by Midge, a woman who, unlike Madeleine, is not a creation of male fantasy. Midge takes Scottie to Pop Lieble, an expert on San Francisco history who reveals that Carlotta was a cabaret dancer who came from a Spanish mission somewhere south of the city. She became the mistress of a wealthy man who later abandoned her, taking with him their only child. Having lost both her romantic and motherly roles, she went mad and eventually killed herself.

Madeleine, the male-created image of feminine perfection, is inextricably linked to this victim of patriarchical oppression. She claims to be possessed by Carlotta, her great-grandmother, who is leading her to suicide. The character of Midge, Carlotta's story, and its relationship to Madeleine all reflect the dilemma of the female spectator and her Oedipal difficulties. As Teresa de Lauretis has argued, in order to "consent to her seduction into femininity" and to fit the male ideal of perfect womanhood, a woman must give up the boyish ways expressed by Midge and strive for the ideal that Madeleine, the creation of the male gaze, represents (1984: 134). Carlotta's story suggests that patriarchical prescriptions demand that in order to accomplish this transformation the woman must sever her connection with her mother and with the mother's experiences of patriarchal oppression. One who accepts the male conception of feminine perfection must also accept male dominance, submit completely to male authority, and never even admit to her oppression. She must be willing in de Lauretis's terms to be "seduced into femininity." Scottie strongly encourages Madeleine to do just this, to reject the maternal figure of Carlotta. If he can get her to repudiate Carlotta and by implication the knowledge of patriarchal oppression that Carlotta represents, she will succumb entirely to his desire and make her own desire an exact replica of his. Unfortunately for Scottie, Madeleine does not succumb; instead, she clings to her identification with Carlotta and refuses to make the Oedipal leap from her Imaginary union with the mother to Scottie's waiting patriarchal desire in the Symbolic. Her apparent suicide, a literal leap that symbolizes this refusal, is examined by patriarchal authority at the coroner's inquest, and Scottie is condemned for his failure to make his dream of perfect femininity a reality.

This condemnation leads Scottie to a mental breakdown. Reduced to a catatonic state in a mental hospital, he is visited by Midge, who hopes to lift his spirits with recordings of Mozart. Why Mozart should be seen as possessing magical curative qualities is never explained, and in any case he fails miserably. Midge's soothing words of "Mother is here" fall on deaf ears, and we last see her slowly walking down a hospital corridor, having admitted to Scottie's doctor: "I don't think Mozart is going to help at all." Midge's final realization here in the hospital corridor that her type of womanhood can never satisfy Scottie's desire should have been clear to the spectator for sometime as a result of a curious interlude set among the sequences showing Scottie's developing obsession with Madeleine. Midge invites Scottie to her apartment to view a work of art that she created in which she has inserted her own face into a caricature of Carlotta's portrait. This scene, combined with Midge's failure in the mental hospital, graphically illustrates the incompatibility of male desire with female individuality and independence as expressed in the character of Midge. The film suggests that in order for a woman to establish a successful relationship with a man in patriarchal society qualities in direct opposition to Midge's motherly power and independence must be cultivated, qualities embodied in the image of Madeleine, whose physical beauty and mysterious eroticism literally drive Scottie insane.

When Midge walks out of the film, the female spectator finds herself without a female figure of identification. The early uneasy identification with Midge might give way during the scenes involving Scottie's growing obsession with Madeleine to a longing to merge with Madeleine's ideal, but distant and inaccessible image. Hitchcock's excessive use of subjective camera encourages both male and female spectators to experience Scottie's longing for Madeleine, but after her death, Scottie's breakdown, and Midge's departure from the film, viewers find themselves almost as bereft as Scottie. This loss is accompanied by the abrupt termination of subjective point of view shots from Scottie's perspective, releasing spectators of both genders from identification with his gaze. Then, the character of Judy appears to provide a new figure of identification for the female spectator, but again it is an uneasy identification because Judy is a less-than-glamorous department store clerk and certainly no Madeleine. She is, nevertheless, still presented as a woman who really exists, not an ideal image like Madeleine, and thus seems to fill the space in the narrative left vacant by Midge. In the famous flashback, in which Judy's thoughts are revealed and the mystery of Madeleine's death is resolved, the spectator is even allowed to enter Judy's consciousness. The break from Scottie's perspective is complete because this flashback provides the audience with knowledge that Scottie does not yet know. For the spectator, Judy, unlike Madeleine, is not at all inscrutable, and immediately after the flashback, the film investigates in some detail her feelings for Scottie as she prepares to run away and tries to write him a confessional farewell letter. Contrary to Mulvey's belief that the film keeps us throughout absorbed in Scottie's perspective, once the flashback has broken our visual link with Scottie by allowing us a glimpse into Judy's thoughts and providing us with information not available to Scottie, the film cannot reinvolve us so thoroughly in Scottie's point of view as it had earlier. As Scottie attempts to transform Judy into Madeleine, subjective point of view shots from Scottie's perspective begin again, but the spectator's identification with him seems to be much less complete. Scottie's fantasy life is now exposed in its violent and artificial imposition on Judy. We see all too clearly her painful attempts to maintain her own personality although she knows that to win Scottie's love she must submerge her identity completely into the persona of Madeleine.

In de Lauretis' terms, Scottie sets out to resolve his Oedipal problems by recreating Judy in Madeleine's image, by seducing her into consenting to the male ideal of femininity. To do this, he must impose an Oedipal crisis on Judy and personally engineer its resolution. We are led to see not just Scottie's satisfaction in this process but also the pain it causes Judy as she tries desperately to relinquish her real personality and deny her own desire in order to adapt to Scottie's desire. Thus, the successful resolution of the male and female Oedipal dramas is shown not to result in the coming together of the man and woman in a perfect heterosexual romantic union but rather to involve the woman's painful alteration. She is made to deny her true self in order to fulfill the male fantasy of femininity.

In *Vertigo*, the triumph of heterosexual romance, exceptionalized cinematically by the famous 380-degree turn during Scottie and Judy's kiss, is very brief in duration because Judy, having allowed herself to be transformed into Madeleine, is unable to maintain the charade. Although she may appear to have stopped consciously trying to fight Scottie's demand that she sacrifice herself to meet his feminine ideal, as noted above, she puts on a necklace that she had worn as Madeleine and that was said to have once belonged to Carlotta. Whether this is a conscious attempt to get Scottie to finally see who she really is or the result of her real personality's unconscious struggle for survival is unclear. What is clear, however, is that when Scottie sees the necklace, he recognizes the truth: Judy has not overcome the Oedipal difficulties he imposed upon her, she has not been transformed into his ideal of femininity, and she is still mired in the Imaginary, connected inextricably to the Mother, and able only to make her desire the mirror of his through sham and falsity. Scottie once again is forced to see "the lack" in the absence of his feminine ideal in Judy, just as he had seen his lack in his inability to save his fellow officer in the opening rooftop scene. Scottie also can be said to have discovered, in seeing Judy/Madeleine's inseparable union with Carlotta, that his own Oedipal drama has not been resolved. If Judy is one with the figure of the mother, then Scottie's union with her places him still in the Imaginary. He has not managed to break with the mother but has rather entered into yet another union with her in the guise of romantic love. As a result of this revelation, Scottie returns to the scene of his final betrayal by Madeleine, to the mission tower where she consummated her union with Carlotta in suicide. Here, he submits Judy to a reenactment of Madeleine's, and of course really her own, falsity and deceit. In Mulvey's terms, having failed to control Madeleine/ Judy by the power of the gaze, by his fetishistic scopophilia, Scottie turns to voyeuristic means, to an investigation of her guilt and the meting out of her punishment. He takes her to the mission where Madeleine's death was staged, drags her up to the tower, and as they climb the stairs, relives every detail of his humiliation at her hands. His anger overcomes his vertigo, his Oedipal difficulties are finally resolved, and he is cured. Judy, who by this time is reduced to a state of complete masochistic submission, still wants him, they kiss once again, and it appears that both of their Oedipal dramas have been concluded successfully, if not happily.

The psychoanalytic critic might say that, here at the end, male and female spectators alike – identifying with Scottie and Judy respectively – feel a sense of relief that they have been released from the film's painful reenactment of their difficult Oedipal transformations. But once again the film turns against them and shows that this perfect heterosexual union in romantic love is only momentary because Judy's Oedipal transformation remains problematic by patriarchal standards. Although she has repudiated her falsity and pledged her love to Scottie in this final kiss, she is still guilty of conspiring to kill the real Madeleine Elster, yet another mother figure. Thus the resolution of the woman's Oedipal drama under patriarchy, demanding as it does the mother's symbolic death, leaves the daughter plagued with guilt, a guilt that she cannot escape through heterosexual union, but only through death. Scottie, after having successfully weathered his Oedipal transformation, is left with an empty triumph. Suddenly confronted with the figure of a nun who has come up to the tower apparently to ring the bell, Judy falls or jumps from the tower to her death. What does the nun represent? Perhaps she is the good woman that Judy realizes she can never be because of her past involvement with murder, a specter reminding Judy that she cannot escape her guilt, or the asexual woman with whom Scottie is left after Judy's death.

This psychoanalytic reading of Vertigo interprets it as both a re-enactment of the male and female Oedipal dramas and an enactment of the dilemma of the female spectator in watching the film, which tries to position her in the situation of the male subject but cannot prevent her from shedding her "transvestite clothes" (Mulvey 1989a: 33) and assuming a female identification. In the course of the narrative, the problematic nature of this identification is revealed as the concept of femininity in patriarchal society is shown to be a male fantasy construct, a denial of the irrevocable mother/daughter bond, and a suppression of female being. Even the source of this repression can be seen in the fear of matriarchy that is expressed in the strong hereditary transference of female power and unity from Carlotta, a "phallic," pre-Oedipal mother figure, to Madeleine/Judy, her symbolic daughter. Using Claire Johnston's terminology, this psychoanalytic analysis of Vertigo reveals the film to be an internally self-critical text, which seems on the surface to support patriarchal ideology but has an underlying subversive meaning that actually reveals the problematic nature of that ideology. As Mulvey suggests in her discussion of the film, Vertigo turns spectators' fascination with Scottie's male gaze against them. When Mulvey looks at the visual elements in the film, however, she identifies this fascination only with fetishistic scopophilia and sadistic voyeurism, both of which are used to counteract the threat of castration symbolized by the female form. As the psychoanalytic reading proposed above demonstrates, the film is much more complex both visually and narratively than this analysis would suggest because the power of the gaze is contained within a narrative and visual structure that calls it into question. Contrary to Mulvey's analysis, Scottie is not always "backed by a certainty of legal right" in the film (1989d: 23). At the coroner's inquest, he is condemned by legal authority. Judy is not the consummate exhibitionist and masochist that Mulvey labels her; instead, she fights against the suppression of her real personality, and the revelation of the "perverted side" of Scottie's gaze is not just "a twist" in the film's structure, as Mulvey (1989d: 23) suggests, but a crucial element in its narrative design. Following the ideas of Gaylyn Studlar (1988), who posits a masochistic regime of filmic pleasure, one can even argue in contradistinction to Mulvey that *Vertigo* places its spectators, both male and female, in a visual position of submission to its fantasy of Scottie and Judy's Oedipal transformations; posits a formidable female figure in the character of Carlotta Valdes, who symbolizes pre-Oedipal maternal power not lack and castration; and creates fluid, multiple, and mobile spectatorial positions that encourage transgender identification for all viewers. The narrative and visual design of *Vertigo* suggested by this psychoanalytic reading is extremely rich and demonstrates the gendered spectator's very complex response to the film.

We might, however, ask what the response of the feminist cultural studies critic would be to *Vertigo* and to the psychoanalytic reading proposed above. First, a cultural studies critic might question the designation of the film as unique in its status as an internally self-critical text, arguing that it is simply polysemous, as are all films. Like other film texts, *Vertigo* opens itself up to various reading possibilities ranging from patriarchal to anti-patriarchal ones. Cultural Studies theorists might follow Virginia Wright Wexman in pointing to possible readings that would historicize the film by focusing on issues of class and ethnicity as well as institutional factors as they impact the film's narrative structure. Wexman points out that feminist psychoanalytic readings of the film tend to obscure its "commercialized eroticism" (1986: 34), which involves Hitchcock's careful creation of Kim Novak as a "manufactured erotic ideal" in order to assure the film's commercial success. The film has been tied to Hitchcock's reputed obsession with controlling his cool blonde leading ladies. He commented to François Truffaut in their series of interviews concerning Hitchcock's films that he and Novak did not get along well during the shooting of the film because she came in with too many ideas about what she wanted to do with her character (Truffaut 1985: 188). Novak certainly had experience with controlling male figures. She was not only forced to bend her will to Hitchcock's plan for *Vertigo*, but to the control of the President of Columbia Pictures, Harry Cohn, who notoriously called her "the fat Pollack" and forced her to live in her studio dressing room where in order to keep her weight down she was only allowed to eat studio prepared food (Wexman 1986: 35). As Wexman points out, Novak's star image had a great deal in common with her dual characters of Judy/Madeleine. Her star persona partook, as so many star's images do, of the twin characteristics of the ordinary and the extraordinary. She was presented as an ordinary young woman "discovered" and set on the road to stardom, where she became, like Madeleine, an image of "etherealized, aesthiticized beauty" (Wexman 1986: 35). The commercial appeal of *Vertigo* was not limited to Hitchcock's use of Kim Novak and James

Stewart, to give the film star appeal, but extended to the travelogue effect the film creates through the use of San Francisco as the setting for the story. As Wexman points out, Hitchcock shows all the city's famous sights including the Golden Gate Bridge, hilly streets, art museum, then famous Ernie's restaurant, giant sequoias, and surrounding Spanish missions (1986: 36).

Not only do cultural studies critics call attention to industrial factors that influence a film, but also to matters of class, race, and ethnicity. For instance, Wexman argues that the "essentialist methodology and universalizing concepts" of psychoanalytic criticism have led it to ignore these issues (1986: 37). She looks at the triad of female figures in *Vertigo* and sees them as representative of various classes in American society: Madeleine embodies old wealth with her idle, privileged lifestyle; Midge the middle-class woman with her strong work ethic; and Judy the working class woman. The failure of Midge and Judy to satisfy Scottie, who seeks, but also fails to move up into the wealthy class in his attempt to woo Madeleine, demonstrates the lack of class mobility in 1950's U.S. society. Carlotta Valdes' character in a cultural studies reading becomes not just a representative of universalized female exploitation, as she might in a psychoanalytic reading, but her ambiguous Hispanic background renders her a representative not only of American injustice to minority groups, but according to Wexman, even of U.S. imperialist "colonization and plunder" of underdeveloped countries (1986: 38). As Wexman sees the film, "political anxieties about dominance and otherness are displaced in *Vertigo* onto the image of women." She goes so far as to see Scottie's romantic failures as a displacement of cold war xenophobic fears of communism and the film's "abrupt unresolved ending" as its ultimate refusal to deal with the implications of all of these class, racial, ethnic, and political issues (Wexman 1986: 37).

All cultural studies critics might not go as far as Wexman in seeing such wide-ranging social and political implications in the film, but the ambiguity of its ending would certainly intrigue them. While the psychoanalytic reading I have proposed here sees the ending as essentially closed in that it shows the failure of Scottie and Judy to resolve their Oedipal crises satisfactorily and form a successful heterosexual union under patriarchy. Cultural studies critics would point to the various different readings critics have given to the film's ending and suggest that this indicates not closure but a polysemy or openness to various interpretive possibilities. For instance, critics seem very divided about the significance of the nun's appearance at the end and Judy's reaction to it. Wexman says the nun represents "religious guilt centered on sexual desire" (1986: 39). In the psychoanalytic reading proposed above, I speculate that she represents more specifically Judy's sense of guilt or Scottie's sense of the impossibility of finding sexual fulfillment with a "good" woman. Others have identified the nun as representing Hitchcock's camera, Hitchcock himself as a spectral figure hovering over his characters, a ghostly maternal figure who represents the child's fear of engulfment by the all powerful pre-Oedipal mother, or a warning that the wish to merge with the Other is a desire in bad faith (White 1991: 931–32).

The cultural studies critic might also point to *Vertigo*'s alternate ending (available on the Legacy DVD of the film), which Hitchcock apparently was required to shot so that it could be added to prints intended for overseas distribution and therefore subject to the approval of a foreign censorship committee. This extended ending has become known as the foreign censorship ending and shifts from Judy's death scene back to Midge's apartment on the night of the same day. Midge is seen listening to a radio broadcast that announces a police plan to track the whereabouts of Gavin Elster, who is reputed to be somewhere in Europe, in order to bring him back to the United States for trial. This news is followed by an account of three college students who were arrested for trying to lead a cow up the steps of a University of California building. This second news item is clearly one of Hitchcock's rather pathetic attempts at comic relief, which were often eventually cut from his films. It comments humorously on Scottie's situation in that cows cannot walk up steps because they become panicked and disoriented, just as Scottie does on the tower stairway. As D.A. Miller explains, "These wanton boys were seeking to induce a case of what can only be called bovine vertigo, the stupid, depsychologized version of Scottie's own predicament." Scottie enters the room, takes up a drink Midge has mixed for him, turns his back on her and the audience, walks to the window, and looks out at the view of San Francisco, as Miller notes, for the first time in the film (Miller 2008–2009: 16). This ending certainly does not add much closure. We do not really know if Scottie will ever have the satisfaction of seeing Elster arrested and tried for his crime or if Scottie will return to his ultimately unsatisfying relationship with Midge, a woman who can never substitute for Madeleine. Perhaps, he is just using Midge as a stopping off point before he resumes his wanderings through San Francisco to find his female ideal. Or does the fact that he is finally looking down over San Francisco suggest that now he is cured of his vertigo and finished with his wanderings? And what does the bovine vertigo joke indicate? Is Hitchcock ridiculing his own protagonist or even his own film as just a ridiculous prank on his audience? From a cultural studies perspective, *Vertigo* emerges as a polysemous text indeed.

Key Terms: *images of women criticism, cinepsychoanalysis, the male gaze, to-be-looked-at-ness, fetishistic scopophilia, sadistic voyeurism, the female spectator, cultural studies, negotiation*

Suggestions for Further Reading, Viewing, and Discussion

1. Claire Johnston characterizes John Ford and Howard Hawks as examples of male auteurs who present female characters as male fantasy figures, but in very different ways. Watch a film by each director and compare/contrast their treatment of female characters. How are they similar/different in their treatment of women? Both directors have extensive careers, so there is a wide range of films from which to choose. You might go to the Internet Movie Database (IMDB.com), which is an excellent film resource, and choose from the lists provided there of all the films they directed. Some interesting ones for Hawks might be *Rio Bravo*, *Gentlemen Prefer Blondes*, *The Big Sleep*, and *Bringing Up Baby*, and for Ford *The Man who Shot Liberty Valance*, *The Searchers*, *She Wore a Yellow Ribbon*, *Young Mr. Lincoln*, and *Stagecoach*. Another interesting project might be to look at the work of two contemporary male directors and compare and contrast their portrayals of women. Would you still say that they present female characters as male fantasy figures? Did Hawks and Ford really present them in that way?

2. Read the introduction to Molly Haskell's *From Reverence to Rape*, Claire Johnston's "Women's Cinema as Counter-Cinema," Laura Mulvey's "Visual Pleasure and Narrative Cinema," and Christine Gledhill's "Pleasurable Negotiations." Compare/contrast their approaches to film. What are the differences and similarities?

3. Is *Vertigo* best described as an ideologically innocuous patriarchal film, an internally self-critical film, or a polysemous text? Can you explain the differences among these three categories? Where would you place *Vertigo*?

4. Consider the ambiguities of *Vertigo*'s ending. How do you interpret the sudden appearance of the nun, Judy's dive from the tower (does she jump or fall and why?), and the final shot of Scottie? Does the ending have symbolic significance? Does the addition of the foreign censorship ending change one's interpretation of the film? How? Does it provide more closure, maintain, or perhaps even increase the film's ambiguities?

5. In our examination of *Vertigo*, we applied the images of women, psychoanalytic, and cultural studies approaches to the film. Choose a contemporary film and see what different aspects of the text emerge as you apply these three feminist approaches to it. Which approach led you to the most interesting interpretation of the film?

6. There are many good anthologies of feminist film criticism. The ones listed in the bibliography by Thornham, Erens, Penley, Kaplan, and Carson

et al. are all excellent. Read some of the original essays discussed in this chapter and other feminist criticism found in these anthologies.

7. Watch other films by Hitchcock with his construction of female characters in mind. Some films that might provide interesting viewing in this regard include *Frenzy, Marnie, The Birds, Notorious, Shadow of a Doubt, Suspicion*, and *Rebecca*, but really you might choose any Hitchcock film as an object of study. You might also read Tania Modleski's excellent book on Hitchcock's portrayal of women, *The Women who Knew Too Much*, and compare your ideas about Hitchcock's women to hers.

Chapter 2

Women and Genre Films
From the Woman's Film to Chick Flicks

Genre films are Hollywood movies that establish themselves as recognizable products by a range of shared visual and narrative conventions, such as common icons (props and stars like the machine gun in the gangster film and John Wayne in the western), plot formulas (the narrative pattern of an entire film like the detective plot of film noir), plot conventions (individual scenes repeated from film to film like the attack of the monster in the horror film), and stylistic conventions (aspects of cinematography, editing, and mise-en-scène such as chiaroscuro lighting in film noir and horror). Feminist critics have investigated the roles of women in most major film genres, but certain genres have proved particularly fertile ground for investigation. Film noir, the genre of detective and criminal films so popular in the 1940s, has been analyzed in particular for its representation of the femme fatale. In psychoanalytic terms, feminist critics have labeled this mysterious, sexually aggressive, manipulative, and possibly murderous female character as representing male castration anxieties, and in sociological terms as expressing male fears of women's power and career success and as empowering female viewers with her assertive femininity and expression of female anger. The "to-be-looked-at-ness" of female characters as the objects of spectacle in the musical and the role of the female victim in horror have also been examined extensively. There seem to be few genres that feminist critics have ignored, but there is one to which they have given special attention, and that is the woman's film, a genre that developed through several stages to become the chick flicks of today.

While the woman's film has gotten considerable attention from feminist critics, other theorists have called its very existence into question. Steve Neale, for instance, points out that although the types of films traditionally considered woman's films are still being made, the term itself has fallen out of fashion (2000: 4). The fact that the woman's film is composed of so many diverse subcategories and does not really exhibit a distinctive visual style also renders it a problematic generic entity. Conventionally, it has been associated with melodrama, but this connection has been questioned in light of melodrama's position as the dominant mode of all Hollywood filmmaking. As

Linda Williams points out, to characterize woman's films as inherently more melodramatic, meaning more fraught with heightened emotion, than other film genres, identifies melodrama inaccurately with the notion of female sentimentality and ignores its connections with what have been considered traditionally male action-oriented generic forms, such as westerns, war films, and action-adventure dramas (1998: 59).

Another problem is the lack of a definitive history of the woman's film. Most work on the genre has focused on what can be characterized as its golden age in the 1930s and 1940s. Molly Haskell, Mary Anne Doane, Janine Basinger, E. Ann Kaplan, and Linda Williams, among others, have debated the contours and concerns of the genre in that halcyon time in its history, but its inception in the silent period has hardly been examined. As Steve Neale has pointed out, D.W. Griffith's woman-centered melodramas, such as *True Heart Susie* (1919), *Broken Blossoms* (1919), and *Way Down East* (1920), represent silent predecessors of the woman's film, and the same can be said of serial queen films, like *The Woman Who Dared* (1911), *The American Girl* (Harry Solter, 1911), *The Exploits of Elaine* (Louis J. Gasnier, George B. Seitz, and Leopold Wharton, 1914), and *Ruth of the Rockies* (George Marshall, 1920) (Neale 2000: 192). These films indicate that the woman's film's origins are not really attached to the sphere of domesticity and romance, as has often been argued, and that at least some of its early representatives fall into the category of the adventure film, a sub-genre of the woman's film that has been revived by contemporary action-adventure films with female heroines.

This problem of exactly what types of films constitute the major categories of the woman's film also troubles discussions of the genre. The woman's film has been traditionally associated with domesticity, romance, and sentiment; nevertheless, when critics attempt to define it, they point to other general characteristics. Both Mary Ann Doane and Jeanine Basinger suggest that the genre is defined by the centrality of its female protagonist, its attempt to deal with issues deemed important to women, and an address to a female audience. This definition encompasses a wide range of films branching out from the central stalwarts of the genre in the 1940s that Doane, Basinger, and Molly Haskell before them examine, all of which could be considered women's melodramas. Other prominent categories of woman's films are career woman comedies, female biopics, and adaptations of women's novels. Additionally, the contemporary chick flick has extended the genre's constraints to include female friendship films, nineteenth-century literary adaptations focused on female protagonists, and women's action-adventure films. Because of its wide-ranging generic composition, Rick Altman has proposed that the woman's film is a critic-created entity, a "phantom genre" not even recognized by the film industry and comprising "a succession of already existing genres" brought together as a way to study films aimed at a female audience (1999: 72). Altman insists the term has come "to take on a life of its own, drawing to its corpus virtually any film apparently addressed to women," and not just films, but television soap operas and gothic romance novels as well. For Altman, the term woman's film represents nothing more than a "multi-media banner" for feminist critical analysis, useful to feminists perhaps, but unrelated to the realities of film production and consumption (1999: 77).

In spite of these objections, the woman's film remains an important area of feminist criticism and its study has foregrounded issues of importance to feminist film scholarship. Analyses of 1930s and 1940s woman's films have been especially important in highlighting debates concerning the female spectator. As Neale points out, feminist scholars have closely focused on "the extent to which these [women's] genres and forms allow for the articulation of a female point of view, and on the extent to which that point of view – and the fate of female protagonists – may be channeled, distorted, recuperated or dictated by patriarchal contexts of production, circulation and reception" (2000: 184). An issue that feminist theorists have only tangentially addressed, but one that warrants much fuller study is the relationship of these 1930s and 1940s woman's films to their contemporary successors. Tania Modleski (1982) in *Loving with a Vengeance* and Christine Gledhill (1987) in *Home Is Where the Heart Is* have made strides in this area in their attempts to tie the woman's film to soap operas and other forms of woman's fiction, and in my book, *In the Company of Women: contemporary female friendship films* (Hollinger 1988a) and my afterword to the volume *Chick Flicks* (Hollinger 2008), I have tried to outline the development of recent woman's films. Still the area of contemporary woman's films or chick flicks, as they have come to be labeled, remains largely untheorized and under-investigated. We will try to undertake some of that investigation here.

A long history of Hollywood cinema essentially targeted to a female audience runs between contemporary chick flicks and the woman's films of the 1930s and 1940s. Both generations of women's cinema examine "women's issues," but the plots of 1930s and 1940s woman's films indicate that the issues filmmakers deemed important to women in that time period involved romance and domesticity, rather than career and female friendship, two of the dominant themes of contemporary chick flicks. Altman questions whether the older woman's films and the chick flicks of today can even be said to form a cohesive genre or whether they merely represent a loosely defined group of films that share three common characteristics: their focus on a female protagonist, emphasis on issues deemed important to women, and appeal to a female audience. Perhaps looking at how feminist critics have approached the history of the woman's film as it developed into the chick flick will allow us to decide if we want to see them as constituting two generations of the same genre or just somewhat related cinematic forms.

As noted above, the woman's film became a privileged genre for feminist film critics primarily because of its ostensible address to a female audience. The relationship of woman's films to their female viewers became a matter of considerable feminist debate at the same time that the issue of female spectatorship began to dominate feminist thinking in the 1980s. The woman's film in its 1930s and 1940s incarnations has been analyzed most extensively by Molly Haskell, Mary Ann Doane, Tania Modleski, Jeanine Basinger, and Linda Williams. One film in particular, the popular maternal melodrama *Stella Dallas* (King Vidor, 1937), precipitated an extended debate between Linda Williams and E. Ann Kaplan in the scholarly publication *Cinema Journal*. We will analyze this debate in depth in our Films in Focus segment of this chapter, where we will also look at *The Devil Wears Prada* (David Frankel, 2006), a contemporary chick flick that focuses, like *Stella Dallas*, on the relationship between two generations of women.

As we noted in Chapter 1, the pioneering feminist analysis of the woman's film was done by Molly Haskell. She devotes one chapter to the genre in her larger study, *From Reverence to Rape: the treatment of women in the movies* (1974 and 1999). Her work is particularly significant because she was the first to take the genre seriously and counter the woman's film's dismissal by male critics. At the same time, it must be said that Haskell's analysis constitutes a very mixed appraisal. She laments the "low caste among highbrows" and the "untouchable" reputation woman's films have had, suggesting that the amount of critical opprobrium launched against them reflects not the films' inherent lack of quality but the widespread belief that their subject matter, "women, and therefore women's emotional problems, are of minor significance" (Haskell 1999: 154). At the same time, Haskell proposes that the majority of 1930s and 1940s woman's films offer their female viewers masochistic scenarios of female victimization. As she describes the films, they "embrace the audience as victims, through the common myths of rejection and self-sacrifice and martyrdom as purveyed by the mass media" and create a world of masochistic feminine self-pity in which women reconcile themselves to their misery rather than rebel against it (Haskell 1999: 160–61). Haskell also argues, however, that the fact that women needed the type of opiate for their woes that the woman's film offers indicates that there was a great deal of disillusionment, frustration, and anger among the female population at the time. She also suggests that these masochistic woman's films represent only the lowest common denominator of the genre. Not all woman's films remain at this level. The ones Haskell champions deal with extraordinary women who are, according to Haskell, emancipated "aristocrats of their sex" or with ordinary women who become extraordinary by rejecting their initial status as victims and overcoming pain and hardship in order to control their own fate (1999: 160–61).

For Haskell, woman's films can be either socially conservative or progressive. Many simply provide women with the opportunity to spend endless "wet, wasted afternoons" resigning themselves to the patriarchal status quo and crying over their sad lot (1999: 154). Others offer their female viewers some sense of accomplishment and pride by celebrating the exceptional woman who transcends the traditional role of the female victim. According to Haskell, all of these films are worthy of study, not because of their inherent merit, although she does believe a number of them are artistically accomplished, but because they are "the closest thing to an expression of the collective drives, conscious and unconscious, of American women" (1999: 168) that can be found in classical Hollywood cinema. In Haskell's opinion, these drives involve a complicated mixture of conscious adherence and unconscious resistance to the established patriarchal order, especially in terms of its treatment of women.

Haskell mentions a number of woman's films, some of which, like *Stella Dallas*, *Letter from an Unknown Woman* (Max Ophuls, 1949), and *Mildred Pierce* (Michael Curtiz, 1945), would be analyzed extensively by subsequent feminist critics, but she does not extend her analysis much further than to present plot summaries of the films and divide them into sub-groupings in terms of focus (on extraordinary women, ordinary women, and ordinary women who become extraordinary) and thematic content. Thematically, she delineates four groupings, as follows:

1. Films of sacrifice: self for children, children for their own good, marriage for a lover, a lover for marriage or his own good, career for love, or love for career (examples: *Stella Dallas*, *Back Street* [John Stahl, 1931; Robert Stevenson, 1942], *To Each His Own* [Michael Leisen, 1946]).
2. Films of affliction: the protagonist dies unblemished or is cured by her doctor-lover (*Dark Victory* [Edmund Goulding, 1939], *Magnificent Obsession* [John Stahl, 1935; Douglas Sirk, 1954]).
3. Films of choice: between two lovers (*The Seventh Veil* [Compton Bennett, 1945], *Daisy Kenyon* [Otto Preminger, 1947]).
4. Films of competition: the protagonist battles another woman for that woman's husband and usually ends up finding that she likes the other woman better than the woman's husband (*The Great Lie* [Edmund Goulding, 1941], *Old Acquaintance* [Vincent Sherman, 1943]) (Haskell 1999: 163–64).

What Haskell offered was a introduction and at the time greatly needed defense of the genre, as well as an appreciation of the contributions to the woman's film of major actresses, such as Joan Crawford and Katherine Hepburn. What her analysis lacks is what the images of women approach to the representation of women in film also lacks: a clear feminist theoretical base.

Haskell's theoretically naive appraisal of the woman's film was followed in 1987 by Mary Ann Doane's highly theoretical book-length study *The Desire to Desire: the woman's film of the 1940s*. Doane's work is heavily influenced by developments in 1960s and 1970s film theory. She utilizes concepts of spectator positioning, gaze structure, and subject formation gleaned from apparatus theory and cinepsychoanalysis to look not just at the images of women presented in film, but at how these images are constructed by the cinematic apparatus and how spectators are positioned to read them in certain ways. Largely accepting Mulvey's argument that the spectator in Hollywood cinema is posited as male, Doane investigates 1940s women's films as examples of what happens on those rare occasions when Hollywood attempts specifically to address a female spectator. Her resulting appraisal is extraordinarily negative and condemning. Although she recognizes that because of their address to a female audience woman's films commonly offer a female gaze, she insists that this gaze is given to the female spectator only to be used against her. Doane sees the woman's film as inevitably placing its female viewers in "a masochistic position defined as 'the (impossible) place of a purely passive desire'" and offering spectatorial pleasure that is too often associated with pain, suffering, and aggression turned against not only female characters but also the female spectator herself (1987: 7). In the final analysis, according to Doane, the woman's film not only offers its female spectator masochistic scenarios of women's victimization but denies her any possible subject position except a masochistic one. Following Mulvey's theorization of female spectatorship as oscillation between male and female poles of spectatorial positioning, Doane suggests that the woman's film de-eroticizes the gaze (does not allow the spectator to look erotically at the film's characters) and in the process de-eroticizes the female image, essentially denying women "the space of a reading" by eliminating the feminine pole of spectator positioning in which the female viewer ostensibly identifies with her eroticized like on the screen (1987: 19). In attempting to address a female audience, the woman's film manages only to alienate the female spectator from its de-eroticized female protagonist and to implicate her all the more fully in a male perspective that victimizes or pathologizes her screen representative.

Like Haskell, Doane divides the woman's film into sub-genres: the maternal melodrama, love story, medical discourse film, and paranoid gothic film. Doane describes maternal melodramas as the paradigmatic representative of the genre. Their "scenarios of separation, of separation and return, or of threatened separation – dramas which play out all the permutations of the mother/child relation" (Doane 1987: 73) established sacrifice and suffering as the essence of the genre and were largely responsible for giving the genre its derogatory label as the woman's weepie. This subgenre seems to have reached its high point fairly early in the woman's film cycle in the late 1930s with *Stella Dallas* and *Madame X* (Sam Wood, 1937), but it continued on into the 1940s, aligning maternal sacrifice with other themes like war propaganda in *Since You Went Away* (John Cromwell, 1944) and women's careerism in *Mildred Pierce*. Although it expanded its thematic concerns, the maternal melodrama always stuck close to the topic of woman's role within the family, especially in terms of her relationship with her children and what constitutes a "good" mother. It is also strongly associated with eliciting a feeling of pathos in the female spectator, who Doane believes is thereby manipulated into assuming a feminized masochistic spectatorial position. The second subgenre that Doane discusses deals not with the topic of motherhood but with the formation of the romantic couple. Its aim seems to be to reposition its protagonist, who has somehow gone astray, in her "proper" role as an object of male desire, but at the same time, the love story is the sub-genre of the woman's film that holds the most subversive potential because, as Doane points out, in working to make its protagonist the object of her lover's desire it also must acknowledge the possibility that she might possess her own erotic desire (1987: 118). While female desire may be recognized, it is thwarted in every conceivable way because the love story is plagued by delays, blockages, missed opportunities, coincidental occurrences, and unhappy endings that prevent the heroine's "desire to desire" from ever being fulfilled. Thus, Doane says the films only serve to re-enact "the impossible position of women in relation to desire in patriarchal society" (1987: 122).

If the maternal melodrama is plagued by loss and the love story by delay and unhappy endings, the medical discourse and the paranoid gothic subgenres are even darker. In the former, the female body is presented as symptomatic, the site of disease, most often mental but sometimes physical, and this symptomatic woman is put under the control of a male physician. For Doane, this illness and submission to masculine medical control has a contagious effect with female spectatorship itself becoming associated with pathology and the need for complete submission to male control (1987: 68). Paranoid gothic films associate the female spectator not with illness but with fear. This category of the woman's film is characterized by the "formulaic repetition of a scenario in which the wife invariably fears that her husband is planning to kill her – the institution of marriage is haunted by murder" (Doane 1987: 123).

For Doane, each of these four sub-genres constructs in its own way a masochistic female spectator (1987: 94). The maternal melodrama submits the female body to loss, the love story to the thwarting of her desire, the medical discourse film to medical control, and the paranoid gothic film to terror. Doane goes on to draw from this dreary analysis a conclusion that seems to be a direct attack on feminist cultural studies. She suggests that feminist critics are often drawn to genres directed to a female audience because they want to find in them something that belongs to women and "escapes the patriarchal stronghold" (Doane 1987: 180). As a result, they approach these texts redemptively, reevaluating as positive characteristics what should be seen as negative or neutral in significance. The resulting evaluation often involves championing traditional feminine qualities as hierarchically superior to male attributes. Doane rejects these sorts of redemptive readings as essentialist and as postulating a too narrow definition of femininity that identifies womanhood with a limited set of positively reevaluated feminine characteristics. She objects as well to another type of redemptive textual analysis that emphasizes not how a film positions its spectator but how real female viewers use mass cultural texts for their own purposes, producing more positive and empowering readings than the texts seem to warrant.

Doane condemns this approach as reading viewers rather than texts (1987: 180). In her evaluation of the woman's film, Doane definitely looks at texts and not viewers. What she finds is absolutely nothing that "escapes the patriarchal stronghold" and belongs to women. This is not to say that Doane sees these films as unrelated to women's culture or to individual women viewers. She suggests that the films follow a mass cultural tradition termed "respeaking" (Doane 1987: 180). Popular culture texts "respeak" the real socially rooted needs, desires, and identities of the social groups that produce and consume them. In the process of this "respeaking," an "echo of our actual or virtual collective speaking" is heard, but something gets lost in the translation, and that something makes the message very different than what it echoes (Doane 1987: 180). For Doane, the woman's film represents just such an echo of women's experiences with the real experiences lost in translation.

Critics of Doane have argued that her insight into the woman's film seems partial at best because she ignores gaps and fissures in the texts that allow readings that her strongly psychoanalytic approach does not recognize. She has also been accused of prescribing politically correct pleasure and fantasies for female audiences and ignoring moments in texts that lend themselves to resistant readings (Rabinowitz 1990: 157–58). Tania Modleski, for instance, in analyzing a paradigmatic paranoid gothic woman's film *Rebecca* (Alfred Hitchcock, 1940) as a female Oedipal drama argues that there is another option that does not repeatedly show how women's silence is inscribed in film texts, but that identifies resistant discourses in woman's films, finding places where women speak if only in a whisper of their discontent with patriarchy (1988: 2). Writing in 1993, Jeanine Basinger adopted Modleski's approach in her study of 1930s and 1940s woman's films. She describes these films as double-voiced, or as she puts it, "two-faced, providing [female] viewers with escape, freedom, release, and then telling them that they shouldn't want such things; they won't work; they're all wrong" (Basinger 1993: 23). Modleski's and Basinger's ideas are clearly influenced by the cultural studies orientation that swept over feminist film studies in the 1990s and that Doane, a staunch psychoanalytic critic, condemns. Like other cultural studies theorists, Modleski and Basinger insist that real women viewers use films in ways that empower them in spite of the regressive messages that scholarly close readings like Doane's might suggest are inherent in the texts. Basinger claims that, beneath the conservative stance that woman's films take on the surface, the texts offer women a sense of temporary liberation. These films allow female viewers to escape for a brief time at least into romantic love, sexual awareness, a luxurious lifestyle, and the temporary rejection of traditionally feminine roles (Basinger 1993: 13).

Linda Williams takes yet another approach to the genre. Oddly enough, she sees it as one of three body genres, the others being pornography and horror. Each of these genres is excessive either in terms of presenting gratuitous amounts of sex (pornography), violence (horror) or emotion (the woman's film). According to Williams, the salient feature of these body genres involves the spectacle of the female body caught in the grip of intense sensation or emotion. In the woman's film, that emotion is an overwhelming sense of pathos caused by intense sadness and loss (Williams 1999: 270). As a body genre, the woman's film tends to promote strong audience involvement in the emotions of the characters. Williams argues that this emotional involvement in the film leads to a lack of a critical aesthetic distance, over-involvement with the characters' emotions, and a feeling of being manipulated. Using psychoanalytic theories of fantasy structures, Williams connects this over-involvement with sadomasochistic fantasy scenarios originating in childhood fantasies that attempt to deal with the major enigmas confronting the child: the origin of sexual desire (dealt with in pornography through fantasies of seduction), the origin of sexual difference (confronted in horror through fantasies of castration), and the origin of the self (taken up in the woman's film through fantasies of loss reactivating the separation from the pre-Oedipal mother) (1999: 278). These fantasy structures allow the spectator to oscillate between passivity (watching the suffering woman) and activity (empathetically suffering along with her). For Williams, the spectatorial position offered by the woman's film, like that of other body genres, encourages the breakdown of masculine and feminine poles of spectator positioning to allow all spectators to engage in multiple identifications (1999: 275). Although Williams still employs the psychoanalytic approach, she comes to a much less negative evaluation of the woman's film than Doane. For Williams, body genres should not be dismissed as "evidence of monolithic and unchanging misogyny, either pure sadism for male viewers or masochism for females"; instead, they should be seen as performing the function of all genre films, which she believes to be "cultural problem solving." By this, Williams does not mean that genres really solve society's problems. The audience appeal of body genres actually involves their ability to deflect basic social problems by displacing them into different terms (Williams 1999: 280). In the woman's film, one could say that the social problem of women's positioning within patriarchy is raised but displaced into masochistic scenarios of loss and suffering that evoke pathos as a response. Citing Italian critic Franco Moretti's theory of why viewers cry in films, Williams argues that we cry in response to woman's films not just because we witness the sadness and suffering of a female character, but we cry at the moment when that character realizes, as we do, that her situation is hopeless and her desire futile (1999: 279). In some ways, Williams returns to Haskell's characterization of woman's films as providing "wet, wasted afternoons" for female viewers, but for Williams there is nothing wasted about these films because even masochistic pleasures can be accompanied by a sense of power and control (1999: 280).

The sub-generic divisions of the woman's film that Doane discusses were transformed in the 1970s into what some critics have called the new woman's film. This regeneration occurred after woman's films had fallen into a period of hiatus during the 1950s, when family melodramas, aimed much more at mixed male and female audiences, began to predominate. Major examples of the 1950s family melodrama include *Written on the Wind* (Sirk, 1954), *East of Eden* (Kazan, 1955), and *Giant* (Stevens, 1956). The new woman's films of the 1970s altered the contours of the genre by dealing with two issues initiated by the growth of the woman's movement in this period: the independent woman and female friendship. Films such as *An Unmarried Woman* (Mazursky, 1978) and *Alice Doesn't Live Here Anymore* (Scorsese, 1974) featured a woman attempting to make it on her own after divorce or the death of her spouse. Female friendship films also proliferated in this decade, notable examples being *Julia* (Zinnemann, 1977), *The Turning Point* (Ross, 1977), and *Girlfriends* (Weill, 1978).

As I argue in my book *In the Company of Women: contemporary female friendship films* (Hollinger 1998a), women's friendship came to dominate the woman's film market in the 1980s. While other types of woman's films are still evident in this period, they were not produced in even close to the same numbers as female friendship films. Films dealing with independent women actually began to die out in the 1980s, or they merged with preexisting film and television genres. As a result, the more patriarchally challenging aspects of the 1970s independent woman films, which openly championed female independence, were muted. For instance, movies that might be categorized as independent mother films modified their female protagonist's sense of independence by combining it with her devotion to motherhood, a much more traditionally feminine trait. Examples include *Stella* (John Erman, 1990; the remake of *Stella Dallas* starring Bette Midler), *Terms of Endearment* (James L. Brooks, 1983), *The Good Mother* (Leonard Nimoy, 1988), *This Is My Life* (Nora Ephron, 1993), and *Anywhere But Here* (Wayne Wang, 1999). The paranoid gothic woman's film was largely transformed into the victimized-woman's-revenge film in *The Accused* (Jonathan Kaplan,1988), *Sleeping with the Enemy* (Joseph Rubin, 1991), and *Enough* (Michael Apted, 2002). The scenario of the abused woman also became a staple of made-for-television woman-in-jeopardy movies, and other television dramas continued in the tradition of earlier medical discourse films by focusing on plot formulas that involve a woman's courageous struggle against a debilitating illness.

From among these various categories of new woman's films, the female friendship film found the widest audience and the greatest mainstream popularity. Beginning in the late 1970s and extending through the 1990s, films centrally concerned with the issue of female bonding were produced in large numbers by Hollywood and even independent filmmakers. Representing a mixture of progressive and regressive elements, these films affirm their female audience by presenting positive female characters who can serve as sympathetic figures of identification, validating the self-worth of the female spectator. The female friendships portrayed also offer an alternative to women's complete dependence on men and family for self-affirmation. On the other hand, these female-affirmative qualities are repeatedly harnessed to discourses that neutralize their potentially progressive effect on women viewers. The feminist ideas expressed often seem appropriated merely to provide a basis for a popularly entertaining narrative rather than to offer a serious consideration of women's concerns. Even when issues important to women are broached, their presentation is typically rendered on such a personal level or the solutions proposed are so simplistic and unrealistic that the significance of women's problems is minimized rather than accentuated. Rather than taking a strong stand on any matter, what most notably characterizes the female friendship film cycle is its cultivation of varying and even contradictory viewer responses, ranging from the progressive to the conservative. The films' mixture of progressive and regressive elements makes them particularly open to multiple reading possibilities, a characteristic that connects them to the cultural studies notion of polysemy. Like other woman's films before them, they represent a highly negotiated cinematic form that offers neither a progressive challenge to the patriarchical status quo nor reactionary support for the dominant ideology; instead, the films are complex instances of the intricate process of negotiation that exists between the competing ideological frameworks of their creators and their audience.

In *In the Company of Women*, I broke female friendship films down into five categories: sentimental, manipulative, political, erotic, and social. Each category addresses the female spectator in a slightly different way. Sentimental female friendship films (such as *Beaches* [Gary Marshall, 1988] and *Steel Magnolias* [Herbert Ross, 1989]) with their focus on close, emotionally effusive ties among women and their emphasis on the nurturing and psychologically enriching qualities of these relationships offer female friendship not as a route to political action and social change but as a means of female social integration. In contrast to these sentimental female friendship films, which came to dominate the cycle and at the same time to contain its most regressive qualities, female friendship films that focused on women's maturation and psychological development offered more progressive possibilities. Films such as *Desperately Seeking Susan* (Susan Seidelman, 1985), *Housekeeping* (John Forsyth, 1987), and *Mystic Pizza* (Donald Petrie, 1988) concentrated on women's need for both relatedness and autonomy in their formation of a sense of female identity. While they left their audience with the image of women's autonomous self-determination, they were able to offer few practical suggestions for where this autonomy might fruitfully find expression. Less emotionally intense but much more patriarchally challenging political female friendship films had a short-lived popularity. *Thelma & Louise* (Ridley Scott, 1991) was unquestionably the most politically "radical" female friendship film, connecting women's discontent with violence. Its radicality, however, precipitated the quick demise of this branch of the cycle. The rarity of political female friendship portrayals demonstrates how limited the anti-patriarchal potential of the cycle really was. Also rare were erotic female friendship films, like *Desert Hearts* (Donna Deitch, 1985) and *Go Fish* (Rose Troche, 1994), and female friendship films that deal with race and ethnicity, such as *Mi Vida Loca* (Allison Anders, 1994) and *Waiting to Exhale* (Forest Whitaker, 1995). Surprisingly, manipulative or anti-female friendship films always remained a rarity in the female friendship film cycle. The dominance of sentimental female friendship portrayals that thematically support women's acclimation to the existing social structure rather than their rebellion against it seems to account for this lack of overt cinematic attacks on female friendship. There was no need to have films that portray female friendship as evil and destructive if female friendship portrayals were serving to acclimate women to an acceptance of patriarchal norms. Anti-female friendship films, like *Single White Female* (Barbet Schroeder, 1992) and *The Hand that Rocks the Cradle* (Curtis Hanson, 1992), prominent really only in the single year of 1992, represent a short-lived response to the politically challenging association of female friendship with violence and social rebellion found in films like *Thelma & Louise* and *Mortal Thoughts* (Alan Rudolph, 1991).

Although these 1980s and 1990s portrayals of women's friendship are the direct ancestors of today's chick flicks, with a few notable exceptions, such as *The Sisterhood of the Travelling Pants* (Ken Kwapis, 2005) and its sequel (Sanaa Hamri, 2008), the female friendship cycle ran out of energy in the late 1990s. I would suggest two reasons for this decline beyond the obvious one of an exhaustion of plot formulas. First, the increasingly conservative climate in the late 1990s and into the 2000s made the female friendship film, which was inspired by feminist notions of sisterhood, anathema to mainstream film-making. Second, the 1990s also witnessed a significant rise in women's involvement in the film industry as producers and directors, as well as an increase in the clout of female stars, who became more involved in production. Despite their foregrounding of female characters and what are generally considered women's issues, Hollywood female friendship films have been overwhelmingly the products of male directors and production executives. The entry of women into directorial and managerial roles changed the contours of woman's films in a direction that led to the appearance of the contemporary chick flick.

One of the first changes women's greater involvement in filmmaking brought about was a return to classic women's literature as a source of female-centered plots and characters. This "return to the classics" movement began in the mid 1990s with the remarkable popularity of the film adaptations of Louisa May Alcott's *Little Women* (Gillian Armstrong, 1994) and Jane Austen's *Sense and Sensibility* (Ang Lee, 1995), both of which focus on sisterly relationships as drawn by prominent women writers of the past. We will discuss this cycle of films more fully in our chapter dealing with female-oriented literary adaptations. It suffices to say here that this cycle produced a veritable deluge of Jane Austen adaptations, as well as other significant films such as *The Portrait of a Lady* (Jane Campion, 1996) and *The House of Mirth* (Terence Davies, 2000). Many of these films are notable for being adapted to the screen by female screenwriters, and often female directors and producers as well, primarily from novels written by female authors, focusing on female protagonists. This female-oriented return to the classics movement, however, very quickly ran its course in the late 1990s and gave way to a new sub-genre of the woman's film, the chick flick.

The chick flick has been defined variously as escapist entertainment for women, any film that men don't like, examinations of the empowerment of capable independent female characters, emotional "tearjerkers," tales of female bonding, and the antithesis to male-oriented action films. At the core of the chick-flick cycle, however, is the romantic comedy which looks at the lives and loves of contemporary young women, mixing in disparate elements, such as female empowerment, solidarity among women, consumerism, old-fashioned sentimentality, and fairy-tale elements. As Carol Dole points out, the result of this rather odd recipe is films whose mixture of feminism and traditional femininity gives them a strong connection to third-wave feminism (1998: 59). Films like *Bridget Jones's Diary* (Sharon Maguire, 2001), *Legally Blonde* (Robert Luketic, 2001) and their sequels, as well as the extremely popular television series *Sex in the City* (HBO, 1998–2004), are core chick flick texts. These films appeal to the postfeminist sensibilities of a twenty-to-thirty-something audience by conveying the third-wave feminist notion that women can have it all. They can be whatever they want to be and have whatever they want to have. The films also show a renewed acceptance of traditional notions of femininity that were largely rejected by second-wave feminism but have been revived in the postfeminist era. They combine an acceptance of conventional femininity in terms of dress, looks, and the importance of love relationships with feminist calls for female independence and equal opportunities for women in the public sphere. Additionally, a notable group of chick flicks are teen-pics or female-oriented maturational comedies, such as the popular *The Princess Diaries* films (Gary Marshall, 2001 and 2004). These teen-pics resemble other chick flicks aimed at a more mature audience in that they show their adolescent female protagonists entering young adulthood ostensibly with the freedom to select what is right for them from a wide range of life choices.

Many chick flicks, teen or otherwise, fall into the makeover film category, showing a young independent woman who does not meet the criteria of conventional beauty experiencing an external transformation that places her much more in accord with mainstream beauty standards. The changes she experiences in terms of her looks not only internally alter her sense of identity and self-confidence but also bring her the external joys of love and/or marriage. As we will see, *The Devil Wears Prada* fits within the makeover formula. Another group of chick flicks is the mid-life romantic comedy that centers on the sexual re-awakening of a woman in middle age, such as

Something's Gotta Give (Nancy Mayers, 2002) and *Under the Tuscan Sun* (Audrey Wells, 2003). These films make somewhat progressive statements about the ultimately enriching effects of a middle-aged woman's reassertion of her sexuality, but like their younger chick flick counterparts, these older female protagonists end up having it all: happy marriages, fulfilling careers, and good sex.

In fact, the life-is-pretty-rosy-for-women-today message is the form of address to female audiences that dominates the contemporary chick-flick cycle. One might argue that the chick flick represents considerable progress in comparison to earlier woman's films, but the question really comes down to whether they actually offer their female viewers a different type of spectatorial position than their predecessors. In some ways the answer to this question is clearly yes, but one must still regard these films with a certain amount of caution. Unlike their woman's film predecessors of the 1930s and 1940s, chick flicks offer not a lament for female loss and unhappiness under patriarchy but a celebration of women's glorious triumph over patriarchal restrictions and their ability to do so while still maintaining many aspects of traditional femininity. If we use the images of women approach to assess these films, their protagonists are unquestionably more positive, or at least happier than those in earlier woman's films, yet questions arise about the unambiguously progressive nature of chick flick heroines, just as they did about earlier woman's film characters: Do these films really address women in ways that challenge women's prescribed gender roles or do they ultimately just return women to a long-standing and very limiting idea of true femininity? Do they embody the complexities of women's lives or merely reflect an unthinking celebration of the you-can-have-it-all philosophy? Can they in any way be said to present positive or realistic images of women? In light of the many questions that remain about how chick flicks address their female audience, the effect these films have on women viewers remains open to question. The messages offered in these contemporary woman's films seem in many ways just as conflicted as those offered by their woman's film predecessors. Perhaps they are conflicted in different ways, but nevertheless considerable ambiguity remains under the seemingly progressive surface of all of these films, and the ultimate question becomes the one that feminists for decades have been asking about the woman's film: In the final analysis are these films good or bad for women? To put it in another way, do they really offer an alternative to male-conceived cinematic representations of women? Since these films undoubtedly affect women's thinking about themselves and about their role in society, it seems important that we examine both an example of an older woman's film and a more recent chick flick in terms of their address to their female audience. We will now look at *Stella Dallas* and *The Devil Wears Prada* in just those terms.

Films in Focus: *Stella Dallas* and *The Devil Wears Prada*

The Stella Dallas *Debate*

Molly Haskell early recognized *Stella Dallas* (King Vidor, 1937) as the paradigmatic woman's film, and it has long been regarded as a quintessential representative of the subgenre of the maternal melodrama with its emphasis on
motherly sacrifice and loss. It was not until Linda Williams published her 1984
essay "'Something Else Besides a Mother': *Stella Dallas* and the maternal
melodrama." in *Cinema Journal*, however, that the film became the center of
intense feminist interest. Williams' essay was seen as a response to an earlier
article by E. Ann Kaplan, "The Case of the Missing Mother: maternal issues
in Vidor's *Stella Dallas*," published in the feminist journal *Heresies* in 1983. In
Kaplan's view, the film perpetuated oppressive patriarchal myths of motherhood that either idealize mothers as all-nurturing, self-abnegating, and self-
sacrificing or disparage them as sadistic, neglectful and selfish, rather than
treating them as complex individuals in their own right (Kaplan 1990: 127).
Kaplan saw Stella (Barbara Stanwyck) as a combination of maternal stereotypes.
At times she is the good, long-suffering mother, but at others she is selfish and
hurtful or silly and ridiculed with her outlandish dress and unsophisticated personality rendering her the embodiment of embarrassing female spectacle (Kaplan
1990: 128). She also resists her proper role under patriarchy by asserting herself,
refusing to accommodate to upper-class norms, and determining to be a mother
who also has "fun," as she tells her disapproving upper-class husband.

Stella is a working-class woman who marries above her social position and
finds that she cannot easily adapt to her husband Stephen's (John Boles)
expectations. According to Kaplan, the female spectator is made to identify
with Stephen's disapproval of Stella's lower class behavior and to approve of
his decision to leave her and their daughter. As the film progresses, Stella
becomes for Kaplan more and more a negative spectacle, especially in comparison to Stephen's new upper-class love interest, Helen Morrison (Barbara
O'Neil), a wealthy widow who is portrayed as the ideal mother to her young
sons and the perfect potential wife for Stephen. For Kaplan, Stella's relationship with her daughter Laurel (Anne Shirley), on the other hand, is presented
as involving an unhealthy excess of mother-daughter devotion (1990: 133).
While we might feel a certain amount of sympathy for Stella as an abandoned
wife and mother, Kaplan sees the film as unremitting in its determination to
turn us against her so that at the end we will approve of her decision to give
up her daughter. Kaplan suggests that by the film's conclusion both Stella and
the female spectator are convinced that Laurel's proper place is with her father
and Helen. In order to persuade Laurel to leave her and take up residence

with Stephen and his new wife, Stella must pretend she is tired of her motherly role, she wants to be "something else besides a mother," and she is indifferent to giving up the daughter who throughout her life has meant everything to her.

Kaplan believes that the film's ending is particularly important in leading the female spectator to view Stella negatively. We come to approve her decision to break all ties with her daughter, give her over to Stephen and Helen, and thus allow Laurel to enter into the upper-class lifestyle where the film suggests she naturally belongs. *Stella Dallas* ends with a tear-drenched final sequence. We are positioned with Stella as she stands outside in the rain and watches from a distance as Laurel marries a wealthy suitor who we are to assume would have never married her if he had to witness the spectacle of her lower-class mother at the wedding. So Stella must watch through a window as her daughter takes her wedding vows. Conveniently, the drapes are left open by the empathetic Helen, who intuits that Stella will be out there watching. Stella stands in the rain smiling and crying at the same time and begging a police officer who tries to persuade her to leave that she just wants to see her daughter's face when her groom kisses her. In spite of the pathos of this scene or really because of it, Kaplan proposes that we are lead by the inexorable

Figure 2 Barbara Stanwyck as Stella in the emotionally wrenching closing scene of *Stella Dallas*.

movement of the narrative to see the rightness of Stella's placement as a distant spectator excluded from her own daughter's wedding. By extension, "we learn what it is to be a mother in patriarchy – it is to renounce, to be on the outside, and to take pleasure in this positioning" (Kaplan 1990: 134).

Williams sees the film quite differently. She believes the female spectator is not led to disapprove of Stella, as Stephen does. In fact, she sees Stephen as the most unsympathetic character in the film. For Williams, we do not identify with any single character but with multiple conflicting points of view. At times, we are aligned with Stella in her love for her daughter and even in her innocent attempts to have "fun" with her friend Ed Munn (Alan Hale), with Stephen in his affection for Laurel and his essential incompatibility with Stella, with Laurel in her conflicted feelings of love for her mother and what the film presents as her natural upper-class inclinations, and with Helen Morrison in her sympathetic understanding of Stella's decision to sacrifice her own relationship with her daughter so that Laurel can live a better life. These multiple conflicting points of view lead the female spectator to identify with contradiction itself, a position to which women are accustomed as their lives under patriarchy are riddled with contradictory and conflicting demands. Thus, the film appeals to the female spectator by illustrating through its narrative that contradiction is at the heart of the prescribed female roles of daughter, wife, and mother under patriarchy (Williams 1984: 17).

Williams reads the film's ending very differently than Kaplan. For her, the structure of multiple identification prominent throughout the film is continued in the final scenes. We see the situation not just from Stella's point of view, but also from Helen's and Laurel's. We see Stella's mixture of joy and sorrow as she watches her daughter's wedding, but just before this, we are shown Laurel telling Helen how sad she is because her mother will not be there to see her get married. Defending Stella, Helen says that surely if there were any way for Stella to come she would, and then Helen deliberately leaves the drapes open so that, if Stella is by chance watching outside, she will be able to see Laurel take her matrimonial vows. Williams believes that the presentation of these multiple points of view prevents the female spectator from accepting the correctness of Stella's decision. Laurel's sadness, Helen's tender sympathy for Stella, and Stella's own pitiful state outside crying in the rain keep us from approving of Stella's decision. We do not believe in the "happy ending" offered to us because we see the cost to the daughter of her mother's self-abnegating stance. In fact, what the female spectator is led to see at least partially is "how we are led to consent to our own eradication" (Williams 1984: 22).

One reason why Williams sees the severance of the mother–daughter bond at the film's conclusion very differently than Kaplan is because she takes a contrasting view of the mother–daughter relationship presented in the film. For Kaplan, Stella's relationship with Laurel is unhealthy for both of them because it is involves an excess of devotion, but for Williams there is nothing unhealthy about it at all. In fact, to see it as unhealthy is to accept a very patriarchal interpretation of bonding between women. According to Williams, the exchange of loving gazes between mother and daughter in Stella Dallas is not a symptom of improper devotion that should more properly be given to a male love object, but rather a moment of resistance to patriarchal restrictions on female bonding. Because the great love between Laurel and her mother is a threat to patriarchal dominance, it must be broken. The film's ending shows the sadness created for both Stella and Laurel by the patriarchal injunction that the daughter through marriage must be lost to her mother.

The Stella Dallas debate went on in Cinema Journal throughout 1985 and 1986 with Kaplan arguing in a reply to Williams that Williams' reading of the film's ending is untenable. Kaplan insists that the film's female social audience in 1937, the women who actually watched the film when it was released, would not have read it as Williams does. For Kaplan, Williams' idea that female viewers might resist seeing Stella's final decision as the correct one presupposes that these viewers would possess a feminist sensibility based on an acquaintance with contemporary feminist theory. Kaplan insists that the female audience in 1937, and even most female viewers today, including herself, will not read the film's ending as Williams suggests it might be read. According to Kaplan, the film makes no attempt to have them do so; in fact, its mechanisms do everything possible to lead viewers to see Stella as having made the proper choice in giving up her daughter (1985: 41). For Kaplan, Williams' interpretation of the film's conclusion is more a product of her own feminism than it is of the workings of the text.

Other feminist critics Patrice Petro and Carol Flinn came to Williams' defense, arguing essentially that her conception of the female spectator as multiply identified is better than Kaplan's because it opens up a greater range of possibilities for feminist critics in thinking about the film, whereas Kaplan's position closes down feminist reading possibilities and regards the film as merely a mouthpiece of patriarchal ideology. Petro and Flinn believe that Williams' reading opens up various possibilities for feminist interpretation because it seeks out "textual moments when woman's voice is heard" (1985: 51) and considers how women's social experience could shape their interpretations of the film. One might question whether one reading of a text should be privileged over another simply because it is considered better for feminist criticism. This perspective led Tag Gallagher, clearly not a feminist critic himself, to comment that Williams' reading of Stella Dallas "raped," "castrated," and "prostituted" the film by refusing to treat it as a work of art and instead merely using it as an example of her pre-conceived feminist ideas (1985: 65–66). Williams responded to Gallagher by pointing out that analyses of films have always been inspired by theoretical positions and that his objections to her reading of the film demonstrate his opposition not to theory itself as a basis for interpreting films, as he proposes, but just to feminist theory (1986: 67). Regardless of Gallagher's possible anti-feminism, one certainly might question Petro and Flinn's position that a reading which is better for feminism is necessarily a better reading of a text. Gallagher's accusation that applying theoretical ideas to a film is raping it, however, goes too far.

Another participant in the *Cinema Journal* debate, Christine Gledhill, placed *Stella Dallas* within the larger category of film melodrama, the history of which can be traced back to nineteenth-century fiction and drama. Gledhill proposes that melodramatic narratives typically contain characters who suffer emotional agonies due to factors that are beyond their control and that they do not fully understand. These works produce intense pathos by having the spectator understand the causes of the character's suffering although the character does not, thus creating a sympathetic spectatorial response (Gledhill 1986: 46). The movement of the narrative is from misrecognition to recognition, concluding with the final revelation of the character's true worth and goodness. Gledhill claims that in *Stella Dallas* the basic question is whether Stella is really a good mother. Because her maternal goodness is affirmed at the film's conclusion, Stella gains the viewer's sympathy not as a result of our seeing her decision as correct or because we have a feminist consciousness, but because the melodramatic structure of the film finally confirms her essential goodness. Gledhill does not make clear whether she thinks seeing the film this way supports Williams' or Kaplan's reading or whether it actually leads to yet another interpretation.

Years after the debate about *Stella Dallas* had subsided, Anna Siomopoulos pointed out that Williams' theory of multiple identifications had become accepted as the "definitive" one not only in regard to *Stella Dallas* but also for the woman's film as a whole (Siomopoulos 1999: 13). Siomopoulos' essay, again published in *Cinema Journal*, calls many of Williams' ideas about the film into question. She places the film within the context of 1930s New Deal liberalism and the concept of the Welfare State. Siomopoulos does not see Williams' notion that *Stella Dallas* promotes multiple spectatorial identifications as necessarily leading to progressive readings. According to Siomopoulos, the film's multiple identifications produce a feeling of empathy for all of the major characters, leaving viewers to feel that no one is to blame and no one is wrong. As a result, the solution to the problems of gender and class difference raised by the film seems to require just more liberal empathy, which Siomopoulos sees as the philosophical position behind the Welfare State's ethic of charity to the suffering have-nots. What liberal empathy does not create is a radical questioning of class and gender stratification that would lead to real social change (Siomopoulos 1999: 10).

According to Siomopoulos, Williams believes the viewer leaves *Stella Dallas* angry and frustrated with Stella's self-denial, and Siomopoulos argues that this reading ignores the ambivalence the film actually produces in its audience (1999: 13). I would argue, however, that Williams' does acknowledge this ambivalence. She actually states that the viewer only partially questions Stella's self-sacrifice. For Williams, we are led to accept Stella's fate, while also feeling saddened by it and at least partially questioning it (1990: 157). Siomopoulos interprets Williams as seeing the film's spectator at the end as much more critical of Stella's decision than Williams actually suggests. Siomopoulos' major objection to Williams goes beyond this argument, however. She proposes that Williams sees the multiple identifications promoted by the film as having a potentially progressive effect because they create spectatorial resistance to Stella's actions. This aspect of her reading of Williams seems to me to be right. Williams does argue for a progressive component to *Stella Dallas*, while Siomopoulos sees no progressive effect whatsoever. Like Williams and Kaplan before her, Siomopoulos hinges her argument on a reading of the film's ending. For her, the multiple perspectives on Stella's decision to give up her daughter provided from the points of view of Stella, Laurel, and Helen do not make female viewers identify with contradiction itself, as Williams suggests, but lead them to understand and sympathize with everyone. As a result, we do not blame anyone for the situation, and Stella's sacrifice of her daughter is presented as admirable, if regrettable in terms of its consequences for Stella (Siomopoulos 1999: 15). Siomopoulos' thinking seems persuasive here. One could easily hold any one of the female characters responsible for the way things have turned out. Stella surely could have found a better way to keep from embarrassing her daughter than totally giving her up. Laurel might have had the insight into her mother's character to know that she would never choose the alcoholic Ed Munn over her beloved "Lollie," and Helen might have done something more for Stella, perhaps encouraging her to come to the wedding and helping her dress more elegantly, rather than merely opening the drapes so that Stella could watch the wedding from out in the rain. Siomopoulos argues that the structure of multiple identifications throughout the film and especially at its end and the resulting creation of liberal empathy does not lead to anything progressive. It does not promote a commitment to social change, but offers only a facile solution to ingrained social problems based on empathy for and charity to those, like Stella, who have suffered. Ultimately, it encourages liberal complacency rather than a commitment to the eradication of class and gender inequalities.

The major issues raised in this *Stella Dallas* debate reflect long-standing feminist queries concerning the woman's film. Does the fact that woman's films are aimed at a female audience mean that these films are in some sense progressive or at least that they contain a limited expression of a female point of view? To put it another way, are women's films internally self-critical texts or ideologically innocuous ones that completely support dominant patriarchal ideas? Or are they better seen as polysemous and open to multiple readings? Feminist critics have disagreed about the best way to answer these questions. Where do you position yourself in this debate?

The Devil Wears Prada: *Is It Really Different?*

Feminist theorists have discussed contemporary chick flicks in terms remarkably similar to the debate about *Stella Dallas*. Do chick flicks, as products of the male-dominated Hollywood industry, represent any progress over earlier woman's films in terms of the messages they are sending to their female audience? An analysis of the popular chick flick *The Devil Wears Prada* (David Frankel, 2006) might provide us with some answers. Like *Stella Dallas*, *The Devil Wears Prada* is based on a female-authored novel, but it was directed by a man. The novel, written by Lauren Weisberger, was considered a *roman à clef* in which Weisberger, who once worked for the formidable American editor of *Vogue* Anna Wintour, skewered not just her ex-boss but the fashion industry as a whole. Unlike the screenplay for *Stella Dallas*, which is attributed to four screenwriters, two male and two female, *The Devil Wears Prada*'s screenplay is credited to Aline Brosh McKenna although the original screenplay is said to have been written by Peter Hedges with additional uncredited work by Howard Michael Gould, Paul Rudnick, and Don Roos. A clear difference between earlier woman's films and contemporary chick flicks is that the later have more female input, especially on the level of screenwriting, yet there is still significant male influence, and ultimately, as is the case with *The Devil Wears Prada*, a man is very often in the director's chair. In order to accommodate to the chick flick formula, the film considerably alters the book, both in terms of its presentation of the fashion industry and the female editor Miranda Priestly, a thinly disguised portrait of Wintour.

Debates about the chick flick center, as did earlier ones concerning the woman's film, on the films' address to their female audience. In many ways, *The Devil Wears Prada* in spite of its comedic tone is a maternal melodrama.

While it does have a conventional heterosexual romance plot, as Andy (Anne Hathaway) struggles to prevent her career from destroying her relationship with her boyfriend Nate (Adrian Grenier), the really intense connection is between Andy and her imperious boss, Miranda Priestly (Meryl Streep). In psychoanalytic terms, Miranda represents the all-powerful phallic mother whom Andy must reject in order to establish an independent adult femininity. From a feminist perspective, the relationship between Miranda and Andy can also be seen as a generational one with Andy representing third-wave feminism and Miranda standing for what a postfeminist might see as the worst aspects of second-wave feminism. She puts career above everything else and loses her femininity in the bargain, whereas Andy wants a career but not if it means becoming a hard-edged professional woman like Miranda. Yet, as Martha P. Nochimson points out, the Miranda of the book has been changed to the film's much more appealing figure. It would have been easy for the movie to recreate Miranda as the sadistic harridan she is in the book, shrilly berating all her employees and constantly making unreasonable demands upon them. This portrayal would have placed her right in line with "Hollywood's usual demeaning portrait of women in the workplace" (Nochimson 2006: 48) and with what Diane Negra has called the chick flick convention of presenting older career women in a negative light (2008: 54).

Negra and others have painted the chick flick as a whole in a negative light, while making exceptions for certain texts, like the HBO sitcom *Sex and the City*, which many consider a positive, if still problematic, representative of chick flick culture. Negra says *Sex and the City* breaks many chick flick conventions in order to move in somewhat progressive directions. Looking at the chick flick phenomenon as a whole, however, Negra and Yvonne Tasker characterize chick flicks as superficial sketches of female subjectivity that hype empowerment for women but have a "hollow quality" because they take female equality as a given and associate women's career achievement with loss and unhappiness (2005: 108). Negra believes that the films appear to offer politically innocent, escapist narratives for women but really have a clear ideological message that is essentially anti-feminist. They portray women enjoying the benefits of feminism, yet they show a disdain for feminism itself (Negra and Tasker 2005: 108). Abandoning feminist political goals, what is championed is the idea of a "free-floating [female] desire," linked to consumerism and sexuality (Negra 2004). While chick flicks often focus on working women, they avoid important workplace issues, like the gendered pay gap and the need for child care (Negra and Tasker 2005: 108) in favor of the hackneyed question of whether women can find a way to balance career and romance.

Looking at the specifics of what Negra outlines as the problematic characteristics of the chick flick, it is unclear whether *The Devil Wears Prada*
transcends these negatives or adheres to them. Looking at the images of women
presented in chick flicks, Negra argues that they offer a problematic view of
the single woman as a "solipsistic single girl" who is either pathetically inept or too
tough in her dealings with others (2008: 63 n. 6). She is most often a young
career woman, whose ambitions are presented as "misguided at best, troubled
at worst" (Negra 2008: 53). Additionally, the chick flick heroine is a "girlie-
girl," cultivating childlike looks and behavior, and to make things even worse,
her perpetual girlhood is celebrated rather than problematized (Negra and
Tasker 2005: 109). As Suzanne Ferriss points out, there is often a makeover
component to these films. Following a long tradition of female makeover films
from *Funny Face* (Stanley Donen, 1957) through *Moonstruck* (Norman Jewison,
1987) to *My Big Fat Greek Wedding* (Joel Zwick, 2002), many chick flick protagonists undertake a major physical transformation in order to make themselves
more attractive to men and in doing so they are able to attract the male
lovers who heretofore had escaped them. This outer transformation often
involves the heroine's inner realization that she is not as independent as she
thought she was and she needs the love and companionship only heterosexual
romance can provide (Ferriss 2008: 41). Inspired by the Pygmalion myth and
Cinderella fairy tale, the chick flick protagonist's struggle to become more
beautiful is very male-focused. She changes to attract a man and under the male
guidance provided either by their future lover or another helpful male mentor.
As Ferriss suggests, Hitchcock's *Vertigo* presents the dark side of the makeover
formula (2008: 43), and one might add that it is a very dark side indeed. Chick
flicks, on the other hand, with their comedic tone take a decidedly upbeat
slant on this makeover scenario, offering female viewers the hope that self-
transformation is within the grasp of every woman through makeup, hair styling,
and expensive clothing (Ferriss 2008: 55) and that once a woman has sufficiently
beautified herself she can find true happiness with the man of her dreams.

While *The Devil Wears Prada* has many of the characteristics outlined above,
it also turns them in a more progressive direction. Andy (Anne Hathaway), the
film's protagonist, is not the solipsistic single girlie-girl that Negra describes.
She is an intelligent journalism school graduate who has turned down a chance
to go to law school to establish herself as an investigative reporter in New
York. Like the conventional chick flick protagonist, she has youthful energy,
yet she does not seem particularly childlike or inept in dealing with others.
Her career ambitions are presented as neither misguided nor troubled, but
merely as stifled by a lack of job opportunities. She is given two job choices:
one as the second assistant to the renowned editor of the prominent fashion

magazine *Runway* and the other as a member of the staff of an auto magazine. All her attempts to move into serious journalism have been unsuccessful, and she hopes that the position with *Runway* will be a stepping stone to what she really wants to do. Although she never looks like she needs to change at all and repudiates her makeover at the film's end, Andy does decide to physically transform herself in order to fit in better with her coworkers at *Runway*. She does it, however, not at all to attract a man, but because she realizes her job is in jeopardy if she refuses to change her appearance. Andy's boyfriend Nate seems actually to prefer her before she cultivates a high couture look, and he cares for her either way. Andy finally rejects a man whom her physical transformation does attract when he turns out to be a very willing player in conspiratorial business machinations against Miranda. As Nochimson points out, the film misses the opportunity to foreground the fact that Andy is beautiful before, during, and after her transformation and that she even rejects her high couture look at the film's end (2006: 50). As a Hollywood film after all, *The Devil Wears Prada* cannot resist showing Andy as the fetishized object of the gaze of everyone, male or female, who encounters her madeover self. At the same time, however, it engages in the double-voiced discourse that Jeanine Basinger (1993) identified as characteristic of earlier woman's films by portraying Andy's makeover as unnecessary, yet showing it to have still made her more attractive.

Figure 3 From left, Meryl Streep as Miranda Priestly and Anne Hathaway as Andy Sachs in *The Devil Wears Prada*.

In dealing with Andy's career ambitions, the film pits her against Miranda Priestly, its representation of the older professional woman, a figure to whom chick flicks have not been kind. She is often played by accomplished actresses (Negra 2008: 54), and in Meryl Streep *The Devil Wears Prada* has the most accomplished Hollywood actress of her generation. Still older career women in chick flicks are almost always portrayed in a negative light, as they are in Hollywood films in general. Their career triumphs cover over wrongdoing, intense personal loss, and/or extreme vulnerability (Negra 2008: 54), and their bitterness leads them to work against their younger counterparts' career success. As in many other areas, *The Devil Wears Prada* both follows and works against this formula by portraying Miranda Priestly is both a villain and a symbol of female empowerment.

In the featurette on the DVD release of the film, its director David Frankel and screenwriter Aline Brosh McKenna stress that one of the major changes they were determined to make involved the book's tone, especially what they saw as its harsh critique of Miranda Priestly and the fashion industry. McKenna says that she wanted to give both Priestly and the industry the respect that the novel denied them. Ferriss maintains that the book presents Priestly as a "cartoonish harridan," whereas the film transforms her into a sympathetic overworked mother (2008: 52). I don't know if I would go quite that far. Is Miranda really presented as sympathetic, or is McKenna's conception that she is given respect more accurate? The film seems to grant Miranda a certain amount of credit for the position of power she has attained and for her ability to manipulate and intimidate others, but she is hardly a sympathetic figure. The scenes of her family life do not really present her as an overworked wife and mother, as Ferriss suggests, but rather as an unsuccessful one. She is being divorced by her third husband, who accuses her of neglecting him for her job and humiliating him in public. She totally spoils her twin daughters. They want the unpublished manuscript of the next Harry Potter book, so she assigns Andy the nearly impossible task of getting it for them. Rather than a sympathetic portrait, this seems to be a fairly conventional Hollywood representation of the successful career woman who has attained professional success at the expense of her personal life.

The characterization of Miranda in the film seems more accurately described as her transformation from the book's "whining bitch to a figure of mythic power" (Nochimson 2006: 48). Nochimson even describes the film's Miranda as deified and a "mystification of the power of a magisterial woman" (2006: 50). For Nochimson, Miranda is a much more compelling character than Andy, whom she describes as boring. Nochimson points to Miranda's grand entrance into the film as placing her "beyond ordinary life" (2006: 48). Miranda's house is conceptualized almost as the "inner sanctum of the gods," and Andy's task to deliver laundry and a layout for the next issue of *Runway* there is presented as a ritual initiation (Nochimson 2006: 49). The novel's Miranda lacks a grand entrance or a mythic house. In the book, she is first heard rudely giving Andy instructions on her cell phone and seems sadistic rather than godly. There is also the film's presentation of Miranda's reaction to her third husband's demand for a divorce. The film keeps her husband almost completely off-screen, putting into play the issue of the failure of their marriage but refusing to dwell on it. In a scene out of 1930s and 1940s melodrama, Andy goes to see Miranda when they are on a business trip to Paris and finds her distraught after just learning that her husband wants a divorce. Streep, who insisted on doing the scene without makeup, plays it ambiguously. Miranda does look quite upset, but when Andy offers her what Nochimson calls "girl-on-girl" sympathy (2006: 49), she refuses to accept it. The film does not linger on the question of her relationships with the men in her life and whether or not she can be complete without a successful romance.

The career world and consumerism are portrayed ambiguously not only in terms of the figure of Miranda Priestly but in a larger sense. Whereas the book is "an indictment" of the fashion industry for its superficial capitalist exploitation of women, the world of fashion largely evades critique in the film (Ferriss 2008: 54). To a large extent, the film defends the fashion industry and critiques the notion that it is run by "airheads devoted to a frivolous consumer culture" (Ferriss 2008: 41). It not only shows the industry to be run by very intelligent and business savvy women like Miranda Priestly, but it connects fashion with women's self-creation and agency. Feminine display and consumer culture are shown to have a positive role in women's lives (Ferriss 2008: 42). Dave Carr even calls the film "a paean to the transforming power of fashion" (quoted in Nochimson 2006: 50), and Hilary Radner argues that fashion was used in the film's promotion to create "a buzz," attract media attention, and establish it as a "female event film" (2011: 142). As Ferriss points out, the film portrays fashion as a tool for female "self-fashioning" and a way for women to shape and reshape their identities by trying on new clothes and performing different fashion roles (2008: 55). Rather than critiquing the fashion industry as a means of capitalist exploitation, the film provides a form of window shopping for female viewers with fashion presented as a visual treat and the stuff of fantasy (2008: 54). As Radner points out, in many ways *The Devil Wears Prada* is a "girly film" that focuses on its protagonist's makeover, the importance of appearances, and the centrality of consumer culture in the life of the feminine subject (2011: 143).

Negra proposes that the chick flick's presentation of its heroine follows what she calls a "miswanting formula," which portrays women's career ambition as misplaced. Professional ambition is shown repeatedly in these films to interfere with romance, which is posited as the most important element in a woman's life (Negra 2008: 53). The heroine finally finds happiness when she gives up her career for love or at least downsizes her professional ambition to make more room for personal relationships. Again, The Devil Wears Prada both follows and modifies this formula. Nochimson argues that the film's plot suggests that Andy was tempted by the satanic lure of the fashion industry but is able to save herself in the end by returning to her original virtuous path of investigative reporting and true love (2006: 49). On the other hand, Ferriss says that, although the film does "question whether professional ambition can substitute for personal happiness," it ends by showing Andy to have found happiness through neither her career nor romance (2008: 54). In accord with the "miswanting formula," Andy experiences an epiphany when she realizes that she does not share the values of Miranda Priestly. In most chick flicks, when the heroine comes to the conclusion that her romantic and career ambitions are incompatible, she gives up her career or at the very least downsizes it for her man, a plot trajectory Negra calls "retreatism" (2008: 56). This is not exactly what happens in The Devil Wears Prada. Andy does reject Miranda's cutthroat professional philosophy, but she does not give up her career goals. She merely rechannels them back into investigative journalism, the field she had always preferred. She does seek out her boyfriend Nate and asks his forgiveness for neglecting him for her Runway job, and he seems to hold out the possibility that they can work things out. The likelihood of this happening seems doubtful, however, because he has found a position as a sous-chef in Boston and her investigative journalism job is in New York. It seems unlikely that this long-distance romance will be much different than the stress and strain of Andy's Runway stint, but the film leaves its ending open in this sense.

As Negra points out, in spite of their focus on femininity, chick flicks always deal with the importance for women of being able to distinguish authentic from inauthentic masculinity. The Devil Wears Prada may seem to keep men peripheral to the central plot, which "hinges on relations between women" (Radner 2011: 145), but this is not entirely the case. An important subplot involves Andy's struggle to choose between two men: her original boyfriend Nate (Adrian Grenier), a would-be chef who represents male authenticity and stability, and Christian Thompson (Simon Baker), a writer she meets through her job at Runway. While Christian seems exciting and worldly, he turns out to subscribe to the same cutthroat values that Miranda advocates and that Andy finally realizes she cannot accept. The film interrelates its two choice plots: Andy must decide between two men, representing authentic versus inauthentic masculinity, and between two career paths, representing false versus genuine values. In the end, the film suggests she makes the correct choice in both instances, yet the conclusion is more ambiguous than these obvious choices would seem to indicate.

Negra proposes that chick flicks most often end with complete and positive resolution in support of a conservative retreatist message. *The Devil Wears Prada* attempts exactly this type of positive closure, but with less than complete success. Its ending actually contains considerable ambiguity and can be read variously. As noted above, Ferriss says that Andy finds satisfaction in neither career nor romance (2008: 54), whereas Nochimson contends that she ends up getting both career success and her boyfriend back (2006: 49). It seems to me that neither is really the case. As Nochimson admits and many reviewers have suggested, the film's ending falls rather flat. Nathan Lee sees Andy as given two options: being a part of the glamorous fashion industry or writing boring earnest articles for serious publication and living happily ever after with her dull boyfriend (2006: 72). The film finally comes out in support of serious writing and a boring man, but it doesn't seem really to believe what it is saying. As Nochimson argues, it asks us to cheer for Andy "opting to be less, as the film construes it" (2006: 50). The problem is that the movie has built up the fashion industry so much, made Andy's fashion transformation seem so glamorous, and mythologized Miranda Priestly's powerful position to such a degree that it is difficult in the end to backtrack from all that. What the film wants finally to say is that Andy has done the right thing in rejecting all the power and glamour of the fashion world because she has learned she could never really accept its cruel cutthroat tactics, but by the film's conclusion we are so immersed in the interactions among the characters at *Runway* that it is hard simply to turn against them or even to believe that Andy would.

The film's ending also involves yet another important element, and that is the resolution of Andy's relationship with Miranda Priestly. It refuses to end with the wing-clipping of the career woman that is so common in other chick flicks (Nochimson 2006: 49). Although Andy does reject Miranda and her cruel and unethical business tactics, Miranda is not punished in any way. In fact, she emerges triumphant, managing to outsmart those conspiring to replace her at *Runway* and to keep her powerful position as editor. For support, she still has her adoring first assistant Emily (Emily Blunt) and a new mousy second assistant whom she can intimidate and abuse. Her character is given a final added dimension in the closing sequence. The film does not end with Andy securing the job she always wanted or with her reconciliation with her boyfriend, but with her seeing her previous employer on the street as Miranda gets into a limousine. The two exchange enigmatic glances. Ferriss reads this final sharing of a "knowing look" as suggesting "mutual respect if not gratitude for each other's existence" (2008: 54), yet what seems to be indicated is even more than this. It is almost mother–daughter affection. After all, earlier in the film Miranda told Andy that she reminded her of her younger self. Perhaps what is implied is that the two generations of women do in the end come together in mutual admiration and respect. Again, we might ask if any part of this ending is convincing. Why would Miranda recommend Andy after she abruptly abandoned her right in the middle of a major fashion show in Paris? Nothing else we have seen Miranda do explains this sudden change of heart. That the harridan suddenly becomes motherly in the end seems a bit of a stretch.

In the final analysis, the question really is does *The Devil Wears Prada* suggest that chick flicks are, as Ferris and Young propose, complex ambiguous texts that on one level "reinscrib[e] traditional attitudes and reactionary roles for women," yet in other ways are "pleasurable and potentially liberating entertainments assisting women in negotiating the challenges of contemporary life" (2008b: 1)? Or are they, as Negra insists, superficial sketches of contemporary women that seem progressive and empowering on the surface, but really present plot formulas that are reactionary vehicles for patriarchal ideas? What is their relationship to earlier woman's films? Do we see substantial progress in moving from the woman's film to the chick flick? These are the types of questions feminist critics investigate in looking at genre films and that you should consider yourself in thinking about *Stella Dallas* and *The Devil Wears Prada* from a feminist perspective.

Key Terms: *genre film, the woman's film, chick flicks, melodrama, female friendship films, maternal melodramas, love stories, medical discourse films, paranoid gothic films, body genres, new woman's films, makeover films, postfeminism, third-wave feminism*

Suggestions for Further Reading, Viewing, and Discussion

1. Consider the issue of why many viewers cry at the end of *Stella Dallas* and at the end of many other woman's films as well. Some of the explanations critics have given are that viewers cry because they realize the hopelessness of the situation and recognize that the character is experiencing this same sense of futility (Moretti), they aesthetically appreciate the beauty of Stella's sacrifice (Kaplan), the woman's film as a body genre contains an excess of emotion that is connected to the pre-Oedipal loss of oneness with the mother (Williams), they over-identify with the image of the suffering mother (Doane), or they feel intense pathos because they know more than *Stella* does and therefore feel sympathy for her suffering. Why do you think viewers cry? Analyze some woman's films of the 1930–50s with their tear-inducing qualities in mind.

2. Is Kaplan right that the ending of *Stella Dallas* leads us to accept the correctness of Stella's decision to give up her daughter? Do the multiple identifications that Williams suggests occur in one's viewing of *Stella Dallas* really lead viewers to question Stella's decision? Or is Sionopoulas correct that these identifications actually promote greater understanding and hence acceptance of Stella's sacrifice? How did you react to the ending of the film?

4. Does *The Devil Wears Prada* represent significant progress over *Stella Dallas* in terms of its presentation of women or are both texts polysemous mixtures of progressive and patriarchal elements? Watch other woman's films from the 1930s–50s and some contemporary chick flicks with their possibly progressive, patriarchal, or polysemous nature in mind. The selected filmography below offers some suggestions, but there are many more films from which you might choose.

5. Watch a number of chick flicks and woman's films with the question in mind of whether chick flicks are the descendants of earlier woman's films or are a different type of film altogether? Is it a mistake to see a connection between them or is drawing this connection a useful way to think about these two chronologically distinct forms of women's cinema?

6. Compare Stella and Mrs. Morrison in *Stella Dallas* to Amanda Priestly in *The Devil Wears Prada*. You might also compare Laurel in the former film to Andy in the latter. What changes do you see in the images of these two generations of heroines as you move from the woman's film to the chick flick?

7. Is Amanda Priestly a villain or hero in *The Devil Wears Prada*? Why or why not?

8. Does Andy's decision at the end of *The Devil Wears Prada* "fall flat" as many reviewers have suggested? Why or why not?

9. Read Lauren Weisberger's novel on which the film version of *The Devil Wears Prada* is based. What are the differences and similarities between the two works? Why do you think the changes were made?

10. Nora Ephron and Nancy Meyers could be considered major chick flick auteurs. Watch a number of films by each. How do their films use chick flick conventions? Do they represent the genre in similar or different ways?

Selected Filmography of Woman's Films and Chick Flicks

Woman's Films

All That Heaven Allows (Douglas Sirk, 1955) and Todd Haynes' contemporary remake *Far From Heaven* (2002)

Back Street (two versions: John M. Stahl, 1932 and Robert Stevenson, 1941)

Dark Victory (Edmund Goulding, 1939)

Gaslight (George Cukor, 1944)

Imitation of Life (two versions: John M. Stahl, 1934 and Douglas Sirk, 1959)

Letter from An Unknown Woman (Max Ophuls, 1948)

A Letter to Three Wives (Joseph L. Mankiewicz, 1949)

Magnificent Obsession (Douglas Sirk, 1954)

Mildred Pierce (Michael Curtiz, 1945 and Todd Haynes' 2011 TV min-series remake)

Now, Voyager (Irving Rapper, 1942)

One True Thing (Carl Franklin, 1998; a contemporary maternal melodrama)

Rebecca (Alfred Hitchcock, 1940)

Since You Went Away (John Cromwell, 1944)

The Snake Pit (Anatole Litvak, 1948)

Stella (John Erman, 1990; a contemporary remake of *Stella Dallas*)

Chick Flicks

Bridget Jones's Diary (Sharon Maguire, 2001)

Bridget Jones: The Edge of Reason (Beebon Kidron, 2004)

Bridesmaids (Paul Feig, 2011)

It's Complicated (Nancy Meyers, 2009)

Julie & Julia (Nora Ephron, 2009)

Legally Blonde (Robert Luketic, 2001)

Legally Blonde 2: Red, White and Blonde (Charles Herman-Wurmfeld, 2003)

Maid in Manhattan (Wayne Wang, 2002)

Party Girl (Daisy von Scherler Meyer, 1995; an independent film that tries to subvert the genre)

Sex and the City (TV, Darren Star [creator], 1998–2004)

Sex and the City (Michael Patrick King, 2008)

Sex and the City 2 (Michael Patrick King, 2010)

Sleepless in Seattle (Nora Ephron, 1993)

Something's Gotta Give (Nancy Meyers, 2003)

Chapter 3

Women in Avant-garde and Documentary Filmmaking

Although much feminist criticism and theory has focused on mainstream narrative films, especially those produced by Hollywood, many female film-makers responded to feminist concerns about the representation of women in popular films by turning to avant-garde or documentary filmmaking as potentially progressive alternatives. Both avant-garde and documentary films have been defined variously, but central to every definition is their characterization as "the Other" of mainstream cinema with a focus on experimentation for the avant-garde and on non-fiction for the documentary. Both types of films do not merely run parallel to dominant cinema, but take a reactive stance that is oppositional in terms of form, content, production and exhibition. In this chapter, we will look at the various qualities of avant-garde and documentary films that have lead to their recognition as forms of feminist opposition to mainstream filmmaking.

The Feminist Avant-Garde

The otherness of the avant-garde takes various forms, which include formal and thematic experimentation, such as non-linear narratives or non-narrative structures, short formats, anti-naturalistic performance styles, obtrusive camera work, unconventional editing, challenging content, and production and exhibition outside of major channels (Petrolle and Wexman 2005: 3). Their aims particularly distinguish avant-garde films, which seek to subvert, challenge, or at the very least separate themselves from the mainstream by asking their audience to rethink fundamental and long-established ideas about the nature of cinema itself. As Murray Smith explains, the avant-garde sets out to be thought-provoking and stimulating with little or no attempt to create pleasure in the conventional sense as it is found in mainstream films (1998: 405). Influenced by artistic and literary modernism, avant-garde films offer major challenges to mainstream ideas of realism and narrative development (Smith 1998: 396). From a modernist perspective, realism creates passive spectators by presenting a story as expressive of truth or reality. To challenge and subvert this truth-effect, avant-garde films either do away with narrative entirely or displace, deform, or reformulate their storytelling aspects (Smith 1998: 397). Additionally, they may combine formal experimentation with challenging content that emphasizes "discovery, inquiry, and innovation," rather than "culturally-dominant thought-forms" (Petrolle and Wexman 2005: 5).

Critics have divided avant-garde films into four categories with each category focusing on one of the major characteristics of the avant-garde: experimental, independent, underground, and art films. Experimental films formally experiment with the medium in ways not seen in conventional narrative film. Independent films may actually be quite similar in their narrative and formal structures to mainstream films but are funded and distributed through non-mainstream channels and strive much less for commercial success. Underground films express views and images that can be perceived as shocking or radical, and art films are commercial products that are aesthetically and thematically at odds with Hollywood. Avant-garde films can also be divided into those that contain political content and those that do not; however, since often formal experimentation and challenging political content work hand in hand in avant-garde cinema, this division seems rather simplistic (Smith 1998: 398). Another possible division is between what has been labeled the first avant-garde, pre-World War I experimental films (for instance, Dada and surrealist works), and the second avant-garde, postwar films that have taken myriad forms from politically leftist to abstract experimental films. Despite the problem of dividing political content from experimental form, both of which have always been central to avant-garde filmmaking, critics have often seen the first and second avant-gardes as diametrically opposed. The first stage of avant-garde cinema is generally regarded as setting out with the specific intention of challenging traditional art forms, whereas the second phase is more concerned with reshaping rather than destroying these forms (Mounsef 2003: 38). Another possible division that will be of major concern to us can be located in the 1970s with the development of a feminist avant-garde cinema quite distinct from the pre-seventies male-authored avant-garde. P. Adams Sitney (1979), one of the most prominent early scholars of avant-garde films, characterized them as very personal works that can best be described as products of the imagination of an individual artist. When Sitney was writing in the 1970s, it was assumed that avant-garde artists, who were seen as expressing their personal imaginative visions, would invariably be male (Blaetz 2007: 18, n.5). Early avant-garde auteurs were rarely female with the notable exception of two major avant-garde figures, Germaine Dulac and Maya Deren, the later of whom we will study in depth in our Films in Focus section for this chapter.

Although their contributions were not always recognized, women were involved in avant-garde cinema from its inception. Germaine Dulac was a major figure in the 1920s French avant-garde and Maya Deren in early American experimental cinema in the 1940s. There has been considerable debate, however, about whether these two avant-garde pioneers can really be considered "feminists in a contemporary sense," or whether they became identified somewhat inaccurately with feminist filmmaking in the 1960s when women's film festivals promoted their films as containing incipient feminist elements (Kaplan 1983: 87). As we shall see in examining Deren's most famous film, *Meshes of the Afternoon* (1943), it has not always been interpreted as feminist cinema. Feminist experimental filmmaking did not really become well established until the advent of the woman's movement of the 1960s when, as we have seen in Chapter 1, feminist critics, like Laura Mulvey and Claire Johnston, condemned Hollywood for objectifying women and representing them as sexual spectacle. The avant-garde became seen as a place where women filmmakers who sought to challenge mainstream images might find many attractions. These attractions included the reduced financial investment needed to achieve the avant-garde's less glossy filmmaking style; its traditional concern with personal expression as a way to express inner experience, sensations, feelings, and thoughts; the formal challenges it often posed to the mainstream in terms of its political themes; its seeming rejection of Hollywood illusionism; and its potential to allow lesbian filmmakers to represent their sexuality without co-optation as male pornography (Butler 2002: 57; Kaplan 1983: 88–89). Yet the special relationship feminist filmmakers thought they might be able to establish with avant-garde cinema actually did not come about.

There are several reasons why avant-garde filmmaking did not turn out to be the panacea that feminists of the 1960s and 1970s thought it might be. First, the misogyny of so many male-authored avant-garde films should have immediately called into question the idea that the rejection of Hollywood filmmaking traditions would necessarily lead to progressive images of women. A classic example is Luis Bunuel's *Un chien andalou* (1929), which opens with the shocking scene of a man, played by Bunuel himself, sharpening a razor and cutting a woman's eyeball. Really, avant-garde films by male directors have not been centrally concerned with issues of gender at all or with portraying progressive images of women. Second, while women might be able to get into avant-garde filmmaking more easily than into Hollywood, they have seldom reached the highest levels of the avant-garde directorial pantheon (Butler 2002: 58–59). The work of women experimentalists has often been undervalued and ignored because it challenges not only mainstream filmmaking styles but also avant-garde traditions. Also, woman avant-garde filmmakers, being a rather iconoclastic lot, have not always self-identified as feminist or consistently expressed feminist ideas (Petrolle and Wexman 2005: 1). Women's avant-garde filmmaking can perhaps best be characterized as caught between the radical aestheticism associated with the male avant-garde and allegiance to the women's movement's demands for realistic portrayals of women's activities and activism (Mounsef 2003: 38).

In spite of this rather conflicted relationship between feminism and the avant-garde, we can still identify a distinct set of progressive characteristics and concerns associated with feminist experimental filmmaking as it developed in the 1960s and 1970s. Alison Butler, for instance, identifies the "central problematic" of the feminist avant-garde as a wholesale rejection of the positioning of women in mainstream cinema. She sees avant-garde feminist filmmakers as attempting to make their female characters more than merely "an element of plot space," give them agency in their stories, and construct them as filmic embodiments of their authors (Butler 2002: 60). These goals have lead to a central focus on the female body, which involves a range of approaches from almost total exposure to complete elimination (Blaetz 2007: 11). As a challenge to Hollywood's objectification of women, a pervasive avant-garde feminist strategy is to interrogate the female body as a cultural and linguistic sign, rather than to portray it as a natural expression of an essential femininity (Blaetz 2007: 12). In the course of this interrogation, there is a tendency to blur the line between performer and author in the films. Thus, the "trope of authorial inscription" (Butler 2002: 59) becomes central as avant-garde feminist filmmakers challenge women's positioning as objects in rather than the subjects of mainstream films. A number of different strategies are used to reach this goal, such as the filmmaker appearing as the main character in her film, placing the film in an autobiographical context, or using a female voice-over on the film's soundtrack (Butler 2002: 61). All of these strategies emphasize that the woman is not merely a visual image in the film, but notably its subject of inquiry. Another important strategic turn is to destroy the pleasure derived from the film through identification, narrative involvement, and the eroticization of femininity by the "surprising and excessive use of the camera, unfamiliar framing of scenes and the human body, [and] the demands made on the spectator to put together disparate elements" (Mulvey 1989b: 125).

The issue of authorship is central to the feminist avant-garde in terms not only of the filmmaker's attempts to inscribe her presence into the film, but also to establish herself as its author, or as film scholarship would have it, its auteur. Women experimental filmmakers have, in fact, never been reluctant, even when faced with poststructuralist arguments against authorship, to declare themselves as the auteurs of their films, and critics have followed suit. Female avant-gardists tend to position themselves both as performers within their films and active agents in creating them, placing their subjectivity as the films' central concern (Petrolle and Wexman 2005: 2). In spite of this tendency to authorial inscription, avant garde women filmmakers are often regarded as "conduits of a gendered female consciousness," rather than as individual artists (Petrolle and Wexman 2005: 2). They are seen as expressing the views of all women and offering feminist opposition to the masculinist aesthetic of the male avant-garde through both formal and thematic innovations. Jean Petrolle and Virginia Wright Wexman, as well as Robin Blaetz, have identified certain innovative filmmaking strategies that they believe render the feminist avant-garde very different from male-authored experimental texts. For instance, avant-garde women filmmakers often tend to deploy what appear to be contradictory strategies in their films, such as juxtaposing narrative and non-narrative elements, rather than choosing to use one or the other; thus, their films alternate between narrative pleasure and narrative disruption. They provide opportunities for viewer identification, while also encouraging a critical distance, and routinely go beyond the short format films and primary concern for formal innovation that characterize the male avant-garde; instead, feminist experimental filmmakers favor hybrid feature-length films that combine avant-garde filmmaking strategies with popular genres and filmmaking modes (Petrolle and Wexman 2005: 3). As Robin Blaetz points out, the feminist avant-garde expresses a sense of opposition to both mainstream filmmaking and traditional male experimental films that is expressed through the creation of a sense of something being missing, incompleteness, and even the impossibility of full expression, rather than the construction of a feeling of fulfillment and completion (2007: 9).

There are also certain recurring forms and techniques that dominate feminist avant-garde filmmaking. Blaetz says male critics have described avant-garde films by women as predominantly falling into the categories of diary, dance, and lyrical films. These categorizations seem rather limited and, as Blaetz suggests, represent male critics' failure to examine women's films closely as well as their discomfort with any deviations from the traditions of the male avant-garde (2007: 9). Actually, feminist avant-garde films are quite varied in style and theme ranging from the more visibly political, which Blaetz identifies in particular with lesbian filmmakers such as Barbara Hammer, to the less overtly political, like the work of Yvonne Rainer, for example (2007: 10). One type of film that can be unquestionably associated with the feminist avant-garde is what has been called the feminist theory film. These films developed in the 1970s in direct response to feminist calls for an alternate women's cinema that would challenge dominant filmmaking both formally and thematically. Examples of prominent feminist theory films include Laura Mulvey's *Riddles of the Sphinx* (1977), Sally Potter's *Thriller* (1979) and a film that we will study in depth, Chantal Akerman's *Je, tu, il, elle* (1976).

The feminist critique of mainstream cinema in the 1960s led feminist filmmakers in two rather contradictory directions. As we shall see later in this chapter, some embraced the realist aesthetic advocated by the images of women critics and set out to capture the lives of "real women" through the documentary form, somewhat naively believing documentaries afford the unique opportunity to capture unmediated reality. Others, deeply suspicious that any form of realism merely hides an ideological agenda under its claims of verisimilitude, saw realist documentaries as strategically unworkable. They turned to avant-garde filmmaking, insisting that it is essential for the feminist filmmaker to foreground the constructed nature of her film through experimental techniques and to use feminist theory overtly as a thematic inspiration. Thus was born the feminist theory film. Following Claire Johnston and Laura Mulvey's calls for a feminist counter-cinema, these avant-garde filmmakers combined a number of theoretical perspectives ranging from structuralism and semiotics to Marxism and psychoanalysis in an attempt to demystify realist representations by showing film to be a conveyor of ideology rather than a direct account of events within the real world. Major characteristics of the feminist theory film include:

- drawing attention to the film's status as a construction by using techniques that break the illusion of realist representation;
- divorcing the spectator from the text through the use of methods of distanciation that prevent viewer implication in the narrative or identification with the film's protagonist;
- eschewing forms of pleasure associated with mainstream film based on recognition of similarity and emotional identification in favor of alternate pleasures associated with cognition and learning; and
- mixing film forms, such as documentary, autobiography and fiction, to create "a tension between the social formation, subjectivity, and representation" (Kaplan 2000b: 138).

Stylistic elements also vary from techniques that experiment with the medium, such as non-linear associative or disjunctive editing, the disconnection of sound and image, and a rough or "dirty aesthetic," to the use of images from popular culture (Blaetz 2007: 13–14). Although audiences accustomed to mainstream cinema unfortunately often see these techniques as rendering the films incoherent or difficult to understand, they stand instead as challenges to both Hollywood filmmaking and the male avant-garde. Women experimental filmmakers are too often branded as incompetent or amateurish, rather than being seen as executing very deliberate and formally complex challenges to traditional filmmaking modes (Blaetz 2007: 11). Blaetz proposes that the variety of feminist experimentation stems from a common thematic source, the desire to look beneath the surface layering of images and sound to reveal the emotion underneath (2007: 15). The seemingly amateur style of many of these films is also a product of what Blaetz describes as the feminist-inspired non-hierarchical and collaborative production practices that these filmmakers employ, which have been misunderstood to signal a lack of confidence or expertise, rather than a pioneering mode of production (2007: 10).

If they have often gone unrecognized, the contributions of women filmmakers to the history of the avant-garde are nevertheless significant and can be found in every period of experimental filmmaking. They include, to name only a few prominent figures, Mary Ellen Bute and Claire Parker in the U.S. amateur film movement of the 1920s and 1930s; Germaine Dulac in the French surrealist and "cinema pur" movements in the 1920s; Maya Deren's formative influence on the American avant-garde; Marie Menken's invention of the diary film in the 1940s; Shirley Clarke's formally innovative and thematically controversial representations of drug culture and street life in the 1960s; post-World War II European experimentalists like Helke Sander, Marguerite Duras, and Chantal Akerman; Laura Mulvey's and Sally Potter's feminist theory films of the 1960s; and Barbara Hammer's and Su Friedrich's experimental lesbian films. If for no other reason than to recognize the accomplishments of these important filmmakers, it is important to study feminist avant-garde films, although many viewers accustomed to mainstream cinema find them puzzling, difficult, and even off-putting. As Petrolle and Wexman point out, women's experimental filmmaking has accomplished much. It has expanded women's public presence as cultural agents, innovatively represented women's subjectivity in ways not seen in mainstream films, and formed "a coherent cinematic tradition and a powerful sociopolitical force" (2005: 5). Thus, the study of feminist avant-garde films must also be multi-dimensional. First, it must involve rediscovering women filmmakers working before the advent of feminist film theory in the 1970s and re-examining their work for feminist elements. In the Films in Focus section of this chapter, we will study how this revisionist analysis can be applied to Maya Deren's *Meshes of the Afternoon*. Taking another tack, we will then look at an avant-garde film directly influenced by feminist ideas, Chantal Akerman's feminist theory film, *Je, tu, il, elle*.

The Documentary: The Other "Other" Of Mainstream Cinema

Like the avant-garde film, the documentary seemed to offer women filmmakers an alternative to the mainstream, but again it was an alternative of a rather uncertain nature. The very definition of a documentary film has been open to considerable debate. As Dave Saunders suggests, the most fundamental assumption behind the documentary form is that it offers a representation of the sociohistorical world with an implicit claim to convey fundamentally accurate information about that world (2010: 15). At the same time, however, many critics of the documentary have argued that its seemingly unbiased depiction of the world is shaped by a particular perspective – namely, that of the filmmaker. As Bill Nichols defines it, the documentary film represents a "creative treatment of actuality, not a faithful transcription of it," oscillating between a rendering of the real world and a response to that world (2001: 39). According to Saunders, the general rule is that a documentary filmmaker can present a case for a particular interpretation of reality, but should do so without falsifying information. Saunders also admits, however, that objectivity matters less to some filmmakers than to others (2010: 23–24). This issue of objectivity or accuracy of representation has led to a strenuous debate in documentary studies between the realist and anti-realist positions. This debate has deeply impacted the work of woman filmmakers, many of whom adopted the documentary form because they saw it as a way to capture the reality of women's lives.

The realist/anti-realist debate centers around the question of the documentary's capacity to provide an objective view of sociohistorical reality given that its presentation of that reality may, and some say necessarily must, involve creativity, distortion, dramatic license, poetic accentuation, amplification, or distillation for the purposes of entertainment, education, polemic, or propaganda. Documentary films also tend to blur the distinction between fact and fiction. Events may be staged for the camera to replicate what is believed actually to have happened, and the filmmaker may intervene in the action or conduct interviews with the film's social subjects. Even the very presence of a noninterventionist director and crew can conceivably affect what happens before the camera. In other words, rather than being an objective account of a pro-filmic event (a record of something that just happened in front of the camera), documentaries seem to be complex combinations of reportage, education, entertainment, consciousness-raising, propaganda, the personal essay, and the expose. In addition, the seeming photographic accuracy of the film medium tends to obscure the filmmaker's construction of, perspective on, and bias toward the film's subject. As Diane Waldman and Janet Walker suggest, we can question whether documentaries really have a unique connection to reality not found in narrative films or whether this is an illusion that covers over the necessarily constructed, mediated, story-telling basis of all films (1999: 11).

Feminist critics got involved in this realist/anti-realist debate as soon as feminist directors began to turn to documentary filmmaking as an alternative to mainstream fiction films in the 1960s. The hope was that the documentary's unique connection to reality could provide a perfect vehicle for images of women that would counter the negative stereotypes found in Hollywood films. This hope turned out to be rather naive and simplistic as the documentary showed itself to offer many different possible forms, all with ambiguous relationships to the elusive notion of reality. These forms characteristically involve either interventionist or noninterventionist approaches by the filmmaker. Bill Nichols describes the interventionist documentary mode as requiring the filmmaker's active interference in the presentation of events and as falling into five different categories, as listed below:

1. Expository: involving an authoritative narration, often provided by what has been termed a voice-of-God narrator who describes, comments on, and even interprets events.
2. Interactive: the filmmaker interviews the documentary's social actors or otherwise intervenes on the pro-filmic events as they take place.
3. Reflective: involving a contemplation and questioning of the assumptions of objectivity underpinning the documentary film, as well as of the

filmmaker's involvement in, construction of, and effect on the events being presented.
4. Poetic: the mood, emotions, and/or intellectual response of the filmmaker is expressed through the way the documentary images are presented.
5. Performative: a personal experimental approach that emphasizes the subjective or expressive aspect of the filmmaker's engagement with the subject and with the film's audience (Nichols 2001: 33–34).

The non-interventionist documentary form is less varied and is commonly labeled observational or direct cinema. Its aim is to capture the unmediated reality of everyday life by observation with a camera that remains as unobtrusive as possible (Nichols 2001: 33).

In addition, Linda Williams has proposed that recent documentaries have developed a new mode of engagement that actually straddles the interventionist/ noninterventionist divide. She calls this documentary form postmodern, characterized by the paradoxical exhibition of a clear sense of its manipulated, constructed nature, while at the same time still claiming to reveal a sense of ultimate truth (Williams 1993: 12). She singles out as instrumental in establishing this form Errol Morris's critically lauded documentary *The Thin Blue Line* (1988), which investigates the questionable conviction of a male drifter in a murder case in Texas. The film uses an intrusive self-reflexive style, extensive interviews, restagings of events, and temporal manipulation of the progress of the investigation to show the partial, contingent and contradictory nature of truth itself. At the same time, it still in the end seems to argue that if we piece together all the competing truths about the crime we can construct what actually happened, so in a sense we can attain ultimate truth, which in this case is that the man convicted of the crime was innocent (Williams 1993: 13). Thus, the postmodern documentary suggests that through interventionist means it can, in fact, establish more clearly a sense of unmediated reality than is found in the non-interventionist observational documentary.

Feminist documentaries, even the earliest such as *Janie's Janie* (Geri Ashur, 1971) and *Union Maids* (Jim Klein, Miles Mogulescu, and Julia Reichert, 1976), always in a sense resembled the postmodern documentaries that Williams describes. They tend to straddle the divide between the interventionist and noninterventionist modes although not always with the clear sense of their constructed nature that Williams finds in postmodern documentaries. They often use unacknowledged interventionist techniques while still claiming to present an unmediated picture of the real lives of women. As Julia Lesage points out, many early feminist documentaries show the daily lives of ordinary women as they struggle to deal with a male-dominated world (1990: 222), but the films' observational sequences alternate with interventionist sections, which are commonly termed talking-heads segments in which the women speak directly to the camera or are interviewed by the filmmaker about their experiences, struggles, and accomplishments. Early feminist documentaries also often involved the director's strong identification with the women in her film and were presented as collaborative efforts by the filmmaker and her subjects to bring the truth of women's lives to the screen. The ultimate goal and intended effect was feminist consciousness-raising, providing the women in the film, behind the camera, and in the audience with the mutual support and collective strength needed to combat patriarchal society and change women's lives. These films were what Julia Lesage calls "committed documentaries" that had clear goals. They hoped to show women as they really are, create a wider range of female images, critique and correct past film depictions of women, and allow women for once to tell their own stories. Their ultimate aim was to "depict and encourage a political 'conversation' among women" (Lesage 1990: 234) that would lead them to work to change their lives and the lives of all women on both the personal and political level, yet the strategies of these early feminist documentaries soon began to be questioned. As E. Ann Kaplan points out, documentary films had an attraction to women filmmakers for the same reason as did avant-garde films. They seemed to represent an escape from oppressive and artificial Hollywood representations of women (Kaplan 1983: 87). Documentaries were seen not only as a way to present images of women that would contradict those presented by Hollywood, but also as affording women access to filmmaking with less costly, lightweight, accessible 16mm and eventually video equipment that necessitated less expense and training (Waldman and Walker 1999: 5). Soon, however, it became obvious that the documentary form had many of the same problems found in mainstream films and feminist critics quickly began to question its efficacy as a means of countering mainstream images of women.

As early as 1973, Claire Johnston in "Women's Cinema as Counter-Cinema" argued that the documentary form could actually be dangerous for feminist filmmakers because the realist techniques it so often uses are actually shaped by capitalist ideology and go unrecognized as such (1973: 131). Noel King suggested that realist documentaries by women, such as *Union Maids* and *Harlan County, USA* (Barbara Kopple, 1976), seem to investigate social injustice while actually suppressing the larger systematic causes of the social problems they examine by stressing instead the individual's moral responsibility to bring about social change. These attacks on documentary realism led feminist filmmakers to regard realist documentaries as strategically limited and to abandon the documentary form in favor of avant-garde theory films (Kaplan 1983: 137). Ellen McGarry, in particular, launched a vigorous attack on feminist documentary realism, arguing that no matter how much a filmmaker was determined to avoid controlling the pro-filmic event decisions about subject choice and shooting location, preconceptions of the director and crew, and even their very presence during shooting all act to control and manipulate reality (Kaplan 1983: 11). Thus, feminist critics began to agree overwhelmingly with Johnston's early suspicion that documentary filmmaking might not provide the key to countering mainstream images of women that some feminist critics thought it might. In fact, the documentary form came to be seen by many feminist critics and filmmakers as holding up the unrealizable goal of non-intervention when it was actually much more effective for women filmmakers to intervene decisively and overtly in the way images of women are presented on the screen. This type of intervention became the goal of avant-garde feminist theory films, which tried to avoid the mystifying truth-claims of documentary realism. According to Johnston, these pretensions to truth only served to create a passive spectator who failed to question the film's depiction of reality (Waldman and Walker 1999: 7).

In the Films in Focus section of this chapter, we will look at three films: Maya Deren's avant-garde classic *Meshes of the Afternoon*, Chantal Akerman's feminist theory film *Je, tu, il, elle*, and Barbara Kopple's realist documentary *Shut Up & Sing* (2006). You might think in particular about which film is most effective in its depiction of women's experiences and poses the strongest challenge to mainstream images.

Films in Focus 1: *Meshes of the Afternoon*

Maya Deren is generally credited as the most significant figure to emerge in the postwar U.S. avant-garde. An avid promoter of both her own films and avant-garde films in general, she has been dubbed "the mother of the avant-garde," a title that is perhaps not entirely flattering. While it does suggest the importance of her filmmaking and promotional work in stimulating interest in experimental films, it also tends to trivialize that work by seeming to displace it from the public into the domestic sphere (Pramaggiore 1997: 25). Critics have recognized Deren's most famous film, *Meshes of the Afternoon* (1943), as the first American avant-garde narrative film, made at a time in the 1940s when male avant-garde filmmakers tended to reject narrative in favor of formally experimental and abstract films (Geller 2006: 140). Critic J. Hoberman even dubbed *Meshes* "probably the most widely seen avant-garde film ever made" (quoted in Rabinovitz 1991: 72); indeed, the film and Deren's promotional activities in support of avant-garde filmmaking were of key importance in establishing experimental film as a vital force in American cinema. Deren worked not only to gain recognition for avant-garde film, but to organize filmmakers into an artistic community and obtain distribution and exposition outlets for experimental films (Pramaggiore 1997: 24). Also significant is her role in developing autobiographical avant-garde cinema by starring in her own films and choreo-cinema or film-dance by introducing dance sequences and movements into her works (Satin 1993: 41). Additionally, she wrote and lectured extensively on experimental films. Her ideas were published in literary, dance, art, and photography journals and in a theoretical monograph, *An Anagram of Ideas on Art, Form and Film*, published in 1946. In her theoretical works, Deren condemned both documentary and Hollywood films for failing to live up to the real goals of filmmaking, which she believed involved creatively shaping and altering photographic reality into a constructed image, rather than merely attempting mimetic representation (Rabinovitz 1991: 74).

From a feminist perspective, there is much to admire in Deren's work. She broke ground as a woman director and theorist in the early days of American experimental filmmaking when there were no other avant-garde women filmmakers and only one woman prominent in Hollywood, Dorothy Arzner. Deren established herself as a major figure in an avant-garde art world that was not just masculinist, but overtly sexist; her films and her campaign against dominant representations of women in film were "met with vehement resistance by a rabidly patriarchal and frequently misogynist, avant-garde film culture that did not hesitate to conflate Deren herself with her films in their attacks" (Geller 2006: 140). For instance, Lauren Rabinovitz documents Deren's experiences on a panel at a film symposium in 1953 where her male co-panelists openly ridiculed her theories of film form in a way that would have been unthinkable in regard to a prominent male director's views (1991: 76–77). In spite of derision and personal attacks, Deren within her films as well as in her public appearances and writings stood resolutely in opposition to Hollywood filmmaking, attacking it as a barrier to true artistic cinematic expression (Rabinovitz 1991: 50). She especially sought to break with the fetishistic objectifying representations of women characteristic of both Hollywood and male avant-garde films and set out to investigate the female psyche in new and provocative ways. Breaking conventional gender boundaries of the time, she established herself as a female auteur and film theorist, self-inscribed herself in her films by assuming the role of their protagonist, and introduced more women into the industry by using female crew members. She even trained the first woman camera operator (Fabe 1996: 143).

In spite of her myriad accomplishments, feminist scholars have been some-what reluctant to embrace Deren as a major feminist filmmaker, although she seems unquestionably to deserve that designation. This reluctance may stem from a tendency to identify the 1960s woman's movement and the resulting outpouring of feminist film criticism in the 1970s as the watershed period for feminist filmmaking (Geller 2006: 154). Additionally, feminist critics have not always been entirely positive in their discussions of Deren's work, ignoring her feminism in favor of her role as an important figure in the fledgling avant-garde movement. For instance, while Laura Mulvey promoted the concept of Deren as the mother of the avant-garde, she, nevertheless, still proposed that women were not a major force in experimental filmmaking until the 1960s (Geller 2006: 154). E. Ann Kaplan went so far as to say that the avant-garde was really founded by men and to imply that women filmmakers, like Dulac and Deren, got undue recognition because they were the only two female directors whose work was shown at early women's film festivals (1983: 87). Both Kaplan and Lauren Rabinovitz describe Deren as "not feminist in a contemporary sense" (Kaplan 1983: 87), completely ignoring the fact that feminism in a contemporary sense did not even exist in the 1940s and 1950s when Deren worked. Kaplan characterizes Deren's films as "shocking, forceful, violent" and "heavily surrealist" explorations of female alienation, jealousies, and night-mares, and Rabinovitz argues that Deren's critique of dominant postwar ideology lacks an understanding of "how the cultural institutions, including the family, constructed and organized women's social subordination" (Kaplan 1983: 88; Rabinovitz 1991: 3).

Deren's life and self-presentation have also led feminists to see her as a rather troubling foremother. For instance, Maria Pramaggiore points out that the ways in which Deren promoted herself as an avant-garde star do not always fit well with a feminist politics. It is perhaps surprising that Deren, whose films consistently exhibit an anti-Hollywood rhetoric, publicized herself as a star-director through interviews, photo images, live appearances at film screenings, lectures, and other promotional activities by utilizing many of the same strategies the Hollywood industry employed to create its female stars. She repeatedly played the major role in her own films; changed her name from Eleanora to the more exotic Maya, which is Hindi for illusion; publicized her Russian heritage, Greenwich Village Bohemian lifestyle, reputed dance background, writing of poetry, and interest in voodoo; cultivated an unconventional look in terms of fashion; and used as her signature image the famous still from *Meshes* in which she poses very theatrically with her face against a window. This photo, which Anais Ninn characterized as having a "Botticelli effect," is remarkably similar to the type of glamour photography Hollywood studios use to mythologize their female stars (Pramaggiore 1997: 21). Lauren Rabinovitz describes the contradictions within Deren's image as reflecting her desire for power combined with her need to cultivate a traditional feminine appearance. Deren comes across not only as "strikingly beautiful" and exotic, but also as a woman with a "forceful, self-centered personality" who always craved attention and was given to flights of high drama (Rabinovitz 1991: 50). Yet her

Figure 4 The iconic shot of Maya Deren from *Meshes of the Afternoon.*

tireless self-promotion was directed at establishing herself, not just as a celebrity, but as a serious filmmaker who was creating works of art. As Rabinovitz suggests, Deren's self-image is particularly troubling from a feminist perspective because it involves a rejection of conventional Hollywood gender norms, while it is still largely defined by the very norms against which it rebels (Rabinovitz 1991: 51–52).

Deren's troubled relationship to feminism also stems from what we know of her life story, which, as it has come down to us, takes on the air of Hollywood melodrama. Deren was born in 1917, the only child of a prominent Russian Jewish family in Kiev. Her father, a psychiatrist, fled Russia in 1922, and only brought his family with him later after much persuasion. Her parents' marriage was deeply troubled with numerous separations, and Deren lived with and was apparently very close to her mother. She rarely saw her father. In later life, however, after her father's death she became estranged from her mother, claiming she was always closest to her father and resented her mother for keeping her from him when he was alive. In 1935 at the age of eighteen, she married a socialist union organizer, moved to Greenwich Village, and became involved with the Young People's Socialist League (Fabe 1996: 145–50). Her socialist involvement as well as her Jewish background were aspects of her life that she did not include in her self-promotional campaigns, probably because of anti-Semitic and anti-communist sentiments at the time (Pramaggiore 1997: 38 n. 26). She was highly educated, earning an undergraduate degree in English from NYU and a Masters from Smith. In 1942, after divorcing her first husband, she became the personal secretary and editorial assistant to modern dance choreographer Katherine Graham, who stimulated Deren's interest in dance and voodoo culture.

As part of a west coast tour with Graham, Deren met and married Alexander Hammid, a Prague-born cameraman working in Hollywood as a documentary editor and director. Under his influence Deren became interested in film. Her output as a film director is not large, and includes only a small number of significant films. Her first film, *Meshes of the Afternoon*, a collaboration with Hammid (more on this collaboration later), is by far her most celebrated work, but some critics argue that it is surpassed in quality if not renown by her later films, *At Land* (1944) and *Ritual in Transfigured Time* (1946). In the late 1940s, she went to Haiti to research a documentary on voodoo. She shot over two-hundred feet of footage, but never finished editing the film, which she entitled *Divine Horsemen: the living gods of Haiti* (1961). It was edited and released only after her death. Married thrice, she claims in her diaries to have used aggressive sexual seductions as a means to assert control over men and to gain power in a male-dominated society (Rabinovitz 1991: 50). Having been introduced in the early 1940s to a New York physician who would become infamous for prescribing amphetamines to celebrities, Deren became addicted to drugs. She died suddenly at the age of 44 from a series of cerebral hemorrhages that were most likely tied to her drug use and possible high blood pressure (Rabinovitz 1991: 54). In accord with her exotic image, however, Stan Brakhage suggests in *Film at Wit's End* that Deren's death was related to her involvement in Haitian Voodoo (1991: 108).

While accounts of Deren's life and her self-created image may be problematic, the nature of her work as a filmmaker is what should be most important to our consideration of her status as a feminist figure. Does her work accomplish the aim of feminist theorists of the avant-garde, who called for female filmmakers to move beyond Hollywood images of women as sexual spectacles and take cinema in new directions? Do her films overcome the problem of audience non-acceptance often faced by directors who attempt to do something new and different? In order to try to answer these questions and assess Deren's position as a major feminist avant-garde filmmaker, we will examine *Meshes of the Afternoon* in some detail. There are a number of issues that can be raised about the film beginning interestingly with who actually was its director, extending to what it is really about, and finally interpreting what it actually means.

The issue of authorship is a fascinating one. The film's opening titles list it as a collaboration between Deren and her then husband, Alexander Hammid. Several male critics, including notable figures of the avant-garde like P. Adams Sitney and Stan Brakhage, have argued that the film was actually Hammid's and that Deren got undeserved credit as its director because she promoted it and herself so heavily. Sitney calls it "Hammid's portrait of his young wife" and claims that the fluid shooting style and character movement, surrealist effects, and even the use of doubles, the multiple "Mayas," were all Hammid's idea (1979: 10). He implies that Deren never finished anything and that she was merely Hammid's muse rather than the creator or even co-creator of the film (Geller 2006: 150). Brakhage says about the same thing, but in a somewhat less coherent way. As Marilyn Fabe points out, Brakhage's comments regarding the film's authorship are "contradictory to the point of incoherence" (1996: 151 n. 3), but seem to come down in the end to support for Hammid as the film's auteur. Brakhage proposes in *Film at Wit's End*: "Essentially Hammid was the photographer; but the real force of the film came from Maya herself. In fact, it has always been assumed that *Meshes* was mainly her film; but from knowing him personally and from studying the film, I have good reason to know it is Sasha's" (1991: 93). Although calling Deren "the real force of the film" does seem to present her as the creative presence behind it, the gist of Brakhage's argument still seems to be that she was merely the muse behind Hammid's directorship.

Hammid himself was contradictory in his comments on the making of the film, describing his collaboration with Deren as "so involved between the two of us that it's hard to separate what was one person's idea and what was the other's" (quoted in Rabinovitz 1991: 55), yet he also insisted that he was only executing her ideas, shooting images from her imagination, and visualizing her poetry, not originating anything (Fabe 1996: 138). Deren's description of the film seems much clearer. She said that, once she had conceived the idea for the film, she decided she could not act in and shoot it herself, so she waited for Hammid to be free from other commitments to "develop further the concept of the film and to execute it with me" (quoted in Rabinovitz 1991: 55). Thus, Deren clearly claims to have initiated the project. On her inheritance after her father's death, she even bought the inexpensive 16mm camera with which she and Hammid shot the film, which in its entirety cost only $260 to make (Rabinovitz 1991: 55). The gesture of using her inheritance to make the film seems an act of defiance on Deren's part against her father, who had strongly disapproved of her artistic ambitions (Fabe 1996: 147).

On the other hand, the film does appear stylistically to resemble a much earlier film that Hammid made as a young filmmaker in Prague, *Aimless Walk* (1930), which even includes the iconography of the doubled self (Pramaggiore 1997: 27). Critics have argued, however, that while there are stylistic and conceptual similarities between the two films, *Meshes'* "intense emotion and overall mood" are entirely different (Rabinovitz 1991: 56). Also, Hammid, who was known primarily as a documentarist and cameraman, never made another significant experimental film, whereas Deren made several with *At Land* (1944) and *Ritual in Transfigured Time* (1948) considered major achievements. One could also argue, however, that when Deren ended her marriage and collaboration with Hammid her filmmaking career deteriorated rapidly (Rabinovitz 1991: 77). In spite of these questions regarding the film's actual director, feminist critics have not hesitated to credit the film to Deren and have been quick to discredit objections to her authorship. They see the male critical establishment at the time of the film's release as waging a sexist campaign against Deren's recognition as the film's auteur. Feminist critic Marilyn Fabe, for instance, unequivocally proposes that Deren was the auteur of the film because she conceived the idea behind it, it grew out of her life experiences, and it expresses her psychological state at the time (1996: 138). The feminist view can perhaps be most succinctly summed up as stating that *Meshes* represents an expression of Deren's artistic vision that Hammid merely helped execute by acting as her cinematographer.

If the authorship of Deren's film has been disputed, the nature of its narrative structure has also precipitated considerable disagreement. What exactly happens in *Meshes of the Afternoon?* Does it even have a narrative? Experimental films are not always, or even usually, organized around a story structure. Their organizational form can instead be described more accurately as associational or abstract. In a film organized associationally, the various parts are assembled not to tell a story, but to reflect upon each other in some way either by similarity, contrast, or other forms of relatedness. An abstract film is non-representational, meaning that the parts do not necessarily represent objects in daily life, but instead relate to each other through the repetition and variation of forms, shapes, sizes, and/or movement. *Meshes* calls on both narrational and associational strategies to shape its formal structure. As a result, its narrative seems rather disjointed and unintelligible to viewers accustomed to the strong narrative and representational nature of Hollywood films.

One can, however, find a coherent narrative of sorts in the film. Some critics have even tried to fit it into Hollywood narrative form, which it seems rather determined to complicate or even repudiate. The following plot summary on the Internet Movie Database is a perfect example of the determination to fit the film into the Hollywood mold:

> A solitary flower in a driveway, a key falling, a door unlocked, a knife in a loaf of bread, a phone off the hook: discordant images a woman sees as she comes home. She naps and, perhaps, dreams. She sees a hooded figure going down the driveway. The knife is on the stairs, then in her bed. The hooded figure puts the flower on her bed, then disappears. The woman sees it all happen again. Downstairs, she naps, this time in a chair. She awakes to see a man going upstairs with the flower. He puts it on the bed. The knife is handy. Can these dream-like sequences end happily? A mirror breaks, the man enters the house again. Will he find her?

This summary, while inaccurate in terms of what actually happens in the film, does manage to place it squarely within the formula of the Hollywood suspense film, and it must be said that *Meshes* does in a sense play upon this formula, as it does in regard to a number of other Hollywood genres, such as film noir, the woman's film, and horror.

Lauren Rabinovitz argues that *Meshes'* popularity may in large part stem from its accessibility to non-avant-garde audiences (1991: 72). Because its narrative resembles those found in popular Hollywood genres, viewers unfamiliar with avant-garde cinema can more easily relate to it. The film's domestic setting has all the accouterments of the woman's film, including a stairway, record player, kitchen table, mirror, flower, and bedroom. As in paranoid gothic woman's films, the protagonist finds herself in a home that suddenly turns threatening, even deadly, and she seems to fear that her husband may have malevolent designs on her. As several critics have suggested, the film also draws on the conventions of film noir, especially the noir depiction of heterosexual romance as fraught with danger and aggression (see, for example, Mellencamp 1990, Rabinovitz 1991, and Sitney 1979). The threatening atmosphere, especially surrounding the mysterious robed, mirror-faced figure, creates an atmosphere reminiscent of the horror genre as well. If *Meshes* calls up images from all of these Hollywood genres, it is certainly a genre film with an avant-garde difference.

What really does happen in the film? A woman, played by Deren herself, comes home and picks up a flower in the middle of the pathway in front of her house. She sees a man just heading out of sight as he turns the corner in the distance ahead of her. She goes to the door of the house and drops her key as she takes it from her purse. We watch it fall down the stairs. She retrieves the key and enters the house, which she finds in some disarray as she enters and walks up the stairs to the bedroom. A knife falls out of a loaf of bread, there are newspapers scattered on the floor, the phone is off the hook, and a record player is playing. She returns downstairs and falls asleep in a large comfortable-looking chair. A shot through a cylinder suggests we are now entering the world of her dream. We see a robed figure with a mirror face walking with the flower in her hand out on the path, and a dream double for the woman chases this figure but is unable to catch it. The dream double enters the house once again, which now is not only in disarray but has become a threatening, even horrifying environment where the double finds herself buffeted from wall to wall as she walks up the stairs and enters the bedroom. There, she is again blown about and nearly catapulted out of the window. The robed mirror-faced figure enters the house and places the flower on the bed, and three dream doubles of the protagonist sit at the kitchen table turning over a key. When the last double turns it over, her hand turns black, the key transforms into a knife, and she turns, now wearing eye-popping goggles. With the knife held threateningly in her hand, she walks over to the chair where the protagonist is sleeping, but as we see a close-up of her feet, they are walking through sand, dirt, and grass. She approaches the woman in the chair seemingly about to cut her throat. We see the sleeping woman's eye open and what she encounters is not the dream double, but a man, played by Hammid, who is trying to awaken her. They go up to the bedroom, he strokes her body in what appears to be the initiation of a sexual encounter, but there is a knife or mirror next to her head. She throws it at the man's face, which cracks like a mirror itself, and we see mirror fragments on a sand beach with ocean waves beating the shore. Then, an abrupt cut shows us the man returning home yet again as the woman had at the beginning of the film. He enters the house only to find the protagonist lying dead in the chair with mirror fragments next to her on the floor, seaweed draped over her body, blood running from her mouth, and her throat cut.

This is what happens. There seems definitely to be a narrative, but what that narrative means is less apparent. Contrary to the summary on the Internet Movie Database, this is far from a typical Hollywood thriller plot. Combining narrative and associational formal elements, the intricate structure is based not only on a story of sorts but also on repetitions and variations on the initial sequence with an ending that is both doubled and mysteriously ambiguous. Deren, who liked to explain her films in her appearances at film screenings, described the plot very simply: "The first sequence of the film concerns the incident, but the girl falls asleep and the dream consists of the manipulation of the elements of the incident. Everything which happens in the dream has its basis in a suggestion in the first sequence—the knife, the key, the repetition of the stairs, the figure disappearing around the curve of the road" (quoted in Fabe 1996: 139). A careful look at the film's structure, however, indicates that it is considerably more complex and the dream sequence more horrifyingly vivid and obsessive than Deren's description fully articulates. In fact, the film's form seems to be spiral, to return upon itself, and to convey the protagonist's inner psychological state. The plot has been called surrealistic in this regard, and Deren said of the film that it "does not record an event which could be witnessed by *other* persons" (quoted in Pramaggiore 1997: 28; emphasis Deren). Sitney even compared *Meshes* to Bunuel's surrealist classic *Un chien andalou* (1929). While *Meshes* does seem to be what Sitney called "a trance film," a recounting of an "interior quest" into the protagonist's mental state (1979: 11), that state seems less related to the irrationality of the Freudian unconscious that surrealist films try to access, than to an internal vision characterized by both narrative and associational logic.

Deren was militantly opposed to psychoanalytical interpretations of her films. She said *Meshes* was intended "to create a mythological experience" and the "tendency toward personalized psychological interpretation could impede the understanding of the film" (quoted in Sitney 1979: 13). The aspect of the "mythical experience" that Deren has created in *Meshes* that has caused the most consternation among viewers accustomed to the unambiguity of mainstream films is the seeming psychodrama that the film's mix of dream and external reality cultivates. This mix creates great difficulty for the viewer in distinguishing where the dream begins and especially where it ends. Although the whole film contains a dream-like atmosphere, the actual dream per se appears to begin when we see a close-up of the woman's eye closing and then a shot through a cylinder that seems to signal an entrance into the internal vision of her dream state (Geller 2006: 144). Where this dream state ends is much less certain. Several critics claim there is a double ending (Sitney 1979: 7, Geller 2006: 147), but it could almost be said to be triple: the first ending would be when the woman seems to awaken to see the man apparently waking her up, the second when she throws the knife or mirror at his face, and the final ending when he returns home to find her dead. Most critics agree that this series of endings suggests a merging of dream and reality, and this merging has lead to one of the major ways in which the film has been interpreted.

Interpretations of the ending take two distinct directions. Some critics regard the conclusion as intimately related to and acting as a culmination of all that went before it, whereas others see it more as a coda that is almost separate from the earlier narrative and serves as a commentary upon it. Within this larger division, there are four primary avenues of interpretation, focusing on the themes of the merging of dream and reality, the split self, the confrontation with the male gaze, and finally women's ambivalent reaction to heterosexual romance. The first interpretation, concerned with the film's merging of dream and reality, derives directly from Deren's own comments that the film's ending shows how "the imagined achieved for her [the protagonist] such force that it became reality" (quoted in Sitney 1979: 9). Deren also proposed that what she wanted to show was the feeling a person experiences about an incident, rather than the incident itself (Butler 2002: 65). This led Sitney, and many who followed him, to see the ending as an "affirmation of dream over actuality" (1979: 14). Others have suggested from a more feminist perspective that the conclusion shows "the power of images – and importantly, women's images of themselves – to produce their own realities" (Pramaggiore 1997: 30). These critics have gone on to propose that Deren sought to illustrate a woman's subjective vision and the volatility this vision might give to the world (Pramaggiore 1997: 66). Another possibility is to read the ending not so much as a confrontation between reality and the inner life of dream and imagination, but rather as focusing more on the dream doubles and their attack on the protagonist. In this reading, the film represents a study of the destructive force of the split female psyche that "effects, experiences, and observes her own demise" (Satin 1993: 50). Most feminist critics connect this splitting of the female self to the protagonist's positioning as both subject and object of the male gaze.

In fact, the confrontation with the male gaze and the disastrous effects of female objectification form the main thrust of a number of feminist analyses of the film's ending. These critics see the scene in which the protagonist attacks her lover in the bedroom as representing a woman's aggressive defiance of the male gaze, her determination to return the look, and her attempt to destroy her objectification (Mellencamp 1990: 33, Geller 2006: 151). The film's final ending is regarded either as a recuperation of this earlier scene or as a further comment on it. One interpretation sees the film as finally suggesting that a woman who refuses objectification, usurps the male gaze, and rejects the power behind it destroys herself in the process (Rabinovitz 1991: 65). A more positive analysis might argue instead that the protagonist's death at the end should not be seen as a literal death, but a figurative one in which her previously objectified self is destroyed, precipitating a rebirth into a new empowered femininity. A final possible interpretation returns to the idea of the split female psyche but sees this split as a product of ambivalent feelings women have in regard to heterosexual relationships, which stem from a lack of complete individuation from the mother. In this reading, the protagonist kills herself because she both desires and fears engulfment by a lover-mother figure embodied in both her husband and the robed, mirror-faced figure. Her ambivalence leads her to turn the psychic defenses she has build against a union with another against herself. As a result, she becomes self-destructive and kills herself (Fabe 1996: 141).

Readings of the film have sought to decipher not only its ambiguous ending but the symbolic meanings behind its wealth of imagery. Pramaggiore even suggests the "mood of obsessive, ritualistic reiteration" of images with suggested symbolic significance displaces the narrative as the film's primary concern (1997: 28). This almost obsessive accumulation of symbolism has lead some critics to insist the film demands psychoanalytic interpretation (Fabe 1996: 144), even though, as noted above, Deren fought against such a reading. Meshes' major symbols include the female body; the house; various domestic objects, notably the stairway and knife; the flower; the mirror-faced figure; and finally the dream doubles. The film's representation of the female body is its central symbol and is complicated by the fact that Deren plays the role of the protagonist herself. Deren's presentation of her own body is contradictory in that the protagonist is portrayed as both active and passive. Deren appears to be in a trance-like state, passive in contrast to inanimate objects which seem to take on a malevolent activity, yet she is also always moving. Her use of mannered acting, repetitive ritualized gestures, and dance-inspired movements was influenced by her background in dance and her interest in Haitian voodoo rituals (Pramaggiore 1997: 26). These aspects of the presentation of the female protagonist give the film a surrealist depersonalized feel and contribute to the sense of the female character as almost hypnotized by her surroundings.

Although constantly in motion, she seems nevertheless "controlled by forces different from and larger than the individual will" (Pramaggiore 1997: 26). The implications of this portrayal for the film's presentation of gender are profound. Deren seems to be exploring the implications for women of occupying the contradictory positions of subject and object, observer and observed, actor and the one acted upon. This effect creates not so much a reversal of the conventional gender dichotomy between active male and passive female, but rather a destructive multiplication of the protagonist's inner self that culminates in her death. At the film's conclusion, when the gaze to which the protagonist has assumed over the course of the narrative both an active and passive relation is returned to the male figure, the woman is destroyed, and the man is left with the last look, but it is a look that encounters only female self-destruction (Fabe 1996: 143).

Other central images all seem to reflect on the film's female figure and the critique of gender relations she offers. The domestic setting takes on particular importance as a symbolically charged, aggressively malevolent space alive with mysterious, threatening objects. As noted above, the film uses images familiar from Hollywood woman's films, film noir, and horror to present its female figure as "progressively entrapped, ensnared, enmeshed" (Fabe 1996: 144) within the dangerous confines of her own home. The stairway, for instance, which feminist critics have identified as a privileged setting for female to-be-looked-at-ness in the woman's film, becomes a site of terror and a "symbolic prison" (Rabinovitz 1991: 61). The knife, which jumps of its own accord into a loaf of bread, returns later in the film to become the vehicle of the protagonist's destruction. The flower, conventionally associated with female domesticity in the form of gardening and with female sexuality, here becomes a frightening object connected to the robed, mirror-faced character.

This enigmatic figure, which seems to be directly extracted from Hollywood horror films, becomes the film's central enigma, and critics have offered a wealth of interpretation of its significance. There is not even general agreement about how to describe it. In her production notes, Deren refers to it merely as "a tall woman with a mirror face" and says both she and Hammid played the figure at different times during shooting (quoted in Fabe 1996: 139–40). Following Sitney, however, many critics have described it as a nun (1979: 9) and others as an androgyne (Geller 2006: 144), but all see it as threatening and horrific, and most connect it to the protagonist's male lover. We can just vaguely see him disappear around the bend in the path in the opening sequence, just as the mirror-faced figure will later disappear in the dream; he puts the flower on the bed in the concluding segment, just as the figure had earlier; and his face breaks like a mirror when the protagonist strikes it. Thus,

Fabe claims that the protagonist's lover becomes transformed in her dream into the figure, and this links him to "a magical, holy mother, a mother superior, the all powerful mother of infancy" (1996: 140). This connection leads Fabe to construct a psychoanalytic reading of the figure that one can imagine Deren with her antipathy to psychoanalysis would strongly reject. Fabe believes the connection between the male lover and the mirror-faced figure reflects a female tendency to identify male lovers with the figure of the pre-Oedipal mother and to suffer in romantic relationships from a resulting oscillation between the attraction and fear of engulfment one first felt in responding to the all-powerful mother of infancy (1996: 140). In a similar psychoanalytic reading, Geller sees the mirror-faced figure as "the Other" whose face never reflects back the protagonist's look (2006: 144). For Geller, the figure is a representation of a maternal failure to reflect back an adequate image of the child in the mirror stage, leading to the child's progressive infantilization as an adult and marring her future love relationships. In a less psychoanalytic reading, the figure's connection to the male lover might be interpreted simply as the fear of abandonment, of his leaving her, or of her inability to establish a true connection with him.

In all of these readings, whether psychoanalytic or otherwise, the mirror-faced figure is seen not only as a symbol of horror, but also as ultimately unfathomable and related to the protagonist's ambivalence, her desire and dread of a romantic union with her lover (Fabe 1996: 141). Fabe gives this ambivalence a biographical connection to Deren's own insecurities as a female artist. She argues that the mirror-faced figure is connected to the art of filmmaking with its face symbolic of the camera reflecting back the events it records. In a reading that makes perhaps a few too many unsubstantiated assumptions about Deren's life, Fabe connects the mirror-faced figure to Deren's possible ambivalence about usurping Hammid's directorial role in making the film. Thus, the mirror-faced figure represents the woman artist who both desires and fears entering the traditionally male artistic realm. Women's anxieties are also expressed in the dream doubles who assemble to plot the murder of the sleeping protagonist. Spawned by the female character's fragmented psyche, they become destructive alter-egos signifying a "terrifying state of ego boundary confusion in which the self is felt to be so intricately part of an other that destructive impulses aimed at the lover can only rebound on the self" (Fabe 1996: 142).

If Deren's film utilizes and at the same time challenges Hollywood conventions in terms of its narrative and symbolic structure, it does much the same in regard to style. The challenge that early feminist theorists posed to women filmmakers was to contest Hollywood in terms not only of content but also through stylistic innovation, and critics have disagreed about whether Deren really achieves these twin goals. For instance, Alison Butler argues that Deren's filmmaking techniques are quite conventional and modeled on those used in Hollywood (2002: 65), whereas Marilyn Fabe proposes that Deren systematically subverts Hollywood conventions (1996: 138). Butler's argument rests on Deren's use of visual elements taken from the Hollywood genres of film noir, horror, and the woman's film. Film noir and horror do provide much of the inspiration for Deren's use of high contrast lighting, extreme camera angles, and subjective point of view shots, and the woman's film supplies the essential elements of her mise-en-scene, such as the claustrophobic domestic atmosphere with the hypersignification of domestic objects (Rabinovitz 1991: 61). The question really comes down to whether Deren assembles these stylistic elements to achieve not just an imitation but a subversion of the Hollywood style. Does Deren take Hollywood stylistic features in unconventional directions? Certainly, a viewer might find her style reminiscent of Hollywood, but it would be hard to mistake Meshes for Stella Dallas, Double Indemnity (Billy Wilder, 1944), or Dracula (Todd Browning, 1931). What makes Meshes so different?

In terms of shooting style, editing, mise-en-scene, and sound, this is no Hollywood film. First, the opening sequence lacks an establishing shot to situate us comfortably within the setting. We never see an extreme long shot of the outside of the house. This in itself causes a sense of disorientation and discomfort very uncharacteristic of Hollywood. The first section prior to the movement into dream is dominated by first person optical point of view shots in a way that is hardly characteristic of Hollywood, and this subjective camera is identified with a woman, not a man. The female protagonist's assumption of optical point of view in the opening segment has disastrous effects for her. Inanimate objects take on malevolent agency and multiple female alter-egos appear, all with what Butler calls a "specular pathology," signified most chillingly by the murderous alter-ego's eye-popping goggles (2002: 66). The film's optical point of view shots also convey a sense of female interiority, as if we are entering the protagonist's mind in what Sitney famously termed an interior quest, one that is hardly characteristic of Hollywood, where women's minds are rarely, if ever, investigated in such depth. Editing also adds an anti-Hollywood dimension to the film by the use of abrupt cuts, off and canted angles, cutting-on-action across disconnected spaces and sudden changes in location, close-ups of objects and body parts, and non-diegetic inserts. The mise-en-scene may employ Hollywood conventions associated with popular genres, but it stretches these conventions to extremes and combines them with highly stylized ostensive acting that is more characteristic of silent film or dance. Throughout the film, Deren maintains an impassive expression, except to raise her hand to her face, open her mouth, or widen her eyes to suggest fear. She seems to be sleepwalking through a defamiliarized domestic setting that conveys none of the cosy comfort of Hollywood melodrama; instead, the mood is one of uncanniness, horror, and claustrophobia. As Rabinovitz suggests, the film's mise-en-scene finds "a strong sense of subject fragmentation, psychological disturbance, and dislocation" in everyday activities within the home (1991: 62), and this sense is far more extreme than conveyed in any Hollywood genre film.

A final aspect to be considered is the film's meaning, and here *Meshes* yet again opens itself up to various interpretative possibilities, both feminist and otherwise. Critics at the time of the film's release either did not regard it highly enough to even merit extensive interpretation or saw it as a surrealist or trance film. Many early male critics were vicious in their attacks, directing their criticism not only to the film but to Deren herself. Manny Farber called it "lesbianish" (whatever that means exactly he left unclear), "cluttered with corny, amateurishly arranged symbols and mainly concerned with sex, hop[ping] too confusingly from reality to dream." To his criticism, Deren responded simply, "This is exactly the point" (quoted in Geller 2006: 148). Similarly, Jonas Mekas labeled *Meshes* "a conspiracy of homosexuality" by an "adolescent film poet" who makes "home movies," whose "supposed depth" is "artificial," and who lacks the technical expertise to evoke universal sympathy for her characters or subject (quoted in Geller 2006: 148, 152). Those who gave it any credence at all as a filmic text worthy of analysis likened it to 1920s French surrealism, especially Bunuel's *Un chien andalou*. Sitney was perhaps the first to really take the film seriously, offering his highly influential character-ization of it as a trance film in which the protagonist wanders through a threatening environment enacting a "personal psychodrama" (1979: 18). As noted above, he also perceptively described it as "an interior quest" for "the erotic mystery of the self" that "offers an extended view of a mind in which there is a terrible ambivalence between stable actuality and subconscious violence" (Sitney 1979: 11, 14).

Deren offered her own interpretation of the film. She would travel with her films or write production notes explaining to her audience how her films should be interpreted. Rabinovitz suggests that Deren had little confidence in viewers' interpretive abilities and often abrasively insisted upon her own interpretations of her films as the only accurate ones (1991: 76). Deren's comments concerning *Meshes* suggest that she saw the film primarily as a study of the power of dream to overtake reality and a study of the inner workings of the mind of a suicide. While it did not stop him from insisting the film is a surrealist personal drama, Sitney quotes Deren's warning against psychoanalytic readings of the film and against seeing it as a personal representation of her real life (Sitney 1979: 13). She described *Meshes* as "concerned with the interior experiences of an individual" and how "the sub-conscious of an individual will develop, interpret, elaborate on an apparently simple casual incident converting it into a critical emotional experience" (quoted in Sitney 1979: 9). She felt the film's key sequence was when the dream double, who rises from the table with a knife in her hand and wearing mirrored goggles, walks over a varied landscape of changing scenery to the sleeping protagonist. Deren said this was intended to show that "you have to come a long way – from the very beginning of time – to kill yourself" (quoted in Satin 1993: 49).

More recent feminist critics have taken the film up as women's discourse. Feminist interpretations of Deren's major thematic concerns fall into five categories: women's self-expression, female identity as related to the male gaze and Hollywood cinema, male–female love relationships, the violent expression of women's anger, and women's relationship to the domestic space of the home. A number of feminist critics have seen *Meshes* as a cautionary tale about the consequences of female artistic, intellectual, sexual, and cinematic self-expression in a male-dominated world. Marilyn Fabe, for instance, proposes that Deren is making a statement about "the self-destructive conflicts of the twentieth-century American woman artist and intellectual, conflicts which pit both love and artistic success against one another and make both fatal attractions." For Fabe, the film reflects the struggle between love and art that Deren experienced in her own marriage to Hammid, and it presages her failure to develop fully as an artist (1996: 45).

A related interpretation sees *Meshes* as an examination of male–female relationships in general and in particular Deren's relationship with Hammid. This interpretation began with Sitney, who read the film as a personal psy-chodrama reflecting the psycho-sexual tensions within the Deren–Hammid relationship. In this reading, the film is said to enact the inner life of a woman suffering from "a repressed and resistant female sexuality and subjectivity" (Pramaggiore 1997: 28). The woman's quest for a stable identity is doomed by the splitting of her sense of self caused by her resistance to culturally accepted femininity and the "gender disempowerment" she feels as the object of male sexual desire (Geller 2006: 151). Some critics have taken this interpretation in a psychoanalytic direction in spite of Deren's obvious antipathy to this type of reading. For example, Fabe argues that the failure of the film's love relationship illustrates a "quintessentially female psychological dilemma" related to con-flicting desire for and dread of heterosexual union. This inner conflict stems from women's difficulty in separating from their mothers, consolidating their identity, and coming to terms with their sexuality (Fabe 1996: 141). In *Meshes*, this dilemma has disastrous consequences with the protagonist feeling, as Fabe suggests Deren did, "a desperate yearning for her mother," represented in the pursuit of the mirror-faced figure, and "a self-destructive identification with her dead father," expressed through her final suicide (1996: 150).

More recent feminist readings see the film as focused not so much on female artistic or sexual expression, as on the idea of the multi-faceted female sense of self. Lesbian-feminist avant-garde filmmaker Barbara Hammer said Deren was a major inspiration for her because she explored the "complexities of the human psyche, discovered the many inner selves of the female person-ality, and tried to project them into images" (quoted in Kaplan 1983: 87). These "complexities" and "many female inner selves" represent not only the difficulties involved in female self-expression and the problems of heterosexual love relationships, but also women's inability to find true fulfillment within the domestic sphere. A number of critics have taken up this line of interpretation and focused on *Meshes'* portrayal of female anger, violence, and self-destruction, stemming from feelings of discontent and imprisonment within "a traditionally female world of domesticity that has suddenly become noiresque" (Rabinovitz 1991: 63). Confinement in the domestic sphere is shown to create a female subjectivity divided against itself, split, destabilized, fragmented, and prone to violent expressions of anger. This anger is initially directed against men, who the film suggests regard woman merely as an appendage and reflection of male desire, rather than as a separate being in her own right with her own needs and desires. Eventually, however, this anger is turned back upon the woman herself in the form of suicidal "narcissistic rage" (Mellencamp 1990: 33).

A related reading of the film with a slightly different emphasis sees *Meshes* as the story of a woman suffering from a fragmented sense of self as a result of her objectification, fetishization, and eroticization by the male-controlled Hollywood film industry. This interpretation sees the film as "a woman's dis-course that rewrites Hollywood's objectification of women" by portraying its female protagonist as destroyed in her attempt to "contend with her own objectification," refuse the male gaze, and exercise an active female subjectivity (Rabinovitz 1991: 56). The female character's unwillingness to sacrifice her own subjectivity to the male gaze, yet her inability to free herself from it, leads inevitably to her self-destruction, showing the cost to the female subject of women's objectification, fetishization, and eroticization by the male-created and male-controlled cinematic apparatus (Geller 2006: 147).

Given all that we have said about Deren's style, narrative form, and struc-ture of meaning in *Meshes of the Afternoon*, the final question we might ask is whether she has done enough to fulfill the aspirations of feminist theory for a female cinema that dismantles mainstream masculinist structures of seeing and creates a new woman's filmic discourse. Was Deren doing this in the 1940s, even before feminist theorists began to call for a restructuring of cinematic form to express female desire and a woman's perspective? Does she provide an early model of women's auteurism in the avant-garde or is it necessary to turn to Chantal Akerman's 1970s feminist theory films to find a true model of feminist experimentation?

Films in Focus 2: *Je, tu, il, elle*

Chantal Akerman was part of a notable group of feminist film directors of the 1970s who responded to the feminist call for a new woman's cinematic discourse. With the films of Laura Mulvey, Sally Potter, and Yvonne Rainer, Akerman's works have been singled out as quintessential feminist theory films that directly challenge mainstream cinema and attempt to forge a new structure for the cinematic gaze. A matter of some critical dispute, however, is whether or not they actually succeed. Born in Brussels of Jewish parents, Akerman worked in Belgium, the United States and is now based in Paris. Considered a major European auteur, but largely unrecognized in United States, she has made over forty films including features, shorts, video essays, and experimental documentaries, and in the 1990s she began creating video installations for art museums and gallery exhibitions. As a filmmaker, she has moved from marginal film production to commercial cinema, where she currently works. In the 1970s, she became renowned for one work in particular, *Jeanne Dielman, 23 Quai du Commerce, 1080 Bruxelles* (1975), which almost immediately upon its release began to be discussed as a feminist classic. With a running time of 201 minutes and recounting in real-time the daily domestic activities of a Brussels housewife who is also a prostitute, the film can be an endurance test for many spectators. Its provocative evocation of the drudgery and imprisonment of a woman's life within the domestic sphere has led it to be hailed as a masterpiece of women's cinema and a key feminist text. Equally interesting, although not as celebrated (or as prohibitively lengthy) as *Jeanne Dielman*, is the film that we will consider in depth, *Je, tu, il, elle* (1975), which is also a response to feminist theorists' calls for a deconstruction of mainstream film and an entirely new way of portraying women on screen. Clocking in at a mere 90 minutes in comparison to *Jeanne Dielman's* epic length, *Je, tu, il, elle* is a more accessible film that is just as unique and challenging as its more famous counterpart. The film was shot by Akerman in Paris in approximately one week on a minuscule budget with a crew of two, a camerawoman and a friend whom Akerman describes as "helping" (quoted in Martin 1979: 30). It is Akerman's first feature-length film although it was not released until after *Jeanne Dielman* became such a feminist *cause celebre*.

Of interest in considering Akerman's work is her position as a critically acclaimed feminist auteur who does not identify her work as feminist. Critics, such as B. Ruby Rich, have labeled Akerman's films "profoundly feminist" and regard her as one of the most prominent feminist filmmakers in Europe (1998: 169). Her films in the 1970s have been seen as especially groundbreaking. When asked how she situates herself in relation to women's cinema, however, Akerman replied, "I wouldn't say I'm a feminist filmmaker ... I'm not making women's films. I'm making Chantal Akerman films" (quoted in Martin 1979: 28). She does not even seem to believe that a feminist cinema is currently possible. When asked if she sees "the feminine look as having a different view of the world," she said that she thinks a feminine language will only be possible "if we achieve real decolonization" (quoted in Martin 1979: 36). She does concede that women may "have a rhythm, if only sexually, physically, biologically, which is different from that of men," but she also insists that Hollywood films do not express a men's rhythm but "the rhythm of capitalism and fascism" (quoted in Martin 1979: 36–37). She says she is aware of the problems of women, but they are not her main concern in making her films. When she makes a film, she does not set out to make "feminist points or to change social structures"; instead she says she is just "interested in style, in expression" (quoted in Martin 1979: 28–29). Akerman claims she did not experience sexism in the industry because she started out on the margins, raised her own money for her films, and "didn't care whether anyone was interested or not" in what she made (quoted in Martin 1979: 28). Although she concedes that the American feminist movement was an important influence on her in the 1970s when she lived in New York (Bergstrom 1999a: 278), she sees herself as feminist only in her confidence about what she does and her conviction that her thoughts are no less valuable because she is a woman (Martin 1979: 28). Can Akerman be considered a feminist filmmaker if she does not identify as one? Perhaps an examination of *Je, tu, il, elle* can answer this question.

Je, tu, il, elle (note that in French only the first word of the title in capitalized) translates to *I, You, He, She* in English although the original U.S. release title was changed to *Personal Pronouncements* (Martin 1979: 30). The film was based on a short story Akerman wrote in 1968. When she first wrote the story, she did not see it as a film, but later she decided to convert it into a screenplay (Rosen 2004: 123). Told in three parts, the story is deceptively simple. We first see a young woman, played by Akerman, locked in a room by herself. She rearranges the furniture, attempts to write a letter to an unknown correspondent, and eats sugar from a bag. She then undresses, hears children's voices outside, and sees a man, who appears to be just a passerby, peering into the room through a sliding glass door. Finally, we see her lying naked on a mattress. The segment is accompanied by the woman's first person voice-over, which informs us of events that never happen or do not happen when the voice-over describes them. It ends when she dresses and leaves the room. In the second section, the woman hitches a ride with a male trucker, listens to him talk about his job and his life with his wife and children, stops with him at a diner to eat, and accompanies him to a bar where they meet some other people. Finally, she masturbates him while he drives the truck, and the segment ends with her watching him shave in a gas station restroom. In the third and final segment, the protagonist arrives at the apartment of another woman, who tells her immediately that she cannot stay. She asks for food, and the woman makes her sandwiches, they have sex, and the protagonist leaves.

This description of *Je, tu, il, elle*'s minimalist plot hardly conveys the complexities of a film that Akerman has labeled "very impressive – very rough too" (quoted in Martin 1979: 30). It is a film that has fascinated feminist critics, if perhaps not all audiences. B. Ruby Rich has called it Akerman's most radical film (1998: 171). It strongly diverges from mainstream film not only in narrative content, but also in its structure and visual style. This divergence can be off-putting to audiences accustomed to watching Hollywood cinema because the film offers the viewer nothing but conundrums from start to finish, rather than the straightforward answers so often offered by mainstream narratives. These conundrums begin with the title, which has fascinated commentators, who have speculated about the exact references of its four pronouns? Critics generally identify the "I" with the main character, the "he" with the trucker, and the "she" with the female lover (Mayne 1990: 134; Butler 2002: 79). The "you" is rather baffling, though. Some have suggested that it may refer to the unnamed addressee of the letter that the protagonist is writing in the first segment, to the relationship of the protagonist with the other two characters (Butler 2002: 79), or "to the space of the spectator" outside of the text (Longfellow 1989: 86). Others have proposed that maybe the "you" just "floats, never assigned" (Turim 2003: 14), refers to each character at some point in the film (Mayne 1990: 134), suggests that the troubled protagonist does not understand the difference between self and others (Foerster 1990: 9), or implies that she is a combination of all four pronouns (Mayne 1990: 134). Judith Mayne even came up with the bizarre suggestion that the "tu" is not intended to mean "you" at all, but rather to suggest "tue," which means "kill" in French, so the title would then read, "I kill him, her" (1990, 134). How exactly that relates to the film Mayne does not explain.

If the title baffles, the film's narrative form is just as perplexing. Every commentator tries to interpret the significance of the three-part structure which seems so simple, but actually turns out to contain various elements that confound easy explanation. Judith Mayne is perhaps correct in saying that there is really no category of film that adequately describes *Je, tu, il, elle* (1990: 133). Its narrative form is certainly very unlike what mainstream audiences are used to seeing. It has been described as anti-realist, minimalist, structuralist, and anti-illusionist (deconstructing the mainstream illusion of presenting reality), yet in spite of its anti-realist qualities some critics have suggested that it has autobiographical roots in Akerman's own life and conducts "an open flirtation with realism" (Turner 2003: 98). The three-part narrative structure diverges radically from the Hollywood norm and can be seen as a deliberate deconstruction of that norm either for purposes of formal experimentation or to make a feminist statement. There is no clear narrative progression from beginning to end, no real sense of character development, no closure at the conclusion, no cultivation of spectator identification with the characters, and no attempt to hide the fact that what we are seeing is a film and not an unmitigated representation of reality. There is minimal plotting and a sense of distance from what is happening that suggests the director's interest lies elsewhere than in the presentation of story and characters.

The film's three-part structure raises several interesting possibilities for interpretation. One issue that a number of commentators have raised deals with whether the film demonstrates a sense of progression from one segment to another. Maureen Turim suggests that as a minimalist-structuralist work *Je, tu, il, elle* leaves each section autonomous and detached from the others, so that the audience must make any connections themselves (2003: 10). She believes the film, therefore, benefits from being viewed more than once and that one's interpretation can change with repeated viewings (Turim 2003: 13). Others have insisted that there is a modicum of connection, even some sense of progression, from segment to segment. These critics claim the film as united either as a dark fairy tale, a journey of sexual self-discovery, or a cynical mockery of rites of passage narratives. If there is a sense of unity, is it based on some sense of narrative progression, and if it is, to what exactly does the protagonist progress? Is it a progression from isolation through a failed heterosexual connection to a final intense lesbian sexual union, or does the film reject and even mock any notion of development or the possibility of connection with others? Jean Narboni has argued that the movement of the narrative is actually circular and the voice-over's declaration at the very beginning of the film, "And I left ... ," actually refers to the protagonist leaving her female lover at the film's conclusion (1977: 10–11). Others have said that the film repudiates and even ridicules the very possibility that the protagonist might develop in any way from her experiences, which seem to be characterized only by a "directionless mobility" (Margulies 1996: 111). According to Mayne, the film's final section provides absolutely no sense that the bond between the two woman at the end represents the central character's assumption of "a more satisfactory, more complete, more successful sexual identity" (1990: 132). The only explanation Akerman offered of the film's structure was that the three parts could be entitled a time of subjectivity, a time of the other or reportage, and a time of relationship

(Margulies 1996: 236 n. 33), but she never explained how these titles relate to the narrative.

The first section has a number of fascinating aspects that directly challenge mainstream conventions. Probably, the most distinctive feature is the disembodied female voice-over that dominates the segment. Rendered in first person, it provides unreliable or at least mismatched commentary on the protagonist's actions as she navigates the confined space of her room. For instance, the voice-over says, "I painted the furniture blue," but we do not see her doing this, and even if we did we could not verify this information because the film is not in color. As noted above, the voice-over begins with the protagonist saying "And I left," but she does not leave the room until the end of the segment, and as noted above, Narboni even proposes that the phrase actually refers to her leaving her female lover at the very end of the film. This running voice-over commentary that fails to describe events accurately helps to set the mood of the whole first section, which really establishes the tone and thematic concerns of the film as a whole. First, the disembodied voice-over directly responds to feminist calls for women's cinema to challenge mainstream conventions by refusing to bind the voice of its female characters to their bodies and in this way granting them discursive power and control. It contributes to Akerman's strong inscription of her own presence in the film, which establishes her as its unquestionable auteur. There is a very troubling quality to the voice-over's disjunction of voice from image that helps create the overall mood of this segment, which oscillates between a meditative, almost ritualistic tone and outright mockery. Certainly, the idea of a voice-over that does not describe what is happening or describes actions when they are not happening can be seen as cultivating a mocking tone. Add to this that the voice-over describes the actions of a woman who is never named and is locked in a room where she compulsively moves furniture, eats sugar, writes a letter to someone whose identity is never revealed, and then strips naked and lies on a cot. Taking all of these aspects into consideration, seeing the whole segment as a mockery of the very idea of coherent narrative seems entirely reasonable.

It seems wrong, however, to see the tone of this opening section as entirely ironic because the protagonist and her actions are presented in a way that is too serious and even pathological to be laughable. If this is mockery, it seems deadly serious in its intention. In fact, many commentators have argued that we should see the film's female protagonist as psychologically disturbed, although there is little agreement on what her psychological problems actually are. She has been described as pathologically narcissistic, obsessive-compulsive, hysterical, tormented by loneliness and feelings of abandonment, clinically depressed, anorexic, confused about her sexual identity, or suffering from the complete dissolution of identity. Her confinement in the restricted and "oppressively barren space of her ground-floor apartment" is so disturbing that it can be seen as a metaphor for her troubled mental condition. She can be said to have regressed to a state of infantile confinement in her apartment's womb-like environment (Longfellow 1989: 86) possibly due to her inability to deal with the desperate life of a "single woman in a modern industrial world" (Foster 2003: 1). We might question, however, if the female character is really psychologically troubled or if she is merely, as some critics have seen her, a young woman of unformed sexual identity on a journey to experience "the extremes of pain and lust" (Foerster 1990: 9). Perhaps, even trying to analyze the protagonist's mental state misreads Akerman's minimalist strategies of characterization. Akerman seems to refuse to present characters realistically or psychologically, instead portraying them through what some commentators describe as a process of "interminable, 'senseless,' addition" that creates not psychological complexity but "a dense, suggestive opacity that cannot be penetrated" (Margulies 1996: 124; Bergstrom 1999a:279).

If we place *Je, tu, il, elle* within the context of Akerman's other early films, the psychologically pathologizing readings of her central character do seem to hold some validity. In her first short film, *Saute ma ville* (*Blow Up My Town*, 1968), with a running time of just 13 minutes, Akerman plays a young woman whom we first see cheerily humming as she enters her apartment. There, she begins to perform everyday activities. She eats, cleans the cabinets, and scrubs the floor, but these activities become increasingly frantic and demented until finally she lights a newspaper on fire and turns on the gas on the stove. The image cuts to black and we hear an explosion, followed by the cheery humming and singing previously associated with the woman. The woman's behavior in *Saute ma ville* seems both eerily similar to the actions of the protagonist in the opening segment of *Je, tu, il, elle* and clearly indicative of psychological problems. Janet Bergstrom describes *Saute ma ville* as "a cry of distress, a plea for attention and perhaps an unconscious expression of transgressive aggression" expressing "the despair of a failed attempt to communicate" (1999a: 281–82), and the same can be said of the first segment of *Je, tu, il, elle*. After making *Saute ma ville*, Akerman requested funding to make a film about an eight-year-old girl who poisons her parents and is happy about it, but her request was rejected by the Belgian Ministry of French Culture (Bergstrom 1999a: 282). In interviews, Akerman describes a film that she made at about the same time as *Je, tu, il, elle* in New York entitled *New York, New York bis* (1984), which she says she lost. It dealt with a woman, again played by Akerman, who arrives in New York, goes to a friend's apartment, the friend tells her to wait because she is busy, and the woman then kills herself (Bergstrom 1999a: 281–82).

Akerman's penchant for playing these seemingly deranged characters herself is troubling enough, but it becomes even more so when one considers the unusual nature of her performance style, which has been described as "obtuse eccentricity" (Butler 2002: 81). She assumes a "montage of postures ... witnessed externally" and staged like an enactment or performance piece (Turim 2003: 13). Akerman has said that she played the part herself in *Je, tu, il, elle* because "It was a matter of putting across a 'malaise.' I started to direct an actress and soon I noticed that her perfection went against the project. I also thought [it] more appropriate ... to oppose the mise-en-scene's rigidity with my own uneasiness" (quoted in Margulies 1996: 112). She has since confessed that she finds it difficult to watch her performance: "I can't stand seeing myself doing those things in the film." She says when she shot the film she did not feel self-conscious because it was just her, the camerawoman, and a friend who was helping her on the set, and because she was only a fledgling director, she did not yet have a sense of having "a relationship with the public" or of "how strong it would appear" (quoted in Martin 1979: 30).

In fact, commentators have described Akerman's presence in the film as so strong that the work as "saturated with authorial signature" and seems to be directed almost in a "narcissistic frenzy" (Mayne 1990: 129–30). Like Deren, Akerman appears determined to make her authorial presence known, which can be seen as yet another direct response to the calls of feminist film theorists. In the 1970s, feminist theory suggested that one way to counteract long-standing prejudices against women in a directorial role was for women filmmakers to imprint their authorship strongly on their films. Marking her protagonist indelibly as a combination of author, character, and performer seems to make the viewer acutely aware of Akerman's authorship throughout the film, yet some commentators have proposed that it has exactly the opposite effect. Akerman provides no confirmation in the film that she is playing the lead role, identifying the performer playing the main character in the end credits instead as "Julie." Additionally, her performance is so eccentric that Angela Martin says it appears as if she "is not doing her own portrait. She is speaking of woman, of a woman at the same time abstract and universal. She is an abstraction of women, a concretization of all women" (Martin 1979: 39). Critics also have remarked that Akerman's performance presents the female body in a way that "eludes gender stereotypes" (Turim 2003: 9). Claire Clouzet proposes that Akerman's presence in the film differs from the way male directors present themselves when they appear in their works. According to Clouzet, Akerman "puts herself, naked, in her own films and talks about her 'difference,' using words and images without reference, since women don't have an aesthetic or literary past, or very little of one" (quoted in Martin 1979: 39). Similarly, Maureen Turim suggests that Akerman presents herself in a way that is completely unique and "not stereotypical of female bodily display." For Turim, Akerman's performance renders her young protagonist a study in contradictions. She is sensuous, yet lacking in refinement; soft, yet strong; voluptuous, yet strikingly adolescent, awkward, and unsure of her own allure; not typically feminine, yet still lacking definite signs of androgyny (Turim 2003: 9).

When the protagonist finally leaves the apartment, an abrupt cut to a high-angle outdoor shot of her standing by the side of a highway signals the beginning of the film's second segment. This transition is also marked by a switch to a much more grainy image than was used in the first segment, but really the style of this section contrasts in almost every way with the first part. The voice-over, which tells us that the protagonist hitched a ride with a trucker, is much less prominent, and the soundtrack is dominated by long silences interspersed with equally long monologues by the trucker. The protagonist seems almost marginal to the narrative here, either inhabiting the borders of the frame or off-screen entirely as the trucker's image and voice assume the dominant role. We find out a great deal about him and his family, but nothing more about the protagonist, who seems fascinated with, yet distant from him. Unlike the first section in which we were confined entirely to the apartment, here close shots inside the narrow space of the trucker's cab alternate with more distant shots of the trucker and female character eating in a diner or stopping at a bar. A sense of where exactly we are becomes even more ambiguous in this section. In the opening segment, the exact location of the apartment is unclear, but because we are so completely confined to that one room, its locale hardly seems to matter. In this segment, where we are is more important because of the outdoor setting and the constant sense of movement, yet signals of an exact location are not only unclear but decidedly confused. Both the trucker and protagonist speak French, but the sounds we hear in the cab and the diner are in English from U.S. radio and television.

When Akerman was asked about this segment in an interview, she said she feels it conveys a sense of the importance of having a "neutral listener, some-one who enters your life for a brief moment and disappears afterward" (quoted in Bergstrom 1999a: 289 n. 11). The film's protagonist is the one who assumes this role of passive listener, perhaps suggesting her domination by the strong male presence of the trucker, but the female character does more than just listen. She also is an active participant in a rather shocking sexual episode near the end of the segment. As we see a close shot of the trucker driving and looking directly into the camera, he in minute detail instructs the protagonist, completely off-screen for the whole time and for the first time in the film, as she masturbates him. The appearance of this scene in the film is so sudden and its presentation so singular that it has provoked considerable critical discussion. There is no preparation for the abrupt transition to this sexual episode, and it is rendered all the more discomforting by the fact that the trucker provides a detailed description of what he is experiencing, and what we never see. As Alison Butler points out, his speech clearly exceeds any erotic or narrative purpose (2002: 80).

The meaning of the scene is ambiguous at best, totally obscure at worst. It may be intended to show the trucker as the object of the female gaze (Mayne 1990: 244 n.11) or the woman as absent from the man's recognition except as a means of providing his sexual satisfaction; hence, she is not even present on screen. The unusual shooting style in this scene, which identifies the protagonist with the camera, has the trucker's direct address to the audience provide "explicit acknowledgment of what we know, that the fictional character within the film is identical to the filmmaker" (Mayne 1990: 130). That this implied recognition of the unity of author and character takes place during a scene of sexual service to a man makes the whole episode all the more uncomfortable for viewers. After the trucker ejaculates, he launches into yet another extended monologue describing his less than satisfactory sex life with his wife, his attraction to his teenage daughter, and his proclivity for sexual encounters with female hitchhikers he picks up on the road. Again, we learn nothing about the protagonist, whose life seems of absolutely no interest to the trucker, and the segment ends as she gazes at him adoringly while he shaves in a truckstop restroom. Are we to see this as an encounter that is only fulfilling for the male figure and reduces the protagonist to his devoted servant or as a subversive reversal of the gaze structure with the man reduced to an object of erotic female contemplation? Should we read it as an instance of attempted, but ultimately unsuccessful heterosexual union or as the establishment of an unconventional, yet strong communicative and sexual bond between the two characters? The segment ends without providing any clear answer to these questions.

If section two has been the crux of considerable debate, section three has provoked a veritable avalanche of critical discussion. After a "monosyllabic verbal exchange" (Butler 2002: 8) and the almost completely wordless consumption of sandwiches, the protagonist and another woman engage in a prolonged sexual encounter. It really does not seem to be much of an exaggeration to say that this sex scene is unlike any other recorded on film. Narboni proposes that it gets "as close as possible both to porn and its destruction" (quoted in Martin 1979: 40). Akerman says she conceived the scene as divided into three movements, which perhaps correspond to the three long takes into which it is divided: the movement of discovery and the collision of bodies, followed by a more tender moment, and culminating in something more erotic (Martin 1979: 39). One might even suggest that these movements recapitulate the central issues found in the film's three segments, which involve a quest for self-discovery, tenderness and connection, and sexual eroticism (Mayne 1990: 128).

Critical discussion of the scene has focused largely on its relationship to film pornography. The length and graphic explicitness of the segment take it very close to lesbian pornography and some commentators do say they find it erotic, yet it is filled with so many elements that violate every pornographic code that the experience of watching it is rendered much more uncomfortable and embarrassing than erotically pleasurable. There are no romantic or adventurous implications. The fact that it is prefaced by the female lover feeding the protagonist could be regarded as sensual, but she feeds her sandwiches and milk, rather than a sensuous feast. Both women's actions are robotic, awkward, repetitious, and even seem rather violent. They certainly do not convey heated passion or sexual frenzy, and the scene looks more like two naked people engaging in a wrestling match than a romantic encounter. The lovers' bodies are not glamorized as they are in Hollywood love scenes; instead, they are shot in a manner that minimizes their eroticization and fetishization. The background setting is a plain, unadorned room; the camera remains static, maintaining a discrete distance in medium long shot; and there are no cut-ins to close ups. There is absolutely no fragmentation of the women's bodies to heighten sexual titillation, and the soundtrack acts not to eroticize the scene, as it does in mainstream films, but actually to de-eroticize it. Instead of romantic music, we hear panting, howls, slapping bodies, shuffling sheets, and an odd murmuring voice that does not seem to come from the two figures, but from a mysterious voice-over that extends throughout the scene. The final de-eroticized moment occurs when the protagonist gets up and emotionlessly walks out the door. Most commentators read this to mean that she has left the apartment, but then we hear the sound of a woman and children singing. One commentator believes the lyrics they sing are from a nursery rhyme that repeats the phrase "Kiss whomever you wish" (Turner 2003: 98), whereas another proposes that the protagonist is singing in the shower (Bergstrom 1999b).

Many critics have contrasted this sex scene to the one with the trucker, and questioned whether it privileges lesbian over heterosexual sexuality. The two scenes are opposed in some ways, yet parallel in others. Akerman's character is completely off-screen in the first and decidedly onscreen in the second, the first is shot close up and the second from a distance, the first is saturated with the trucker's monologue and the other has no speech whatsoever. On the other hand, both are similarly shot in long takes in a dispassionate, reportorial manner; both are notable for their "self-conscious display of dehumanization and lack of visual pleasure" (Foster 2003:1); and both seem intended to mock almost every convention of mainstream sex scenes. Gwendolyn Audrey Foster even believes there is a sense of camp humor exhibited in the two scenes (2003: 1). Critics disagree about what exactly the similarities and contrasts between them indicate. Are we to see the protagonist as having progressed from an unsatisfying heterosexual encounter to a more equitable and fulfilling lesbian one? The length of the lesbian sex scene and the more mutual involvement of the two participants supports this reading, but the de-eroticized, cold, almost scientific way both scenes are shot suggests, on the contrary, that this relationship is not much more fulfilling than the earlier heterosexual one. As Mayne points out, the whole third section indicates not a sense of "lesbian triumphalism" over a failed heterosexual connection, but rather the "ritual of two women's simultaneous attraction to and distance from each other" (1990: 128). The connection the lesbian relationship has with hunger, pain, neediness, and rejection could even open the film up to a homophobic reading. Both relationships are more intriguing, however, if seen in a meta-cinematic

Figure 5 From left, Claire Wauthion and Chantal Akerman as lovers in the ambiguous closing segment of *Je, tu, il, elle.*

light as part of a larger attack the film launches against mainstream cinema and its presentation of romance and sexuality.

The film's meta-cinematic visual style fits almost perfectly with feminist calls for women filmmakers to challenge and subvert mainstream conventions. Stylistically, Akerman is the ultimate rebel, constructing through her "confrontational minimalism" (Turim 2003: 25) a "continual risk-taking anti-cinema" (Foster 2003: 2). She violates so many mainstream conventions and frustrates so many of the pleasures that we are used to experiencing when we watch a film that theoreticians find her work enormously powerful, but too often it is unpleasurable, off-putting, and even annoying to viewers. *Je, tu, il, elle* is so drastically antithetical to Hollywood that its difference seems to represent calculated mockery with a biting edge, yet the film also has a hybrid nature that makes its violation of mainstream norms even more frustrating to many viewers. We are led in some ways to expect a conventional film and then we get hit with an Akerman film instead. *Je, tu, il, elle* resembles a mainstream film in that it is feature-length, has a fairly coherent narrative, and contains characters who on the surface at least are realistically presented. Thus, it can be considered an amalgam of commercial, avant-garde, art cinema, and women's auteur cinema, yet its style unquestionably takes it in a unique and very different direction.

Je, tu, il, elle is structured in a way that seems stylistically to represent a complete denial of every form of conventional filmic pleasure. It simply does not set out to entertain its audience in the way Hollywood films do by building tension and suspense, offering characters with whom one can identify, and employing a shooting style that draws the spectator into the story. What Akerman offers can almost be called a mode of non-involvement. Rather than drawing us into the story and cultivating identification with the characters, what her minimalist style provides is significant distance from both plot and characters, projecting her audience into a state of contemplation as if the film were a mental exercise or puzzle to be worked on and thought out. Thus, her films are much more fun to think about afterwards than to watch. Seemingly stripped down to the absolute basics, her minimalist style just does not give us enough information about setting, characters, or events to spark immediate interest, but probably the most off-putting characteristic of her work is her use of what is called real-time pacing. As Akerman explains, this actually involves slowing down the actions of the actors during shooting so that time is "totally recomposed, to give the impression of real time." To audiences accustomed to the rapid pacing of Hollywood films, this recomposed timing can provoke frustration and disinterest, rather than what Akerman says she hopes to stimulate in her audience: a contemplative distance from which "we feel our existence. Just by the fact that we're somewhere beyond the merely informative" (quoted in Rosen 2004: 125).

Akerman also uses a long list of other stylistic distancing devices that resist the classical Hollywood model and its satisfactions. She eschews shot/reverse shot editing and cut-ins to close-ups which draw the viewer into involvement with characters. Her films are generally composed of blocks of long takes with a low-level static camera (in her early films such as *Je, tu, il, elle* the camera never moves); no changes in camera angles; no optical point of view shots; an artificial-seeming, almost perfectly symmetrical mise-en-scene; no zooms; and shots held for what seem like excessive amounts of time. Sound is also used in ways that are disjunctive, with the frequent use of a disembodied female voice-over and visual/sound counterpoint. B. Ruby Rich describes the effect as "filming degree zero," in which "shots are held so long that meaning dissolves into play, interest into detachment, detachment back again into involvement" (1998: 170). Janet Bergstrom calls the style "splitting" in that Akerman always maintains a distinct separation between the field occupied by the camera and thus associated with the director's vision in contrast to the field observed by the camera and connected with the characters. A careful distance is always kept between that which is being represented in contrast to the person who is doing the representing and those who are experiencing that representation. For Bergstrom, the effect is to create a split approach to reality which takes objective reality into consideration but at the same time disavows and replaces it with an anti-reality produced by desire (1999a: 280). Whether one describes Akerman's style as splitting or filming degree zero, it comes very close to ful-filling Mulvey's call for a feminist cinema that is able to "free the look of the camera into its materiality of time and space" (1989d: 26). Whether this is enough to release "the look of the audience into dialectics, passionate detach-ment," as Mulvey suggests it might, seems to lead us directly to a consideration of the film's major themes (1989a: 26).

Thematically, *Je, tu, il, elle* might strike one as totally mystifying or indeci-pherable. Indeterminacy seems to reside at the heart of the text, which at every point refuses "interpretive completion and certainty" (Turim 2003: 21). Interestingly, in spite of the film's structural and stylistic peculiarities, most critics still tend to read it realistically as a study of psychological pathology. As noted earlier, they see the protagonist as suffering from some form of psychic disturbance ranging from mere loneliness to obsessive-compulsive disorder and suicidal depression. Akerman has lent support to this reading in several comments she has made about the film. For instance, she describes the plot as about "someone who is in a crisis precisely because things don't work out with another person – this other girl," and, as indicated previously, she said she had to play the protagonist herself because she was the only one who could convey the sense of "malaise" that she wanted to express (quoted in Margulies 1996: 112). Even if Akerman's remarks tend to endorse a realist reading, we might still question whether this interpretation fits with her minimalist strategies of characterization and plot development. Is the protagonist really that psychologically disturbed or is she better described as on a quest for self-fulfillment, sexual knowledge, connection with another, and/or a resolution of her ambiguous sexuality? In interviews, Akerman has said that "nomadism" plays an important role in her films and that it reflects her own feelings of homelessness as a Belgian Jew whose mother, a holocaust survivor, only settled in Belgium after the war. Extrapolating from her own feelings, Akerman proposes that no one ever really finds one's true "place" in the world and that she personally does not feel a relationship of origin with Belgium, even though she was born there (Bergstrom 1999a: 287). *Je, tu, il, elle* can be read as a tragic text about just this sort of nomadic existence with its protagonist attempting to find a sense of place at first within herself in the isolation of her own apartment and then in sexual connections with both male and female lovers. Every attempt fails to fulfill her desire and in the end she leaves in despair of finding either a secure sense of self or an intimate connection with another.

Judith Mayne has raised the issue of whether the film should be read as a lesbian text that shows its protagonist moving from being "sealed in the hermetic space of her own narcissism" to becoming a sexual being first in a heterosexual encounter with the trucker and finally by finding "a more satisfactory, more complete, more successful sexual identity with her female lover." Mayne is really rather undecided about what to make of the film's lesbian content. She proposes that *Je, tu, il, elle* does not fit comfortably in the category of the lesbian film because it is not addressed to a lesbian audience and fails to offer an affirmation of lesbian identity; instead, it tends to identify lesbianism with pain, narcissism, infantilism, and neediness. On the other hand, the film does in a sense affirm sexual desire between women as a complex source of female creativity and associate explicit lesbian desire with the author–text relation (Mayne, 1990: 132). Thus, Mayne proposes that the text contains some elements that exhibit what she calls "the radical otherness" of lesbian sexuality and identity (1990: 133).

If the film's narrative components lead to realist interpretations of its story and themes as related to psychological malaise, the search for identity, and lesbianism, its stylistic features move in an entirely different direction. They open it up to being read as a meta-cinematic feminist theory film, the major concern of which is to counter the representation of women in mainstream cinema, rather than to present a realistic story. By creating a visual style that mocks Hollywood codes of female representation at every turn and even attacks the "cynically voyeuristic attractions of pornography" (Rich 1998: 171), Akerman seems to have created exactly the feminist anti-mainstream masterpiece that 1970s feminist theory advocated. The question we might finally ask ourselves, however, is if the displeasure so many viewers feel in watching this film calls her strategies for destroying mainstream pleasures into question or if she succeeds in replacing these pleasures with exactly the "passionate detachment" that Mulvey among others advocated.

Films in Focus 3: *Shut Up & Sing*

Unlike Deren and Akerman, Barbara Kopple chose the documentary form as her mode of expression. Kopple has been a documentary filmmaker for over twenty years. She is a politically committed director who nevertheless claims to adhere strongly to a non-interventionist approach to filmmaking. She began in documentary work in 1974 by recording sound for the anti-Vietnam war documentary *Hearts and Minds* (Peter Davis) and earlier worked with the famous documentarists the Maysles Bros. on their cinéma vérité classic, *Salesman* (1968). Her crowning achievements thus far are two labor documentaries, both of which won Academy Awards, *Harlan Co. U.S.A.* (1976) and *American Dream* (1990). Like all her films, her labor documentaries straddle the divide between the interventionist and non-interventionist documentary modes in ways that illustrate the problematic nature of claims to documentary realism. As we shall see, Kopple has repeatedly made non-interventionalist claims for all her films although she has consistently failed to live up to these claims in practice.

Kopple's career has been varied. She has done projects for television as well as film and directed a number of biographical documentaries on prominent male figures: *A Conversation with Gregory Peck* (1999) in which she interviewed the famous Hollywood actor, *Wild Man Blues* (1997) which follows director Woody Allen and his jazz band on their European tour, and *Fallen Champ: The Untold Story of Mike Tyson* (1993) on the career of the controversial boxing great. Kopple has also been involved with overtly political projects like the anti-Vietnam war documentary *Winter Soldier* (1997); *Beyond "JFK": A Question of Conspiracy* (1992), a reconsideration of the factual basis for the 1991 Oliver Stone movie on the Kennedy assassination; and *WMD: Weapons of Mass Deception* (2004) on the media's role in promoting the Iraq war. In addition, she co-directed the television documentary *Bearing Witness* (2005) on women journalists reporting in war zones and even ventured into narrative filmmaking with *Havoc* (2005), which focuses on two affluent teenaged girls who clash with Latino gang culture in Los Angeles.

Most of Kopple's films do not deal with feminist issues as their primary topic, but with *Shut Up & Sing* (2006), which she co-directed with her friend Cynthia Peck, Kopple moved into the realm of the feminist documentary. The film chronicles the off-stage lives of the all-female country group The Dixie Chicks as they found themselves embroiled in a major controversy after their lead singer Natalie Maines criticized President George W. Bush's handling of the build-up to the U.S. invasion of Iraq. On March 10, 2003, Maines told an audience at the Shephard's Bush Empire Theatre in London: "Just so you know, we're on the good side with y'all. We do not want this war, this violence, and we're ashamed that the President of the United States is from Texas [which the Dixie Chicks consider their home state]." The resulting controversy led their songs to be banned on country radio, much of their country fan base to desert them, and even death threats to be made against Maines. Overwhelmed by the enormity of the backlash against the band in country music circles, Maines quickly apologized to the President on March 14, admitting that her "remark was disrespectful" and that "whoever holds that office [the Presidency] should be treated with the utmost respect." Notably, she did not say that she supported his stance on the war or that she regretted having said otherwise. The apology, which seemed rather half-hearted at best, did nothing to quell the vitriolic attacks on Maines or to get the band's music back on the radio.

Before the controversy erupted, the Dixie Chicks turned Kopple and Peck down when they approached them to do a documentary on what turned out to be the Chicks' ironically named Top of the World Tour. Once the brouhaha about Maines' remark began, the band must have concluded that a sympathetic feature length documentary could only help what quickly appeared to be their seriously damaged career. They approached Kopple and Peck to undertake the project after all, reputedly choosing them over more high profile documentarists Michael Moore and D. A. Pennebaker (Smith 2007). In assembling the film, Kopple and Peck used footage they shot themselves combined with footage already shot during the Top of the World Tour and archival material on the Chicks' earlier performances and career (Brooks 2006). The resulting film takes the form of an apologia for the Dixie Chicks and a critical appraisal of those who attacked them. Kopple, who always claimed that her documentary approach is entirely non-interventionist, found herself making statements about the film that contradict its actual content.

Like so many other women documentarists, while expressing strong support for the realist aesthetic, Kopple has employing film techniques that are clearly interventionist. For instance, she declared, "What I would call a really good documentary is one in which you never feel the presence of the camera or the filmmaker. It's like peeking under a blanket when you're not supposed to look and seeing real life and real people unfold" (quoted in Legiardi-Laura 1992: 38). She also proposed that what she considers a great scene is when her subjects just forget the camera is there and the story takes over (quoted in Stubbs 2002: 217). If a filmmaker wants to get something "real and sincere," she claims the director must have "no agenda" and allow "the characters to take you on a journey with them." She further describes her approach as removing from her mind everything she ever thought about her subjects, allowing their story to emerge, and then following it (Smith 2007).

At times, Kopple describes her process totally in realist terms, claiming to approach her films "with an open mind. I don't go into a film with a particular agenda – I rarely know how a film will end when I start filming" (quoted in Brooks 2006). At other times, however, she describes herself as a very politically committed filmmaker, and her films bear out this self-description much more than they do her realist claims. Her filmmaking techniques actually appear to be decidedly interventionist. For instance, in order to portray the 1973 miners' strike in *Harlan Co. U.S.A.*, she lived with the miners for thirteen months. Because they came to trust her, she was able to capture their experience of the strike in intimate detail. Thus, her film is hardly a distant, clinical analysis of the situation in a non-interventionist mode, and Kopple even admitted to being committed to the miners' cause. She said she regards the miners, and American workers in general, as "my heroes, the people I care about" (quoted in Legiardi-Laura 1992:36) and that she would always take their side (Legiardi-Laura 1992: 38). As E. Ann Kaplan points out, *Harlan Co. U.S.A.* is a "highly structured argument about the strike from the miners' point of view" (1977: 12), and Kopple even described the film as in essence an organizing instrument for the miners' cause (Kleinhans 1977: 4). At the same time, she also claimed to have taken pains to present every side of the story of the strike so that her audience could "understand the dynamics, the complexities, and the layers within the film" (quoted in Legiardi-Laura 1992: 38).

Kopple's interventionism goes beyond a sense of involvement and solidarity with her subjects to her use of a penetrating shooting style. She describes herself as "a very intimate filmmaker. I like to be able to get underneath what people think" (quoted in Legiardi-Laura 1992: 37). In order to make *Harlan Co. U.S.A.*, she not only lived with her subjects, but her camera entered into every facet of the strike from the miners' meetings to their violent encounters with company thugs on the picket lines. Kopple employs a shooting style that "plunges us into the midst of the actuality of the event" (Kaplan 1977: 12). On the picket lines, Kopple even filmed her own altercation with one of the company thugs who tried to intimidate her and get her to stop shooting. There are several scenes in *Harlan Co.* in which Kopple not only penetrates into the details of the strike but also into the personal lives of the miners. Notable instances of this penetration are scenes Kopple shot of the miners' wives organizing their protests, picketing the entrance to the mine, blocking scabs from breaking the picket lines, and standing up to a state trooper who tries to get them to disperse. They go so far as to lie down on the road to prevent the scabs from entering the mine and to allow themselves to be arrested. As Kaplan points out, Kopple shows the women to be central actors in the strike and captures both their strength and their suffering. The women "trusted her enough to be relaxed in front of the camera" and thus exposed their pain without seeming to be acting (Kaplan 1977: 12). This trust is particularly evident when Kopple is allowed to film the funeral of a young striker who was killed on the picket lines allegedly by company thugs. The camera is there as the man's pregnant wife and elderly mother pass by his casket with the mother hysterically sobbing. It is a scene that some critics found too intrusive, almost exploitive of the family's grief. As Paula Rabinowitz suggests, it is particularly disturbing because there is a sense of "raw feeling spilling out inappropriately for public consumption" (1999: 59).

In *Harlan Co.*, Kopple's interventions do not just involve her interest in and partisan involvement with her subjects. Her documentaries are so powerful because she shapes the disorganized reality of pro-filmic events into a tele-ological narrative with a clear social and political message. Interestingly, Kopple has always strenuously denied that she does this at all. She insists that she never sets out to fashion a story from the events she films. When an inter-viewer proposed that her films work so well because, like a fiction filmmaker, she creates dramatic tension, she interrupted him to insist, "I don't *create* tension" (quoted in Legiardi-Laura 1992: 37), suggesting that the narrative tension is already there in the events themselves. She seems to want to believe that she simply allows things to unfold before her camera and these incidents form a dramatic narrative entirely of their own accord. She claims to just follow along recording things as they happen, but there is strong evidence within her films themselves that this is hardly the case and that Kopple shapes events into highly dramatic, and some critics have said overly melodramatic, stories with very distinct messages. Much of the dramatic effect of *Harlan Co.*, for instance, comes from Kopple's effective use of traditional protest songs, often sung by female folk artists in the rich musical tradition of Appalachia. This music both adds to the film's melodrama and raises the miners' struggle to the level of a mythic event in a long tradition of working-class social protest. It is difficult to come away from *Harlan Co.* without the feeling that the film is a carefully constructed "meditation on the eternal plight of the miner" (Biskind 1977: 4), as well as on his enormous strength and courage. What Kopple conveys, and it seems very deliberately, is the story of the miners' ongoing struggle with the forces of big business that seek to stifle their heroic attempts to improve their working and living conditions.

Kopple's statements about *Shut Up & Sing* are just as contradictory as her comments on *Harlan Co. U.S.A.* and her other earlier films. Despite her deter-mination to claim adherence to a non-interventionist credo, it was extremely difficult for her to propose that she took an entirely non-interventionist approach to presenting the story of the Dixie Chicks' run-in with the country music establishment. In discussing *Shut Up & Sing*, Kopple yet again proposed that she does not like to "go into a film with an agenda," but she also admitted that she knew from the beginning that she believed the Dixie Chick's situation involved the suppression of free speech and that she respected their refusal to back down in the face of intimidation and threats from the country music industry and fans. Yet, in many of her interviews about the film, Kopple still tried to argue for a non-interventionist approach, proposing, "I didn't want it to be solely about the comment and its immediate aftermath. I wanted to see how this experience changed them as humans and musicians" (quoted in Brooks 2006). Whether Kopple wants to see it as such or not, the film does not just observe how the Dixie Chicks' experience changed them, but presents them as heroic defenders of freedom of speech and plucky survivors who refused to let opposition from the country music establishment derail their careers. When asked how she saw *Shut Up & Sing* fitting in with the rest of her films, Kopple said that the majority of her films are "all about people who are fighting for social justice and people who are standing for what they believe in, and people who won't be silenced. ... It's just people whose stories you might not know – or who you might think of in a totally different way." She went on to describe the Dixie Chicks as not just talented singers but as "so complex, so bright, such great businesswomen," and she said she wanted her audience to see them in a new light. She was especially anxious for those who were against the Chicks to understand where they were coming from. She describes her goal somewhat melodramatically as to get people to see that it is important to be "true to yourself" and it is wrong to try to destroy someone just because that person has openly expressed her beliefs (quoted in Smith 2007).

Although the film goes to great lengths to persuade the viewer that the Dixie Chicks as a band and as remarkable women were not destroyed by the aftermath of Maines' remark, that this is actually the case seems doubtful. Their career as a country music band has never recovered from this incident, and Maines is no longer even currently recording with the two other members of the group, Martie Maguire and Emily Robison, although they claim the band has not broken up and that they will all be recording together in the future. One would not gather that the Dixie Chicks were in any danger of dissolution from Kopple and Peck's documentary. Cultivating a hagiographic tone, the film portrays the Chicks as strong feminist role models who refused to be defeated or to allow the attacks on them to destroy their solidarity as a group. As Kopple describes her conception of what happened, the country music industry thought that because the Dixie Chicks are women they would just crumble when under attack, but they "had no idea who they were dealing with" (quoted in Smith 2007). The film repeatedly shows the band members sitting together strategizing to find new ways to revitalize their flagging career, declaring their refusal to be intimidated, and supporting each other unequivocally throughout their ordeal. As Gavin Smith has pointed out, Kopple and Peck present the Chicks not only as "martyrs for free speech, ... savvy strategists and hard-driving business women," but also as "women in control." Kopple said that she admired them because "nobody told them what to do," they refused to back down, showed tenacity in the face of a crisis, and insisted on their right of free expression, even though it cost them most of their fan base (quoted in Smith 2007).

Figure 6 The Dixie Chicks in *Shut Up & Sing*.

Although Kopple has never been comfortable admitting to an agenda, she and Peck obviously made gender issues a prominent aspect of their film. In the course of the documentary, the Chicks are extolled more and more as feminist heroes. They fight sexism everywhere within the country music industry, even within their own entourage. As J. Martin Daughtry suggests, the film includes archival footage that shows deeply misogynist speech used against the Chicks by their opponents and even by their handlers, especially their male manager, who uses sexist language and a patronizing tone in speaking with them (2009: 271). Kopple and Peck also focus on the strong feeling of sisterhood the Chicks exhibit as they fight to protect their rights and salvage their career. Kopple has said the strength of their friendship and how they pulled together as a unit particularly impressed her (Smith 2007), and she and Peck document this female bonding not only in the repeated scenes of the Chicks' strategizing sessions, but most movingly in an emotion-packed scene in which Martie breaks into tears as she talks directly to the camera (Smith 2007). She explains how worried she is about Natalie and that she would gladly sacrifice her fame if she could just bring her peace. The scene is certainly emotional, if perhaps a bit overly melodramatic and contrived, but it demonstrates without doubt that Kopple and Peck's intentions were to establish the feminist solidarity found among their subjects.

In interviews, Kopple emphasized repeatedly the admiration she felt for the Chicks because they refused to apologize to their fans or to country music radio for Maines' remark and continued to insist on their right to free speech. This is unquestionably the position Kopple and Peck's film takes, but it is not so clear that this refusal is actually what happened. Did the Chicks really refuse to apologize? They did not retract their opposition to Bush's Iraq policy, but as mentioned earlier, Maines did admit her comment that they were ashamed to be from the same state as Bush was disrespectful to the President and his office. She also said that she wished she had not made the remark that she had and that it was something she should not have said. Because Kopple and Peck wanted to emphasize the Chicks' defiant stance, the documentary does not focus on Maines' apologies. In fact, it barely mentions them. What it does emphasize is the violent and sexist nature of the attacks against her by fans, music radio, and even other country stars like Toby Keith. Kopple has said in interviews that she thinks the country music establishment got so angry at the Chicks because they just assumed they were conservative and were shocked to discover that there were in their midst liberal country artists who did not completely agree with right-wing ideas. She also proposed that she did not believe that if a male artist had made the same remark that Maines made he would have been treated with such contempt (Smith 2007). It was because the Chicks were women insisting on their right to speak out and express what was on their minds that country music became so enraged. The aftermath of the remark with the Chicks refusing to be completely contrite just fed the flames. As noted above, Kopple argued that country music thought these female performers would fall apart under their attacks, and it is clear she and Peck fashioned their documentary to emphasize the Chicks refusal to do so. As Kopple put it, she wanted to show that the country music establishment "had no idea who they were dealing with" (quoted in Smith 2007).

Kopple said she and Peck also wanted to include scenes to provide some background on who exactly the Dixie Chicks are, so that the audience could relate to them more easily. To this end, the documentary contains a considerable amount of footage of the women at home with their husbands and children. Kopple said including this footage made the time sequencing in the film "tricky" (quoted in Smith 2007), and the film's structure does jump achronologically to scenes from different time periods in a way that can be somewhat confusing and is certainly not conventional in documentaries on music stars that are intended for a mainstream audience. Kopple said she felt this intimate family footage was needed to get the audience to know the Chicks so they would care about what happened to them (Smith 2007). These scenes more specifically seem intended to win over conservative viewers and present the Chicks as less radical and unconventional than their opponents portrayed them. They are shown to be devoted mothers and loving wives after all, just like many of their conservative fans, and not at all wild-eyed subversives out to attack the President. As Kopple said, one of her goals in the film was to get those who were opposed to the band to come to understand who the Dixie Chicks really are and therefore come to an understanding of the position they took.

Perhaps also reflective of this strategy is Kopple and Peck's decision to leave out of the documentary much of the footage of the band's performances. This makes Shut Up & Sing a decidedly unusual music documentary, one that eschews documenting its subjects' performances. We get very little sense of the "glittery glory" of the Chicks in concert (Smith 2007) or even of the extent of their talent. Why was this group so popular before Maines made her remark? What put them at the "top of the world" of country music at the time? Kopple and Peck are not interested in these questions; instead, they focus on what Kopple describes as the maturation process the band went through as a result of their rejection by country music. As Kopple and Peck saw the Chicks' story, it was about three strong women who courageously faced the ordeal of having to confront not just criticism from country music radio, declining music sales for their albums, and a severe falloff in ticket purchases for their concerts, but also hatred, taunts, and even death threats from their former fans. Shut Up & Sing presents them as refusing to crumble as a result of these events; instead, they are shown to have undergone a personal and artistic transformation and, as Kopple sees it, "became totally comfortable in their own skins and went on to write a wonderful album" that dealt with "everything from politics to infertility to love, all of the universal themes that are so much about who we are" (quoted in Smith 2007). Thus, Kopple transformed an unfortunate incident that could be seen as having completely ruined a very popular band's career into an inspirational feminist chronicle of their strength and courage in the face of extreme and unfair attacks.

In interviews, Kopple said that everyone involved in the film saw it as showing that the current political climate in the U.S. was one in which basic freedoms of speech, protest, and dissent were in danger. She proposed that the film's structure never really came together until the editing room where she and Peck were able to weave together all the disparate material to highlight both the personal impact and political significance of the Dixie Chicks' story (Brooks 2006). The personal impact that Kopple and Peck wanted to portray is clear. They convert what could be seen as the devastating destruction of a popular country group into a feminist parable of female tenacity, courage, intelligence, sisterhood, and ultimate triumph. What the film says about the larger political issue of free speech is much less apparent. Kopple has stated unequivocally that she went into the film knowing she wanted to tell people that they need to stand up for what they believe and not let anyone silence them or stop them from expressing their views (quoted in Smith 2007). She said that she wanted the film to show that "when you stand up for your rights, people will be there to support you, and follow your lead (quoted in Brooks 2006).

Despite Kopple's adherence to the aesthetic of non-interventionism, *Shut Up & Sing* is very much constructed to express Kopple and Peck's particular perspective on the Chicks' experiences. Those experiences can be seen quite differently, however, and the film can be read against the grain as not so much about three female advocates for free speech who spoke truth to power and won, but as a cautionary tale warning of the watch-what-you-say attitude that surrounded the war in Iraq and the devastating effects this political climate had on the lives of those who spoke up in opposition to government policy. While Kopple and Peck take pains to present the Dixie Chicks as having beaten their adversaries and come out on the top of the world after all, the trajectory of their career during the time of the film and after does not entirely support this teleological progression. Their career has not recovered from the effects of Maines' comment, and at the current time it looks like it will never do so. Other issues that the film pushes to the side in order to argue for the Chicks' ultimate triumph also complicate the free speech issue. For instance, does the Chicks' experience really show that free speech was stifled at the time, or do the protests and counter-protests concerning Maines' remark actually demonstrate that free speech is, in fact, alive and well in the U.S.? After all, don't those opposed to what she said also have a right to free speech? But was this even primarily a free speech issue or one of a powerful media organization exercising a form of censorship to stifle dissent? Were country music fans really so outraged by what Natalie Maines said, or were they the dupes of right-wing commentators and bloggers who stirred up a frenzy with their irresponsible attacks on the Chicks?

These are some of the issues that the film never even gets close to addressing. It does not really seem even to be interested in them. What it is interested in is presenting a feminist tale of the Dixie Chicks as strong female role models, women who stood up for themselves, waged a battle against those who would silence them, and won. That this story does not entirely accord with the facts of the situation seems hardly to have troubled Kopple and Peck. One aspect of the film that does seem clear, however, is what it indicates about Barbara Kopple as a documentary filmmaker who always has taken pains to present herself as a non-interventionist, even when the form and content of her films suggests otherwise. With *Shut Up & Sing*, it seems apparent that her devotion to non-interventionist filmmaking lost out to her feminist concerns. But is this really a loss or is non-intervention in the documentary form an unrealizable goal, a myth that women filmmakers like Kopple should refuse to propagate?

Key Terms: *experimental films, surrealist films, abstract films, feminist theory films, the realist aesthetic, interventionalist documentary filmmaking, non-interventionalist documentary filmmaking, minimalist, meta-cinematic, real-time pacing*

Suggestions for Further Reading, Viewing, and Discussion

1. The title *Je, tu, il, elle* was changed when the film was first shown in the U.S. to *Personal Pronouncements*. How does this U.S. title relate to the film? Does it?

2. Should Deren, Akerman, and Kopple be characterized as feminist filmmakers even though none of them have claimed that their work is feminist? View some films by other women avant-garde and documentary filmmakers and do some research to determine if they self-identify as feminist or not. Compare and contrast their work to each other, and to the filmmakers we have studied in this chapter.

3. Both Deren and Akerman star in their own films, but *Meshes* has been repeatedly seen as autobiographical, whereas *Je, tu, il, elle* has rarely been examined as such. Why do you think this is so? How does the fact that the female directors play the roles of the protagonists in their films affect your reaction to them? Barbara Kopple, on the other hand, tends to efface her presence from her films. How do you explain the difference in technique and what are the effects of this difference? Does it reflect differences between the avant-garde and documentary modes of filmmaking or just the personal styles of the filmmakers?

4. How does Deren and Akerman's use of an experimental style and Kopple's use of the documentary mode affect the way you react to their films? Does it enhance or destroy your viewing pleasure? Explain why? Are these film forms too different from mainstream film to be pleasurable? If the films are pleasurable, how is this pleasure different from that found in mainstream narrative film? Or is it different?

5. What is your view of the authorship controversy surrounding *Meshes*? Should Deren be considered the auteur of the film or has Hammid been unfairly denied that position?

6. Does the narrative of *Je, tu, il, elle* create a sense of progression or not? Does the protagonist develop in the course of the film? How?

7. How do you interpret the ambiguous endings of *Meshes* and *Je, tu, il, elle*? Does Kopple's ending contain any ambiguity or does it provide complete closure to the Dixie Chicks' story?

8. As noted in the chapter, although she did not give them titles in the film, Akerman named the three parts of *Je, tu, il, elle* a time of subjectivity, a time of the other or reportage, and a time of relationship. How do these titles relate to the three sections of the film? Do they? Do you think the titles should have been included in the film?

9. Do you think the avant-garde and documentary forms really do offer women filmmakers a less patriarchal type of cinema in which to work? Why or why not? Which mode of filmmaking do you see as more effective as a feminist form?

10. View works by other women avant-garde and documentary filmmakers and consider how they fit with some of the qualities of feminist filmmaking outlined in this chapter. The selected bibliography below offers some suggestions for films, but there are many more from which you might choose.

Selected Filmography of Avant-garde and Documentary Women Filmmakers

Documentaries

Joyce Chopra: *Joyce at 34* (1972)

Connie Field: *The Life and Times of Rosie the Riveter* (1980), *Have You Heard from Johannesburg* (2010)

Jill Godmillow: *Antonia: A Portrait of the Woman* (1974), *Far from Poland* (1984)

Jennie Livingston: *Paris Is Burning* (1990)

Saroya Mire: *Fire Eyes* (1994)

Pratibha Parmar: *A Place of* Rage (1991), *Warrior Masks* (1993), *Jodie: An Icon* (1996)

Lourdes Portillo: *Corpus* (1999); *The Devil Never Sleeps* (1994); Las Madres: The Mothers of the Plaza de Mayo (1985)

Leni Riefenstahl: *Triumph of the Will* (1935), *Olympia* (1938)

Helke Sander: *The Germans and their Men — Report from Bonn* (1989), *Liberators Take Liberties: War, Rapes, and Children* (1991/92)

Monica Treut: *Gendernauts* (1999), *Warrior of Light* (2001)

Agnes Varda: *The Gleaners and I* (2000), *Les plages de Agnes* (*The Beaches of Agnes*, 2008)

Trinh T. Minh-ha: *Reassemblage* (1983), *Surname Viet Given Name Nam* (1989)

Avant-garde and Experimental Filmmakers

Chantal Akerman: *Jeanne Dielman, 23 Quai du Commerce, 1080 Bruxelles* (1975)

Michelle Citron: *Daughter Rite* (1979)

Shirley Clarke: *The Cool World* (1964), *Portrait of Jason* (1967)

Germaine Dulac: *The Smiling Madame Beudet* (1923), *The Seashell and the Clergyman* (1928)

Marguerite Duras: *Nathalie Granger* (1972), *India Song* (1975)

Su Friedrich: *Damned If You Don't* (1987), *Sink or Swim* (1990), *Hide and Seek* (1997)

Barbara Hammer: *Dyketactics* (1974), *Nitrate Kisses* (1992), *Tender Fictions* (1995)

Laura Mulvey: *Riddles of the Sphinx* (1979)

Sally Potter: *Thriller* (1979), *Orlando* (1992), *The Tango Lesson* (1997)

Yvonne Rainer: *Lives of Performers* (1972), *The Man who Envied Women* (1985)

Helke Sander: *The All-Round Reduced Personality—REDUPERS* (1977)

Joyce Wieland: *Reason over Passion* (1969)

Chapter 4

Lesbian Film Theory and Criticism

Theoretical approaches to the cinematic representation of lesbianism represent a particularly complex and fruitful area of feminist film study, as well as one filled with substantial debate. Issues arise, for instance, concerning the exact definition of a lesbian film as well as the relationship between lesbian films and those that focus on other forms of female bonding, like women's friendships, mother–daughter relationships, and sisterhood. Other areas of debate include the usefulness of psychoanalysis for the investigation of lesbian films and the various categories of lesbian cinema. Lesbian films can be divided into ambiguous as opposed to openly lesbian portrayals, Hollywood productions vs. independent features, and coming-out narratives, lesbian romance films, and representations of lesbian families and communities. Additionally, critics have examined the history of lesbian and gay cinematic representation and theorized the potential challenge these films pose to the patriarchal, heterosexist status quo. Recently, a major issue in lesbian film criticism has centered on whether lesbian theory really should be affiliated with feminist film studies at all or whether it more properly belongs within the growing field of queer studies, which unites lesbian and gay male film critics under one theoretical umbrella and analyzes film representations from the perspective of sexuality rather than gender. Thus, lesbian film critics currently find themselves torn between feminist and queer perspectives. One would hope that this hybrid identity will not sever the connection between lesbian and feminist film criticism because, as we shall see, lesbian criticism has contributed so much to feminist film studies that it would be a great loss if lesbian critics divorced themselves entirely from a feminist perspective.

One area of feminist film studies to which lesbian theorists have made substantial contributions considers the usefulness of psychoanalysis to feminist film theory. Many lesbian theorists reject psychoanalysis as promoting the heterosexist notion that lesbianism is the result of a masculinity complex and regression to the pre-Oedipal mother-daughter attachment. They feel this theorization pathologizes lesbian desire as a case of arrested development, an infantilizing fixation with a narcissistic and dependent early bond with the mother. Other lesbian critics have embraced psychoanalysis as a way to investigate not only cinematic representations of lesbianism, but also its psychic origins and dimensions. Indicative of the use of psychoanalysis to investigate crucial issues in lesbian film theory is the discussion between Jackie Stacey and Teresa de Lauretis concerning their theories of female spectatorship and homoerotic desire. In her 1989 article "Desperately Seeking Difference," Stacey suggested that lesbian portrayals and films that deal with female bonding create similar connections with female spectators. She argued that there is a homoerotic component to films that concern "a woman's obsession with another woman," even when this obsession is not ostensibly of a sexual nature (Stacey 1989: 125). Stacey offered as particular filmic examples *All About Eve* (Joseph L. Mankeiwicz, 1950) and *Desperately Seeking Susan* (Susan Seidelman, 1985), suggesting that the homoerotically charged relationships between the films' central female characters are replicated in the connection formed between the female viewer and the films' female stars. Similarly, in *Star Gazing: Hollywood cinema and female spectatorship* (1994), Stacey again argued for a homoerotic dimension to the female spectator–star relationship. She maintained that one element of cinematic pleasure for all women viewers in watching female film stars involves "a fascination with an idealized other which could not be reduced to male desire or female identification within the available psychoanalytic dichotomies, but rather necessitate[s] a rethinking of the specificities of forms of female attachment" (Stacey 1994: 28).

In "Film and the Visible" (1991) and *The Practice of Love: lesbian sexuality and perverse desire* (1994), Teresa de Lauretis objected strenuously to Stacey's ideas. For de Lauretis, the connection Stacey draws between female spectatorship and homoerotic desire confuses desire with narcissistic identification. According to de Lauretis's orthodox reading of Freudian theory, Stacey's ideas violate the Freudian separation between object libido and narcissistic or ego libido. As de Lauretis explains, Freud conceived of object libido as involving "desire, wanting to have (the object)," and ego libido as "desexualized and ha[ving] to do with narcissistic identification, wanting to be or be like or seeing oneself as (the object)" (1994: 116–22). For de Lauretis, following Freud, the two cannot be combined, whereas Stacey maintains, to the contrary, that this dichotomy ignores the fact that "narcissism is not just love of self, but always involves an image of another" (1994: 30). In response to de Lauretis, Stacey argued that rather than confusing identification and desire she was instead arguing for the eroticization of identification. In other words, she was not saying that identification and desire are the same, but that "female identification contains forms of desire which include, though not exclusively, homoerotic pleasure" (Stacey 1994: 29). Stacey's revisionist Freudianism allows her to argue that female spectator–star relationships as well as women's spectatorial positioning in regard to films involving various types of female bonding represent forms of intimacy between women that involve both identification and desire simultaneously. While these relations contain no direct articulation of homosexual object choice, they possess, nevertheless, an element that is more than the mere expression of identification devoid of erotic pleasure or desire, as de Lauretis insists. According to Stacey, the intensity and intimacy involved in these female spectator–text interactions articulate more than just the desire to become the female star or character on the screen; these intensely intimate female bonds express a "homoerotic pleasure in which the boundary between self and ideal produces an endless source of fascination" for female viewers (1994: 173).

For de Lauretis, Stacey's attempt to draw together films that deal with female bonding and those that portray lesbian relationships threatens the very existence of lesbian cinema, which de Lauretis identifies with lesbian independent films rather than with mainstream portrayals. She feels that the conflation of female bonding and lesbianism, which she believes represent two distinctly different types of female relationships, results inevitably in a denial of "the specific difference that constitutes lesbian subjectivity" (de Lauretis 1994: 114). This denial involves "the sweeping of lesbian sexuality and desire under the rug of sisterhood, female friendship, and the now popular theme of the mother–daughter bond" (de Lauretis 1994: 116). According to de Lauretis, these latter relationships can be distinguished definitively from lesbianism because they involve only narcissistic identification between women, while lesbian relationships are based on homoerotic desire. De Lauretis clearly does not accede to Adrienne Rich's formulation of a "lesbian continuum." In her controversial 1980 essay, "Compulsory Heterosexuality and Lesbian Existence," Rich envisioned lesbianism uniting with other forms of female bonding under the umbrella term of woman-identification. For de Lauretis, as for other feminist and lesbian-feminist theorists, many of whom prefer to be labeled queer theorists rather than lesbian feminists, Rich's lesbian continuum oversimplifies and romanticizes the notion of female resistance to patriarchy by identifying it simply as female bonding and underemphasizing the sexual dimension of lesbianism (1994: 190–92). De Lauretis argues that lesbianism is decidedly different from heterosexual female bonding in that it involves a unique configuration of components that are not combined in the same way in other forms of female relationships. For de Lauretis, the lesbian subject's loss of the mother is redoubled by the loss of the female body, providing "a narcissistic wound" that acts as "a fantasy of castration," threatening the subject with "a loss of body-ego, a lack of being" (1994: 261–62). As a result of a maternal failure to validate the child's body image, the lesbian subject through disavowal displaces the wish for the missing female body onto a series of fetish objects.

De Lauretis describes two forms of lesbian fetishism corresponding to butch-femme lesbian roles. The butch adopts fetishes with masculine connotations because they are "most strongly precoded to convey, both to the subject and others, the cultural meaning of sexual (genital) activity and yearning toward women," not, as some theorists have suggested, because they "stand in for the missing penis" (de Lauretis 1994: 263). For the femme, desire for the lost or denied female body is signified by a "masquerade of femininity." According to de Lauretis, "The exaggerated display of femininity in the masquerade of the femme performs the sexual power and seductiveness of the female body when offered to the butch for mutual narcissistic empowerment. This femininity, aggressively reclaimed from patriarchy by radical separatism, with its exclusive reference and address to women, asserts the erotic power of the unconstricted, 'natural,' female body in relations between women" (de Lauretis 1994: 264). Thus, de Lauretis's idea of a lesbian sexuality based on the fetishistic expression of desire is entirely female-directed and female-centered in both its butch and femme incarnations. It contrasts significantly not only with developmental theories of heterosexual female sexuality but also with traditional psychoanalytic accounts of lesbian development which describe lesbianism as either an enduring, active phallic attachment to the mother or a masculinity complex resulting from a regression to the phallic phase consequent upon disappointment of Oedipal love for the father. Lesbianism for de Lauretis represents a decidedly different form of female psychosexual subjectivity, and the lesbian film is a clear expression of this lesbian difference.

The Stacey–de Lauretis debate relates not only to questions concerning the usefulness of psychoanalysis in lesbian film studies, but also to the issue of how best to define the lesbian film. The either/or formulations embodied in their dispute, however, have prevented rather than facilitated an understanding of the relationship between lesbian films and their audience, whether lesbian or heterosexual. Although de Lauretis seems justified in her refusal to conflate lesbian representation with films that deal with other forms of female bonding, her conceptualization of a radical break between them seems extreme. Recognizing similarities does not inevitably lead to conflation. The connection Stacey draws between lesbian films and other types of representations of female bonding seems more accurate, and acknowledging this connection does not prevent a recognition of the distinct qualities that characterize both lesbian subjectivity and lesbian filmic representations. These qualities, together with the elements lesbian films share with representations of other forms of female bonding, need to be considered in any attempt to investigate lesbian cinema.

In contrast to de Lauretis' adamant rejection of a connection between lesbian films and other films of female bonding, Christine Holmlund's theorization of lesbian cinema embraces Rich's idea of a lesbian continuum. In "When Is a Lesbian Not a Lesbian?: the lesbian continuum and the mainstream femme film", Holmlund (1991) suggests lesbian films form a continuum from ambiguous lesbian representations like *Personal Best* (Robert Towne, 1982), *Entre Nous* (Diane Kurys, 1983), and *Fried Green Tomatoes* (Jon Avnet, 1991) to more openly lesbian portrayals like *Lianna* (John Sayles, 1983) and *Desert Hearts* (Donna Deitch, 1985). In *In the Company of Women: contemporary female friendship films* (Hollinger 1998a), I expanded Holmlund's concept to argue that this continuum could serve as a generally applicable model in thinking abut the relationship between lesbian representations and films that deal with other types of female relationships. Rather than regarding lesbian portrayals and films of female bonding as either completely separate or closely connected, I suggested that the two types of films might be better characterized as falling into a range of cinematic representations from films that focus on female friendship, sisterhood, and mother–daughter relationships and contain no erotic implications to overtly lesbian films that make plain the sexual nature of the relationship represented. Standing between these two poles is the ambiguous lesbian film, a type of film that attained considerable mainstream popularity with both lesbian and heterosexual female audiences by refusing to identify itself unequivocally as a portrayal of female friendship or lesbian romance. The sexual orientation of its female characters is never made explicit, and viewers are left to read the text largely as they wish.

The ambiguous lesbian film can be characterized in a number of ways. Typically, these films titillate their viewers with hints of lesbianism between the two principle characters, allowing lesbian spectators to see the two women as lovers while providing heterosexual viewers with reassurance that the characters could be just friends. In this way, they offer their audience the voyeuristic satisfaction of seeing two beautiful women interacting in sexually provocative ways on the screen without overtly challenging heterosexist norms. For instance, both *Entre Nous* and *Fried Green Tomatoes* focus on the intensely passionate relationship that develops between two women whose attachment to each other overshadows the bonds of marriage and comes to involve their sharing a life together, yet in neither film is the women's relationship specifically delineated as lesbian. The viewer is left uncertain of whether the characters' feelings for each other involve only friendship or sexual desire. These films utilize various strategies in promoting this spectatorial uncertainty. First, the films' female characters are typically portrayed as femmes, lesbians who are conventionally attractive and feminine in appearance, so that they can easily be interpreted as heterosexual. Second, although allusive references to lesbianism or to alternative lifestyle choices may be made, the focus is placed on the strong, passionate affectional bonds and the exchange of long, loving looks between the two women, which can be read ambiguously as either erotic or friendly (Holmlund 1991: 145). Holmlund also isolated certain "cliched counter-conventions of continuity editing" that mark a relationship between two female characters as possibly involving lesbian desire: "shot/reverse shots of two women looking longingly at each other, point of view shots where one woman spies on another, and two shots where two women hug, romp, or dance together" (1994a: 36). All of these visual and narrative markers of suggested homoerotic attraction can just as easily be interpreted, and certainly are by many viewers, merely as indicators of admiration and affection between friends. In combination, they create what D.A. Miller in "Anal Rope" has described as the filmic confinement of homosexuality to the level of connotation rather than denotation.

The ambiguous lesbian film's connotative presentation of lesbianism has both negative and positive effects on lesbian viewers. As Miller suggests, ambiguous portrayals of homosexuality construct "homosexual subjects doubtful of the validity and even of the reality of their desire" (1991: 125). They tell their audience that what appears to be lesbianism is really only female friendship, thus seeming to deny the very existence of lesbian identity. At the same time, however, they also arguably possess certain lesbian affirmative qualities. They at least avoid the overt homophobia that has for so long characterized mainstream representations of homosexuality. Their "lesbian" characters are presented as sincere and loving rather than evil and predatory, the women's sexual relationship is neither exploited pornographically, nor are the "lovers" punished in the end by death or separation. In fact, these films may serve an important social function for their lesbian audiences by offering moments of "discursive consent" through which lesbian viewers can engage in lesbian cinematic fantasies rendered socially "safe" within a homophobic society by the film's heterosexual implications (de Lauretis 1994: 121). The safety of these fantasies is both literal and metaphoric: while the films, on the one hand, avoid overt gay bashing, they also minimize substantially the threat their ambiguously lesbian images offer to heterosexist and sexist ideologies. This safety is bought at a significant cost to lesbian subjectivity. As de Lauretis points out, ambiguous lesbian representations act to deauthorize and foreclose cinematic representations of actual lesbianism "in its instinctual, fantasmatic and social complexity" (1994: 122).

Although critics have theorized the relationship of the ambiguous lesbian film to its lesbian viewer, it has largely been seen as offering only a threat to the heterosexuality of non-lesbian viewers. For instance, Miller argues for the radical instability of films that reduce the issue of homosexuality to the level of connotation. By never confirming the sexual orientation of the film's major characters, the films leave the viewer seeing implicit homosexuality everywhere. For Miller, there is a potentially subversive quality to the almost omnipresent homosexual implications of these films because they challenge a simplistic dichotomy between heterosexual and homosexual identities (1991: 125–26), suggesting that the division between same-sex friendship and homoerotic attraction is far from definitive. I have argued that the popularity of the ambiguous lesbian film with heterosexual female audiences indicates that female viewers may not see these films so much as a threat to their heterosexual identity, but, instead, as offering them the same type of "discursive consent" that de Lauretis proposes the films offer lesbian viewers. Ambiguous lesbian films provide their heterosexual female audience with a "safe" means of engaging with a lesbian fantasy scenario by offering at the same time the possibility of denying this fantasy (Hollinger 1998a: 156). While de Lauretis attributes the attraction of ambiguous lesbian films for lesbian viewers to the presence of both same-sex identification and desire within lesbian subjectivity, her attempt to affirm lesbianism's radical difference from other forms of female bonding leads her to deny what appears to be the real possibility that, as Stacey suggests, both identification and desire may also play a key role in heterosexual women's spectatorial pleasure as they view films that focus on relationships between female characters.

Whereas ambiguous lesbian films refuse to make the sexual identity of their characters explicit, openly lesbian films clearly present their central female characters as erotically involved. The openly lesbian film can be sub-divided in a number of ways into different categories of films that develop different strategies of audience engagement. First, the films can be distinguished in terms of their mode of production: Hollywood products like *Personal Best*, *Three of Hearts* (Yurek Bogayevicz, 1993), *Boys on the Side* (Herbert Ross, 1995), and *Kissing Jessica Stein* (Charles Herman Wurmfield, 2001), for instance, typically present heterosexually conceived portraits of lesbianism, while independently produced films like *Claire of the Moon* (Nicole Conn, 1993), *Go Fish* (Rose Troche, 1994), and *Saving Face* (Alice Wu, 2004), made by lesbian filmmakers outside of the Hollywood system, provide an insider's rather than an outsider's perspective on lesbian issues and lifestyles.

Openly lesbian films can also be categorized by plot interest. Some lesbian films like *Lianna*, *Claire of the Moon*, *But I'm a Cheerleader* (Jamie Babbit, 1999) and *Saving Face*, are coming-out narratives following the time-worn formula of the bildungsroman, the tale of an individual's personal development and psychological maturation. The lesbian bildungsroman or coming-out story chronicles its protagonist's movement from the world of heterosexuality to an acceptance of her lesbian identity. Coming-out narratives can conclude with either a happy or tragic ending. In the heterosexually conceived, male-directed *Lianna*, for instance, after considerable struggle the film's eponymous heroine finally succeeds in coming to terms with her homosexuality, but her journey of self-development still ends painfully. After she declares her lesbianism and leaves her husband, her lesbian lover deserts her for another woman, and Lianna (Linda Griffiths) is left to seek consolation from a female friend, who proves in the end to be the only one who is truly loyal to her. The lesbian-directed *Claire of the Moon* and *But I'm a Cheerleader*, on the other hand, build to a climactic love scene which seems intended to symbolize not only their heroines' final acceptance of their lesbian attraction to other women but also their attainment of genuine intimacy in a sexual relationship.

Coming-out narratives often merge with a second common form of lesbian film, the lesbian romance or love story, such as *Desert Hearts* (Donna Deitch, 1986) and *The Incredibly True Adventures of Two Girls in Love* (Maria Maggenti, 1995). In the lesbian romance film, the focus shifts from one character's discovery of her lesbian identity to the formation of the lesbian couple. As we will see, in *Desert Hearts*, the paradigmatic representative of this subgenre, one of the barriers that separates the two women is the internalized homophobia and resulting inability to accept her attraction to another woman that torments one of the lovers, yet the film's plot centers not so much on her struggle to accept her lesbianism as on whether both women will be able to overcome their differences and successfully come together as a couple. A third and much less common form of lesbian narrative combines the lesbian romance with an exploration of life within the lesbian community. While these films may contain at their center a lesbian romance or a coming-out narrative, this story is placed firmly within the context of an exploration of lesbian life-styles and friendship networks. Rose Troche's independent feature *Go Fish* introduced this category of lesbian narrative with considerable success. Although the film does involve a central lesbian romance, its focus alternates between the development of the lovers' relationship and the lives of their lesbian friends. As a result, it becomes not only a lesbian love story but also a celebration of lesbian community. The popular Showtime serial *The L Word* (2004–9) is an example of the successful transfer of this category of the lesbian film to the television serial format. In *The Kids Are All Right*, Lisa Cholodenko (2010) expanded this category to include the lesbian family drama.

As lesbian theorists make clear, these categories of largely positive con-temporary lesbian portrayals have emerged from a long history of negative and distorted mainstream lesbian representations. While cinematic portrayals of lesbians before the contemporary period have covered a wide range of variations, few of these variations were positive. Until very recently, lesbianism was either barred from mainstream cinema entirely, or when it was infrequently represented in films such as *The Fox* (Mark Rydell, 1967), *The Killing of Sister George* (Robert Aldrich, 1968), and *The Children's Hour* (William Wyler, 1962), it was portrayed as sordid, depressing, and deviant behavior resulting either from congenital deformity, arrested psychic development, or patholo-gical gender reversal. Lesbian characters were, and in too many cases still are, presented as sinister villains, victims of mental illness, cultural freaks, or pornographic sexual turn-ons for a male audience. Such homophobic lesbian images are used most frequently to validate the superiority and desirability of heterosexuality. Richard Dyer even describes a heterosexist plot formula central to the structure of mainstream lesbian films (1984: 34). The story involves a struggle for control of the central female character by competing female and male love interests. The woman who is at the center of this contest is portrayed as "without character, unformed. ... nothing, an absence," and because her sexuality is "malleable – she will be had by anyone." In the conflict, the lesbian competitor, is ultimately defeated, and the male character triumphs, "getting the girl," and suggesting, as Dyer indicates, that "the true sexual definition of a woman is heterosexual and that she gets that definition from a man" (1984: 34). Within this plot configuration, gayness is used merely as a way to reinforce the appropriateness of heterosexuality, the hegemony of which is never really challenged. This heterosexually conceived and heterosexist lesbian plot formula can be identified not only in past lesbian representations but in contemporary ones as well. *Personal Best, Three of Hearts,* and *Kissing Jessica Stein* all portray the disintegration of a lesbian relationship and its replacement by a heterosexual romance in ways that follow the structure that Dyer describes. Lisa Cholodenko in *The Kids Are All Right* subverts this formula by having the lesbian lover triumph over her male competitor in the end.

Lesbian theorists have also examined the question of how these various forms of contemporary lesbian representation relate to their viewers. The issues of whether or not they reinforce or challenge the homophobia that has characterized past mainstream lesbian portrayals and how they might best be constructed in the future represent other areas of considerable disagreement in lesbian film studies. Some critics have suggested that the exploitation and distortion that have dominated the history of lesbian representations have led lesbian audiences to reject mainstream lesbian portrayals completely as heterosexually conceived; instead, they have become adept at expropriating through camp reading strategies non-lesbian films that focus on strong female characters. This fear of exploitative and distorted lesbian representations also has contributed to the popularity of ambiguous lesbian films with lesbian viewers. The possibility of portrayals of lesbian sexuality being used by male spectators for pornographic purposes is minimized by the films' refusal to clarify their central characters' sexuality.

In her essay "'A Queer Feeling When I Look at You': hollywood stars and lesbian spectatorship in the 1930s", Andrea Weiss discusses the attraction of lesbian audiences to sexually ambiguous female stars like Marlene Dietrich, Greta Garbo, and Katherine Hepburn. Weiss argues that extra-cinematic rumors and celebrity gossip have always been important in shaping the fantasies of lesbian fans about certain sexually ambiguous stars and authorizing lesbian readings of their films. While these rumors may have been circulated by studio publicity departments to promote male erotic interest, Weiss maintains that they also encouraged lesbian viewers "to explore their own erotic gaze without giving it a name, and in the safety of their private fantasy in a darkened theater" (1994: 331). She also points to specific moments in their films when isolated gestures or movements that were inconsistent or extraneous to the narrative and even seemed to pose an ideological threat to its coherence opened up the possibility of reading the narrative against the grain and uncovering a possible lesbian subtext. As examples of such ideologically threatening moments, Weiss mentions the famous scene in *Morocco* (Josef von Sternberg, 1930) in which Dietrich gives a stage performance dressed in a tuxedo and top hat and kisses a woman in the audience or Garbo's movements, voice, manner, appropriation of male attire, and kiss with another woman in *Queen Christina* (Rouben Mamoulian, 1933). Weiss proposes that this type of subversive reading of Hollywood films gave lesbian viewers a special relationship with certain stars and was particularly important in the 1930s when there were so few images of lesbian desire on the screen and when the images that were shown were so overwhelmingly negative (1994: 334–35). According to Weiss, these fleeting moments and innuendos about stars allowed lesbian viewers to take individual scenes out of context and use gossip and rumor to fashion subversive lesbian readings that were empowering for them (1994: 341). In a similar vein, Patricia White (1999) in *Uninvited: classical hollywood cinema and lesbian representability*, calls attention to lesbian subtexts in mainstream films, like *Rebecca*, *All About Eve*, and *The Haunting* (Robert Wise, 1963), that seem on the surface to contain only heterosexually oriented plots.

Rather than championing camp reading strategies or ambiguous representations of homosexuality, other lesbian and gay critics have argued that the paucity of representations and abundance of negative images of lesbians and gay men in popular films make the creation of positive mainstream images of homosexuality all the more expedient. Yet advocating a simplistic "positive images approach" to lesbian and gay representation which suppresses contradiction and results in unrealistic, static, one-dimensional portrayals seems hardly the answer. One current development which should lead to less stereotypical lesbian representations is the advent of more lesbian filmmakers who can bring to popular cinema their own visions of lesbian life in its various dimensions. Lesbian filmmakers need, however, to be given the opportunity to express through both popular and avant-garde cinema a variety of lesbian experiences and to move beyond the now standard coming-out and romance narratives to create stories of lesbian history, culture, communities, households, and daily life, as well as to present non-exploitative portrayals of lesbian sexuality.

One reason for the lack of mainstream lesbian representations relates to marketing strategies that prompt Hollywood producers to direct their films toward multiple audience groups. Rightly or wrongly Hollywood sees lesbian films as risky ventures with limited appeal. Another proposed explanation for the paucity and the distorted nature of mainstream lesbian portrayals is the subversive effect lesbian representations might have on heterosexual female viewers. The open portrayal of lesbianism has been seen to pose a significant threat to the heterosexist, patriarchal status quo in a number of ways. First, lesbianism represents an alternative to the patriarchal heterosexual couple and challenges female dependence on men for romantic and sexual fulfillment. By providing women with the space to exercise self-determined pleasure, lesbian portrayals threaten mainstream cinema's "unproblematic fit between the hierarchies of masculinity and femininity on the one hand, and activity and passivity on the other" (Mayne 1991: 127). Chris Straayer argues that the lesbian film also "deconstructs male/female sexual dichotomies, sex/gender conflation, and the universality of the male Oedipal narrative" (1990: 50). The very visibility of lesbianism on the screen seems to unsettle the rigidity of sexual categorizations and the maintenance of patriarchal, heterosexist hegemony.

Teresa de Lauretis argues in both "Film and the Visible" and *The Practice of Love* that lesbian representations offer a radical spectatorial position to all female viewers, regardless of their sexual identity. She describes this position as a site of real liberation that creates "a new position of seeing in the movies, a new place of the look: the place of a woman who desires another woman; the place from where each one looks at the other with desire and, more important still, a place from where we see their look and their desire; in other words, a place where the equivalence of look and desire – which sustains spectatorial pleasure and the very power of cinema in constructing and orienting the viewer's identification – is invested in two women" (de Lauretis 1991: 227). According to de Lauretis, this desiring lesbian subjectivity is embodied in the subject position created by independent lesbian films. In these films (she uses Sheila McLaughlin's independent feature *She Must Be Seeing Things* [1987] as an example), two women are brought together who as a "coupled" subject inhabit the film's subject position together, thereby projecting a coupled female spectatorial position that is subversive of patriarchal, heterosexist norms (de Lauretis 1991: 225). Although de Lauretis believes the lesbian coupled subject position is confined to independent lesbian representations, it seems reasonable to believe that it might also be found in mainstream films where the representation of a desiring lesbian subjectivity would offer an even stronger challenge to the conventional structures of film viewing.

As we have seen in Chapter 1, according to Mulvey's classic articulation of looking relations in mainstream cinema, the power of the gaze is invested in the male and the female is typically positioned as the object rather than the subject of desire. The subversive potential of the lesbian coupled subject position, as de Lauretis has theorized it, resides ultimately in its evocation of the lesbian look and in the investment of this look in two desiring women, the coupled lesbian protagonists of the film, each of whom is simultaneously both subject and object of the look and consequently of female desire. I have argued in "Theorizing Mainstream Female Spectatorship: the case of the popular lesbian film" that the active desire invested in the coupled lesbian subject position contains the potential to be transferred through the lesbian look to the film's female spectator, who is thereby offered empowerment as an active desiring female subject. In other words, the lesbian look challenges the exclusive male prerogative to control the filmic gaze and reconfigures this gaze so that it reflects a new female relation to desire. Differing markedly from the male gaze, the lesbian look "requires exchange. It looks for a returning look, not just a receiving look. It sets up two-directional sexual activity" (Straayer 1990: 50). Its radical potential involves not only reciprocity but also an association between female subjectivity and agency and a refutation of an all-encompassing "natural" male–female opposition as the defining principle of subject formation. Although these subversive qualities are not to be found in every cinematic representation of lesbianism, de Lauretis seems too restrictive in designating as potentially subversive only those independent lesbian films in which a lesbian filmmaker, her characters, and the spectator unite in a fantasy of lesbian desire through investment in the lesbian look. While I agree with de Lauretis that most mainstream representations of lesbianism adopt definite means to reduce the possibility of this union, not all are necessarily successful in doing so.

To create a lesbian subject position in a film, it takes more than simply replacing a heterosexual with a lesbian couple, as many mainstream lesbian films do. As we will see, the groundbreaking lesbian romance *Desert Hearts* has come under attack for presenting its lesbian love story in accord with the conventions of heterosexual romance. Many mainstream representations of lesbians blur the distinction between heterosexuality and lesbianism with a resulting failure to affirm the difference of lesbian subjectivity. In what would seem to be an attempt to appeal to a heterosexual audience, they represent lesbianism not as a distinct sexual identity for women, but as really the same as heterosexuality. The lesbian is presented simply as a woman whose sexual desire is similar to a man's, and no light is cast on the specificities of lesbian desire. The potentially subversive effects of lesbian representation on mainstream audiences are also often counteracted by the identification of lesbianism with traditional derogatory forms of female friendship that involve female rivalry and antagonism (for example, *Single White Female* [Barbet Schroeder, 1992]) or imposing an unhappy conclusion on the film's lesbian relationship so that a woman who would dare to exhibit active sexual desire for another woman is shown to be punished for her usurpation of male privilege (for example, *Lianna*). It seems unwise, however, to dismiss all mainstream lesbian films as distorted counterparts of truly subversive independent lesbian representations; instead, they might more profitably be approached as complex texts that open themselves up to various interpretive possibilities and offer their female viewers, regardless of their sexual identification, myriad opportunities for viewing pleasure.

In any case, it seems clear that it would be a great loss to feminist film studies were lesbian theorists to see their affiliation as falling entirely within the compass of queer studies. Lesbian film theory has brought to light a number of significant issues in regard to women and film. For instance, it has questioned the exact relationship between lesbian representations and other films that focus on female bonding. Should lesbian films and films about female friendship, sisterhood, and mother–daughter relationships be seen as closely related forms of female representation, or should they be seen as radically different? Is the notion of a cinematic continuum between lesbian films and other films dealing with female bonding a useful way to think about the impact of lesbian films on female viewers, or does this connection deny the radical potential of lesbian representation? Even within the lesbian film itself, distinctions must be considered between ambiguous and openly lesbian portrayals, various plot formulas, and different methods of characterization which affect spectatorial response and the possibility that the films will generate subversive readings. Two aspects of lesbian cinema that seem to open up subversive interpretive possibilities are the coupled lesbian subject position and the lesbian look. How exactly is this subversive potential enacted in specific lesbian films and what means, if any, are employed to control its effect on female viewers? Clearly, the theorization of the lesbian film has initiated a new understanding of this much neglected area of women's cinema, but it has also raised many unanswered questions. In addition, lesbian film theory has cast new light on the overarching questions of the usefulness of psychoanalysis in feminist film study and the positioning of the female spectator in mainstream films, two issues that have for so long intrigued feminist film theorists. We will now turn our attention in the films in focus segment of this chapter to the groundbreaking lesbian romance film *Desert Hearts* and its relation to the question of female spectatorship.

Films in Focus: *Desert Hearts*

The 1980s represent a watershed period for the portrayal of lesbianism in mainstream American cinema. Prior to this time, it was only in independent and avant-garde cinema that positive lesbian portrayals could be found in the work of Jan Oxenberg, Barbara Hammer, Lizzie Borden, Sheila McLauglin, and Su Friedrich, for instance, but these films did not receive mainstream distribution. The 1982 release of Robert Towne's *Personal Best* marked a significant transformation in mainstream lesbian representations. *Personal Best* took the lesbian film in a new direction by offering at long last a positive mainstream portrayal of a lesbian romance, even if this portrayal was limited by the eventual failure of the film's lesbian relationship and its portrayal as merely a stage in the development of the protagonist, who moves on to what is presented as a more fulfilling heterosexual romance. This new more positive direction in lesbian portrayals was expanded considerably later in the decade as lesbian films in the late 1980s and early 1990s began to offer innovative portrayals of erotic female relationships that went well beyond earlier lesbian portrayals.

The most notable lesbian film of the 1980s was Donna Deitch's ground-breaking lesbian romance *Desert Hearts* (1985), the first mainstream lesbian film by a lesbian director and still by many accounts the most popular lesbian film ever made. *Desert Hearts'* success with both lesbian and heterosexual audiences might lead one to expect that it would initiate a long line of openly lesbian romance films with crossover appeal to both lesbian and heterosexual viewers, but this did not prove to be the case. After *Desert Hearts*, mainstream lesbian portrayals nearly disappeared, and when a major lesbian feature film was finally released in 1992, it cultivated a crossover audience by retreating into the less potentially controversial arena of ambiguous lesbian representation. *Fried Green Tomatoes* gained vastly expanded distribution and was much more popular at the box office than *Desert Hearts*, but it accomplished this success by closeting its lesbian content. It was not until 1994 that the openly lesbian film again reasserted itself, and *Go Fish*, a low-budget, independently made lesbian romance again directed by a lesbian director, Rose Troche, entered mainstream theaters with limited success. Since then, there have been sporadic examples of mainstream films with lesbian content, most made independently and then finding limited mainstream distribution. Examples include *High Art* (Lisa Cholodenko, 1998), *But I'm a Cheerleader*, *Saving Face*, and *The Kids Are All Right*. In a significant development, Lisa Cholodenko has even emerged as a major mainstream lesbian director whose films have crossover appeal to both lesbian and heterosexual audiences.

While *Desert Hearts* is unquestionably the most popular mainstream lesbian film of the 1980s and represents a significant advance in lesbian representation, it has received curiously negative critical attention from lesbian critics, who overwhelmingly condemn it. Teresa de Lauretis, for instance, insists the film casts its lesbian love story squarely in the tradition of Hollywood heterosexual romance. For her, the film's repackaging of heterosexual conventions "as a commodity purportedly produced for lesbians, does not seem … sufficient to disrupt, subvert, or resist the straight representational and social norms by which 'homosexuality is nothing but heterosexuality,' nor *a fortiori* sufficient to shed light on the specific difference that constitutes a lesbian subjectivity" (de Lauretis 1991: 256). Jackie Stacey is almost alone among lesbian critics in recognizing *Desert Hearts'* importance not only as the most popular mainstream lesbian film in contemporary cinema, but also as "the first lesbian romance which offers its spectators an unapologetic celebration of lesbian love" and poses an open challenge to "the traditional definition of lesbianism as 'unnatural,' 'deviant,' 'predatory,' or 'depressing.'" Yet even Stacey sees the film as ultimately a failure. She believes that although *Desert Hearts* rejects older definitions of lesbianism it still "fails to introduce engaging new narrative formulae to replace these older unacceptable ones" and as a result lacks the emotional intensity viewers expect from screen romances (Stacey 1995: 111). Perhaps a close examination of *Desert Hearts* will tell us if these condemnations are justified or if they stem from a failure to investigate fully the attraction the film's story of lesbian love affords to lesbian and heterosexual viewers alike.

Donna Deitch, a photographer as well as an avant-garde and documentary filmmaker, spent six years developing *Desert Hearts* from the time she initially conceived the project in 1979. Her struggle to get the film off the ground began with the task of convincing Jane Rule, the well-known lesbian author of *Desert of the Heart*, the novel on which the film is based, to grant her the rights to film the story. Before Rule would agree, she required Deitch's assurances that she would not exploit the novel's lesbian content for pornographic purposes. Deitch then spent two and a half years raising money for the project and is reputed to have single-handedly raised, primarily from the gay and lesbian community, somewhere between US$850,000 and US$1.5 million (Stacey 1995: 94). In spite of Deitch's herculean efforts to obtain adequate financing, the film's limited budget clearly affected its production values. It was shot in 31 days with few retakes and little room for artistic flourish. Once the film was completed, however, Deitch managed to obtain mainstream distribution by Samuel Goldwyn Productions. Based on Natalie Cooper's screenplay adaptation of Rule's novel and set, like the novel, in 1950s Reno, Nevada, the film recounts the story of the love affair between an Eastern college professor Vivian Bell (Helen Shaver) and a Western casino change-girl Cay Rivvers (Patricia Charbonneau). Vivian comes to Reno in order to divorce her college professor husband, meets Cay at the ranch where they both are staying, and they fall in love. While their relationship is openly presented as lesbian, a comparison of *Desert Hearts* to Jane Rule's novel clarifies sharply the film's extensive adoption of heterosexual conventions. The great majority of the changes made from novel to film render the story considerably less challenging to heterosexual norms than was the novel.

First, the film encloses Cay and Vivian's relationship within an environment dominated by idyllic heterosexual romance. Silver (Andra Akers), Cay's co-worker and best friend, is involved in an intense heterosexual love relationship with her fiance, Joe (Anthony Ponzini), and their romance serves to parallel and comment upon Cay and Vivian's. It is after Silver and Joe's engagement party that Cay and Vivian first kiss, and their love affair is interrupted by their attendance at the couple's wedding. The paralleling of the two relationships suggests that lesbian love is similar to, as intense as, and thus as natural and legitimate as heterosexual romance. Silver and Joe's passionate heterosexuality is also set up as the norm by which the intensity of Cay and Vivian's homosexual relationship is appraised. Although the novel, like the film, includes Silver and Joe's wedding, their relationship is much less idyllic than it is in the film. Rather than serving as a heterosexual parallel to the novel's lesbian romance, Silver and Joe's relationship compares much less favorably with it. In the novel, Silver even serves as a rival to Evelyn (renamed Vivian in the film) for the affections of Ann (Cay in the film). Whereas the film's Silver is a failed singer who feels she has finally found her long-awaited true love in Joe, her novelistic counterpart is an ex-prostitute who is involved with a newspaperman who wants to become a pornographic author. During Joe's frequent absences, Silver invites Ann to spend the night with her, and the two engage in a clandestine lesbian affair. This affair continues throughout Silver's involvement with Joe, and she even invites Ann to stay with her on the night before her wedding. Unlike the film, which presents Silver and Joe's marriage as the culmination of their passionate love affair, in the novel their wedding is precipitated much less romantically by Silver's unintended pregnancy.

In the film, Cay and Vivian's relationship is also implicitly compared to the heterosexual love affair between Cay's surrogate mother, Frances (Audra Lindley), and her now deceased father, Glen. The character of Frances is greatly transformed from novel to film. In the novel, she is supportive of Ann and Evelyn's relationship, whereas in the film she is a controlling, destructive mother figure who is determined to do everything she can to destroy Cay and Vivian's love affair. Frances' opposition seems founded not only on her homophobia and possessiveness, but also on her own sexual attraction to Cay, an attraction that seems to stem from Cay's resemblance to her dead father,

Glen. Frances tells Vivian that Cay strongly resembles Glen in both looks and personality. She describes her relationship with him in terms that Cay will later repeat in describing her relationship with Vivian. Frances proposes that Glen "just reached in and put a string of lights around my heart." Later, after Silver's wedding when Frances tells Cay that she just cannot accept "two women together," Cay repeats Frances's earlier phrase, applying it to her feelings for Vivian and suggesting a parallel between Frances's heterosexual romance and her lesbian one.

Not only does *Desert Hearts* place Cay and Vivian's affair within an exclusively heterosexual context, but it also presents the women's relationship as a matter of exclusionary sexual preference, never as a threat to the heterosexual relationships that surround it. In contrast, Rule's novel suggests that both Ann and Silver are bisexual, rather than exclusively homosexual or heterosexual. In the novel, Ann is said to have ended a long affair with her male employer, Bill (Darrell in the film), not because she realized that she was really attracted to women, as is the case in the film, but because she feared the exclusivity of marriage. Similarly, her clandestine lesbian relationship with Silver in the novel calls into question the exclusive and passionate nature of Silver's heterosexual union with Joe in a way that is completely absent from the film. Deitch's recasting of the sexual relationship between Ann and Silver into a platonic friendship further indicates her determination to make the film less threatening to heterosexual norms. The film contains only vague suggestions of Silver's possible attraction to Cay. In one scene, the two women take a bubble bath together, and Silver gazes at Cay with obvious desire, but Cay does not return the look, as she will later with Vivian. The scene culminates in the two women discussing Cay's attraction, not to Silver, but to Vivian. Joe enters, and Silver turns her attention entirely to him, leaving Cay to look on with embarrassment as they proclaim their undying devotion to one another.

The film replaces Silver as Ann's bisexual lover with Gwen (Gwen Welles), a lesbian one-night stand. Teresa de Lauretis suggests that Gwen serves as a "stock character whore" adapted from the conventions of the Hollywood western. She is coded by looks, pose, makeup, and speech as the "slut" in contrast to Vivian's role as Cay's real love interest. As de Lauretis points out, "*Desert Hearts* does not distance this image and role or reframe them in a lesbian camp tradition or in the lesbian history of the forties and fifties, as it might have done, but only invokes a general fifties mood typical of many films of the eighties" (1991: 256). As a result, Gwen, a conventional Hollywood stereotype with whom a heterosexual audience could feel comfortable, replaces Silver, an unconventional bi-sexual character who might be potentially alienating to heterosexual viewers. The novel's presentation of

Ann's relationship with Silver posits lesbianism as existing within as well as next to heterosexual relationships, a much more subversive statement than the film's contention that the two sexual orientations co-exist harmoniously in non-threatening, mutually exclusive proximity.

The novel and film also differ in their presentation of the relationship between their lesbian lovers. In the novel, Evelyn and Ann's attraction is based primarily on their similarities rather than their differences. While there is a substantial age difference between them, they still resemble each other enough that they are sometimes mistaken for mother and daughter. They are not only remarked upon as mirror images of each other, but they also share similar literary interests. Ann is a cartoonist, not a sculptor as Cay is in the film, she has an extensive library filled with literary classics, and she writes poetry. Evelyn, the college literature professor, represents a potential intellectual mentor to Ann, whom she initially says is "as young as a student" (Rule 1985: 9). While the novel places the women's relationship in what can be described as the "transgressive space" of lesbian sameness (Farwell 1990: 102), the film returns it to the more conventional heterosexual dimension of difference by accentuating the things that divide rather than unite the two lovers. Cay is from the west, and Vivian from the east. Cay is given to wild spontaneous physicality, while Vivian represents the sexually repressed intellectual. Cay advocates risk, luck, and adventure, and Vivian wants order, safety, and respectability. Cay is more aggressive sexually, while Vivian embodies more traditional passive femininity. These personality contrasts are not as evident in the novel as they are in the film. As Mandy Merck suggests, they represent "symbolic dichotomies" written into the film to make the lesbian relationship conform to heterosexual romantic norms by accentuating differences between the lovers rather than sameness (1993: 379).

Given Deitch's watering down of the subversive qualities of Rule's novel to gain crossover audience appeal and lesbian critics foregrounding of the film's limitations, what are the attributes of the film that have for so long attracted female viewers, both lesbian and heterosexual? First, *Desert Hearts'* positive portrayal of lesbian romance succeeds as no film had before it in reversing the overt homophobia that previously characterized representations of lesbianism in mainstream cinema. It was the first mainstream film to present a lesbian romance as sincere and loving and to refuse to use lesbianism merely as a way to show the superiority of heterosexual attachment, nor did it follow earlier films in depicting lesbianism as a regression to a childhood attachment to the mother or as merely a developmental stage leading to a more mature heterosexuality. In *Desert Hearts*, the lesbian love affair ends happily with both women transformed in positive ways by their attachment, rather than following older traditions in which lesbian lovers are ultimately punished or their love relationship is destroyed. These aspects render the film strongly affirmative of lesbianism and would seem alone to be enough to explain its popularity with lesbian viewers.

In addition, *Desert Hearts*' gaze structure and representation of lesbian sexuality are decidedly progressive. The exchange of erotic, desiring looks between Cay and Vivian is so prominent throughout the film that it presents a distinct challenge to mainstream cinema's dominant male gaze. The looks exchanged between the two women are never activated, complemented, and legitimized by the gaze of male characters; instead, they create an active, desiring female subjectivity independent of male control. Vivian and Cay engage in homoerotic visual interchanges that involve mutuality and reciprocity rather than dominance and submission. Their evocation of the lesbian gaze can be said to open up to the female spectator the coupled lesbian subject position theorized by Teresa de Lauretis as characteristic of truly radical lesbian representations. Like more avant-garde lesbian films, *Desert Hearts* creates a lesbian subject position that in de Lauretis's words offers "a place from where the equivalence of look and desire – which sustains spectatorial pleasure and the very power of cinema in constructing and orienting the viewer's identification – appears invested in two women, each of whom is both the subject and object of that look/desire" (1994: 88). Rejecting mainstream norms, the film refuses to recuperate this evocation of an active, desiring female subjectivity by punishing its female characters with death or the destruction of their relationship; instead, they are rewarded with a happy ending. Cay and Vivian not only end up together, but their relationship empowers them to take the necessary risks to find new directions in their lives. Vivian accepts her love for Cay and sets out to persuade her to accompany her back East. Similarly, at the film's conclusion Cay seems about to overcome her fears and embark on a new life with Vivian that will allow her to develop her creative talents fully.

The film's presentation of lesbian sexuality is more problematic than its evocation of the lesbian look. Much of its narrative tension is sustained by the anticipation created by its long-delayed love scene. Unlike Rule's novel which contains several sexual encounters between Ann and Evelyn, the film creates emotional intensity by slowly building up to one climactic sex scene. While this strategy works effectively to involve the audience in the women's desire for one another, the centrality of the love scene seems to define lesbianism primarily by its sexual dimension. The fact that Cay, coded as the more butch character, initiates their sexual relationship by actively pursuing the reluctant, more femininely passive Vivian also preserves norms of masculine dominance and feminine submission associated with heterosexual sexuality. As Jackie Stacey describes the film's presentation of lesbian seduction, it is "painfully reminiscent of pressure or coercion," a "battle of wills" with Cay representing confidence and spontaneity and Vivian repression and denial (1995: 107). The shooting style of the scene also presents a complex mixture of progressive and regressive elements, and critics have diverged sharply in their reactions to it. The scene has been described as portraying hygienic, painfully naive, sentimental, and even reactionary lesbian sex. As Christine Holmlund points out, "it is restrained by the conventions of love scenes in the heterosexual woman's film. Lighting is never harsh. The use of close-ups and medium shots shows a distinct preference for the caress, the kiss and the gaze over anything else. Cunnilingus is, of course, out of the question. Sex, when shown at all, is never rough, and always takes place in relatively tame and traditional places ... " (1991: 153).

In spite of these qualities, other lesbian critics have labeled the scene "one of the hottest bed romps in recent memory" (Holmlund 1991: 160). While it begins with a pursuer/pursued situation reminiscent of representations of heterosexual sexuality, this encounter can be read as "a classic butch/femme, active/passive scenario which contemporary lesbians have come to associate with romance and sexuality between women in the 1950s" (Stacey 1995: 107). As the scene progresses, it breaks down this active/passive dichotomy and conveys the mutuality of the women's attraction to each other. As Holmlund indicates, during its long, almost five minute evocation of lesbian sexuality "a space for homosexual desires for and identification with characters who openly acknowledge and live their homosexuality emerges in a way that it does not in most Hollywood films" (1991: 153). It is not only as a reworking of traditional portrayals of lesbianism that Desert Hearts can be regarded as innovative. As noted above, it presents a lesbian relationship that leads both women to change their unsatisfactory life situations. While the empowerment resulting from the relationship remains primarily personal with the woman remaining isolated from the larger community, it does extend in significant ways out into the public sphere. Vivian not only overcomes her internalized homophobia, but also in attempting to persuade Cay to accompany her back East, she seems to have decided to fight openly against homophobic public opinion. Cay's decision to get on the train with Vivian, at least until the next stop, suggests that their relationship will lead her to take action to alter her life as well. In any event, she seems to be beginning to understand that, as Vivian tells her, she needs "to be with someone who realizes just how wonderful you are." It is on this note of lesbian triumph and self-affirmation that the film ends. Its conclusion is a victory for its lesbian characters not only because it is implied that they choose to be with each other, but also because their relationship seems to be leading them to greater personal development and self-fulfillment.

Figure 7 From left, Helen Shaver as Vivian Bell and Patricia Charbonneau as Cay Rivvers in the final scene of *Desert Hearts.*

While this strategy of spectatorial engagement may fail, as de Lauretis suggests, to cast light on the specific differences that constitute lesbianism, it may make it more likely that the film's image of a desiring female subjectivity will be taken up not just by lesbian, but by all female viewers. Homosexual and heterosexual female spectators alike are offered the "coupled lesbian subject position" that the film creates, and they are granted the "discursive consent" to adopt it. They can identify with the film's female characters as both desiring subjects and desirable objects of the female gaze that is so openly portrayed. Then, they can retreat, if they wish, to seeing the film, as Deitch describes it, as "just a love story, like any love story between a man and a woman" ("Desert Hearts Production Notes" 1985: 1). The film also offers its lesbian spectators identification through the character of Cay with a primal scene of lesbian desire. As Teresa de Lauretis describes this scenario, it presents a restaging of the lesbian original fantasy, the "mise-en-scene of lesbian desire" as a drama of "the loss and recovery of a fantasmatic female body" – not the mother's body but the subject's herself (de Lauretis 1994: 265). Lesbian psycho-sexual development for de Lauretis is distinctly different from heterosexual female development in that the loss of the pre-Oedipal mother is redoubled by the loss of the female body, a narcissistic wound that acts as a fantasy of castration threatening the subject with a loss of body-ego, a lack of being itself. As a result of a maternal failure to validate the subject's body-image, the lesbian subject through disavowal displaces the wish for the missing female body into a yearning toward other women (de Lauretis 1994: 263). Unlike traditional psychoanalytic accounts which associate lesbianism with an enduring, active phallic attachment to the mother, de Lauretis's theory of the original lesbian fantasy has less to do with the recovery of the lost mother than with the loss and recovery of the female body, of the subject's own body image.

Through Cay's relationship with Frances, *Desert Hearts* enacts just such a scenario. Frances tells Vivian that Cay was rejected by her real mother and that she took her in, acting as a mother substitute. As we have seen, however, Frances's strong attachment to Cay stems not so much from her affection for Cay herself, but from Cay's resemblance to her dead father. Thus, Frances's surrogate mothering redoubles Cay's loss of her real mother. Like the mother who rejected her, Frances rejects Cay's female body image and replaces it with Cay's father. By loving Cay for herself, Vivian recovers for her, not her lost mother, but her own body-ego, her sense of self. Indeed, the nurturing aspects of their relationship, with Vivian both desiring Cay physically and offering her the intellectual companionship she needs to develop her talents, completes this "mise-en-scène of lesbian desire." As a result, the film is able to offer its lesbian spectator a means of engaging with the text through this restaging of a lesbian primal scene as well as through the formation of a nurturing lesbian relationship. As Vivian and Cay are shown to experience rebirth through their attachment to each other, the lesbian viewer is encouraged to aspire to the same therapeutic sense of self-discovery. The love relationship between the two women is not a refuge from the world, but a way into it. Vivian finds herself sexually, and Cay artistically. The viewer, nurtured by the film, as the women are by each other, is encouraged to do the same, to take the risk to find her real identity, to express her desiring subjectivity, to achieve a sense of positive self-esteem, and to reach her goals and ambitions, whatever they may be.

The intended effect is perhaps best summed up by Deitch, who inserts herself in the film for a brief, but important, cameo as an anonymous woman identified in the credits only as the "Hungarian gambler." Having won a jackpot at one of the casino slot machines, she is asked by Cay if she wants to play it off. She then announces the film's central theme: "If you don't play, you can't win." It is this risk-taking subject position that the film offers to its female spectators, irrespective of their sexual orientation. The popularity of *Desert Hearts* in spite of its reduction of the subversive potential found in Rule's novel may rest ultimately on its strong sense of female affirmation. In spite of its flaws, it offers its viewers, both lesbian and heterosexual alike, through its representation of female connection as a means of personal development, much to attract them, and as such its popularity is not so difficult to understand.

Key terms: *queer studies, ambiguous lesbian films, openly lesbian films, coming-out films, lesbian romance films, the lesbian look, the coupled lesbian subject position*

Suggestions for Further Reading, Viewing, and Discussion

1. View some contemporary lesbian films. The selected filmography below offers some suggestions for films, but there are many more from which you can choose. Do these films relate to some of the issues or fit into the different plot formulas that we have discussed in this chapter? Do they go in new directions?

2. Read Jackie Stacey's essay "Desperately Seeking Difference" and watch *All About Eve* and *Desperately Seeking Susan* and/or any other films that present friendships between women. Is Stacey correct that these films contain homoerotic components?

3. Read Christine Holmlund's essay "When Is a Lesbian Not a Lesbian?: the lesbian continuum and the mainstream femme film" and view *Entre Nous* and *Fried Green Tomatoes*. What do you see as the effect of these films on lesbian and heterosexual viewers?

4. Examine a group of lesbian films paying particular attention to the exchange of looks between the characters. Does the gaze structure in these films contain subversive possibilities? Why or why not?

5. View several episodes of *The L Word*. How does this popular television series fit in with other lesbian representations?

6. Watch another lesbian romance film or a heterosexual romance film and compare its structure to *Desert Hearts'*.

7. Read Jane Rule's novel *Desert of the Heart* and decide for yourself if it represents a more radical representation of lesbian romance than the film. Which work do you prefer and why?

8. The most prolific and successful current lesbian mainstream auteur is Lisa Cholodenko. Watch some of her films and consider how they fit with the issues and plot formulas that we have discussed in this chapter. Is she taking lesbian filmmaking in new directions?

Selected Filmography of Lesbian Films

Aimee and Jaguar (Max Färberböck, 1999)
The Children's Hour (William Wyler, 1961)
Better Than Chocolate (Anne Wheeler, 1999)
Bound (The Wachowsky Bros., 1996)
Boys Don't Cry (Kimberly Peirce, 1999)
Boys on the Side (Herbert Ross, 1995)
But I'm a Cheerleader (Jaime Babbit, 1999)
Chasing Amy (Kevin Smith, 1997)
Entre Nous (Diane Kurys, 1983)
Fingersmith (TV, Aisling Walsh, 2005)
Fried Green Tomatoes (Jon Avnet, 1991)
Go Fish (Rose Troche, 1994)
High Art (Lisa Cholodenko, 1998)
The Incredibly True Adventures of Two Girls in Love (Maria Maggenti, 1995)
The Kids Are All Right (Lisa Cholodenko, 2010)
The Killing of Sister George (Robert Aldrich, 1968)
Kissing Jessica Stein (Charles Herman-Wurmfield, 2001)
Lianna (John Sayles, 1983)
The L Word (TV, Irene Chaiken, Michelle Abbott, Kathy Greenberg, 2004–9)
The Owls (Cheryl Dunye, 2010)
Pariah (Dee Rees, 2011)
Personal Best (Robert Towne, 1982)
Saving Face (Alice Wu, 2005)
Tipping the Velvet (TV, Sally Head (executive producer), 2002)
The Watermelon Woman (Cheryl Dunye, 1996)
When Night Is Falling (Patricia Rozema, 1995)

Chapter 5

Literary Adaptations, Biopics and Women

Whereas the woman's film and chick flick have gotten significant attention from feminist critics, two types of films with wide popularity among female audiences have not been afforded much critical attention at all: the nineteenth-century literary adaptation and biopics of women. Although they are not often thought of together, these two filmic categories actually have a number of similarities. They are both based on literary sources, either fictional or biographical, and criticism has traditionally focused on their fidelity to these sources. Literary adaptations have been criticized for deviating too far from the fictional works upon which they are based and biopics for playing fast and loose with the facts of their subjects' lives. Both filmic categories have also been critically neglected. In fact, there is not even a critical consensus on their appropriate categorization. They usually are not considered genres because they transcend generic categories, but exactly what they should be called is unclear. Even more unclear is their relation to feminism and their female viewers. It is this aspect of these two filmic forms that will primarily concern us.

The Nineteenth-Century Literary Adaptation

Even though it does not fit neatly into any one genre, the literary adaptation has always been considered a major cinematic mode. Estimates range from claims that half to three-fourths of all films are based on literary sources. Novels are overwhelmingly the most common source, followed by plays, short stories, and even the rare source of the narrative poem. Adaptations can be based on popular works as well as high literature. For instance, two of the most popular sources for adaptations are bestseller fiction and literary classics. Because the literary adaptation is so multi-faceted, it has a wide target audience and can attract viewers of both sexes, but one type of adaptation that takes as its source the nineteenth-century novel seems to hold a particular attraction for female viewers. Beginning in the 1990s, this attraction generated an avalanche of nineteenth-century literary adaptations aimed primarily at a female audience, and often created by female screenwriters, production executives, and directors. The many 1990s literary adaptations include, to name only a few of the most prominent, *The Age of Innocence* (Martin Scorsese, 1993), *Little Women* (Jillian Armstrong, 1994), *Sense and Sensibility* (Ang Lee, 1995), *The Portrait of a Lady* (Jane Campion, 1996), *Washington Square* (Agnieska Holland, 1997), and *The House of Mirth* (Terence Davies, 2000). Based on the work of such respected literary figures as Edith Wharton, Louisa May Alcott, and Henry James, these adaptations all found considerable success, but the queen of the literary adaptation is unquestionably Jane Austen, whose books have been adapted so many times and so successfully that the period of the 1990s has been dubbed the decade of "Austenmania."

The Austen phenomena is somewhat unique in that it involves not only feature film adaptations, but television mini-series, rewritings of and sequels to her novels, and spin-off films loosely based on her life and works. The major Austen film adaptations are *Sense and Sensibility*, *Persuasion* (Roger Michell, 1995), *Emma* (Douglas McGrath, 1996), and *Mansfield Park* (Paricia Rozema, 1999). Television adaptations of Austen's works have been ongoing in every decade since the 1950s, but the contemporary craze began with the extraordinary popularity of the BBC six-part mini-series *Pride and Prejudice* (Simon Langton, 1995), which made Colin Firth the first Austen male sex symbol. Although the 1990s was labeled the decade of Austenmania, the craze has hardly subsided; it has only mutated slightly. The BBC created new television adaptations of some of the major Austen novels and combined them with earlier adaptations to form a whole new series that was shown in the U.S. on PBS's *Masterpiece Classics* during the 2009 television season. Since the novels have been worked over quite thoroughly, new films have been made that are spin-offs from her works or are based on her life. There is an Indian version of *Pride and Prejudice*, entitled *Bride and Prejudice* (Gurinder Chadha, 2004), and one of *Emma*, renamed *Aisha* (Rajhree Ojha, 2010); a Chicana version of *Sense and Sensibility, From Prada to Nada* (Angel Garcia, 2011), another version of *Pride and Prejudice* (Joe Wright, 2005) with a new star in the lead, Kiera Knightly; an imaginative rendering of Austen's early life, *Becoming Jane* (Julian Jerrold, 2007); and even a film adaptataion of a contemporary novel about members of a Jane Austen reading group, *The Jane Austen Book Club* (Robin Swicord, 2007). In development is *Pride and Prejudice and Zombies* (Craig Gillespie, 2013), based on Seth Graham-Smith's bestselling horror spoof of Austen's novel.

Critics have employed several different approaches to the study of the Austen adaptations. Adaptation studies traditionally, and many would say unfortunately, have focused on the issue of fidelity. In evaluating a film adaptation, the critic simply asks how faithful it is to its literary source. The faithful adaptation equals the good adaptation, and that is pretty much it. While it might seem easy to make this determination, it really is more difficult than one would think because the questions of what exactly a faithful adaptation is and whether or not a film's complete fidelity to a literary work is really so desirable are hard to resolve. There are actually many reasons to question whether the fidelity approach is the best way to study adaptations. For instance, Robert Stam, who has set out to redirect adaptation studies in more profitable directions, suggests that the rhetoric associated with the notion of fidelity inevitably leads to the conclusion that the literary text is superior to its film adaptation. This idea is already inscribed in the minds of so many viewers that the simplistic notions that a book is always better than a film and that books are art and film is just entertainment have practically become accepted truisms. The fidelity approach plays right along with these ideas by focusing almost exclusively on what is lost in the translation from literature to film, which implicitly suggests the literary work is inevitably better, more complete, more respectable, and really just more of everything than the film. Stam points out that this is based not on fact, but on prejudice. It involves a series of myths, including what Stam calls the "myth of facility," which expresses a distaste for film based on the idea that films are easy to make and enjoy, and that it requires almost no intelligence to do either. Another myth that contributes to the denigration of film is a type of class prejudice that sees film as popular entertainment for the masses and the literary work as intellectual stimulation for the elite. The film adaptation then comes to be seen as a "parasite" that steals its source's vitality and vampirically drains away its life's blood in order to make a pale, undead cinematic copy of a vital, living literary original (Stam 2005: 7–8).

With the fidelity approach focused almost entirely on evaluation of the film and not the literary work, the film ends up losing no matter what it does. If it is faithful, it lacks originality. If it is unfaithful, it betrays its source. If it attempts to update the source to be more attractive to contemporary audiences, it shows disrespect for the period which the literary work depicts or in which it was written. If it tries to stay within period, it is seen as anachronistic. If it adds sexual scenes to the work, it has vulgarized it, and if it does not contain sex, it is cowardly (Stam 2005: 8). Another problem is the subjective nature of the whole notion of fidelity. Most critics who subscribe to this approach argue that a faithful adaptation is one that successfully transcribes "the essential narrative elements and core meanings" of its source text (Desmond and Hawkes 2005: 2), but what those essential elements and core meanings actually are is open to wide disagreement. As Stam points out, the whole idea of fidelity depends on an essentialist argument that assumes each work of literature contains an essence or core quality underneath its surface that can be unearthed and converted to the screen (2005: 15). What that essence is varies for different readers from basic plot elements to characters, mood, or themes, but the fidelity approach assumes all readers will interpret a literary work's plot, characters, mood, and thematic content in exactly the same way and will agree on which of these features constitutes the work's essence. Contemporary literary theory seriously calls this notion into question, arguing that literary works do not contain a single essence dropped into the text by the author to be extracted through careful analysis by the diligent reader. Texts are actually polysemous and open to various interpretations; thus, it is impossible for a film adaptation simply to extract its source's essence so that it can convert it intact to the screen.

Recent adaptation studies reject the fidelity approach as unworkable, but the idea of the need for fidelity lives on in the minds of the general public. When I teach a course in literature and film, I explain very fully and carefully the problems with the idea of fidelity and point out that it is really impossible and even undesirable for a film to be faithful to a work of literature because literature and film are different art forms. As Stam points out, film is a multi-track medium that engages the full range of the viewer's senses through the performance of actors, the spoken as well as the written word, music, sound effects, and photographic images, whereas literature is a single-track medium that relies entirely on the written word to convey its meanings (2005: 20). To translate a literary work into cinematic form inevitably involves changes. Requiring absolute faithfulness to a source actually denies the adapter his or her artistic input. A completely faithful adaptation would actually lack creativity on the part of the filmmaker. In spite of my lengthy explanation of these problems, I still get student papers that argue vehemently that a filmmaker betrayed, cheated on, defamed, and/or ruined the film's literary source by having the audacity to alter it in any way. The idea of fidelity does not seem to want to go away.

To accommodate the persistence of this notion, a number of critics have proposed what John M. Desmond and Peter Hawkes call a revisionist fidelity approach, which uses a film's faithfulness to its source not as an evaluative, but as a descriptive and analytical tool (2005: 2). This approach divides adaptations into categories based on the level of the filmmakers' faithfulness to the source text. There are a number of different variations on this approach, but they all generally outline three major categories of adaptations: close, loose and intermediate (Desmond and Hawkes 2005: 3). A close adaptation attempts to keep most of the elements of its source's story and theme, a loose adaptation uses its source merely as an inspiration or a point of departure, and an intermediate adaptation maintains some elements of its source, but also departs in significant ways to take its own direction. Thinking of adaptations in this way begins to consider why changes were made and how those changes reflect the technical, stylistic, historical, and ideological contexts of the adaptation. Why was this film made at this particular time and in this particular manner? How does it reflect the historical period in which it was made, and why was it readily accepted or rejected by its audience? These seem to provide much more fruitful avenues of investigation than merely attacking films for their failure to be completely faithful to their source, a task that is impossible to accomplish anyway. In looking at the Jane Austen adaptations and in particular at the most critically praised of them all, *Sense and Sensibility*, we will consider the issue of fidelity because after all a literary adaptation's relationship to its source is an essential issue, but we will consider it only in terms of what it tells us about the remarkable attraction of these films to filmmakers and audiences alike. Our particular focus will be the films' fascination for female viewers, rather than their loyalty to Jane Austen.

Critics have begun to consider this fascination, asking why nineteenth-century novels and Jane Austen texts in particular had such a resurgence of popularity in the 1990s and why the Austen phenomenon has had such longevity. Numerous possible answers have been proposed, some recognizing the importance of the female audience to the Austen phenomenon and others suggesting a wider appeal. The explanations center on the films' creation of a sense of nostalgia for an idealized lost past, the attraction of their evocations of romance, their high culture appeal, and their feminist, postfeminist or anti-feminist ideological interest. One of the earliest explanations of Austen's cinematic appeal places adaptations of her novels into the category of British heritage productions. The heritage genre began in the 1980s with the Merchant-Ivory films and expanded to include not just literary adaptations, but historical films, costume dramas, and biopics. Heritage films are loosely connected in terms of iconography, narrative formula, and spectatorial effect, but they represent a rather amorphous collection of diverse works ranging, for instance, from British productions like *A Room with a View* (James Ivory, 1985) and *Shadowlands* (Richard Attenborough, 1993) to the European financed, French-language *Queen Margot* (Patrice Chereau, 1994) and U.S./ U.K. co-productions like *Chariots of Fire* (Hugh Hudson, 1981) and *The House of Mirth*. In spite of the films' diversity, critics have identified one outstanding element that characterizes a heritage film: a nostalgic image of the past that tends to avoid ideological engagement with the present. Much of the criticism of the genre has been extremely negative. For instance, heritage films have been accused of falling in line with Thatcherite conservative politics, propagating an idealized picture of a glorious conservative British past, wallowing in visual over-indulgence, and lacking artistic interest or merit (McKechnie 2001: 104). Others have been less condemning and have described the films as leisurely in pace, focused on a central love story, containing feminized male characters dressed in attractive retro clothes, offering escapism into a romanticized past, and expressing a "museum aesthetic" that creates a mise-en-scène dominated by spectacular scenery, elaborate costume, and historical detail (Gilligan 2003: 70–71).

The debate over the significance of heritage films really breaks down into the positive vs. negative dichotomy. On the negative side, they are seen as offering an idealized image of the past that acts as a "social emollient," persuading viewers to ignore contemporary social problems connected to gender, race, ethnicity, and class. Their stylish look covers over shallow content and their visually stunning portrait of the past is laced with modern anachronisms and designed primarily to stimulate British tourism (McKechnie 2001: 110–12). On the positive side, the films' representation of the past is said to convey at least some historical knowledge in a way that may actually be more effective for the average viewer than strict adherence to the chronological detail of written historical accounts would be. The films' visual depiction of the past, however dubious in terms of strict historical accuracy, conveys a sensual experience of a period that might otherwise be beyond the intellectual reach of many contemporary filmgoers. A number of critics have also proposed that the genre has progressed in a positive direction from heritage into post-heritage films. Post-heritage cinema differs from its predecessor in that it is concerned less with a nostalgic view of the past as a way to escape contemporary problems and more with using the past as a safe place to examine current issues, especially those related to gender and sexuality (Gilligan 2003: 72). While post-heritage films, such as *Elizabeth* and its sequel *Elizabeth: The Golden Age* (Shekar Kapur, 1998 and 2007), still provide the pleasures of glossy historical spectacle through setting and costume, they also attempt to place contemporary issues within the context of this spectacle. Critics seem to have come to no consensus about the place of Austen adaptations within the heritage/post-heritage dichotomy. Are they heritage films that try to escape current reality through a flight to an idealized Austenian past or do they use that past to reflect on contemporary gender issues? This is a question that our analysis of *Sense and Sensibility* will take up.

In looking at Austen adaptations in particular, it seems clear that the films do not merely retreat into the past, but rework that past in accordance with contemporary ideas. That reworking has often been described as expressing a neo-conservative nostalgia for a lost ideal embodied in a small pre-industrial, pre-urban community where a few families live in a "vague, abstracted, non-specific past" that is free from the complex contemporary social issues of gender, race, ethnic, and sexual equality (Thompson 2003: 21–22). The Austenian cinematic past is a cultured, stable, recognizable, yet exotically distant aristocratic world where appropriate behavior is guided by clear rules of conduct and good manners, as well as an uncontested social hierarchy based on social status and wealth (Margolis 2003: 23). For American audiences, this perfect world of White Englishness is distant enough to be exciting, but not foreign enough to be threatening. It allows viewers to come away from the film feeling that life may have been attractive then, but it is still better in the here and now (Parrill 2002: 7). The films do not focus, however, on the flaws of the earlier era; they ignore the gross social inequality, classism, sexism, racism, and general air of social hypocrisy that characterized Austenian society.

Their analysis of class in particular is extremely limited. As James Thompson points out, the Austen adaptations follow the novels in aestheticizing class with an "elegant feminine gloss" that equates it with style. Class is defined not by the economic, social, and political domination of one social grouping over another, but by the elegance, morality, kindness, and grace of "an aristocracy of the plucky, of the good and the elegant, in which we can perceive morality as style" (Thompson 2003: 23). Carol M. Dole identifies the conception of class found in both Austen's novels and their film adaptations as not entirely in accord with conservative social and political ideas, but rather as expressive of a doubleness that is both regressive and progressive at the same time. Dole admits that Austen's novels and their film adaptations present an idealized portrait of the English landed gentry, but she proposes that they also offer a critique of the gender and class divisions within that society. Although British adaptations of Austen's novels take a harder look at class than their American counterparts, Dole believes that most of the film adaptations, both American and British, engage in a double-voiced discourse that ridicules class snobbery, while at the same time reifying class divisions (1998: 60). As Amanda Collins points out, the rosy picture of an ideal aristocratic past characteristic of Austen adaptations presents a hyperreal imitation of an era that never really existed (1998: 80), but that holds a tremendous attraction to those who fear contemporary gender, class, and racial conflict.

The appeal of the Austen adaptations is based not just on the nostalgic return to the past they offer, but also on the fact that this past is filled with romance and courtship. Certainly, Austen's novels deal with courtship situations, but the films enhance the romantic aspect to the extent that they have even been accused of "harlequinizing" Austen, who always treated romance with a sense of irony (Kaplan 1998: 178). Deborah Kaplan argues that the films heighten the romance found in the novels to the extent that they present love in an "unsurprising, even clichéd way" that is predictable, familiar, attentive primarily to the attractive physical appearances of the characters, and aimed at commercial appeal (1998: 178). Harriet Margolis, on the other hand, proposes that while the films' portrayals of romance may cultivate an appeal to female viewers that is similar to the attraction of harlequin romances, they also have the positive quality of showing courtship from a female point of view and espousing values associated with women's culture. For Margolis, the films, following Austen's novels, advocate use-value rather than exchange-value ethics that express concern for the happiness and well-being of the individual and for how one's actions affect others rather than regarding people as objects in materialistic terms (2003: 26). Additionally, the heightened and revised romance plots found in the films add to Austen's rather austere storylines a soupçon of sexuality (although never of a graphic nature), the reassurance of a happy romantic ending, and the comfort of the simple moral that "lovers deserve to enjoy one another" (Brownstein 1998: 20).

Other critics attribute the appeal of the Austen adaptations to the attraction they have for fans of the novels, but the films' attempts to attain high cultural status as prestige pictures are not aimed at attracting just readers of Austen's novels but also would-be readers, those who never made it through an Austen novel, but wish they had. Almost all adaptions of literary classics play on what viewers may believe is the universal appeal of great literature and on their nostalgia for books they remember fondly from high school or college, and this to a large extent explains why so much of the promotional material for adaptations attempts to gain an air of authenticity through specious claims of fidelity to their source texts. Claims to fidelity by adapters can be dangerous, however, and can do more harm than good in terms of attracting audiences. There is a long tradition of devoted fans of literary works becoming incensed by minute changes in their adored books, especially when the adaptation is based on a literary classic or a work of popular literature that has an avid fan base. A filmmaker's claims of fidelity to a literary source in order to attract readers of the novel really represent a double-edged sword, yet they are still one of the major ways that a film can gain recognition as a prestige picture and bask in the high culture aura of great literature.

Often with Austen adaptations this sense of authenticity and high culture appeal is achieved not so much by fidelity to the novels' plots, themes, and characterizations, but by location shooting in English country homes, panoramic shots of magnificent landscapes, elaborately detailed costuming, and the use of Austen's original dialogue. Not straying too far from the novels seems to be a requirement if some sense of supposed authenticity is to be achieved, and this sense appears to have an appeal to certain elements of the target audience for Austen adaptations. The Austen adaptations have an advantage in this regard in that they are able to bask in the novels' intellectual cachet without incurring too much expense in order to do so. The novels are in the public domain so filmmakers do not have to pay for adaptation rights, there are no special effects needed, and only a small cast is required. At the same time, the films can easily create an expensive period look through setting, costumes and characterization. Austen adaptations are pretty films as well as actors' films known for providing excellent roles for stars and for attracting award nominations.

Interestingly, the success of the Austen adaptations has also been attributed variously to their feminist, postfeminist or anti-feminist qualities. Commentators agree that the films are influenced by contemporary feminist ideas, but they differ on what exactly this influence amounts to. Some have argued that the films heighten and expand the feminism implicit in the novels, whereas others claim that in attempting to make the novels' feminist ideas appealing to mainstream audiences they water them down or even undercut them. A third group proposes that the novels were not very feminist in the first place; instead, they provide the films with plots whose emphasis on courtship and celebration of male and female harmony in a "period of reticence, privacy, intimacy, and repression" are perfect vehicles to assuage contemporary anxieties about gender issues (Thompson 2003: 5). At best, the novels offer only an implicit critique of patriarchy and a limited exploration of women's social inequality. They do not overtly challenge the social structure of Regency England or its treatment of women. The question then becomes what do the films do with the novels. Do they use them merely to attain a patina of timid feminism, while actually under this surface contributing to a postfeminist or anti-feminist backlash? Do they represent a neoconservative postfeminist mainstreaming of feminist ideas that employs the novels' romance plots and happy endings to divert attention from real feminist concerns? Like Austen's novels, the films may begin by critiquing patriarchy, but they go on to reject the idea that their heroines' lives are really negatively impacted in any significant way by patriarchal oppression. The female characters in both the novels and films eventually overcome gender restrictions through successful excursions into the whirl of courtship and romance. One critic even calls the films "patriarchalizations of feminism" (Samuelian 1998: 156, note 2).

Other commentators have gone in a completely different direction, claiming the films are decidedly feminist and progressive and that they even enhance the implicit feminism found in Austen's novels. These critics focus on the novels' and films' dynamic heroines who avoid the passivity so often found in nineteenth-century female characters. They are physically and intellectually active: avid talkers, walkers, and readers. While they may be limited in their pursuits and goals, these limitations are imposed on them by their society not by their own inadequacies (Looser 1998: 164). They are strong, assertive, opinionated, smart, industrious, morally upstanding women who are fully engaged within the traditional female sphere of domesticity and even upon occasion venture forth into the public world of men. One of the biggest attractions of the films may just be their strong focus on these appealing female characters and the sense of sisterhood, family, and community that exists among them. While Austen's novels also have these attractive heroines, they contain a number of female villains as well. The films downplay female villainy in favor of female friendship and community. Women who are unattractive, and even villainous, exist in the films, but they are shown to be outside these communal bonds of sisterhood. Selfish, unfeeling, and materialistic, they act as foils for the films' heroines, who unlike them never show a lack of concern for their fellow women or treat them unfairly or with disdain.

Not everyone agrees that the Austen adaptations fit the feminist mold. Some have proposed that part of their appeal actually stems from their postfeminist qualities. In this reading, the Austen adaptations are seen as the immediate precursors of contemporary chick flicks and as sharing many of the same characteristics. They express the "nice," polite feminism that these critics also find in Austen's novels, rather than the more "angry" feminism of the contemporary women's movement. Their feminism is of the postfeminist variety that is conciliatory, depoliticized, and constructed in "widely palatable terms" to appeal to mainstream female audiences without alienating male moviegoers. While the films cannot be seen as "unmediated feminist texts" or "harbinger[s] of radical change" in their thinking about women, they are not totally conservative either (Looser 1998: 173–74). In a postfeminist fashion, they provide a certain amount of social criticism mixed with self-help solutions that restrict women's problems to an individual level and minimize the difficulty involved in overcoming institutionalized obstacles to women's social equality.

The Biopic

Although related to the literary adaptation, the biopic (fictional biographical film) differs in that it is not entirely fictional. It is a hybrid cinematic form that tells the partly factual, partly fictional story of a real person's life or a significant portion of that life. It combines melodrama, history, psychological drama, biography, and documentary. Although a number of theorists have called it a genre in itself, the biopic really appears, like the literary adaptation, to be a multi-generic filmic form that includes a wide range of films from musicals and comedies to serious dramatic works and historical epics. Dennis Bingham, who is the most recent scholar to write extensively on the biopic, proposes that at its heart is the attempt to get at the truth about someone's life (2010: 10). That truth may be moral, inspirational, or admonitory, and biopics range from celebratory hagiographies of admired public figures intended to provide examples of a life well-lived to dire cautionary tales detailing the downward spiral of a life that has swerved out of control. Lisa Levy points out that plots of contemporary biopics most often focus on both the great work and the great love of their protagonists (2002: 87), whereas earlier biopics concentrated only on their subjects' public accomplishments. In both cases, however, the films seek to provide moral or social edification for their audience by showing their main character's struggle for fame and fortune. It should be added that this main character has overwhelmingly been male, and the biopic has been characterized as one of the most male-oriented film forms.

Like the literary adaptation, the biopic has been both critically neglected and industrially celebrated. Critics have ridiculed, maligned, and despised biopics, characterizing them with a wide range of pejorative descriptors as simplistic, artistically embarrassing, vacuous, formulaic, sentimental, tedious, pedestrian, and even fraudulent. At the same time, however, like literary adaptations, the industry routinely promotes biopics as prestige pictures and star vehicles, and they are known to garner major award nominations. Why then has the biopic found so little critical acceptance? Bingham suggests that critics and viewers alike feel uneasy and distrustful of the biopic's mixture of fact and fiction (2010: 14). The biopic seems to be neither fish nor fowl, not really fiction and not really biography, and as such, not a film that can be trusted or believed. Others have condemned it in ways similar to attacks on the literary adaptation as aesthetically bankrupt and deeply conservative, offering a simplistic backward-looking glorification of the past, which it presents as composed of a succession of great men. The biopic has been accused of reducing complex historical events to the myth of the self-made man and the cult of the individual, while suppressing important social issues in favor of hagiographic accounts of ruggedly individualistic masculine heroes. These qualities seem to support a conservative historical perspective that upholds the status quo and rejects progressive ideas, yet many biopics are more complex and interesting than these blanket condemnations indicate, and they have found long-standing popularity with film audiences.

The biopic extends all the way back to the silent era, although it did not attain major status within the industry until the 1930s with the initiation of a series of Great Man Biopics. The major creative figures behind the studio-era biopics were director William Dieterle at Warner Bros. and the powerful producer Darryl F. Zanuck at 20th Century Fox. Dieterle's major films all employ the hagiographic mode to examine the lives of prominent historical figures: *The Story of Louis Pasteur* (1936), *The Life of Emile Zola* (1937), *Juarez* (1939), and *Dr. Ehrlich's Magic Bullet* (1940). His only film to honor a woman is *The White Angel* (1936), which tells the life story of Florence Nightingale. Zanuck's films, like *The Story of Alexander Graham Bell* (Irving Cummings, 1939) and *Young Mr. Lincoln* (John Ford, 1939), are similar to Dieterle's in that they celebrate the lives of great men. Zanuck is notable, however, for having pushed the biopic as far as possible into the realm of inspirational fiction, insisting that engaging the audience with a "rooting interest" was the key factor in biographical films. Zanuck believed that viewers wanted an underdog for whom to "root" much more than they wanted historical accuracy, which he argued could "choke a story to death" (quoted in Custen 1992: 132). After its heyday in the 1930s, the biopic continued to flourish, moving away from the great man era into a 1950s emphasis on contemporary figures, rather than men of the past. The new biopic subjects were entertainers, athletes, and gangsters, rather than inventors or political figures. The period from the 1960s to the 1980s is seen as one of decline for the biopic as the films took a more ambiguous investigatory form. In the tradition of the faux-biopic *Citizen Kane* (Orson Welles, 1941), these films presented their main characters as complex, deeply flawed individuals who are difficult to understand and with whom one cannot completely sympathize. Notable films in this mode include *Bonnie and Clyde* (Arthur Penn, 1967), *Patton* (Franklin J. Schaffner, 1970), *Raging Bull* (Martin Scorsese, 1980), and *Reds* (Warren Beatty, 1981). The biopic seems not to have really declined so much in these years as to have transformed and developed, and in the 1990s and 2000s it reemerged with complex, multi-perspectival portraits by major directors, such as Martin Scorsese and Oliver Stone. It is Stone who has established himself as the most prolific contemporary biopic director with a consistent output of biographical films including *Born on the 4th of July* (1989), *Nixon* (1995), *Alexander* (2004), and *W* (2008).

The male-oriented content of these films might lead one to wonder if women even have a place in the biopic at all. Biopics are overwhelmingly focused on male protagonists with statistics indicating that the percentage of biopics of women has remained consistent at the low figure of 25–28% in both the studio and contemporary era (Custen 1992: 103; Anderson 1988: 336), yet there have still been notable female biopics. They merit study in particular because it is important not only to look at films that are female-oriented like the woman's film, chick flick, and lesbian film, but also to see where women fit into film genres that are dominated by male content. In his extraordinarily negative assessment of the female biopic in *Whose Lives Are They Anyway?: the biopic as contemporary film genre*, Bingham proposes that the differences between male and female biopics are so great that they should be approached as entirely different types of films. According to Bingham, it is only the male biopic that has progressed, whereas the women's variation has until quite recently been almost completely resistant to change (2010: 20). Calling biopics of women "victimology-fetish biopics," he claims they just repeat gloomy scenarios of female suffering, victimization, and failure that enact an inevitable downward spiral resulting in sorrow, humiliation, defeat, drug addition, and even madness (2010: 217). As noted above, Bingham maintains that all biopics set out to reveal a truth about their protagonist, but this truth is very different for male and female biopic subjects. Male protagonists of biopics ultimately triumph over all obstacles to find success in the public sphere, or they are brought down by dark outside forces beyond their control, but female subjects of biopics are inevitably doomed to disaster once they enter the public sphere, where the films make it clear they do not belong (2010: 218). Bingham sees male biopics as developing through five successive generic stages, as listed here:

1. The celebratory great man films of the 1930s.
2. Flawed/troubled hero biopics (Bingham uses the unfortunate terminology warts-and-all biopics which I find myself unable to use).
3. Investigatory biopics (which examine the lives of complex protagonists who are presented from various perspectives following the model of *Citizen Kane*).
4. Postmodern biopics (which adopt a self-reflexive, ironic, and even sometimes absurdist tone that questions whether piecing together all the aspects of one person's life is really informative or even possible).
5. Parodic biopics (which parody the traditional biopic form either for purposes of humor or criticism) (2010: 10).

According to Bingham, biopics of women have not followed the same developmental pattern as male biopics because they have been unable to progress beyond scenarios of suffering and defeat. He does, however, come up with some sense of progression through the following stages, as given below:

1. "Emotionally busy" queen biopics (which Bingham, as one can readily tell from his word choice, views disparagingly as not so much about royal women engaging in the public sphere as about the ups and mostly downs

of their love lives. I would propose, however, that these films are actually far more complex in their examinations of women's relation to the public sphere than Bingham even begins to suggest).

2. Flawed/troubled heroine biopics of the 1950s (again, Bingham uses the ugly title "warts-and-all biopics" for these films that focus primarily on female entertainers and present their lives as filled with victimization by men).

3. Worst-of-the-worst female biopics of the 1980s (the title here is mine, but it describes perfectly Bingham's attitude to these films, which he says represent "some of the most despairing films ever made about the potential of women in public roles") (2010: 25).

4. Revisionist feminist biopics of the 1990s–2000s (in which women directors attempt to reinvent the female biopic in order to "take back the gaze of the woman's story" and create an empowering genre with a distinctly feminist point of view) (Bingham 2010: 10–11).

Bingham believes that the biopic's time-worn formula of women's victimization is so strong and so extremely difficult to break that the female biopic remains plagued by the same old plot formulas and conventions: the protagonist inevitably fails in her attempts to enter the public sphere; she is shown to be better off remaining in married life, although even there she suffers innumerable tragedies related to failure in love; she is thwarted by the machinations of an evil mother figure; and she is motivated not by her own goals and desires, but by the ambitions of the men in her life, who are really responsible for any success she might have in the public sphere (2010: 213, 222, 214).

While Bingham's overall assessment of the female biopic is overwhelmingly negative, the films he examines present a different picture. Not one completely fits into his victimology formula by chronicling only the "process of a woman's degradation" and the ways "by which women are washed out as human beings, and wash themselves out" (Bingham 2010: 231). Why is this the case? It might be because the female biopic has much more complexity than Bingham grants it. From the Susan Hayward crime drama *I Want to Live!* (Robert Wise, 1954) through the Julie Andrews musical *Star!* (Robert Wise, 1968) to Todd Haynes' parodic *The Karen Carpenter Story* (1989), the Julia Roberts' star vehicle *Erin Brockovich* (Steven Soderburgh, 2000) and Sophia Coppola's revisionist *Marie Antoinette* (2006), the films Bingham discusses do not just wallow in women's victimhood and suffering. Even *Gorillas in the Mist* (Michael Apted, 1988), a film that Bingham loathes, tries to present a complex picture of anthropologist Dian Fossey. It fails perhaps, as Bingham suggests it does, because it tries to do too much. It sets out both to celebrate a remarkable woman and to investigate a flawed heroine, but it just cannot pull those two strands together (Bingham 2010: 302). While it is undeniable that female biopics in contrast to those about men focus more on their protagonists' suffering, this suffering is presented much as it is in the woman's film. It does not degrade the female protagonist but rather shows her ultimate triumph over her misery, or at the very least her success in being able to survive through it all. Consider, for instance, *Frances* (Graeme Clifford, 1982), which is certainly in the category of Bingham's 1980s worst-of-the-worst female biopics. The film, which features a bravura performance by Jessica Lange as the doomed 1930s Hollywood actress, Frances Farmer, is such a depressing victimology narrative that it becomes difficult to watch its repeated scenarios of Farmer's persecution for her failure to fit into the Hollywood starlet mold. If all the audience gets from this film is a sense of Farmer's degradation, however, they are not watching the whole film, which concludes with Farmer's final vindication. She is shown to have been unjustly victimized by the Hollywood industry, her mother's manipulations, the mental health system's failures, and the patriarchical society of the time, but she is also portrayed as having survived it all. The film is a bitter attack on everything that conspired to undo the life of this unconventional rebellious woman, not merely a chronicle of her victimhood. To characterize the female biopic as just wallowing in women's suffering and failure is greatly to underestimate its complexity in the same way that so many critics missed the complex nature of 1930s and 1940s woman's films.

This is not to deny the many differences between biopics of women and those of men. They are different in so many ways: first, the fields in which women distinguish themselves tend to be more limited than those open to men, reflecting the social limitations imposed on women by patriarchy. Women's biopics are much more likely than male biopics to be about entertainers, queens, or headliners (women noted for making the news either in good or bad ways). Male biopics have a much wider range of protagonists from entertainers, athletes, and criminals to political and military figures, scientists, artists, and writers. Failed romance is a much more common component of the female biopic, whereas male biopic heroes commonly have the love of a loyal spouse to support them. Female biopics tend as well to be more critical of their heroines and less hagiographic, but these differences do not render the female biopic as detestable a film category as Bingham suggests.

Biopics of women actually possess a number of positive characteristics: first, many female biopics express women's need to enter the public sphere and establish a sense of autonomy and control over their lives. That the women in these films have not often found complete success in the public sphere is not so much a comment on their inevitable weakness, failure, and degradation, but rather a critique of the patriarchal society that is responsible for this failure and degradation. Like the woman's films of the 1930s and 1940s to which they can fruitfully be compared, female biopics have traditionally had a strong focus on female suffering, but this suffering does not ultimately show women's debasement; instead, it conveys a sense of their strength and triumph over this suffering. The same comment that

Molly Haskell made about the woman's film can be made about the female biopic. The fact that there is so much suffering in these films and that the female audience identifies with this suffering indicates that women do experience a great deal of misery under the constraints of patriarchy. It should also be pointed out that not all female biopics focus on female suffering. The biopics of the 1950s place the strongest emphasis on female victimization, but since that time biopics of women have been slowly moving away from such a strong focus on female misery. A final positive characteristic is that the biopic has throughout its history provided excellent star vehicles for actresses. Consider, to name just a few of the outstanding stars of female biopics: Greta Garbo, Marlene Dietrich, Bette Davis, Kate Blanchett, Judi Dench and Helen Mirren in their brilliant portrayals of queens; Susan Hayward in her 1950s suffering women cycle; Barbara Streisand, Diana Ross, and Angela Bassett in their memorable musical performances as Fanny Brice, Billy Holliday, and Tina Turner; as well as award-winning contemporary biopic performances by Hillary Swank, Julia Roberts, and Charlize Theron. If biopics have done nothing else, they have given some fine actresses the opportunity to create outstanding portrayals of biopic heroines.

In our films in focus section, we will investigate further the appeal of the female-oriented literary adaptation by examining *Sense and Sensibility*, the film that initiated the contemporary phenomenon of Austenmania. To assess the positive and negative aspects of biopics of women, we will then turn to an analysis of Julie Taymor's *Frida* (2002), a major contemporary female biopic that recounts the life of Mexican artist Frida Kahlo.

Films in Focus 1: *Sense and Sensibility*

Released in 1995, *Sense and Sensibility* was the result of the combined creative efforts of a male and female filmmaking team composed of star-turned-screenwriter Emma Thompson, producer Lindsay Doran, and director Ang Lee. Although the director is generally given credit as a film's auteur, the artist who leaves a creative imprint on a film, the case seems to be very different in regard to *Sense and Sensibility*. Producer Lindsay Doran said the film was "the fulfillment of a long cherished dream" (*Sense and Sensibility* Press Book [nd]: 6) for her, and screenwriter Emma Thompson described the project as something she wanted to do for women (Collins 1998: 85). Doran said she first read Jane Austen's novel in the year she graduated from college and decided then that it would make a perfect film adaptation, but it took her 25 years to make this happen. Her first problem was to find the right screenwriter who would not adapt the novel to the screen in a way that was in Doran's words "too polite, or too melodramatic, or too modern, or too arcane." According to Doran, every screenwriter she approached turned out to be a disappointment: "The funny ones weren't romantic and the romantic ones weren't funny." Then, she met Emma Thompson and Kenneth Branagh in 1991 when Doran was producing *Dead Again*, which Branagh directed and in which both he and his then wife Thompson starred. Doran felt she had found the perfect screenwriting and directing team in the husband and wife. She had seen skits that Thompson had written for her British television comedy series, entitled *Thompson*, and she was particularly attracted by Thompson's ability to write comedy in period settings (*Sense and Sensibility* Press Book [nd]: 6). The fact that Thompson was married to Branagh, who had recently directed a very popular film adaptation of Shakespeare's *Henry V* (1989), no doubt also helped stimulate Doran's interest.

Thompson was a first-time screenwriter who describes herself as totally at sea when it came to composing a screenplay. She claims to have begun by dramatizing every scene from the novel, which resulted in a 300-page handwritten manuscript. It took her four years, endless drafts, and the constant collaboration and support of Doran to construct a workable screenplay. As she describes her process, "The novel is so complex and there are so many stories in it that bashing out a structure was the biggest labor. I would write a version, Lindsay would read it and send me notes. Or, if we happened to be in the same city, we would sit down together and talk out the problems. Then I would cry for a while and then go back to work. And that's how it was for three years." Even when Thompson finished the screenplay, she wanted to have it interpreted by actors, so she set up a full-scale read-through at a London theater which included several of the actors who later would be cast in the film, including its major male star, Hugh Grant (*Sense and Sensibility* Press Book [nd.]: 7). In the meantime, Doran set out to sell the film to a studio. She says she shopped it around as early as 1990 to Paramount, Universal, Disney, and Fox and "all said no" (quoted in Alberge 1996: A5). When she was on the point of giving up, Columbia Tristar finally expressed interest. By this time, Thompson and Branagh were in the middle of a divorce, and a new director had to be found. Duran chose Ang Lee, but she and Thompson never allowed him into the inner sanctum of their female creative collaboration. In the film's press book, Doran is said to have been attracted to Ang because she saw him as "an inquisitive outsider with a sense of humor," and an outsider he seems to have remained (*Sense and Sensibility* Press Book [nd.]: 8). Ang himself describes his input largely in terms of visually recreating the historical period of the early 1800s and working with the actors to enhance their performances. Even in regard to casting, Thompson read at all of the call-backs and offered her opinions on all casting choices, although Ang says she did leave the final decisions up to him (Feld 1996: 8). There were, however, several scenes dealing with the plight of Brandon's seduced and abandoned ward that Ang wanted included in the film. These scenes would have darkened the film's mood considerably and perhaps increased its feminist portrait of women's direful social position in nineteenth-century British society, but Doran, who apparently was determined to keep the film's mood light, cut them because she felt they were "too jarring" (quoted in Gray 1997: 82, n. 13).

While Ang obviously had some input, the project was clearly dominated by Thompson and Doran. Thompson even agreed somewhat belatedly to star in a role that was written for a much younger actress (Elinor in the novel is only nineteen years old), most likely because her participation would help assure that the film would be taken seriously by the studio and given an adequate budget. For instance, Ang admits that he was initially attracted to the project by Thompson's presence (Tunison 1995: 6). Even with Thompson attached, the film was budgeted rather modestly for a major studio release at US$16 million (Klady 1995: 8), but it was given a prime release date during the Christmas season in what Duran admits was a blatant attempt to replicate the success of another nineteenth-century literary adaptation aimed at a female audience, *Little Women* (Gillian Armstrong, 1994) (Moore 1995: 18). The strategy worked, and *Sense and Sensibility* became a resounding box office hit, especially with female audiences.

We might begin our examination of the film in the traditional way with the question of its relation to its source. It was based on Austen's first published novel and one that has always been overshadowed by her later works, especially *Pride and Prejudice* and *Emma*, both of which were also given major television or film adaptations in the 1990s. The 1995 six-part television mini-series of *Pride and Prejudice* was first shown in Britain in September 1995 and in the U.S. in January 1996, and it was a huge success, making Colin Firth, as noted above, an instant sex symbol in the role of the handsome, dashing Darcy, who was much more sexy than his character in the novel. *Emma* was adapted twice to film in the 1990s, first in a very loose modernized adaptation as *Clueless* (Amy Heckerling, 1995), and later in a more faithful adaptation that stays in period, *Emma* (Douglas McGrath, 1996), the film that made Gwyneth Paltrow a star. It has also had several television adaptations, as has *Sense and Sensibility*. Whereas the novel versions of *Pride and Prejudice* and *Emma* surpassed *Sense and Sensibility* in literary prestige, the film and television versions of these more critically acclaimed Austen novels did not outstrip *Sense and Sensibility*'s reputation as the most accomplished Austen adaptation, a film that made "cinematic art from one of Austen's least successful novels" (Parrill 2002: 44). Like all Austen adaptations, the film attempted to evoke the literary prestige and attract readers of the novel by claiming complete fidelity to its source, but when critics have looked closely at it, they have concluded that, while staying in period, it also modernizes the novel considerably to attract a contemporary female audience, making changes in plot, characters, and theme.

As we have discussed, ascertaining a film's fidelity to its literary source is a tricky business for many reasons, not the least of which is that critics of a novel rarely agree on a single interpretation. To say that a film is faithful to the essence or core of its source novel becomes difficult when critics are not in complete agreement about what that essence might even be. In the case of *Sense and Sensibility*, there isn't even critical agreement on the novel's major theme. Many commentators argue that the novel centers on the conflict between sense and sensibility suggested in the title and embodied in the characters of its twin heroines, Elinor and Marianne. There is little agreement, however, about exactly what Austen wants her reader to glean from this conflict as it is worked out through the two sisters' experiences. Some have proposed that Austen is entirely on the side of Elinor, her center of consciousness in the novel and the character whose thoughts and feelings are most clear to us. Elinor is the sensible sister who is proper, upright, rational, and emotionally controlled, whereas Marianne is associated with sensibility, which in 1811, when the novel was first published, meant an overindulgence in emotion, imagination, feeling, and sentimentality. Many reviewers assume Austen sided wholly with Elinor and felt Marianne's ideas were in dire need of reformation. What she needed was to become more like her sister, which at the novel's end is exactly what happens. It might be said then that the novel preaches a rather simplistic moral message, presenting Marianne's character as a warning of the dangers of over-indulgence in sensibility at the expense of sense, yet many critics have been attracted to Marianne's liveliness, genuineness, and touch of rebelliousness. They consider Austen's ending with a chastened Marianne led to marry the much older, dour, and dull Colonel Brandon in order to please her family and reward him for his loyalty and generosity to them to be a terrible betrayal of this attractive character. In this reading, Austen is seen as torn between her intellectual approval of Elinor's sense and her instinctive attraction to Marianne's sensibility. Some have even suggested that the seemingly perfect Elinor comes across as too stiff and uptight and is herself in need of considerable reformation. For these critics, Elinor learns by the novel's end to be more in touch with her feelings and expressive of her emotions. One might wonder, though, whether her marriage to another dull man, the uptight would-be minister Edward, really seems to predict a future of intense emotional expression.

One might also wonder, as several critics have, whether the novel is really as concerned with the conflict between sense and sensibility expressed in its title as it is with other conflicts, such as the one between the values associated with nineteenth-century female domesticity and those of male society. In many ways, Austen's *Sense and Sensibility* is more an attack on the selfishness, self-absorption, and over-indulgence in sentimentality that Willoughby and to a certain extent Marianne embody. These qualities are contrasted with Elinor and Edward's selflessness, sense of propriety, and concern for the welfare of

Figure 8 From left, Emma Thompson as Elinor Dashwood, Kate Winslet as Marianne Dashwood, and Gemma Jones as their mother in *Sense and Sensibility*.

others. In this reading, Austen's major concern is Marianne's need to be educated in the altruistic ways of her more mature sister. It is this altruism that she finally attains at the novel's end when under the encouragement of her family she marries a man whom she respects but does not really seem to love.

What can we say about these men that Austen offers as possible marriage partners for her heroines? Why did she chose to divide her male characters into the boring, physically unattractive, but responsible Edward and Brandon versus the exciting, handsome, but caddish Willoughby? Some commentators have proposed that there is a feminist message here. By furnishing her heroines with rather unexciting suitors, Austen was trying to show how limited the options open to women in the nineteenth century actually were. In a society that did not allow women to earn their own living, they were doomed either to marry dull, but responsible men or be betrayed by exciting caddish ones, but then maybe for Austen Brandon and Edward were not as boring as critics see them. It is not easy to portray a good, upstanding character as interesting. Perhaps Austen just was not up to the task, or maybe her point was that excitement is not necessarily the best indicator of a good husband.

Another major area of disagreement about the novel is whether or not it makes a feminist statement about women's limited social roles in nineteenth-century British society. Did Austen want to show her heroines as stifled by oppressive social constraints? Is the novel a protest against those constraints, or does it simply offer advice on how women might make the best of their lives under limitations that Austen accepted as inevitable? Again there is little agreement on these issues. Critics either commend the socially progressive or lament the socially conservative Austen, so when they move to assessing the film adaptation's fidelity to the essence of the novel, it is difficult to know exactly what that essence is. Thus, it seems more profitable to leave the question of fidelity behind and move on to more interesting questions. For example, we might consider what the film does to make the novel more appealing to a largely female contemporary audience and how successful it is in this endeavor.

Judging from its overwhelmingly positive critical reception and impressive box office success, *Sense and Sensibility* seems to have been quite successful in creating mainstream appeal. How exactly it did this, however, is somewhat more difficult to determine, but the changes made in moving from novel to film tell us much. Rather than look at these changes with the question of fidelity in mind, it might be more profitable to consider them in terms of their contribution to the popular appeal of the film. The first obvious change is in the characterization of the two heroines. The film maintains the novel's strong focus on Elinor and Marianne, but in order to exploit the then current popularity of Hollywood female friendship films, it places much more emphasis on the affection between the two sisters. In order to accentuate the theme of female bonding, Thompson added scenes and dialogue in which Elinor repeatedly expresses her devotion to her sister, refers to her as "dearest," and even becomes extremely emotional when Marianne becomes ill. Elinor's more passionate attachment to her sister in the film contributes to the feeling that she undergoes a character change in the course of the narrative. Through her own ordeal in coping with Edward's prior engagement to Lucy Steele, as well as watching the course of Marianne's disastrous involvement with Willoughby, the film's Elinor becomes more in touch with her own emotions. This is not so clearly the case in the novel. In fact, many critics have seen the novel's Elinor as so completely perfect right from the beginning that her admirably sensible nature is hardly in need of improvement. In the film, we see her suppressing her feelings early on, but learning to become more in touch with her emotions not only in terms of her relationship with Edward, but also through her growing expression of love and support for Marianne. Elinor's ultimate transformation into a woman who is not only strong and perceptive, but also in touch with her emotional side is expressed in two scenes in which she openly breaks into tears. The first is a scene that Thompson added to the screenplay and that is not found at all in the novel. In this scene, Elinor openly weeps at her sister's sickbed because she fears Marianne's imminent death. In this melodramatic moment, Elinor begs the unconscious Marianne to cling to life and not leave her all alone. In a later scene, Elinor breaks into tears yet again, but this time before her whole family (in the novel she goes off to cry in private) when Edward announces that he has not married Lucy Steele and she realizes he is now free to ask for her hand.

While Elinor's transformation is clear, its effect on the audience's reaction to her character is less so. Rebecca Dickson reads Elinor's transformation negatively as having anti-feminist implications; she feels that the film converts Elinor, a woman whom Austen presented as strong and admirably self-restrained throughout the novel, into someone who is emotionally unable to handle her sister's illness and who breaks down into "loud, wailing tears" when she learns Edward is free to marry her. According to Dickson, Elinor embarrasses herself in front of Edward and her whole family, whereas Austen had her leave the room and cry alone with dignity (1998: 54). Dickson takes a very harsh view of the film's Elinor, characterizing her as having to learn from her interactions with men how to express her emotions, how to be more dependent on men's actions and advice, and how to become nearly "emotionally unhinged" when she realizes she can marry one of them (1998: 5–6). Other critics see her quite differently and praise Thompson for creating an admirable balance in her characterization of the two sisters. The film, unlike the novel, presents both Elinor and Marianne as in need of reformation. They must find the perfect balance between prudence and individualism, between sense and sensibility, a balance that Austen seems in the novel to have believed only Marianne lacked (Dole 1998: 62).

If the film's Elinor is in need of character development, Marianne is even more so. In both novel and film, she suffers greatly as a result of her overly emotional and excessively romantic inclinations, but in the film she is a much more likeable character. Marianne's likability might be attributed to Kate Winslet's attractive star persona, Thompson's greater sympathy for Marianne's romantic notions, or her desire to make Marianne more appealing to a female audience. For whatever reason, the self-destructive, willful, thoughtlessly impulsive Marianne who is carried away by her romantic fantasies in the novel becomes in the film the naive, charming, beautiful young woman seduced and abandoned by a handsome, but callous rake. The alteration in Marianne is demonstrated most clearly if we look at the changes Thompson made in the events leading up to Marianne's near fatal illness. In analyzing the novel, many critics have been quite critical of Marianne's actions preceding her illness, which they see as either brought on by her selfish wallowing in her own misery after Willoughby rejects her or even by her self-induced, exaggerated, psychosomatic, hysterical reaction to this rejection. Thompson takes a much less critical view of Marianne. In the novel, Marianne is taken ill after she gets her feet wet from walking in the wet grass in an attempt to catch a glimpse of Willoughby's estate. In the film she is caught in a thunderstorm, totally drenched, and dramatically rescued by Colonel Brandon in a scene obviously constructed to equate his actions with Willoughby's earlier gallantry in carrying Marianne back to her home after she sprained her ankle walking in the fields with her younger sister. Marianne's illness in the film is not only provoked by a more dire situation than in the novel, but also is of a much more serious, genuinely life-threatening nature. It is difficult to see the film's Marianne as bringing about her own illness by her selfish wallowing in misery, as exaggerating her symptoms, or as merely experiencing an hysterical episode. Elinor and Brandon's, as well as the Palmers' and Mrs. Jennings', reactions at her sickbed rule out such an interpretation. Marianne in the film is really near death, and her illness as precipitated not by her own willful behavior but by Willoughby's callous insensitivity.

Another major change that Thompson made in adapting the novel to film also adds to the narrowing of interpretive possibilities in regard to Marianne. Thompson decided to delete a scene in which Willoughby arrives at the Palmers' estate during Marianne's illness. This is a crucial scene in the novel that has received considerable critical attention in regard to its impact on Willoughby's and Elinor's characters. In the novel, having learned of Marianne's illness, Willoughby arrives gallantly on horseback to inquire about the state of her health. He remorsefully confesses to Elinor his love for her sister, insists he initially had honorable intentions toward her, and claims he suddenly learned during their romance of his dire financial situation, which made it impossible for him to marry for love rather than money. Austen, who is reputed to have experienced a similar romantic episode in her own life, presents Willoughby's situation somewhat sympathetically. Thompson said she did not include the scene because she had trouble writing it effectively for the screen and felt it interfered too much with the Marianne–Brandon love story, which she wanted to focus on at this point in the film (1996: 272).

Whatever Thompson's motivation, the effects of the deletion are wide ranging. Its removal not only allowed Thompson to place greater emphasis on Marianne's fight for life and Elinor's emotional reaction to her illness (Gray 1997: 78), it also increases our sympathy for Marianne by making Willoughby more of a consummate villain. Additionally, if the scene had been included, it might have detracted from the singularity of Elinor's affection for Edward. Kristin Flieger Samuelian proposes that Elinor's expression of sympathy for Willoughby in this scene in the novel indicates that she is "aroused" by him in a way that she never is by Edward (1998: 152). Samuelian believes Thompson did not include the scene because she did not want it to cast suspicion on Elinor's total devotion to Edward. Thompson also added a number of other scenes to the film in which Elinor demonstrates her attraction to Edward. In one such scene, he seems about to confess his love for her and explain his prior engagement to Lucy Steele as Elinor gazes at him with obvious affection (Samuelian 1998: 154). Samuelian's argument that Elinor's sympathetic reaction to Willoughby's confession of love for her sister in the novel represents sexual arousal seems rather unconvincing. A much more plausible explanation for why Thompson felt the need to cut the Willoughby scene is that she thought a contemporary audience would not understand why Elinor, who in the film is so emotionally distraught because of her sister's illness, would be understanding of Marianne's seducer. Thompson may also have wanted to keep Willoughby playing the part of the evil villain and acting as a foil to the heroines' proper love interests, Edward and Brandon.

Probably the biggest change that Thompson makes to Marianne's character concerns her relationship with Brandon and her transformation at the film's ending. As in the novel, the film's Marianne experiences an epiphany as a result of her illness. She realizes that she should have been more circumspect in her relationship with Willoughby and even tells Elinor that she will strive in the future to be more like her, but the film's ending makes this transformation seem less complete than it is in the novel. As noted above, Marianne's vibrant personality seems to be totally subdued at the novel's end as she enters a respectable but seemingly passionless marriage of convenience with Brandon, a much older father figure for whom she feels respect and gratitude but not love. She marries him not to please herself at all but to please him and her family. In giving up her selfish ways, she seems to have become just a bit too selfless, relinquishing all hope of romance or love. The situation in the film is quite different. The film's Marianne is actively courted by Brandon, who loves her as she is and does not require her to change at all. It is he who changes for her. We see him devotedly engaging in the same activities with Marianne that Willoughby did. They read poetry together, he buys her a pianoforte so they can enjoy music together, and in the film's final triumphant wedding scene Marianne glows with happiness and love for her dashing husband, who does not look old at all, but rather handsome and virile in his red military uniform. As she sits in their wedding carriage in a state of marital bliss, he throws out coins to the wedding guests in an enactment of a quaint British tradition that Thompson added to the film. Money will not interfere with the love and happiness of this ideal couple. It seems clear that Thompson did not feel a contemporary female audience would react favorably to the type of marriages Austen fashioned for the novel's heroines, with both women entering into unions that are best described as practical rather than passionate. In the film, their marriages are not only practical in that they marry men who can support them, but romantic in that both women marry men they truly love and who truly love them.

In order to bring about this romantic ending, Thompson had to extensively remodel the novel's men, and the alterations she made to Edward, Brandon, and Willoughby are the biggest changes from novel to film. Was she unfaithful to the novel? It seems obvious that she was. Did the changes she made benefit the film to make it more attractive to a female film audience? I think the answer to this question is that they absolutely did. Thompson gave Austen's men the qualities they needed to become romantic figures capable of offering the film's heroines ideal companionate marriages. Critics have repeatedly described the novel's Edward and Brandon as rather unattractive matches for Elinor and Marianne. Austen describes Edward as not particularly handsome, difficult to get to know, and emotionally inexpressive. He is upstanding per-haps to a fault in holding himself to his promise to marry Lucy Steele, whom he does not love, and he is genuine and decent, but never even comes close to being a romantic figure. Thompson changes all that and transforms Edward into a paradigm of what Devoney Looser calls the contemporary "New Man."

While both he and Brandon may seem emotionally distant on the surface, underneath their reserved exteriors lie "truly caring and more equal partners, caregivers, rescuers" than are found in the novel (Looser 1998: 170).

Edward, for instance, is introduced in the film through his loving, nurturing relationships with both Elinor and her younger sister Margaret. He consoles Elinor as she mourns her father's death and is sensitive to the plight of her family in losing their home. His playful and affectionate friendship with Margaret also shows that he is good with children and thus has the potential to be a caring husband and father. As portrayed by the handsome Hugh Grant, Edward seems merely shy, not emotionally distant as in the novel, and he demonstrates a playful sense of humor and a ready wit. Grant's facial expressions show his understanding and sympathy for Elinor and her whole family in their time of mourning. He also demonstrates respect for Elinor's intelligence and presents himself as her ideal partner both intellectually and morally. Brandon is similarly transformed from the novel's dour old man in a flannel vest into a handsome mature love interest for Marianne. In his black suits and cavalier hats, he emerges as a Byronic figure with a brooding sexual presence. His distant reserve is shown to be a reaction to his earlier disappointment in love; Alan Rickman said he played Brandon as "a man thawing out after being in a fridge for twenty years" (quoted in Casey 1998: 181). Rickman definitely played Brandon to the hilt as a romantic hero, more suitable as a husband for Marianne than Willoughby in every way. His concern for his ward Beth even though she has been disgraced by pregnancy out of wedlock and the deep consideration he shows and support he provides to Elinor during Marianne's illness reveal him to be not only a nurturing caregiver, but also a very dashing one. With his shirt collar opened at the neck as he leans disconsolately against the door to Marianne's sickroom looking terribly distraught by her illness (and with Willoughby's dramatic visit excised from the film), Brandon emerges as Marianne's truly devoted lover. He begs Elinor, "Give me an occupation, Miss Dashwood, or I shall run mad." This is a line that Austen's Colonel Brandon in his flannel vest could never have uttered.

The final male figure that Thompson transforms is Willoughby, and here the transformation moves in a negative rather than a positive direction. As noted above, Willoughby becomes much more of a villain in the film than he is in the novel. The elimination of his emotional confession scene with Elinor as Marianne lies ill does much to make him seem more reprehensible, but it is not only this. His rejection of Marianne at the ball is particularly callous and cruel. In the novel he is exonerated somewhat when he tells Elinor that his actions at the ball and the hurtful letter he wrote to Marianne explaining his lack of feelings for her were really orchestrated by his jealous wife. Austen and the women of her time were perhaps more understanding than are contemporary women of men whom economic necessity compelled to marry women of wealth, rather than those they loved. Thompson knew that a contemporary female audience would be much less likely to understand such behavior, so she did not grant Willoughby the understanding that Austen gives him in the book. James Thompson offers an interesting interpretation of the significance of Willoughby in the film. He suggests that the casting of the American actor Greg Wise in the role with his "unBritish unantiquated accent" and his "contemporary male beauty" identifies Willoughby's expedience and selfishness with the contemporary age rather than with Austen's time. In the end, we see Willoughby, as a figure of contemporary society, looking longingly from a hilltop at Marianne's joyous wedding below (something Willoughby in the novel does not do), just as the audience is meant to look longingly on the film's representation of an idyllic past so distant and so much better than the present (Thompson 2003: 26).

Does Thompson really represent the past as so much better than the present? Certainly, it is romanticized in a way that it is not in Austen's novel, which in spite of its focus on courtship maintains an ironic distance from and a distrust of romantic notions. Thompson abandons Austen's distance and distrust almost entirely. Her men are transformed into passionate figures of romance, Marianne is not asked to give up her sentimental qualities, Elinor actually becomes more sentimental and emotional as the film progresses, and it concludes with a glorious celebration of love and marriage. While Thompson increases the film's romanticism, she at the same time, enhances its feminism, making the film's expression of feminist sentiments much more overt than the novel's. As noted above, the novel's feminism has been seen as questionable, and Thompson has even been accused of reducing its underlying feminist thrust. It seems clear, however, that on the surface at least the film makes its feminism much more apparent than the novel does. The novel does criticize male arrogance, duplicity, and sexism, but it attacks powerful women as well (for instance, the venial characters of Mrs. Ferrars and Fanny Dashwood) and satirizes female foolishness (the silly and unwise characters of Mrs. Palmer and Lucy Steele). Austen even concludes the novel by placing her intelligent, active female characters in traditional roles, and seems to glorify those roles. For instance, we are asked at the end of the novel to accept Marianne's apparently loveless marriage to a wealthy older man and to applaud the smart and talented Elinor's achievement of the dubious distinction of becoming the wife of a dull rural minister whose living is barely enough for them to live comfortably. This is not the stuff of which contemporary feminists' dreams are necessarily made.

Elements of feminism can be found in Austen's novel, most notably in its opening pages when we are presented with the tragic situation of the Dashwood women. When their husband and father dies, they lose their home as a result of an unusual inheritance arrangement according to which the estate could only be inherited by a male heir. In the novel, this situation is the result of the unique nature of the will of Mr. Dashwood's uncle, from whom he inherited the estate. The women become largely dependent on their male relatives for support. Their older brother John, who inherits their father's property, under the influence of his malicious and venal wife Fanny, fails to provide for them, and it is only a distant relative, Sir John Middleton, who offers them a cottage in which to live. Thompson replicates this situation in the film, but increases its critique of women's precarious position in the patriarchal society of the 1800s. She eliminates the issue of the will, which established the Dashwood women's situation as unusual rather than representative, and has Elinor tell her youngest sister Margaret simply that their home is no longer theirs because women are unable to inherit property (an historical inaccuracy). The feminist critique is stronger because the situation is presented not as unique to the Dashwoods particular situation, but as the common lot of women at the time.

Thompson also accentuates nineteenth-century women's total dependence on men by adding a conversation not found in the novel between Elinor and Edward in which Elinor expresses very explicitly her frustration with the roles allotted to women: "You talk of feeling idle and useless – imagine how that is compounded when one has no choice and no hope whatsoever of any occupation." To this, Edward replies that they are exactly in the same situation, but Elinor points out, "Except that you will inherit your fortune. We cannot even earn ours." Several critics have suggested that the seriousness of Elinor's comment is deflated by the humor of Edward's response: "Piracy is our only option." But does his rather cavalier attitude really diminish the seriousness of Elinor's remark or does it indicate that as a man he really does not understand their situation? Regardless of Edward's failure to take her seriously, Elinor's words still convey a strong feminist critique of the economic limitations placed on women in the nineteenth century and even today.

Another feminist addition that Thompson made involves the recasting of the role of Margaret, the youngest Dashwood sister. In the novel, she is an underdeveloped character who seems merely to be following in her older sister Marianne's overly sentimental and romantic footsteps, but in the film Thompson makes her a pre-adolescent symbol of feminist revolt. As Sue Parrill points out, Margaret seems to be a budding feminist who openly criticizes the status quo, advocates equal opportunities for women, and exercises the mobility and independence her older sisters have learned to repress (2002: 37). Although her aspirations to enter the male world are portrayed comically through her desire to be a pirate, she seems intended to show what nineteenth-century women could have been like if their natural inclinations were not quashed by a repressive society. Her role unquestionably adds a stronger feminist critique to the film than is found in the novel.

Even with these changes, a number of critics have characterized the film as expressing only a conciliatory, depoliticized, watered-down popular feminism. These critics propose that although the film does make its feminism overt in its opening scenes it moves on to heighten the romance of the novel, which acts to undercut the earlier feminist message. As noted above, Thompson alters the courtships of the Dashwood sisters considerably. In the novel, the only passionate love affair that is portrayed is between Marianne and Willoughby, and in the end this is shown to be based on deceit on his part and gullibility on hers. The women's romances with the dull and physically unattractive Edward and Brandon are presented as financially and socially advantageous but hardly deeply romantic. Thompson changes all that. In the film, Edward makes a touching proposal of love to Elinor once he is free from his engagement to Lucy Steele. He announces: "I have come with no expectations. Only to profess, now that I am at liberty to do so, that my heart is and always will be yours." The film then concludes with its celebratory wedding scene in which Colonel Brandon and his new wife are seen triumphantly exiting the church where their wedding just took place, looking deeply in love and ecstatically happy. They are followed by Edward and Elinor also beaming with love and happiness. The feminist critique of the situation of women in the nineteenth century is significantly reduced by this ending, which suggests that even in an oppressively patriarchal society women who are smart enough and good enough actually can overcome all obstacles and find perfect happiness in the arms of ideal men. In the novel, the heroines are only rewarded with unexciting, but reliable husbands and providers. In the film they get perfect men who are both exciting and reliable.

The question in analyzing *Sense and Sensibility* is thus not one of fidelity. The film is in some ways faithful to the novel and in other ways not, but this is really only a peripheral question. The more interesting issue involves what the changes Thompson made in moving from nineteenth-century novel to twentieth-century film tell us about the female audience for whom the film was largely intended. What the film does very effectively is heighten both the romance and the feminism of Austen's text. This feminism is not radical and can perhaps be best characterized as a nice conciliatory feminism that does not go very far in attacking the abuses of patriarchy, but it is more emphatically stated in the film than in the novel. Does the film's increased romanticism and emphasis on the happy-ever-after ending totally derail its feminist message? This is a question about which critics do not agree, and one that seems much more significant to ponder as we think about the film, rather than merely spending our time evaluating it as faithful or unfaithful according to how closely it sticks to a two-hundred-year-old book.

Films in Focus 2: *Frida*

A surface analysis of Julie Taymor's biopic *Frida* (2002) might dismiss it as a paradigmatic example of what Dennis Bingham calls the "victimology-fetish biopic" that wallows in its female protagonist's suffering. Frida Kahlo, the renowned Mexican artist whose life the film recounts, certainly experienced a great deal of pain from the physical injuries she suffered from a streetcar accident when she was a young woman and from the emotional effects of her stormy marriage to the brilliant, but notoriously womanizing Mexican artist Diego Rivera. It would be easy to dismiss the film as a typical woman's biopic that dwells on Kahlo's misery and neglects her art, but I think this is too hasty an analysis. To really investigate this film, it is necessary to view it not just as a woman's biopic, but also as an artist biopic and to consider carefully whether it does something more than merely reduce its heroine to a state of victimization and abject suffering.

Painters are not a common subject for biopics, and women painters, of which there have been so few, are even more rarely given biopic treatment. If one is to consider entertainers artistic figures, and they certainly are artists in the popular realm, then they overwhelmingly dominate the category of the artist biopic, but when we think of artists, we usually think of painters, writers, or musicians, and these occupations have had little appeal to biopic filmmakers. The biopic subject of choice has traditionally been men of action, rather than those whose work, like the artist's, is cerebral, internal, and solitary. Political figures, sports celebrities, and military heroes have always been more popular biopic subjects than those in artistic professions. Ronald Bergan speculates that artistic accomplishments are so difficult to portray on the screen and artists so highly romanticized in the popular imagination that viewers find it difficult to accept artist biopics as realistic (1983: 21). Painter biopics have fallen very much in line with this view. As critics repeatedly point out, they portray their subjects as eccentric, tormented, tragic figures, rather than dedicated craftspersons. The artist's fragile psyche is presented in a melodramatic, overdramatized, and sentimental narrative that wrings as much emotion as possible from the creative struggle and the artist's mythical conflict with a society that just cannot understand the nature of artistic talent. Artist biopics promise, as Bingham suggests all biopics do, to reveal some essential truth about their subjects, and in the artist biopic this truth concerns what is presented as the almost magical origin of genius. This origin, however, is portrayed as very difficult to uncover. As a result, artist biopics rarely tell us much about the artist's work or about the nature of art itself. In fact, they usually do not spend much time even showing the artist in the process of artistic creation, since artistic endeavors are notoriously difficult to make interesting on the screen.

How long can we watch a painter painting before we want to move on to something else? That something else is inevitably the artist's life, which is usually presented in melodramatic, sentimental detail and envisioned as the source of the artist's creative accomplishments.

Few artist biopics have found great popular success, but notable films within the subgenre include *The Moon and Sixpence* (Albert Lewin, 1942, based loosely on the life of Gaugin), *Moulin Rouge* (John Huston, 1952, on Toulouse-Lautrec), *The Agony and the Ecstasy* (Carol Reed, 1965, on Michelangelo), and more recently *Basquiat* (Julian Schnabel, 1996, on Jean Michel Basquiat), and *Pollock* (Ed Harris, 2000, on Jackson Pollock). Unquestionably, the most successful and critically praised artist biopic and the one that established the conventions that would become most associated with succeeding films is *Lust for Life* (Vincente Minnelli, 1956). This seminal biopic of Vincent Van Gogh was considered ground-breaking for its time. Its episodic narrative structure breaks Van Gogh's life into five parts with each segment visually designed to express his current emotional state and the stages in the development of his work (Casper, 2006). In many ways, *Lust for Life* is the model not only for other biopics that followed it, but in particular for *Frida*, which does not so much follow the formula of the woman-as-victim biopic, as it does that of the artist biopic set by *Lust for Life*. The portrait of the artist established by Vincente Minnelli's much praised Van Gogh biopic appears to be the real inspiration for Taymor's film.

In the mold of *Lust for Life*, *Frida* tells the story of a suffering artist. Like Van Gogh (Kirk Douglas), Frida Kahlo (Selma Hayek) converts her tormented life into her art, and the film shapes its mise-en-scène around that art. Both films use as a template for their stunning visual presentations of their protagonists' lives the replication of their most famous paintings. They also both seem torn between hagiography and expose. In the 1950s, *Lust for Life* was hailed as transforming the traditional artist biopic by employing a no-holds-barred-tell-all approach, what Bingham refers to as the warts-and-all technique. This approach ostensibly reveals the inner turmoil behind Van Gogh's works, yet the film does not entirely abandon the hagiographic "great man" mode that characterized earlier biopics. It still glorifies Van Gogh's amazing artistic achievements and even renders them more remarkable by the mental struggles he suffered in their creation. Similarly, *Frida* celebrates its protagonist's art, as well as her struggle to produce it, given her deteriorating physical condition and the emotional ravages of her tempestuous relationship with Diego Rivera (Alfred Molina).

Also, both films were promoted as gaining a particular intensity from their stars' feelings of a special connection to their characters. Kirk Douglas claimed he knew he was destined to play Van Gogh, not only because of his marked physical resemblance to the artist, but also because of a similarity in temperament (Casper 2006). Selma Hayek also proposed that she had a special connection to Frida Kahlo. Before *Frida*, Hayek was typecast in film roles that required her to play the "Latina spitfire," a character who is presented as voluptuous, sexually available, and emotionally temperamental (Guzman 2007: 119). Not seen as having the acting ability to undertake the role of Frida or the star status to sell the movie, Hayek had to fight to get the part, notably against Jennifer Lopez, who was also very interested in the role. To promote herself, Hayek "exploited the nationalistic rhetoric of ethnic purity and homogeneity to argue that as the 'true' or 'pure' Mexican" she could more effectively play the part. Interestingly, if Hayek did have an ethnic connection to Frida, it would be based not on the purity but on the hybridity of their ethnic heritage: Frida's father was German and Hayek's Lebanese (Guzman 2007: 123, 125). As Isobel Molina Guzman suggests, Hayek is connected to Frida much more in terms of their similarities as "independent, racially unde-termined, ethnically hybrid women who problematize discourses of Latina bodies and racial and national purity" (2007: 27). Promotion for the film, however, played up Hayek's "physical likeness [to Kahlo], Mexican identity, and heritage" as evidence of her "ethnically privileged and biological connection to the role" (Guzman 2007: 123). Although Hayek admitted to not even being familiar with Kahlo's work until her late teens when a friend introduced her to it and not having initially liked it, she also claimed she channeled her admiration for the artist into her portrayal. She is credited as one of the film's producers, and was said to have worked to get Taymor to direct the film and her then boyfriend Edward Norton to do an uncredited script rewrite (Briley 2003: 76).

Even though the films were made almost fifty years apart, *Frida* actually has much more in common with *Lust for Life* than it does with biopics of women artists that immediately preceded it in the 1990s. Two notable biopics of the period, the British-made *Carrington* (Christopher Hampton, 1995) and the French import *Artemisia* (Agnes Merlet, 1997), both represent dismally unsuc-cessful attempts to portray the female artist. Actually based on Michael Holroyd's biography of Lytton Strachey, not on the life of Dora Carrington, *Carrington* almost entirely ignores its ostensible subject's art in favor of her love affair with the gay writer. The film's focus on Carrington's (Emma Thompson) adoration for Strachey (Jonathan Pryce) renders it almost entirely a study of obsessive love and not at all of female artistic accomplishment.

Whereas *Carrington* was received with critical indifference, *Artemisia* raised considerable controversy concerning its distortion of the life of the seventeenth-century female painter Artemisia Gentileschi, one of the first women to gain recognition as an artist. In fact, Gloria Steinem was so incensed by the film's portrayal of Gentileschi that she circulated a fact sheet with art historian Mary

Garrard, who had earlier written a feminist analysis of Gentileschi's work. The fact sheet, "Now You've Seen the Film, Meet the Real Artemisia Gentileschi," calls for a boycott of the film and outlines the major ways in which it distorts Gentileschi's life. Garrard and Steinem's critique of *Artemisia* is so devastating that it led Miramax, the film's U.S. distributor, to withdraw the claim that it was a true story from the film's publicity (Pollock 2001: 32). Gentileschi is known not only for her art but for the notoriety she gained from her involvement in a lengthy rape trial. Her father, also a painter, sued Agostino Tassi, an artist whom he had hired as his daughter's teacher, accusing him of having raped Artemisia. The trial transcript is extant and indicates that no evidence of a love relationship between Tassi and his student was presented to the court and that even under torture Artemisia maintained her accusation of violent rape. She admitted to having had sex with Tassi after the rape, but claimed to have done so only because he promised to marry her if she did. Tassi was convicted of rape, but the sexual scandal still ruined Artemisia's reputation, branding her as a seductress bent on revenge against the man who rejected her. Even her most famous painting, "Judith and Holfernes," has been read as a portrait of a sexy murderess attacking her lover (Pollock 2001: 32–33).

The film alters Gentileschi's story considerably, reversing its major elements to convert it into the tale of doomed lovers. Tassi is portrayed as having been misled by Artemisia's desire to understand human anatomy, which he believed reflected not the determination of a dedicated young artist to improve her art, but the longings of a sexually active young woman. In the film, Artemisia does develop an attraction to Tassi after the rape, and they initiate an ongoing sexual relationship. When her father learns of it, he initiates the rape trial even though Artemisia refuses to say she was raped. At the trial, she is tortured because she will not identify Tassi as her rapist, not as in real life because she refused to retract her testimony that he did rape her. In the film, Tassi admits to the rape in order to protect Artemisia from further torture. The effect of these changes is enormous: the film completely alters the personality of Tassi, who was accused at the real trial not only of having raped Artemisia, but also of having impregnated his sister-in-law and arranged the murder of his wife, whom he had raped before their marriage (Garrard and Steinem 1998). The film transforms him from a liar, brutal rapist, and possible murderer into a devoted lover who was reluctantly drawn to Artemisia by her irresistible charms and at the trial was willing to sacrifice himself for her. Gentileschi's artistic accomplishments are presented not as the result of her talent, hard work, and dedication to her craft, but as stemming from her sexual longing for the lost lover that her father denied her. The film even has her painting "Judith and Holofernes" in reaction to her relationship with Tassi, who it is implied was the model for Holofernes, which was not the case in real life. The painting was actually done long after the rape, and most art historians identify the Judith figure as a symbolic representation of "the self-creating [female] artist," not the frustrated seductress (Pollock 2001: 36). The feminist outrage that greeted the film is easy to understand from this comparison of the film's portrayal of the rape to the real historical record, but there is more. The film also leaves out many other details that actually support a feminist interpretation of Gentileschi's life and work, such as her subsequent marriage to another man, motherhood and mentorship of artistic daughters, successful career as an artist after the trial, self-negotiation of commissions for her works, and earning of her own livelihood from sales of her paintings (Pollock 2001: 36).

A careful examination of *Frida* might lead us to consider whether it belongs with these other 1990's failed biopics of women artists or with *Lust for Life*'s more successful examination of the male artist. Many scholarly critics have argued that the film falls in with traditional portraits of female artists, but if we think of *Carrington* and *Artemisia*, *Frida* seems to be decidedly different. The film is based on Hayden Herrera's 1983 biography, which is the most influential treatment of Kahlo's life. As Tina Olsin Lent points out, Herrera's biography adheres closely both narratively and thematically to the established conventions of female artist biographies. Taymor's film, however, deviates considerably from Herrera's treatment and from the conventions of the female artist biography as Lent describes them. *Frida* actually follows many of the conventions of art-historical monographs dealing with male, rather than female artists. Like these male biographies, it presents Frida's life as explaining her art, her talent as evident early in life, and her success as based not on hard work, skill, and training but on intrinsic god-like genius. It also presents her as different from others, divorced from normal society, and "an outsider whose self-centered, tormented, solitary existence was the price demanded by [her] art" (Lent 2007: 70). Lent suggests that biographies of female artists usually conform to the male model in that they express the idea of the artist's life as inspiring her art, but they deviate from it in numerous other ways. Conventionally, the female artist is not represented as god-like, but as exceptional only among women. She is shown to be dependent on a male mentor to encourage her and elicit her talent. Her commitment to her art stems from a transformative event that forced her to turn to artistic achievement for fulfillment because she is unable to find happiness in the conventional female roles of wife and mother. Finally, she is portrayed as unlike the male artist in that his sexuality benefits his creativity, whereas her sexual desires are seen as unnatural or deviant and as making it difficult for her work to be taken seriously (Lent 2007: 71).

Lent criticizes Taymor's film for following Herrera's biography too closely and thus remaining too much within the mold of the female artist biography, but is this really the case? Lent argues that the film actually owes as much to the woman's melodrama as it does to the artist biopic. She proposes that it presents the trolley accident in which the teenaged Frida was so badly injured as a transformative event, even a symbolic rape trauma, that led Kahlo to regard herself as a grotesque figure who could only restore her sense of wholeness through her art (Lent 2007: 71). She also sees the film as taking from women's melodrama an excessive emotionalism, the valorization of love and family over success, a concentration on the domestic, a reliance on the "woman's weepie" love story, and a determination to move the viewer to tears by Kahlo's long-suffering womanhood (Lent 2007: 74). But in many ways *Frida* actually rejects a number of the conventions that Lent sees it as embodying. While it does present Kahlo's work as related to her life, it also makes clear that it was her genius that allowed her to transform her life experiences into art. This genius is demonstrated early in her life, even before the trolley accident. Kahlo's passion for art becomes clear when, as an adolescent school girl, she sneaks in to watch Rivera work on a mural. In the tradition of the female artist biography, Rivera does in a sense occupy the role of the male mentor who stimulates Frida's talent, but he could as easily be seen as one of the problems in her life that combines with her physical debilitation to interfere with her work. While Kahlo appears to be obsessed with Rivera and devastated by her inability to have a child with him, the film does not unequivocally endorse love and family over success. In fact, it could be interpreted as a critique of exactly this notion. Frida's dedication to romance and the idea of family actually leads her to an unhealthy obsession with the lecherous, womanizing Rivera. This obsession makes her life miserable and prevents her from concentrating on her art. The film also refuses to condemn Frida for her sexuality or for her bisexual affairs, which are presented as neither unnatural nor as minimizing the significance of her artistic endeavors. Finally and importantly, Frida is hardly portrayed as a complete female victim. She uses her art to transcend her suffering, and the film recognizes her for her courage and determination to live a full life in spite of her physical disabilities and marital difficulties.

In spite of these progressive elements, most critics have strongly condemned Taymor's film. Taymor said that her intention was to avoid the external presentation of her protagonist's life that is so often characteristic of biopics, and instead present a subjective view of Frida from Frida's own point of view in order to uncover what inspired her paintings (quoted in Lent 2007: 73). Lent proposes that in the process Taymor became interested in the mystery of Frida's personality much more than in the source of her artistic creativity (2007: 74), but it would seem that for Taymor the two are intimately intertwined. While Taymor does focus heavily on Kahlo's life, her technique of using tableaux vivants, in which episodes from Kahlo's life are transformed before our eyes into her paintings, does not diminish her as an artist; instead, it demonstrates her genius in converting the events of her life into art. Does this mean, as Carol Kino suggests, that we learn nothing from the film about how Kahlo actually created her works? Well, perhaps not as much as we would like, but this is true of all artist biopics, and in *Frida* we at least do see Kahlo's art in remarkable visual sequences that show her life experiences visually transpose into her surrealist paintings before our eyes. In comparison to *Lust for Life*, which uses Van Gogh's art merely as punctuation between scenes, Taymor's attempts to show Kahlo's paintings are much more visually striking.

Critics have also criticized the inauthenticity of Taymor's portrayal of Kahlo both in terms of the facts of her life and the film's presentation of her Mexican ethnicity. In the tradition of the biopic, which by its nature combines fact with fiction, *Frida* plays fast and loose with the actual events of Kahlo's life in order to create a more compelling story. Although the film was promoted as based on Kahlo's own diaries and the Herrera biography, there are still many omissions and inaccuracies, including the failure to acknowledge all of Kahlo's many love affairs, the neglect of her artistic training and later her teaching, and the avoidance of the very dark side of her life. Kahlo's addiction to drugs and alcohol as a way to deal with the pain from her disability, her use of repeated surgeries to gain Rivera's attention (known as the Munchausen Syndrome), her idolization of Stalin, and her bizarre cremation, in which her body sat up as it was being burned, are all eliminated from the film. Additionally, some have criticized the presentation of Kahlo's dedication to Mexicanidad, which the film characterizes as a way in which she connected her passion for life to the spirit of pre-modern Mexico. The film takes up Kahlo's embrace of Mexicanidad, the ideology of post-revolutionary Mexican intellectuals who saw Mexico's Indian and folk heritage as its true cultural patrimony and rejected European influences. Through her mise-en-scène, which emphasizes Kahlo's fascination with the folk art, clothing, and rituals of pre-modern Mexico, Taymor presents Mexicanidad as one of the major means by which Kahlo transformed her life into art (Lent 2007: 72). Kahlo's collection of paper-mache Judas figures, skeletons, calaveras, pottery, artifacts, and indigenous plants and animals in her Casa Azul residence is presented as inspiration for her art and her signature style of dress. In real life, it was Rivera, not Kahlo who was most associated with Mexicanidad and who encouraged Frida to wear traditional Mexican Tehuanna skirts and huipils (Lent 2007: 71). In the film, Taymor downplays Rivera's influence in this regard and portrays Kahlo as independently making herself into an "animated piece of folk art" (Lent 2007: 73). For Ellen McCracken, Taymor's portrayal of Kahlo's attraction to Mexicanidad amounts to a fetishistic use of supra-ethnicity as a way to counteract the threat posed to U.S. audiences by the film's images of Kahlo as a "third world other" (2008: 256).

Figure 9 Selma Hayak as Frida Kahlo and Alfred Molina as Diego Rivera in *Frida*.

One of the major criticisms of *Frida* is that it reduces Kahlo's life to a love story centered on her obsessive attachment to Diego Rivera. Ron Briley sees the film as failing to portray Kahlo as an "independent woman who articulated her vision within the masculine art world" and instead presenting her as "a submissive figure dependent upon the approval of the men in her life." According to Briley, the film suggests that Kahlo just wanted "to settle down, making art and love with Diego Rivera," whose penchant for sexual promiscuity unfortunately made her desire for domestic bliss impossible

(2003: 76). Briley sees Frida as totally dependent on male approval and the male gaze; even her provocative dance with the famous Italian-American photographer and actress Tina Modotti (Ashley Judd) is not portrayed as a challenge to gender conventions, but merely as an attempt to gain the attention of Rivera and his male cronies (2003: 76). Taymor said she conceived the film as a love story and believed Kahlo's love for Rivera was integral to her life and ultimately triumphant. At the same time, however, she proposed that the film was really about Kahlo's love for life itself (Lent 2007 71). Perhaps, Taymor saw the two as intimately related, even though Kahlo's relationship with Rivera was a mixture of constructive and destructive elements. As Joan M. and Dennis West suggest, the real mystery of the film is why Kahlo was so determined to stay married to Rivera in spite of his compulsive philandering. The only answer the film offers is that she loved him as he was, which seems shallow given the complexity of their relationship (West and West 2003: 40). Briley even suggests that the film portrays Kahlo as so upset that she could not have a child because she believed a baby would save her relationship with Rivera, as preferring a "conventional bourgeois marriage" to artistic success, and as engaging in a "libertine lifestyle" only as a way to make Rivera jealous (2003: 76). There is no question that Kahlo's attachment to Rivera seems obsessive in the film, but not as much as it appears to have been in real life where she is believed to have undergone surgeries just to attract his sympathy and bring him back to her side. Taymor presents Kahlo's passion for Rivera not so much as obsessive love, but rather as part of her passionate engagement with life itself, a passion that also motivated her art.

Certainly, *Frida* can be criticized for concentrating too much on Kahlo's personal tragedies rather than her artistic talent, making her appear too dependent on Rivera, using English instead of Spanish to increase the film's appeal to U.S. audiences, sending an "implicit message of exoticness through the sexualized commodification of ethnic otherness," emphasizing Kahlo's sexuality over her Communist political affiliation (Guzman 2007: 123,125), refusing to explore her bisexuality (West and West 2003: 40), and glamorizing her pain and suffering (McCracken 2003: 252). On the positive side, however, it unequivocally presents her as an artistic genius, celebrates her embrace of her Mexican ethnicity through her cultivation of Mexicanidad, presents her relationship with Rivera as both constructive and destructive, includes a number of visually stunning representations of her art, and emphasizes her determination to live her life to the fullest despite her disabilities. This is no small feat in the biopic genre, which has the reputation for either failing to represent women at all or presenting them through the lens of victimhood.

Frida may portray its protagonist as a victim in some ways, but it also shows her to be an accomplished artist and a complex, fascinating woman. To see the film simply as a victimology-fetish biopic would be a serious mistake.

Key Terms: *the issue of fidelity, heritage films, post-heritage films, great man biopic, victimology-fetish biopic, revisionist feminist biopic*

Suggestions for Further Reading, Viewing, and Discussion

1. Compare the female biopic to the woman's film, nineteenth-century female-oriented literary adaptations, and the chick flick. What qualities do these different types of female-oriented cinema share?

2. View other nineteenth-century literary adaptations (or adaptations of Austen's novels in particular) and compare them to *Sense and Sensibility*. Do you see them as feminist, anti-feminist, or postfeminist? The selected filmography below offers some suggestions for possible film choices.

3. View more female biopics from different periods and in the various categories outlined by Dennis Bingham. Are they all victimology-fetish biopics or are they more complicated than this? The selected filmography below offers some suggestions for film choices.

4. Should literary adaptations and biopics be considered genres or not?

5. View some of the biopics of male artists mentioned in the chapter. How do they compare/contrast with *Frida*?

6. View a film adaptation of a nineteenth-century novel and read the novel. What major changes were made? Why do you think they were made?

Selected Filmography of Nineteenth-Century Literary Adaptations and Biopics

Clueless (Amy Heckerling, 1995)

Emma (two versions: Douglas McGrath, 1996, TV, Jim O'Hanlon, 2009)

The House of Mirth (Terence Davies, 2000)

Jane Eyre (three versions: Robert Stevenson, 1943; Franco Zeffirelli, 1996; Cary Fukunaga, 2011)

Little Women (three versions: George Cukor, 1933; Mervyn LeRoy, 1949; Gillian Armstrong, 1994)

Mansfield Park (Patricia Rozema, 1999)

Persuasion (two versions: Roger Mitchell, 1995; TV, Adrian Shergold, 2007)

The Portrait of a Lady (Jane Campion, 1996)

Pride and Prejudice (three versions: Robert Z. Leonard, 1940; TV, Simon Langton, 1995; Joe Wright, 2005)

Sense and Sensibility (TV, John Alexander, 2008)

Washington Square (Agnieszka Holland, 1997)

Biopics

Angel at My Table (Jane Campion, 1990)

Elizabeth (Shekhar Kapur, 1996)

Elizabeth: The Golden Age (Shekhar Kapur, 2007)

Elizabeth R (TV, McWhinnie & Whatham, 1971)

Erin Brockovich (Steven Soderbergh, 2000)

I Want to Live! (Robert Wise, 1958)

Lady Sings the Blues (Sidney J. Furie, 1972)

Madame Curie (Mervyn LeRoy, 1943)

The Notorious Bettie Page (Mary Harron, 2006)

The Passion of Joan of Arc (Carl Theodor Dreyer, 1928)

The Private Lives of Elizabeth and Essex (Michael Curtiz, 1939)

The Queen (Stephen Frears, 2006)

Queen Christina (Rouben Mamoulian, 1933)

Rosa Luxemburg (Margarethe Von Trotta, 1986)

The Rosa Parks Story (TV, Julie Dash, 2002)

The Scarlet Empress (Josef von Sternberg, 1934)

The Virgin Queen (Henry Koster, 1955)

What's Love Got To Do With It (Brian Gibson, 1993)

Chapter 6

Feminist Film Studies and Race

Although African American and postcolonial feminist film theory are distinct categories of feminist film scholarship, they share so many ideas and concerns that it seems useful to think of the two approaches together. Although African American theory focuses on the representation of Black women in U.S. films and postcolonial criticism concentrates on a global context, both put race at the forefront of their feminist analyses of film. African American and postcolonial feminist film theory was born in the late 1980s and early 1990s from a feeling of frustration and disappointment, and that feeling was not just in response to the obvious absence and distortion of images of women of color on the screen. It was also based on the perception that feminist film studies was following in the footsteps of cinema itself and ignoring issues related to race. Race-oriented feminist scholars have set out to show exactly how wrong Toril Moi was when she notoriously asserted in her overview of feminist theory, *Sexual/Textual Politics*, that the feminist analysis of race could have no real theoretical significance because it deals with the same theoretical problems and uses the same methodology as White feminism (Thornham 1997: 138). Race-oriented feminist film theory argues in particular that feminist film studies as a whole has not only failed to interrogate the images of women of color on the screen, but has actually worked against the investigation of those images. Two interrelated facets of feminist film studies seem to account for this neglect. First is the conception that White feminism speaks for all women regardless of differences of race, nationality, class, and sexuality, and the second is the feminist reliance on cine-psychoanalysis as a major analytical tool, even though Freud's theories are notoriously blind to national and social differences. In response to this critical neglect, race-oriented feminist critics have set out to make their primary subjects of investigation screen images of African American and Third World women, the works of African American and postcolonial female filmmakers, and the distinctive responses to film texts that characterize women of color.

Although postcolonial and African American feminist film studies are similar in that both share a concern with the issue of race, they diverge in that African American criticism has a unified focus, whereas postcolonial theory is so wide ranging in terms of its object of study that it can be said to lack a clear focus. Its central subject is the films and filmmakers of what have been termed postcolonial nations or the national cinemas of the Third World, but both of these designations are rather murky in terms of definition. Postcolonial nations are generally identified as countries in Asia, Africa, South America, and the Caribbean that fell under European imperialist domination during the nineteenth century and gained their independence as separate nation-states sometime thereafter, but there are a number of problems with this designation. First, it lumps together very different countries under the label postcolonial, which tends to homogenize discordant areas, ignoring the unique issues, problems, and peoples that characterize different countries and even continents. Second, it identifies these diverse areas by their status as former colonies, rather than by their current very different national situations. At the same time, it erroneously implies that once the colonial period was brought to an end and national independence was won, the effects of colonialism, including the extreme poverty in many Third World countries, were completely obliterated (Rajadhyaksha 1998: 413). Ashish Rajadhyaksha suggests that postcolonial theory is so fragmented that its many different areas "do not talk to each other" and terms such as colonial, postcolonial, Third World, imperialism, and neo-colonialism are used in ways that confuse their meanings (1998: 413, 422). There are further problems with the divisions of First (Western nations associated with the United States and Europe), Second (Eastern European nations formerly in the U.S.S.R.), and Third World (everything else). This tripartite division seems too simplistic and tends to promote thinking that "papers over class oppression in all three worlds, while limiting socialism to the now non-existent Second World, ... flattens heterogeneities, masks contradictions, and elides differences" (Shohat 1997: par 8). It also ignores the fact that an important aspect of postcolonial film involves works created by diasporic artists who work outside of their native country. These problems have lead many critics to question whether using concepts such as postcolonial and Third World are even useful ways of thinking about global concerns.

It does appear, however, that many crucial issues concerning the work of a wide range of important filmmakers and the representation of diverse groups of people have been brought together under the umbrella designations of postcolonial or Third World. For this reason, it is important to recognize feminist postcolonial criticism as an important theoretical approach to film studies. As Alison Butler suggests, issues united under the rubric of postcolonial film theory all deal with "the complexities involved, for filmmakers and critics, in posing feminist questions in a world of unequal transnational exchanges" (2002: 123). These issues can be organized into two categories: those related to the effects of colonialism and national identity and those connected to globalism and the transnational. The former issues center on the long-term effects of negative stereotypes imposed on subaltern women under colonial rule, as well as how best to counteract these stereotypes and formulate a new sense of postcolonial female identity. This strain of feminist postcolonialism is heavily influenced by post-World War II nationalist movements in newly emancipated countries. These movements called for indigenous nationalist realism as a filmmaking strategy and for cinematic portrayals that would present the history of newly liberated peoples in a different way that would provide them with authentic self-images in contrast to the negative stereotypes imposed on them under colonial rule (Rajadhyaksha 1998: 417). The advocacy of this approach led to strenuous debate by postcolonial feminist critics concerning whether using realism as a way to create positive images of subaltern woman was a naive and simplistic approach to the fight against colonialist gender stereotypes or whether realism even with its limitations was still a useful strategy at least temporarily to create countermyths against the damaging inferiorization of subaltern people by their colonialist oppressors (Thornham 1997: 153).

A second category of postcolonial feminism moves beyond a backward-looking analysis of the effects of colonial rule to a consideration of the current global and local situations in which the people of the Third World find themselves. This type of postcolonial feminist theory considers transnational issues, such as the roles that Third World and White Western women should play as critics, theorists, and filmmakers in shaping postcolonial criticism and Third World filmmaking. A major stumbling block to the establishment of a productive relationship between First and Third World feminism is White Western women's culpability for supporting colonial and imperialist domination of the Third World and the destructive racist ideology that accompanied it. Classic Western feminism showed itself incapable of considering the differences between the oppressive situations of First and Third World women, and early feminists seemed to believe they could speak for all women. Postcolonial feminist theorists have pointed out that this First World feminist arrogance was racist in origin and that it effectively reduced Third World women to a position of exclusion and silence (McCabe 2004: 68). How to move beyond this unfortunate divisive situation and bring feminist critics and filmmakers of both worlds together to work against patriarchal domination and for women's liberation everywhere is a matter of major concern to postcolonial film theorists.

Postcolonial feminist film studies perhaps because of its neglect within classical feminist thought has drawn heavily on the ideas of postcolonial male thinkers, who do not specifically address the effects on women of colonial rule or women's situations under postcolonial nationalist regimes. Important postcolonial thinkers such as Franz Fanon, Edward Said, and Homi K. Bhabba, who are not feminist per se have contributed important ideas to postcolonial feminist film criticism and theory. Fanon's *Black Skin, White Masks*, first published in 1952, has been particularly influential for its use of psychoanalysis to explain the long-lasting effects of colonial rule and racial oppression on the colonized and how White racism came to structure colonized people's experience of themselves and their world. Fanon proposed that Black men under colonial rule were led to accept idealized images of their White oppressors and to internalize racist notions of their own inferiority. According to Fanon, this inferiorization of the colonial male subject reflects not only the White colonizer's need to justify his oppressive rule but also his insecurity about his own sexual completeness (McCabe 2004: 68–69). Edward Said's concept of Orientalism, coined in his book of the same name, has also had an important impact on feminist film theory. Said used the term to refer to the myths and misconceptions that dominate Western thinking about the East and portray Asian and Middle Eastern men as the antithesis of everything that Western men like to think they are. Thus, Eastern men are characterized as weak, feminized, inferior, and welcoming of Western domination. Building on Said's theory, Homi K. Bhabba developed additional influential ideas that focus on the use of inferiorizing stereotypes as a way to justify the Western conquest and domination of The Third World. In *The Location of Culture*, Bhabba contends that Western myths have characterized colonized men as so savage, sexually insatiable, and anarchic that colonial rule is the only way to control them. Drawing on psychoanalytic theories of voyeurism and scopophilia, Bhabba emphasizes how looking relations establish a disciplinary regime of surveillance that is crucial to the assertion of colonialist power. Expanding on Fanon's concept of the colonized's internalization of an idealized image of the White man, Bhabba developed his theories of mimesis, mimicry, and hybridity. He argued that the imposition of the colonist's culture on subaltern people was not complete. Indigenous peoples melded together their own beliefs and customs with colonial social mores through imitation and mockery to form a hybrid culture that is both similar to and different than that of the colonizer. A final theorist of influence is a woman and a feminist, Gayatri Chakravorty Spivak. Although she does not directly focus on film, her postcolonial feminist work has had a huge impact on film studies. Spivak argues that colonialist powers justified their conquest and domination of the Third World by seeing colonized nations as "previously uninscribed" and completely silencing subaltern peoples, especially women, who are regarded as subjects of oppression and nothing more (1988: 271).

Responding to accusations that classical feminism had ignored African American and Third World women and building on the work of these earlier postcolonial theorists, a number of White feminist film theorists began to investigate cinematic representations of race. Jane Gaines' "White Privilege and Looking Relations," first published in 1986, closely examines White feminist film criticism's failure to deal with racial issues. She was one of the first critics to attribute this failure to White feminists' reliance on psychoanalysis and the concept of patriarchy as analytical tools. Gaines points out that psychoanalysis provided feminist critics with a theoretical framework that actually prevented the investigation of oppressions other than those related to gender. Early feminists' acceptance of Freud's belief that his theories of human psychology are universally applicable made it difficult for them even to contemplate racial or national differences or to imagine that the historical situation of African Americans or colonized peoples might render their psychological makeup considerably different from that of White Westerners (Gaines 1990c: 198–99). Gaines does not see psychoanalysis as the only problem, however. She points out that the centrality of the notion of patriarchy within feminist thought tends to emphasize the male–female split so strongly and to view patriarchal structures as so monolithic and universal that it obscures any notion of other oppressions (1990c: 201). This concept of a universal monolithic patriarchy that effects all women in the same way prevented White Western feminists from recognizing that women of color might see White women as complicit in their oppression and that they might feel their strongest bond is with African American or Third World men. Women of color might well feel that patriarchy is not indigenous to their community or nation, but instead actually represents learned behavior adopted by African American and colonized men in imitation of their White male oppressors (Gaines 1990c: 202–3).

In terms of film in particular, the use of psychoanalysis and the concept of a universal patriarchy led to the feminist theoretical emphasis on gaze theory and the voyeuristic male gaze. Gaze theory posits a monolithic male perspective without any recognition that the power of this gaze is invested not in all men, but in White men, and that the object of this gaze is not all women, but White women. Black men have been traditionally denied the power of the gaze or their exercise of it had been regarded as clandestine and illicit, and the object of the look of all men, whatever their skin color, was always the White woman (1990c: 207). Women of color were relegated to a position of absence, eliminated from the screen entirely as either subject or object of the gaze.

Gaines' insights were expanded by another White feminist critic, Mary Ann Doane. In "Dark Continents: epistemologies of racial and sexual difference in psychoanalysis and the cinema," Doane argues for a similarity between the way White women and Black men are envisioned in the White male unconscious. Using a psychoanalytic approach, she contends that both embody castration for the White male, but in different ways. The White woman evokes lack, loss, and absence, whereas the Black man represents excessive sexuality, the overpresence of the penis, and hypermasculinity. Thus, they offer a similar threat to White manhood and must be brought under control through the constant surveillance of the White male gaze. As both Black and female, the Black woman signifies a double threat; therefore, she is almost completely eliminated from the screen, or when she is rarely portrayed, she is equated, as Freud's "dark continent" metaphor suggests, with a promiscuous hypersexual primitiveness that connects her to the natural landscape. In this way, the White colonialist imagination could brand her inferior and justify the exploitation and domination not only of the Black woman but of the African continent itself (Doane 1991: 212–13).

Tania Modleski in "Cinema and the Dark Continent: race and gender in popular film," first published in 1991, took another important step in going beyond just pointing to Black women's absence from the screen. She argues that when women of color have been portrayed it has always been in stereotypical images that reduce them to their biological functions or present them only as surrogates for White women (Modleski 1999: 133). For instance, the mammy figure reduces Black women to figures of reproduction and motherhood and the sexually voracious Black woman presents them stereotypically in terms of images of female sexuality (Modleski 1999: 330–31). Developing on Gaines' ideas, Modleski proposes that White feminist critics have "locked the door" that prevents women of color from joining with them to overturn patriarchal ideology, so it is the responsibility of White feminists to work to open that door and initiate studies of the role of race in film (1999: 334).

One White feminist who has tried to open that door by moving from the analysis of images of women in Western film to postcolonial theory is E. Ann Kaplan. In *Looking for the Other*, Kaplan extended her earlier work on the male cinematic gaze to theorize the Western imperialist gaze. Kaplan argues that the two types of looking relations are similar in that both involve surveillance of the Other, either the female or the non-Western Other. This surveillance establishes an unquestioned sense of White male superiority and domination in which the look of the White male establishes his sense of mastery and control either over foreign lands, indigenous populations, or women through the power of his gaze, a gaze that those subjected to it are not allowed to return. Kaplan sees contemporary Third World women filmmakers producing new ways of looking beyond the dominant male and imperialist gaze. She proposes that these new looking relations are based on the mutual gaze found in the mother–child relationship, and they involve cross-cultural, inter-racial, non-hierarchical ways of looking that refuse to objectify or stereotype the Other, but instead promote dialogue between different races and cultures. Kaplan points in particular to Julie Dash, Clare Denis, Pratibha Parmar, Gurinder Chadha, and Trinh T. Minh-ha as diasporic female filmmakers working to develop this new cinematic gaze (1997: 292–303). In *Trauma Culture*, Kaplan extends this argument to apply to Western filmmakers, who she argues must give up the traditional ethnographic approach to representing the traumatic situations faced by women globally both in the past and present and instead adopt a strategy of what she calls "translation." She envisions critics and filmmakers from different cultures acting as "embodied translators" and trying to convey the experiences of one culture to another by "a sort of feeling out toward the other culture (something which is very different from the condescending stance of traditional ethnographic cinema)." This is not a case of "two known fixed entities" exchanging ideas, but one in which representatives from both cultures create new meanings and "forge new subjectivities in the process of their movement across borders" (Kaplan 2005: 104).

Women of color have not left it entirely to White women to open that door to African American and postcolonial film criticism. Two African American feminist film critics in particular have been extremely influential in developing the investigation of images of Black women on screen, approaches to the work of Black women filmmakers, and theories about the Black female audience. Foremost among these is unquestionably bell hooks, whose "The Oppositional Gaze: Black female spectators," first published in 1992, is perhaps the single most significant expression of African American feminist film theory. hooks reiterates Gaines's criticism of White feminist film theorists for ignoring race, positing gender as the only source of women's oppression, allowing their psychoanalytic framework to obscure socio-historical differences among women, and creating a monolithic universal category of woman that equates all womanhood with White womanhood. hooks goes beyond Gaines in two ways: she proposes the important theoretical concept of the oppositional gaze, and she argues that greater consideration must be given to the work of Black female filmmakers.

hooks' concept of the oppositional gaze is an extremely important one because it ties together the crucial issues of the representation of Black female characters on screen, the importance of the Black female filmmaker, and the need to analyze the distinctive reactions of the Black female audience. hooks proposes that the African American oppositional gaze had its origins in slavery when Blacks were forbidden to look and were forced to usurp that right in order to challenge White portrayals of reality (1993: 288–89). This "illicit" looking is quite different for female as opposed to male African American spectators because the Black male gaze adopts the structures of looking characteristic of White males and takes as its object the White woman (hooks 1993: 290–91). The oppositional gaze that characterizes Black female spectatorship assumes a very different, much more subversive form in reaction to the "violent erasure" of Black womanhood from mainstream film. According to hooks, Black women in film are not allowed to look or to be looked at; these spectatorial viewing positions are reserved for White men and White women respectively. Black women function primarily to validate White supremacy, their presence on screen serving only to enhance the to-be-looked-at-ness and ultra-Whiteness of the White female star (hooks 1993: 291).

In reaction to this situation, hooks proposes that Black female spectators adopt one of three possible viewing positions: they either refuse to watch entirely, become what hooks calls "gaslighted," or adopt the oppositional gaze. The first group sees the portrayals of African Americans on screen as an assault on their self-image and in a gesture of resistance simply refuse to watch mainstream films at all. The second "gaslighted" group is composed of avid moviegoers who turn off their critical sensibility and refuse to critique the images they see on the screen; instead, they adopt what hooks calls an adoring gaze that identifies with the images of Whiteness projected on the screen or a masochistic gaze that wallows in their own cinematic victimization (hooks 1993: 293). The final category of Black feminist spectators does not shut down critique but rather enhances it by adopting the oppositional gaze. They choose not to identify with the cinematic construction of White womanhood as the object of the phallocentric look, and reject both the perpetrators and victims of that look. Through the strategy of distanciation, they divorce themselves from the images they see on the screen and read them against the grain, gaining viewing pleasure from deconstructing cinematic images of Whites and interrogating negative images of Blacks (hooks 1993: 295). Thus, they become not just resisting spectators, but creators of alternative cinematic texts. Rather than just reacting to racist and sexist film images, they project their own desires in terms of both race and gender on the screen (hooks 1993: 300). hooks does not confine her focus to the Black female spectator, however. She concludes her essay by shifting to the African American female filmmaker, whom she sees as being offered the unique opportunity to disrupt conventional racist and sexist representations of Black womanhood and to invite the female spectator to look differently using the deconstructive film practice suggested by the oppositional gaze (hooks 1993: 302).

Another African American critic whose ideas have been extremely influential is Jacqueline Bobo, who, like hooks, focuses in particular on the Black female spectator. In *Black Women as Cultural Readers* and in her earlier essay "Reading Through the Text: the Black woman as audience", Bobo centers her argument on African American female spectators' responses to Stephen Spielberg's film adaptation of Alice Walker's *The Color Purple*. Bobo proposes that Spielberg systematically undercut the feminism of Walker's portrayal of Black women to make the film not about race and the empowerment of Black womanhood, but about the Black man's journey to self-understanding (1993: 272). For Bobo, Spielberg replaces the strong African American female characters of the novel with negative stereotypes like the overbearing matriarch (Sophia), sexually insatiable temptress (Shug), and pathetic victim (Celie) (1993: 275). Celie (Whoopi Goldberg), the abused Black woman who gains a sense of economic independence and self-worth in the book and is unquestionably its protagonist, loses that role in the film to her abusive husband "Mister" (Danny Glover), whose moral development becomes the film's major concern (Bobo 1993: 272, 281). As I have pointed out elsewhere, Spielberg even said in interviews that he did not see the film as about race, but about the triumph of the human spirit, so he divested the plot as much as possible of Walker's attacks on White racism, instead making the female characters victims of "Mister," the film's Black male villain (Hollinger 1998a: 183). Spielberg then went on to center the story on the reformation of this Black male villain who comes to represent the transformation of an oppressive into a benevolent patriarchy. In so doing, he removed the novel's advocacy of Black women's independence, self-worth, and solidarity as means of combating both patriarchy and racism and bringing about a social reformation based on feminist values (Hollinger 1998a: 190). In place of these themes, Spielberg substituted an emphasis on sentimental sisterly affection, a heightening of the novel's emotionality, a feel-good affirmation of a reformed patriarchy, and a female-affirmative message of personal rather than collective empowerment (Hollinger 1998a: 190–91). As Bobo points out, in spite of these changes, which largely eviscerated Walker's novel of its radical feminist content, African American female viewers still responded very positively to the film in a way that illustrates almost perfectly what hooks describes as the oppositional gaze. They created an alternate text that extracts the positive images of Black women from the film and relates those images to their own lives and to other positive Black female images found in contemporary literature by Black women authors (hooks 1993: 285).

One might argue that if African American women can exercise the oppositional gaze it is almost inconsequential what images are actually presented to them on the screen. Regardless of what images are offered to her, the Black female spectator can use her oppositional gaze to render these images affirmatory for her, but Bobo does not end on that note; instead, she concludes with the question of what *The Color Purple* would have been like if it were made by a Black female director. In a 1991 essay entitled "Black Feminism and Media Criticism: *The Women of Brewster Place*" which Bobo co-wrote with Ellen Seiter, she and Seiter actually outline what that type of film might look like. They point to White filmmaker Donna Deitch's television version of *The Women of Brewster Place* as an effective adaptation of Black author Gloria Naylor's novel. According to Bobo and Seiter, the made-for-television film resists conventional television images of Black women by refusing to portray them as having a natural connection to sexuality, serving Whites as loyal domestics, or acting as domineering or restraining forces within the Black family. *The Women of Brewster Place* challenges these stereotypical images by showing instead the economic and social roots of women's oppression, emphasizing the importance of relationships among Black women as a means of sustaining their resistance to oppression, and transforming the genres of soap opera and maternal melodrama to suit an African American context (Bobo and Seiter 1991: 140). Bobo and Seiter suggest that the works of Black female novelists, if adapted effectively, can thus provide a source of positive images for Black female filmmakers.

Lola Young, on the other hand, writing from a Black British perspective, rejects the positive image approach to the representation of Black women. In contrast to African American feminists, she sees psychoanalysis as potentially useful in examining how race, gender and sexuality have been linked to each other and to issues of power, control and subjugation, all of which have been mapped onto the Black female body. In *Fear of the Dark: "race," gender, and sexuality in the cinema*, Young examines eight films that were made in Britain between 1959 and 1987 and that deal with racial issues. According to Young, these films all relate to White fears and anxieties about miscegenation, the stability of the family, and an assumed oppositional relation between Blacks and Whites (1996: 4). She attempts to develop a framework through which to study British cinematic representations of Blacks by using psychoanalysis in conjunction with an analysis of historical, social and cinematic discourses on gender and sexuality. Young sees these discourses as having been racialized by ideas from Britain's colonialist imperialist past. She criticizes the positive images approach to the filmic representation of race for relying on a realist conception of film images which involves "reductionist simplifications" that actually reify the very stereotypes the approach tries to denounce (1996: 9). Young proposes that films need to be seen as constructs and fabrications that are historically related to ideological beliefs of the time when they were made, rather than as authentic representations of reality (1996: 8). She sees stereotypical representations of African Americans in U.S. films as connected strongly to the experience of slavery and its effects, whereas British representations of Blacks are more related to the historical context of British colonialism and imperialist conquest (Young 1996: 10). Although she does point out that cinematic images of Blacks "obsessively repeat well-worn stereotypes of black femininity and masculinity," Young believes it is naive to call for truthful, positive, or realistic images or to ask Black filmmakers to speak with the "authentic voice of 'the black experience'" (1996: 36–37).

Like African American feminist critics, Young also critiques White feminist claims for what she calls an "undifferentiated interracial sisterhood in the name of women's liberation." Like her African American counterparts, she sees these calls for female solidarity as marred by a lack of racial awareness and conscious or unconscious racism (Young 1996: 13). For instance, she points to how White feminists' advocacy of women's right to choose abortion to terminate an unwanted pregnancy and their critique of the nuclear family as a major component of women's oppression ignore the fact that Black women see the family not as a locus of oppression, but as a source of strength in a hostile world (Young 1996: 14). Like hooks, Young argues that the work of White feminists has been "impoverished through being unable to take cognizance of white women's collusion in racial oppression, their relatively privileged social status and the way in which this is manifested in visual culture" (1996: 33).

Using a psychoanalytic approach similar to Doane's, Young links Black women's comparative absence from the screen to the double threat they present to the White male viewer. She points out that because the Black woman is different from the White man in terms of race as well as gender, she represents a "double negation of the white, male self which underlies the notion of sexual and racial difference" (Young 1996: 20). Young proposes that psychoanalysis is actually quite useful in analyzing how White fears of racial and sexual difference became conflated in conceptions of the "Otherness" of both Blackness and womanhood. She sees this conception of Otherness in particular in Black women's stereotypical characterization as less civilized, less rigorously controlled sexually, and more prone to excessive sexual expression. Young connects all of these stereotypes to the repressed sexual longings and desires of Whites, both male and female, rather than to any reality of Black sexuality (1996: 23). Drawing on the ideas of Franz Fanon, Young also uses psychoanalysis to examine the role of film in constructing the Black internalization of racial stereotypes. She points out that films often work to add to feelings of inadequacy and inferiority among Blacks, feelings that have their origin in the heritage of colonialism and imperialism. She also sees psychoanalysis as useful in thinking about the psychic processes that underpin White fantasies about Blacks, the absence from the Black psyche of the Oedipal complex and other neuroses common among Whites, and how White racism structures the Black experience of the world (Young 1996: 24–25). In addition, Young uses Fanon's psychoanalytically influenced concept of Blacks as phobogenic, stimulating anxiety in Whites, to explain why White filmmakers are reluctant to include Black characters or address Black issues. Drawing as well on the work of Homi Bhabha, Young argues that the Black Other represents a threat to the White male's self-definition and his fallacy of psychic wholeness (1996: 29). She finds the psychoanalytic concept of projection particularly useful in explaining how racist cinematic portrayals allow the White male viewer to transfer to a despised racial group his own "intolerable passions and inclinations" (Young 1996: 31).

In an essay co-authored with Claire Pajaczkowska, Young describes further the possible uses she sees for psychoanalysis to examine "how deeply racism permeates not only the institutions of a post-colonial society like Britain, but also the way in which we experience ourselves and others" (2000: 356). For instance, Pajaczkowska and Young see the concept of trauma as particularly useful to an examination of American slavery and colonialist oppression. As defined in psychoanalytical thought, trauma represents an event significant for its intensity, the subject's inability to respond adequately to it, and its long-lasting effects on the victim's psyche. Both slavery and colonialism certainly fit with this definition, and their status as deeply traumatic events helps explain why they can never be represented adequately on the screen (Pajaczkowska and Young 2000: 358). The psychoanalytic concepts of introjection, projection, and the Oedipus complex can be used to demonstrate how deeply imbedded within the psyche of the White racist is the need "to maintain violently exploitive structures of identification" (Pajaczkowska and Young 2000: 359–60). Finally, the concept of disavowal, used as a defense against painful, disturbing, and troubling knowledge, can help explain the widespread negative reaction of so many Whites when they are asked to consider the reality of racism (Pajaczkowska and Young 2000: 359). To explain how Whites have justified the brutal treatment of people of color under slavery and colonial rule, Young and Pajaczkowska develop the term "Negrophobia" and suggest that its victims can use literary and film texts to counteract the negrophobic stereotypes that have been imposed on them. By employing film and literature as versions of Freud's talking cure, African American and indigenous peoples can overcome "historical amnesia and national disavowal," deal with unspeakable trauma, understand their repressed memories, and begin to regain a sense of cultural self-identity (Pajaczkowska and Young 2000: 372).

It seems clear that Young does not just rely on psychoanalysis to ground her ideas; instead, she gives them strong historical underpinnings, tracing images of Blacks and especially of Black women back to racist conceptions used to justify British colonialist imperialist domination. She sees contemporary British cinema as having inherited from colonialist imperialist discourse notions of Blacks as possessing fixed, inferior characteristics that render them primitive, infantile, atavistic, and sexually uncontrolled/excessive. British films have also strongly condemned miscegenation for destroying the purity of the country's White racial composition and its "self-contained, 'pure' white family" (Young 1996: 48, 84). Black women are seen as a particular threat to the purity of the white family, and their absence or lowly status in film is used to accentuate the privileged status of the White woman (Young 1996: 53). An implicit cinematic contrast is set up between White and Black women, with the latter presented as not as fully or purely female as the former. Black women are portrayed as highly sexualized, associated with reproduction, and branded as subordinate. They are presented as women in a sense, yet not women in the same way as White women are because they are regarded as "not pure, not feminine, not fragile, but strong and sexually knowing and available" (Young 1996: 64).

The most significant postcolonial feminist theorist is the diasporic Vietnamese filmmaker and critic Trinh T. Minh-ha. Her two books, *Woman, Native, Other* and *When the Moon Waxes Red: representation, gender and cultural politics,* outline her major theories of postcolonial female identity and the role of the film theorist, critic and filmmaker in representing Third World women. Trinh proposes that there is no authentic postcolonial female identity that can be captured in film because Third World women's sense of self is shaped by fragmentation, hybridity, and in-betweenness. For Trinh, it is impossible to express a single true sense of self because all identities are multiple. There is no true self to be discovered beneath surface layers of false identities, but the self is actually composed of infinite layers, none of which is more or less authentic than the other. She proposes that the idea of difference, which means "difference within as well as between," undermines the very notion of a true or authentic identity (Trinh 1989: 96). At the same time that Trinh denies the existence of a stable identity, she also proposes that the postcolonial subject must resist, reverse, and displace Western hegemonic positions that naturalize and universalize the dominant Western world view and relegate other cultures to the unknowable realm of the Other (1991: 74). In order to dislodge Western ideas from their hegemonic position, Trinh proposes that a new conception of subjectivity, which she calls a "subject-in-process," must be constructed. The "subject-in-process" is never stable; it is "always constituting itself from a multiplicity of identities, truths, and voices, separate but interdependent, which defies easy classification within conventional categories of race, gender, and national identity" (Trinh 1991: 48). The role of the filmmaker and critic is to put this new conception of subjectivity into practice by refusing to speak for or about the Other, but instead "speaking nearby" by never claiming to know the Other, just establishing a closeness that always recognizes distance and difference. "Speaking nearby" is "a speaking that does not objectify, does not point to an object as if it is distant from the speaking subject or absent from the speaking place. A speaking that reflects on itself and can come very close to a subject without, however, seizing or claiming it" (Trinh and Chen 1992: 87).

Trinh does not see the postcolonial critic or filmmaker as speaking from a more authoritative position in comparison to that of the West. She believes that all filmmakers must employ radical film techniques that represent "strategies of dislocation and displacement, juxtaposing techniques of fiction and documentary, history and storytelling, and refusing viewers a singular viewpoint" (Thornham 1997:155). In her two most critically praised films, *Rassemblage* (1986) and *Surname Viet Given Name Nam* (1989), she does just this. She attempts to create new ways of knowing about different cultures. In the former film, the West African culture that is presented is not her own, whereas in the later, it is her native Vietnam. In both films, she employs but also works against the conventions of the ethnographic documentary, offering multiple voices and images and very deliberately constructing a disjunction of sound and image intended to disrupt conventional spectatorial processes and challenge viewers to make their own meaning and even in a sense assemble their own film.

Trinh emphasizes formally innovative strategies of filmmaking which she believes can be used by the postcolonial filmmaker to break with stereotypes of the Third World, but other critics have stressed the need for films simply to offer more representations of people of color and for Western feminists to show a greater sensitivity to the different situations and concerns of Third World women. In looking at portrayals of African women in film and fiction, Lisbeth Gant-Britton, for example, argues that White Western feminists often fail to understand how different the concerns of African women are from their own. First, there is the problem of integrating Western ideas with traditional African culture. Western audiences often do not understand why African women on screen find it so hard to fit into modern urban society, why they are so determined to fulfill their traditional responsibilities to husbands and families, and why they feel so reluctant to give up their traditional and familial support structures. Western viewers do not understand that African women are still expected to have many children, to be totally responsible for child care, and to contribute to food production for their large families. Anti-colonialist struggles for national independence have not often recognized the need to change traditional views and customs in regard to women, so African women for the most part suffer from their status as second-class citizens and their lack of access to leadership positions. An added problem is that, when filmmakers focus on women's oppressive treatment in postcolonial society, this contributes all the more to negative Western stereotypes of Third World nations as less evolved than those of the West and to the tendency to portray the situation of all Third World women exclusively in terms of victimization. Representing postcolonial women as hypervictimized and without power or agency within their societies also tends to place the focus entirely on gender oppression, ignoring the social and political conditions of all Third World people.

Ella Shohat, an Israeli-American critic who has written extensively on cinematic representations of Third World women, characterizes postcolonial women's cinema as launching a two-pronged attack that challenges both traditional feminism and postcolonialism, both of which have relegated the oppression of Third World women to the bottom of their agendas. Shohat argues that, now that Third World nations have established their independence and the European empire has fallen, a new post-Third World era has begun in which the voices of postcolonial feminist filmmakers are being expressed all the more strongly. Post-Third-Worldist feminist film accepts the "funda-mental validity of the anticolonial movement, but also interrogates the divisions that rend the Third-World nation," especially in regard to gender. Thus, it challenges the "masculinist contours of the 'nation'" in order to draw atten-tion to the fact that although the "macronarrative of women's liberation has long since subsided yet sexism and heterosexism prevail, and in an age when the metanarratives of anticolonial revolution have long since been eclipsed yet (neo) colonialism and racism persist" (Shohat 1997: par 5). Post-Third-Worldist feminist filmmakers attack nationalists' "sentimental defense of patriarchal social institutions simply because they are 'ours' ... [as] hardly emancipatory" and argue that Third World nationalist movements have covered over their inherently masculinist and heterosexist discriminatory practices under the banner of national liberation (Shohat 1997: par 9, 11). Moving beyond the anti-colonialist focus of earlier films and the "Third-Worldist euphoria" over the success of nationalist independence movements, post-Third-Worldist fem-inists have begun to express deep concerns about issues that affect women in Third World countries. They criticize anti-colonialist Third World films that make women "carry the 'burden' of national allegory" as symbols of the nation itself, assume a fundamentally unified national identity that ignores issues of "gender, class, ethnicity, region, partition, migration, and exile," and refuse to acknowledge "the layered, dissonant identities of diasporic or post-independence feminist subjects" (Shohat 1997: 14, 24). Shohat argues that post-Third-Worldist feminist fimmakers express a deep skepticism of "'purely' feminist or 'purely' nationalist discourses" as well as grand metanarratives of all kinds in favor of "heteroglossic proliferations of difference within polygeneric narratives, seen not as embodiments of a single truth but as emerging political and aesthetic forms of communitarian self-construction" (1997: par 30).

In the Films in Focus section of this chapter we will examine African American filmmaker Julie Dash's short film *Illusions* (1983) and diasporic Indian filmmaker Deepa Mehta's post-Third-Worldist feminist film *Fire* (1996). Both films illustrate well how contemporary African American and postcolonial female directors are incorporating feminist theoretical ideas directly into their films and constructing complex and challenging representations of racial and gender issues.

Films in Focus 1: *Illusions*

For a short film with a running time of only 34 minutes, Julie Dash's *Illusions* has received a remarkable amount of critical attention. The reason seems clear: the film puts into filmic form many of the major ideas of African American feminist film theory. Dash's later film *Daughters of the Dust* (1991), the first feature-length film directed by an African American woman to receive mainstream distribution, has garnered greater attention, but *Illusions* "offers a more complex vision and theoretical analysis of Black women's cinema, of the responsibilities and challenges confronting Black women in the contemporary fimmaking industry, and of strategies for negotiating these. No other Black women's film offers as insightful and expansive a view of the political vision informing Black feminist filmmaking" (Ryan 2004: 1320). *Illusions* was the first in a projected series of films that Dash said she hoped to make portraying the lives of African American women beginning at the turn of the century and extending into the future (Klotman 1991a: 192). The series was intended to portray Black women at pivotal moments in their lives and crucial times in U.S. history and to show their experiences as they never have been seen before, with the focus placed on Black women's intraracial relationships rather than on their victimization by White society (Davis 1991: 111, 115).

The series is yet to be completed. Chronologically, *Daughters of the Dust* represents the first in the series, is considered by many critics to be Dash's masterpiece, and has in many ways overshadowed her earlier film. Set in 1902, *Daughters* deals with the struggles of a Gullah family with particular emphasis on its female members as they prepare to move to the mainland from the Sea Islands off the coast of Georgia and South Carolina. Critics praise the film for its sumptuous visuals and representation of Black women, but Dash's uncompromising vision, which includes the use of the Gullah dialect by all the characters, limited the film's audience significantly. Dash directed two other films that can be seen as part of the series, although I have not seen evidence that she considers them as such: *The Rosa Parks Story*, her made-for-television biopic of the famous civil rights figure of the 1950s and *Brothers of the Borderland* (2004), a short film made for the National Underground Railroad Freedom Center Museum that chronicles the flight of a slave woman to freedom.

Written and directed by Dash and set in the Hollywood film industry during World War II, *Illusions* tells the story of Mignon Dupree (Lonette McKee), a Black film executive who is passing for White. As a tale of passing, the film fits into a narrative form with a long history and a mixed critical reception. The traditional passing plot "focuses on the consequences of being genotypically black for a character or characters who pass for white, at least intermittently" (Smith 1994: 43). The most critically praised novel employing the plot formula is Nella Larsen's *Passing* and the most acclaimed film is *Imitation of Life*, which has had two notable incarnations: John Stahl's 1934 film staring Claudette Colbert and Louise Beavers and Douglas Sirk's 1959 technicolor cinemascope extravaganza staring Lana Turner and Juanita Moore. Passing stories conventionally follow a timeworn formula with four recurring elements:

1. A light-skinned Black is motivated to pass for White in order to benefit from the wider financial and social opportunities available in a White-dominated society, but the narrative presents the character's motivations for passing as a desire to be White, rather than simply to be rich and successful.
2. The plot presupposes that in passing the Black character is abandoning and betraying his or her race.
3. The Black mother takes on major significance as a sympathetic figure who has been abandoned by her child. She serves as a symbol of the warmth and security of the Black home and the beauty of maternal love and self-sacrifice, all of which the passing character has callously rejected. The mother is an ambivalent figure, however, in that she also embodies the limited opportunities imposed on Blacks by White racism.
4. In the end, the passing character is punished for transgressing racial boundaries by having his or her true racial identity discovered, and as a result, being rejected by White society, losing status and wealth, returning in disgrace to the Black community, suffering the loss of a loved one, and/ or dying (Smith 1994: 44).

As is clear from this plot formula, the passing tale can be quite regressive in its ideological content, but Dash takes a revisionist approach, doing all she can to fashion the story into a progressive form. Some critics have seen her as successful in this revisionist endeavor, while others have not. S.V. Hartman and Farah Jasmine Griffin see the passing formula as so unremittingly racist in its overall message that its reactionary implications cannot be overcome. In their extremely negative evaluation of *Illusions*, they argue that Dash tries to exploit the subversive possibilities of the passing tale without challenging its essential message, which for Hartman and Griffin is aimed at a White audience and seeks to instill in them a sympathetic response to the passing character. This sympathy is intended to lead to a greater understanding of the negative effects of White racism (Hartman and Griffin 1991: 371). In order to accomplish this end, Hartman and Griffin believe tales of passing set up their passing characters as "White Negroes" who are superior to the rest of their race, and they accuse Dash of doing just this with her protagonist Mignon Dupree. Mignon is someone with whom Hartman and Griffin believe Black viewers find it difficult to identify because she is portrayed as superior to them. The Black audience identifies more strongly with Ester Jeeter (Rosanne Katon), the young Black singer who is being exploited by the studio where Mignon is employed. Ester is being paid to dub the voice of the studio's White star in an upcoming film, but she will not be given screen credit for her performance. Mignon tries to help Ester as much as she can by making sure that she is paid fairly, but Ester is still portrayed as a victim of the studio's racist exploitation of Black talent. Hartman and Griffin argue that the Black spectator's rejection of Mignon as a "White Negro" and identification with the victimized Ester leads them to associate Blackness with exploitation, subordination, and inferiority (1991: 370). For Hartman and Griffin, no matter how much Dash revises the passing story it can only promote internalized racism and a sense of self-hatred in the Black viewer.

Other critics are less condemnatory of the passing plot and of Dash's attempted revision of its basic components. For instance, Valerie Smith sees tales of passing as contradictory in their ideological implications, rather than as inherently racist. Smith points out that not all passing plots end with the complete punishment of their protagonist. For male characters who pass, the ultimate consequences are often less dire than for female characters. The text might still condemn his use of passing as a strategy to combat racism, but it allows its protagonist to repudiate his attempt to pass in White society without any major repercussions, return to the Black community re-educated and pre-pared to uplift his race, or even to remain in White society with some measure of success. Smith also points out that passing stories present a strangely ambivalent conception of race, portraying racial boundaries as both insurmountable and indistinct (1994: 45). The Black protagonist's attempt to pass for White is seen as attempting the impossible, yet at the same time the character is also shown to be proving by the very act of passing that one cannot so easily determine racial difference from visual appearances. Smith concludes, there-fore, that the passing tale might actually represent a productive site for considering "the intersectionality of race, class, and gender ideologies," as well as their transgression. She believes Dash's revision of this plot does just this. It reverses the traditional passing narrative to construct passing as a subversive rather than a shameful activity (Smith 1994: 43).

A close examination of Dash's film shows that her revision of the traditional passing plot is extensive. As Smith points out, unlike the major characters in traditional passing narratives, Mignon does not repudiate her connection to African American culture and history (1994: 52). The telephone conversation she has with her mother after meeting Ester makes this very clear. Ester's description of her relationship with her mother, who loyally waits outside the studio for her whenever she has a singing assignment, parallels Mignon's tele-phone call to her own mother. Through this phone call, Mignon affirms her continued connection to her Black maternal roots. Dash makes this explicit when Mignon explains to her mother that her passing is not entirely inten-tional (Gibson-Hudson 1994: 372). She says she never told anyone she was White, but "They didn't ask [if she was Black] and I didn't tell them." Mignon also makes it clear to her mother that her motives for passing are not selfish and that she has not lost her sense of her Black identity (Ramanathan 2006: 54). She says she is passing in order to gain the power within the film industry she needs to be able to work for more positive cinematic representations of African Americans. Hartman and Griffin point out that throughout this con-versation, Mignon's mother is both unseen and voiceless (we only hear Mignon's side of the conversation). Thus, like Julius, Mignon's Black fiancé, whose picture she keeps but whom we never see or hear, Mignon's mother is a symbol of Black "discursive impotence," vulnerability, and passivity (Hartman and Griffin 1991: 367). It is this discursive impotence that Mignon is trying to overcome by passing as White in order to gain the power within the film industry to speak for all African Americans. Thus, Mignon uses passing not as a betrayal of Black culture, but as a way to help bring about greater racial equality. Her reasons for passing break yet another convention of the tradi-tional passing plot. Her primary motivation is not a selfish desire for financial success and material comfort. She passes to work for her race, not to reject it in order to attain wealth or social status.

Another convention of the passing tale that Dash rejects is its concluding punishment of the passing character. At the end of *Illusions*, Mignon does not lose a loved one, relinquish status or wealth, return to the Black community in disgrace, or die; instead, Dash creates an ambiguous ending that takes the film in a direction very unlike conventional passing stories. Traditional passing narratives end as cautionary tales warning Blacks to stay in their place because any attempt to move into White society represents a denial of their African American community and is doomed ultimately to bring about only failure and misery. The denouement of *Illusions* is much more complex. To fully under-stand it, we must go back to the film's climax when Mignon's racial identity is discovered by Lt. Bedsford (Jack Rader), a military officer whose exact role at the studio is never entirely explained. What is clear is that he is sexually attracted to Mignon. He finds the photo she keeps of her Black fiancé and never even considers that she might be a White woman involved with a Black man. He simply assumes that "to be entangled in black sexuality is to be black" (Hartman and Griffin 1991: 365) and concludes that Mignon must be passing. When he angrily confronts her with his discovery, rather than being devastated, as heroines in conventional passing plots are, Mignon fights back, delivering a searing indictment of a racist film industry that has denied her "participation in the history of this country." She declares, "I'm not ashamed of who I am, Lieutenant."

The film ends with Mignon's voice-over prophecy: "We would meet again, Ester Jeeter and I, for it was she who helped me see beyond shadows dancing on a white wall; to define what I had already come to know, and to take action without fearing. Yes, I wanted to use the power of the motion picture, for there are many stories to be told and many battles to begin." This enigmatic conclusion suggests that Mignon intends to continue to work as a production executive at National Studios, even though it is unlikely that in 1942, when the film is set, someone who is discovered to be a Black woman passing for White would be kept on in an executive position. Mignon seems to believe, however, that she will not only keep her position, but that because she has now witnessed Ester's exploitation by the studio she will be inspired to work all the harder to use her influence to bring about more positive representations of African Americans on the screen. Mignon's prophecy even suggests that she will be instrumental in creating a film career for Ester. As Harman and Griffin point out, however, it is difficult to accept the idea that the discovery of Mignon's Black identity will actually bring about her greater empowerment (1991: 368). The film's ending can be seen as a deliberate anachronism on Dash's part to move her story from history to autobiography. As Judylyn Ryan suggests, the ending seems to be Dash's attempt to establish a connection with her heroine by having Mignon end by "ventriloquisting" Dash and declaring her intention to "stay right here and fight" (2004: 1322). In this way, Dash makes a strong association between contemporary Black female film-makers, including herself, who seek to refashion images of Black women on screen, and Mignon, whose determination to bring about change prefigures their endeavors.

Dash's refashioning of the traditional passing plot accords with a number of ideas expressed by African American film theorists. It involves a strong emphasis on female bonding, a repudiation of the male gaze, and a devastating critique of Hollywood filmmaking. At the center of *Illusions* is the relationship that develops between Mignon and Ester as they unite in reaction to the studio's racist policies. Mignon Dupree is a character Dash constructed as a revision not just of female characters in passing narratives, but of traditional screen representations of Black women in general. Mignon is strong, intelligent, ambitious, supportive of other Black women, passionate about transforming Hollywood filmmaking, and neither defined by service to Whites, nor subservience to men. Even with a minuscule budget, Dash managed to get Lonette McKee, an actress on her way to developing an established Hollywood career, to take the part of Mignon without pay and to fit it into her schedule between other projects (Klotman 1991b 193). It seems clear that Dash felt a strong attachment to Mignon's character, especially to her determination to make important films that challenge racism and are empowering for Black audiences.

At the same time, Mignon is in many ways a flawed character who does not reveal her true thoughts or identity. She is first introduced in the film wearing a veil, which takes on symbolic significance both as the shield she has constructed to mask her true racial identity and the intractable racial barrier that separates White from Black society. It is a mask that she is reluctant to remove and an obstacle that she has not really overcome (Gibson-Hudson 1994: 371). In many ways, Mignon is not much different than Ester. She wants to make images that challenge the status quo, but when she presents her ideas to the studio head, he summarily rejects them. In a sense, she is in an even worse situation than Ester because not only is she denied the opportunity to speak in her true Black voice, but when she does speak, her voice is totally ignored. As noted above, she is also a problematic figure of identification for the Black female spectator because by denying her race, or as she sees it, neglecting to reveal it, she has maneuvered herself into a place of social privilege that African American women are in reality routinely denied. As a result, Hartman and Griffin insist she inspires not admiration in Black female spectators, but instead instills in them a feeling of inferiority and self-hatred. Thus, they say the only "healthy response to her for black women viewers is rejection" (Hartman and Griffin 1994: 372).

Hartman and Griffin's reaction to Mignon seems rather harsh. Should Mignon really be seen as a total sellout, who is making no progress at all? She at least does get to express her views to the studio head, and although she does not have enough clout to get Ester the credit she deserves for her singing, she is able to assure that she is fairly paid. By the film's conclusion, she seems to have developed into an heroic figure through whom the film's major themes are expressed. She not only stands up for Ester and forms a bond of sisterhood with her, but also refuses to be intimidated by Lt. Bedsford, one of the film's major symbols of White male authority. She will not let his discovery of her racial identity destroy her; instead, it only makes her stronger and more passionate in her desire to pursue her ambitions and goals. Her determination to change the images projected on the screen remains undiminished, and she comes to realize that her goals are unlikely to be attained by the strategy she has heretofore adopted. Expressing a determination to move in new directions in her struggle to reform Hollywood filmmaking and the racist social structure that it supports, Mignon comes to represent bell hooks' oppositional gaze put into action. She launches a strong attack on Hollywood cinema for propagating images of African Americans and other marginalized groups that support White supremacy and racism. Her attack is not only on Hollywood for eliminating alternative images from the screen, but also on American society itself for excluding marginalized people from the culture as a whole. Mignon's ambitions mirror Dash's in that both women hope to put the oppositional gaze into operation. They seek to become the type of Black female filmmaker that hooks envisioned – one who makes subversive films that challenge the status quo.

If Mignon represents hooks' conception of the progressive Black female filmmaker who puts the oppositional gaze into practice, Ester is the "gaslighted" Black female spectator who has shut down her critical sensibilities in order to become an adoring consumer of White screen images. Ester idealizes Leila Grant (Sandy Brooke), the White female star whose voice she dubs, so much so that she does not even resent the studio's appropriation of her talent (Hartman and Griffin 1991: 366). Even if Ester does not fully recognize the extent of her exploitation, the viewer certainly does. The projection room scene reveals both the depth of her victimization and her unwillingness to recognize it. We see Ester watching Leila Grant on the projection room screen and dubbing her voice with a look of pleasure, even adoration, on her face. It is only Mignon who is upset. Exercising the "metacritical gaze of the black woman producer" (Ryan 2004: 1340), Mignon alone recognizes the extent to which Ester's talent is being appropriated in order to enhance both the screen image of the White female star and her objectification.

Dash adds a component to this scene that a number of critics have found problematic. The voice of Rosanne Katon, who plays Ester, is itself dubbed by a recording of the renowned Black singer Ella Fitzgerald. Hartman and Griffin see this as a betrayal of the film's ultimate message (1991: 369). If the voice of the actress playing Ester is not even legitimate, but an illusion, how can Dash condemn Hollywood's use of the Black voice to substitute for that of a White performer. In a sense, Dash is doing exactly what Hollywood has done for so long. Other critics see Dash's use of Fitzgerald's voice differently. They regard it as a deliberate comment on the constructed nature of all film images, those produced by Hollywood and even oppositional ones, such as those found in *Illusions*. No film images are truly realistic; all are illusions (Smith 1994: 54). Dash might also have used Fitzgerald's famous voice in an attempt to highlight Ester's exceptional talent. Her voice is portrayed as equivalent to one of the greatest voices in recording history, yet because of her race, she is being denied due recognition.

When Mignon and Ester meet in the National Studios' office after Ester's performance to discuss her remuneration, their relationship develops even further. They share feelings of powerless in the face of their exploitation by the White racist film industry. Mignon assumes a protective attitude toward the younger Ester, who in turn acts as a catalyst for Mignon's recognition that her position at National Studios is not that much different than Ester's. They both are exploited and their talents appropriated in the service of the White majority. As they discuss their respective situations, they form a bond of solidarity under oppression. Ester recognizes that Mignon is passing for White, but refuses to condemn her; instead, she accepts Mignon's friendship, and they provide each other with mutual support and recognition. This bond of Black sisterhood is expressed through their exchange of affectionate glances, as well as the physical gestures of affection and understanding they share as they discuss their ambitions and fears. The relationship is pivotal in Mignon's developing consciousness as she moves away from Hollywood illusion and dedicates herself all the more strongly to fight for a diverse and authentic cinematic representation of all members of American society. Female bonding is shown to be crucial to the Black woman's self-healing and her development of the inner strength needed to fortify her for her fight against White racism. This fight pits the Black woman against both the male gaze and the Hollywood film industry. Through the character of Mignon, Dash launches a devastating critique of mainstream cinema as a purveyor of racism. As its name suggests, National Studios, Mignon's employer, purports to represent an egalitarian U.S. society, but this society is shown to be exclusionist at its very core in terms of race, class and gender.

This critique of Hollywood filmmaking is central to the film's structure of meaning. As hooks points out, Lonette McKee's impressive screen presence is in itself subversive. McKee forcefully claims for the Black woman the space of the female protagonist, a space reserved for the White female star in Hollywood cinema (hooks 1993: 300). The film suggests that American film as a representative of U.S. society misrepresents, denies and erases the presence of people of color. Their work both before the camera and behind the scenes goes unrecognized, so that Hollywood can create the illusion of White supremacy. At the same time, American society makes the claim that it represents "a culturally homogenous, uncontested and already attained democracy" (Ryan 2004: 1336). Dash makes her critique of Hollywood as a microcosm of America itself explicit in the film's opening quote from Ralph Ellison: "To direct an attack upon Hollywood would indeed be to confuse portrayal with action, images with reality. In the beginning was not the shadow, but the act, and the province of Hollywood is not action, but illusion." The film uses this quotation, presented over an Oscar statuette revolving in a black void, as a jumping-off point to argue that Hollywood not only replicates social reality but also shapes it by producing illusions that claim to be realistic portrayals. Dash illustrates this point by using Hollywood's very conventions against it. As Patricia Mellancamp points out, *Illusions* is a critical rewriting of the quintessential Hollywood musical *Singin' in the Rain* (Gene Kelly and Stanley Donan, 1952) (1994: 78). Both films offer behind the scenes examinations of Hollywood filmmaking, but *Singin' in the Rain* only appears to demythologize Hollywood film production by revealing its constructed nature. It ends by remythologizing the Hollywood musical as a microcosm of American society and a testament to the ingenuity and talent of the American people. *Illusions*, on the other hand, really does demythologize Hollywood as seeming to represent a land of dreams on the surface, while underneath purveying the racism that acts to destroy for Black Americans the very dreams Hollywood purports to represent.

The film's portrayal of female bonding takes on particular significance as a way for Black women to stand together against the Hollywood film industry and by implication against racist American society as a whole. It offers a way to undermine the White male gaze that is so central to mainstream filmmaking. In *Illusions*, L.L., the head of National Studios, and Lt. Bedsford, the government watchdog, represent the White male gaze. Both men refuse to recognize Mignon as a Black woman, objectify her, and attempt to reduce her to the White woman's position of submission to the male gaze. All the White women at the studio are just "aspiring copies of the glamorized, objectified, and infantilized screen star, Leila Grant ... whose performance of self must be shaped for a phallocentric gaze." Grant, "a languid parasite" who is "intravenously feeding on Ester through the sound apparatus," relies totally on the "enlivening potential of Black women's voices." In contrast, Mignon rebuffs Bedsford's advances and deflects his attempts to visually objectify her. Refusing to submit to his controlling male gaze, she responds only to Ester's gaze of friendship, a gaze that humanizes rather than objectifies her (Ryan 2004: 1337). It is Ester's empowering gaze that leads Mignon to develop a truly critical self-consciousness and fortifies her for her fight against Bedsford's objectifying gaze and L.L.'s demeaning gaze, both of which refuse to even recognize her as she really is.

At the film's conclusion, Mignon not only rejects the White male gaze but sets out to replace it with her own "transformative vision" (Ryan 2004: 1337). It is this vision which she intends to see enacted on the screen. Although we do not know for certain that her ideas will ever find cinematic expression, the film leaves the viewer with the hope that they will, just as Dash's transformative vision is expressed in *Illusions*. This transformative vision expresses a "Black feminist cultural ideology" that insists upon the "complete recognition and understanding of black women's life experiences as valuable, complex and diverse" (Gibson-Hudson 1994: 366). It also calls for an end to the erasure of Black images from the screen and for a termination of the simultaneous exploitation, expropriation, and non-recognition of the talents and contributions of African Americans to U.S. society.

Films in Focus 2: *Fire*

The work of Deepa Mehta provides a good example of post-Third-Worldist cinema. Mehta is an Indian diasporic filmmaker working within the cinematic traditions of both East and West. She has called herself "a hybrid person who can move from continent to continent," prefers to be seen as a mixed Canadian and Indian filmmaker, and dislikes being labeled one or the other (Levitan 2003: 277, 272). Born in India to a wealthy family, she studied philosophy at the University of New Delhi, and after graduation, she started working in film for an Indian documentary production company. She moved to Canada in 1973 with her then husband Paul Saltzman, a Canadian filmmaker. They started their own film production company together, Mehta began making films for Canadian Television, and eventually she moved into feature filmmaking with *Sam and Me* (1991) about the Indian immigrant experience in Canada and *Camilla* (1994), a female friendship film starring Bridget Fonda and Jessica Tandy. Mehta's experience with *Camilla* discouraged her from making films in Canada. She says she lost artistic control of the film, but then was still blamed for its ultimate failure at the box office (Levitan 2003: 277).

Although she fashions herself as a hybrid Canadian–Indian filmmaker, she has complained bitterly of restrictions on government funding for films in Canada, where she believes restrictions intended to prevent U.S. domination also discriminate against immigrant filmmakers, who are channeled into making films confined to the subject of immigration. (Levitan 2003: 282, n. 12). As a result of these restrictions and because of her continued attachment to India, Mehta turned to making films about and produced in her native country. In 1996, her first film made in India, *Fire*, initiated an ambitious trilogy of films, which also includes *Earth* (1998) and *Water* (2005), all of which focus on the lives of Indian women. *Earth* deals with the tragic romance between a Hindu maid and her Muslim lover during the time of India's partition, and *Water* tells the story of a group of widows forced into poverty and destitution by the social restrictions imposed on them. Mehta has said she intended the trilogy to focus on politics: *Fire* on the politics of sexuality, *Earth* on the politics of sectarian war, and *Water* on the politics of religion (quoted in Chitterjee 2007: 76). She is currently working on a film adaptation of Salmon Rushdie's award-winning novel *Midnight's Children* to be entitled *Winds of Change* and scheduled for release in 2012. As the Internet Movie Data Base points out, Mehta is rapidly coming to be seen as the voice of the new India.

We will look closely at the first film in Mehta's trilogy, *Fire*, which was not only a watershed film for Mehta, bringing her international attention, but also a highly controversial film in India that stimulated heated protests. As she did with each film in the trilogy and is currently doing with *Winds of Change*,

Mehta wrote the screenplay for *Fire* herself. Although it was her first attempt at screenwriting, she still completed the script in three days. She prefers to write her own screenplays because she says it gives her a sense of integration between the process of writing and directing, rather than feeling that someone else is telling her how to make her film (McGowan 2003: 285, 291). The story of *Fire* concerns the lesbian love relationship that develops between two women married to brothers and living in a joint-family household where they are expected to fulfill the traditional female role of submission to the will and whims of their husbands and their husbands' family. Through their relationship with each other, the two women eventually find the courage to break away from their oppressive marriages and embark on a life together. Mehta said the film was not based on any people or incidents in her own life, but on a controversial short story, "Lihaaf" ("The Quilt") written in 1941 in Urdu by Ismat Chugtai (McGowan 2003: 289). The story, however, is very different from the film. It concerns a young girl who is staying with an older relative. As she sleeps in a bed next to her aunt, she hears the sounds of the lovemaking between her aunt and her female servant under the quilt on her aunt's bed. Eventually, when the female servant leaves for a short trip, the aunt makes sexual advances on the child, who is shocked and repelled by the aunt's actions. When the servant returns, the aunt returns to that relationship, and the child, who now desperately wishes to return home, is forced again to witness their lovemaking. The story was attacked by the Indian literary establishment and Chugtai was even subjected to an obscenity trial, which she won. Although the story may have provided Mehta's inspiration for *Fire*, the differences between the plot, characters, and point of view of the story and film make it difficult to see the story as providing the basis for the film.

The film, originally shot in English and later translated into Hindi, was made on a very tight US$1.6 million budget. It received the Indian censorship board's seal of approval with only minor changes required and is said to have initially played to full houses in Bombay, especially attracting female audiences, until three weeks into its run when it was closed down by militant Hindu fundamentalist protests (Moorti 2000). The protests were led by Shiv Sena, a rightist religious group whose members disrupted screenings and condemned the film on several counts. As a result of their protests, film exhibitors shut down the film in India, death threats were made against Mehta, and she was even burned in effigy (Levitan 2003: 280). Although the protesters did not always coherently outline their objections to the film, they seem to have targeted three specific aspects of its plot and thematic structure. Initial objections focused on the film's advocacy of women's need to express their desires and make their own choices, sexual or otherwise. This ideological stance was seen as "spoiling" Indian women and introducing Western ideas into Indian culture. The protesters claimed that lesbianism was an "unnatural" Western phenomenon that was foreign to Indian society and completely unknown to Indian women. The introduction of the idea of lesbianism as a possible sexual choice for Indian women was seen as a threat to women's reproductive role in the patriarchal family, and therefore by extension, a danger to the Indian nation itself. Later opposition focused more on the issue of Western imperialism, with Mehta's Canadian citizenship used as evidence that she was merely a pawn of the West who was presenting ideas antithetical to indigenous Indian culture. As Sujata Moorti points out in her very thorough account of the protests waged against the film, the protesters constructed a scenario that pitted "a chaste and pristine India" against "a decadent, licentious, and immoral West." One major source of the protests was the "neo-swadeshi trend" in Indian society, which opposes all Western influences and advocates a "patriotic preference for indigenous goods" and the persecution of anyone who sells Western items (Moorti 2000).

Criticisms of the film extended beyond vocal protests to written critiques, and not just from conservative religious fundamentalists, but from other segments of Indian society. One major objection was that the film attacks traditional values and religion. Many fundamentalists felt the actions of Mehta's female characters, Sita (Nandita Das) and Radha (Shabana Azmi), represent a rejection of religious values and the proper female roles advocated in religious texts (McGowan 2003: 288). The film's critique of traditional religion is most apparent in its references to the *Ramayana*, the ancient Sanskrit epic that is considered a major work of Hindu instruction and mythology. The *Ramayana* chronicles the life of Ram, an incarnation of the god Vishnu, reborn in order to kill Ravana, the King of Lamka, who was harassing the gods. Ram's wife Sita is abducted and held captive by Ravana until Ram rescues her in a great battle. He fears, however, that during her captivity she was raped by Ravana, so she agrees to prove her purity by submitting to the agnipariksha (trial by fire). Although she walks through the fire unharmed, Ram's followers still are not convinced of her purity, and bowing to gossip and what he sees as his duty to his people, Ram banishes her into the forest. There, she gives birth to his twin sons, and then prays to the gods to have the earth swallow her up. Ram realizes too late that Sita was always true to him. In sorrow, he gives his kingdom to his sons and steps into a river to merge with Vishnu (Barron 2008: 71–72).

Hindu fundamentalists interpret the story as a call to Hindu men to work for the reestablishment of a perfect kingdom based on the mythical realm of Ram, who is seen as the "good citizen leader" (Patel 1998: 13). This "ideal" kingdom excludes women from equal rights as citizens and envisions them in the mold of Sita, who is considered to be the perfect woman. She represents the "absolutely virtuous wife" whose name has come to signify "wifeliness, virtue, devotion, and tradition" (Patel 1998: 13), as well as female chastity, subordination, self-sacrifice, and purity (Moorti 2000). By naming her young heroine Sita, Mehta offers a direct challenge to the *Ramayana* and its conception of ideal Hindu womanhood. Sita's female lover, Radha, is also named for a mythological figure, the goddess consort of Krishna whose love for him is presented as perfect, transcendent, and devotional, if also extramarital (Barron 2008: 67). By giving her heroines the names of these archetypes of ideal femininity in Indian culture, Mehta establishes them as symbols of Indian womanhood and the Indian nation and thus assured that her film would be regarded as an overt challenge to Hindu fundamentalism and its sacred texts.

Mehta said she considered the legendary figures of Sita and Radha to be "two wronged women of Indian mythology" (Nae 2000: 520), and she seems to have used their names in order to transform their stories. Sita is changed from a model of devoted, long-suffering womanhood to a modern woman who refuses to be bound by traditional wifely virtues and proscriptions. The trial by fire that the mythical Sita undergoes is transferred to Radha, who is left to die by her husband after her sari accidentally catches on fire during an argument precipitated by his discovery of her lesbian relationship with Sita. Like the mythical Sita, Radha emerges unscathed from her fiery ordeal, but in this case, she does not wait to be banished by her husband; instead, she leaves him for her female lover. Mehta portrays her heroines as rejecting the oppressive traditions symbolized in the stories of their namesakes and determined to overcome the misogyny these traditions embody. Hindu fundamentalists recognized quite rightly that the film's use of the names of these mythical female figures and its transformation of their stories was a direct attack on the *Ramayana* and other mythical texts as oppressive to women and an attempt to turn them around to support advocacy of changes in the way women are treated in Indian society (Barron 2008: 79).

Fundamentalist critics were not only outraged by what they saw as the film's attack on religion, they also disapproved of its social message for women, which they characterized as an attack on the Indian patriarchal family. Rather than presenting the family as the foundation of the Indian nation, Mehta portrays it as a repressive institution that is responsible at least in part for women's oppression in Indian society. The film was attacked for "spoiling [Indian] women" by attempting to Westernize them and convert them to a radical feminism that would render them unfit for their traditional roles as wives and mothers. This corruption of womanhood was presented as inevitably leading to the collapse of marriage and eventually of the entire Indian state (Moorti

2000). The protesters also launched personal attacks on Mehta as a diasporic Indian filmmaker. The most scathing written attack in this regard was by Uma Paramesweren, who insisted that, although Mehta was born in India and claims to spend an equal amount of time there as she does in Canada, she is really a Canadian filmmaker who made the film to appeal to Western audiences (2007: 11). Although Mehta has said that she intended the film as a debunking of Western stereotypes of India (Jodha 2007: 42), Paramesweren insists that Mehta follows in the tradition of other diasporic Indian writers and filmmakers who have exoticized and sensationalized India by associating it with abject poverty and sectarian violence (2007: 11). According to Paramesweren, *Fire* is an artistic failure because it shows a complete lack of understanding of Indian culture, using cultural allusions heavy-handedly and irresponsibly for shock value (2007: 12). Madhu Kishwar in an attack similar to Parmesweren's even went so far as to title his review of the film "Naive Outpourings of a Self-Hating Indian."

Figure 10 From left, Shabana Azmi as Radha and Nandita Das as Sita in *Fire*.

Another criticism of the film related to its social message focuses on Mehta's use of lesbianism as a way to express her female characters' assertion of their independence from tradition and need to make their own choices, sexual and otherwise. Objections to the film's inclusion of lesbianism came from a number of sources not limited to the fundamentalist perspective. Fundamentalist critics condemned the lesbian content as introducing to Indian women a decadent Western notion completely foreign to them (Moorti 2000). Building on this idea, some critics proposed that Mehta was doing a "disservice to the cause of women" because female affection is generally accepted in Indian society and is not identified with sexual feelings. By portraying the relationship between Sita and Radha as lesbian, the film might discourage Indian women from bonding with each other (Nae 2000: 523). Sujata Moorti argues that the protesters really objected to the film's suggestion that lesbianism might be a viable alternative to oppressive patriarchal marriage. Although Mehta insisted that Fire was not really about lesbianism, but about women's need to be able to make their own choices and express their desires (Levitan 2003: 278), Shabana Azmi said she saw the film as an exploration of lesbianism and was reluctant to take the part of Radha because she feared it would hurt her career. Her fears were not unwarranted. Protesters expressed objections to such a renowned actress, who had an impressive 25-year career in the Indian film industry, playing the role of a lesbian. They also accused her of having "besmirched the dignity of Indian women" by playing the part of a Hindu woman when she is a Muslim (Moorti 2000).

Non-fundamentalists also questioned the wisdom of using lesbianism as a symbol of female agency and the expression of women's desire. For Mary E. John and Tejaswini Niranjana, the film suggests that women can be liberated from oppressive social conditions simply by the assertion of sexual choice, which ignores a wide range of oppressive social structures that cause women's subordination to men (2000: 375). A number of lesbian critics were also critical of the film, especially after Mehta disavowed its lesbian content by insisting that she did not really see it as about lesbianism. Mehta said she used "the lesbian angle" merely as "a symbol of an extreme solution" to her protagonists' problems (quoted in Moorti 2000). Needless to say, lesbian critics found Mehta's comments offensive. They felt her remarks attempted to minimize the significance of the lesbian relationship to the film's overall meaning and were particularly insensitive given Indian lesbians' very vocal support of the film against fundamentalist protests (Levitan 2003: 279).

Rima Benerji's attack on the film expresses strongly the negative lesbian response to Mehta's remarks.

> Mehta's refusal to take a public stand supportive of lesbians is insulting and demeaning when originally so much of the hype mentioned the same-sex relationship at the film's core. After all, there is a difference between saying Fire is not a lesbian film (as Mehta has done) versus saying it is not only a lesbian film, and that it has multiple possibilities embedded in it. By

making the former statement, Mehta alienated precisely that segment of viewers which has been at the forefront of defending the substance of *Fire* on her behalf, and protecting it from attack by fundamentalists (quoted in Levitan 2003: 282 n.15).

Benerji also labeled the film an artistic failure, significant only because of the controversy it stimulated, which brought lesbianism out into open debate in India (1999: 18). Like Benerji, V.S. accused Mehta of opportunism in allowing the film's promotion to stress its lesbian content in the West, where the characters' lesbianism was not a subject of controversy, and then when faced with protests in India, claimed the film was not about lesbianism, reportedly announced that she herself was heterosexual, and even proposed that she would be devastated if her daughter told her she was gay. V.S. termed Mehta's stance a "politics of convenience" and accused her of "hypocrisy, defensiveness, and a retreat to the safe shelter of her heterosexuality," as well as a willingness to exploit and commodify the lesbian content of her film to attract viewers (2000: 519).

Based on an examination of the film itself rather than Mehta's comments about it, its lesbian content seems to have both positive and negative aspects. Despite Mehta's disclaimers to the contrary, the lesbian relationship that develops between the two female characters is a major aspect of the film, although it is not the only component of its representation of women in Indian society. On the negative side, a number of critics reacted to the film's representation of lesbianism much as they did to Donna Deitch's *Desert Hearts*. They saw it as "superficially handled and unrealistically depicted" in the form of a conventional heterosexual cinematic love story, rather than as "casting any new light on lesbianism as a political or lifestyle choice" (Benerji 1999: 19). V.S. proposes that Sita and Radha are portrayed as "non-lesbian lesbians" whose relationship is never fully developed or psychologically convincing (2000: 519). The word lesbian is never even used to describe them (Patel 1998: 15), and at the end we do not get a strong sense of how they will sustain their relationship now that they have left their husbands (Benerji 1999: 21). The film uses lesbian desire merely as a symbol of female agency and desire pitted against wifely duty and tradition. Benerji believes that it would have been better if Mehta had taken another tack and shown women's desire and agency as really in accord with rather than as opposed to Indian tradition (1999: 19–20). Setting up the women's decision to enter into a same-sex union as a response to their failed marriages also feeds the stereotype that women only turn to lesbianism in response to male neglect or abuse (John and Niranjana 2000: 375). More positive responses to the film's presentation of lesbianism describe it as challenging homophobic norms by showing that female connections formed within extended family households can be sexual, act as a source of support for women, and serve as an alternative to heterosexuality (Benerji 1999: 19). Additionally, the casting of Shabana Azmi, who is widely regarded as a symbol of the changing image of the heroine in Indian cinema (Moorti 2000), to play Radha associates lesbianism with progressive developments in Indian society. The film also had a progressive extra-textual effect in that it increased the public visibility of lesbianism, portrayed it as indigenous to India rather than as a Western import, mobilized gay and lesbian groups in support of the film, and increased the sensitivity of women's organization in India to gay and lesbian issues (Moorti 2000).

Discussions of the film focused not only on its lesbian content but on other equally important components of its structure. Some detractors saw it as aesthetically flawed because of its overtly polemical nature, which they believed led Mehta to distort the realities of life in India in order to promote her social agenda. For instance, Avinash Jodha claims that the picture Mehta presents of the Indian extended family as isolating and oppressive for women is totally unrealistic. Jodha suggests that Mehta's knowledge of Indian society is extremely limited and even implies that she constructed her whole trilogy to present India as depraved and corrupt in order to appeal to Western audiences (2007: 42, 52). Defenders of the film countered these criticisms by arguing for *Fire*'s positive qualities both as a work of art and a social document. They called the protesters who shut down the film's exhibition in India thought-police who wanted to impose cultural hegemony through a "terror raj" (Moorti 2000). What they believed was really behind the protests was opposition to the film's advocacy of an open secular Indian society as opposed to an insular nationalism that seeks to impose Hinduism on all of India. Defenders also pointed to the protesters' hypocrisy in accepting Bollywood's objectification of women as well as women's everyday social oppression in Indian society, but opposing a film that argues for their right to make choices about their own lives (Moorti 2000).

Like the film's critics, its defenders also used tradition to bolster their arguments by arguing that the film actually fits well with longstanding Indian beliefs advocating tolerance and the assimilation of different viewpoints into Indian society. They also criticized those opposed to the film for making the female body central to their arguments in a way that made the image of woman a "repository of difference ... [that] carries the mark of the authentic India; her body is the terrain where contested definitions of national identity are worked out" (Moorti 2000). As a result, Indian women came to symbolize India itself as caught between tradition and modernity. In addition, the film's defenders insisted that it was really being attacked because it criticized the Indian family, and by extension Indian society, as oppressive to women. They saw opposition to the film as reflective of a "vernacular nationalism" that regards sexism and homophobia as patriotic and refuses to confront the real oppressive conditions that women face in contemporary Indian society (Moorti 2000).

Part of these oppressive conditions involve the attitudes of Indian men. Frequent criticisms made against the film were that it presents Indian men unfairly, parodies Indian masculinity, and offers women only one option in the face of male sexism, and that is to turn to each other for emotional and sexual fulfillment (Patel 1998: 11). The women's husbands do indeed furnish very unflattering pictures of Indian masculinity. Radha's husband Ashok in reaction to their inability to have children takes up the practice of Nationalist Gandhian abstinence. Ghandi, like Ashok's guru, advocated renouncing sexual desire as a way symbolically to reject worldly concerns (Patel 1998: 58). Ashok (Kalbhushan Kharbanda) regularly calls upon Radha to lie next to him in bed so that he can demonstrate his religious asceticism by rejecting her sexually. Jatin (Javed Jaffrey), Sita's husband, represents the "cosmopolitan bourgeois new man" who marries Sita through an arranged marriage only to please his family, but is in love with another woman whom he continues to see even after his marriage (Barron 2008: 78). He expects Sita to be content with her role as his wife and the future mother of his children even though he makes it clear to her that he can offer her no real affection or sexual fidelity.

A final male character who plays a prominent role in the film is Mundu (Ranjit Chowdhry), the family servant. He seems intended as a ribald comic character, an object of ridicule and disdain derived from "the position of the sidekick in Sanskrit drama" and a common figure in Hindi film (Patel 1998: 11). His actions directly challenge the family's matriarch Biji (Kushal Rekhi), who takes on meta-phorical significance as a representative of the repressive, intolerant religious tradition that the film associates with the *Ramayana*. Paralyzed, unable to speak, and in need of almost constant attention, she still maintains an aggressive dom-inance over her family, symbolically representing the repressive force and restric-tive power of "mute traditionalism" (Sengupta 2007: 106). Mundu flagrantly and irreverently challenges both Biji's matriarchal power over the household (Patel 1998: 11) and the moral authority of the *Ramayana*, with which she is asso-ciated. He is charged with taking care of her when everyone else is busy working in the family store. What he is expected to do is to sit with Biji and watch a recorded television production of the *Ramayana*; instead, when every-one else is gone, he substitutes a sex video for the sacred religious text, which is commonly seen as the repository of the rules of proper conduct. Forcing Biji, whose muteness and paralysis render her incapable of protesting, to participate unwillingly in his lewd challenge to the forces of religious authority, he not only makes her watch the video with him but masturbates in her presence as they watch. When Radha discovers his behavior and reveals it to the rest of the family, they forgive his irreverent actions much more easily than they will Radha and Sita's sexual attachment, demonstrating the double standard for male and female sexuality within Indian society (Barron 2008: 76). In retaliation against Radha and out of frustrated sexual attraction to her, Mundu is the one who reveals her relationship with Sita to the family, precipitating the film's dramatic and controversial conclusion.

The film's strongest challenge to Hindu fundamentalism is contained in its ending. The two women decide to leave the household after Ashok discovers them in bed together. Sita leaves first and Radha promises to follow after she has had one last talk with Ashok. Their discussion quickly turns into an argument, and Ashok accuses Radha of infidelity in a way reminiscent of the accusations made against Sita in the *Ramayana*. In a complete repudiation of the *Ramayana*'s portrayal of the ideal submissive wife, however, Radha defends her relationship with Sita and her need for love and sexual fulfillment. In the course of the argument, which takes place in the kitchen, Radha's sari accidentally catches on fire from the stove. Rather than try to save her, Ashok callously leaves her to burn as he runs to save Biji and flee from the house. Radha miraculously survives her trial by fire in what is yet another reference to the *Ramayana*, but again events are reversed. Radha survives not to be exiled by her distrusting husband, but to leave him to join her female lover, and unlike the *Ramayana*, the film is sympathetic to her perspective not her husband's (Barron 2008: 81).

Mehta stages Radha's final reunion with Sita in a Muslim shrine, a plot choice that can be seen as the film's most direct and controversial challenge to Hindu fundamentalism. The women reunite at the shrine to Nizamuddin, a revered fourteenth-century Sufi Muslim poet and mystic who was opposed to all forms of fundamentalism and preached instead the unity of all religions. By setting her ending here, Mehta takes a firm stand against orthodox Islamist fundamentalism, its construction of the Indian nation, and the communal violence its sectarian views have engendered (Barron 2008: 90). The two women unite in what some critics have called a much too happy-ever-after ending outside of the home, the family, and in a sense even the Indian nation (Barron 2008: 71). Sujata Moorti, for instance, suggests that the ending presents a far too rosy denouement that ignores the realities of Indian society, yet one might question exactly how rosy this ending really is. Radha has just barely escaped burning to death and the two women are left without any resources for their survival. What will they do and where will the go? The film's ending seems mixed at best. As Jabir Jain suggests, the image that remains in our minds is

"Radha with her half-burnt clothes, anguished face and an overwhelming consciousness of failure and rejection, very much in need of succor. The loneliness, the rain, all add to the heaviness at the heart of the journey" (2007a: 70). We still do have a classic romantic ending, however, with the lovers reunited after one has escaped from great danger, and we are left to sympathize with their situation and to celebrate their final union (Barron 2008: 88).

As a post-Third Worldist feminist text, Fire centers thematically on three problems presented as prominent in postcolonial Indian society: the denial of women's right to freedom of choice, their oppression within the extended family, and the destructive effects on women (and on the Indian nation as a whole) of the struggle between communalism and secularism within Indian society. The primary theme relates to women's right to make choices about the direction of their own lives, a right that the film argues has been denied them in Indian society (Levitan 2003: 279). The issue of choice is presented through the women's decision to take control specifically over their emotional and sexual lives. Their decision to enter into a lesbian relationship is symbolic of their refusal to have their lives dictated by their husbands, the extended family, or Indian tradition. Critics have suggested, however, that by making the women's sexuality so central to the film Mehta makes sexual freedom the key to the destruction of patriarchal oppression, thus ignoring the multiple oppressions from which women suffer in Indian society and offering a simplistic and reductive solution to a much larger problem (John and Niranjana 2000: 375). The film does not really say this, though. In fact, Mehta makes it clear that the women's exercise of sexual choice is an expression of their desire for freedom in other areas of their lives as well, and the ending indicates that their decision to strike out against their oppression leads to persecution, rather than complete liberation (Kapur 2000: 379).

Additionally, the film does not just limit itself to the issue of women's need for freedom of choice, but also interrogates "the maltreatment of women inherent in Indian culture" through an examination of the tensions found within the extended family household (Nae 2000: 520). Sita introduces modern ideas into the traditional family structure, which results in the women's revolt against their established familial roles. This rebellion precipitates an unresolvable domestic crisis that leads to the family's destruction. Some critics have argued that Mehta constructs a distorted picture of the Hindu extended family that is targeted to appeal to negative Western stereotypes of Indian family life (Nae 2000: 522), but the film's attempt to draw attention to the oppressive conditions suffered by women in arranged marriages seems plausible. Fire is particularly effective in showing how the weight of traditional beliefs tends to thwart women's desires, how women are limited by their restrictive roles in the extended family structure, and how any attempt by women to move out of their accepted roles and reject their ritual-bound existence for some sense of autonomy precipitates unbearable tensions and anxieties within the traditional middle-class family structure (Moorti 2000). The film actually does an impressive job of rewriting the Bollywood portrait of the Indian family, which conventionally resolves the conflict between traditional and modern views of family life by upholding tradition. What Bollywood offers to women viewers is the time-worn creed: "Pray to God, love your parents, live for your husband … and everything will be perfect," but *Fire* shows its female characters decisively rejecting these beliefs and accepting the more modern idea that in some cases women need to place their individual needs over those of their family and by extension their society (Moorti 2000). As in *Fire*, women are often presented in Bollywood films as a disruptive force within the family, but in Bollywood they are condemned and punished for this disruption, whereas in *Fire* they are presented as sympathetic exemplars of female courage and determination (Moorti 2000).

Fire provoked so much controversy not just because of its critique of the Indian extended family, but because this critique extends even beyond the family and the role of women within it. The film can be read as an allegory in the tradition of popular romances in Indian cinema that use a Hindu and Muslim couple to symbolize the tensions within the nation between communal and secular ideas. Rather than developing a romance between different ethnic religious groups, Mehta converted the romantic relationship to one between two women, but the unconventionality of the romance still opens it up to interpretation as a metaphor for the "taint of racial and ethnic contamination" that has traditionally been regarded as infecting the Hindu household and by extension the Indian nation (Chitterjee 2007: 83). In this allegorical reading, the women's union at the film's end would be interpreted as symbolizing the healing of the communal divide through the formation of a secular nation that is accepting of all social groups (Barron 2008: 90–91). Thus, the film becomes not just a critique of women's oppression in Indian society, but of Hindu fundamentalism's intolerance for different racial and religious groups (Barron 2008: 86). This allegorical extension of the film's representation of its same-sex romance does not diminish its strong critique of women's social oppression, but rather extends this critique to include the negative impact on real women's lives caused by the way their image has been used in conceptualizations of the struggle between tradition and modernity in Indian society (Chitterjee 2007: 76)

In the final analysis, how should we see *Fire*? Is it a flawed feminist text that provoked heated controversy because it distorted and misrepresented women's place in Indian society, or a devastating post-Third Worldist critique of the real oppression Indian women suffer as a result of their unequal position in traditional Indian culture? Was the opposition to the film largely a rightist reaction to an Indian diasporic female filmmaker's attack on the oppression of women as a deeply rooted aspect of postcolonial Indian society? The merit of this controversial representative of global feminist film culture perhaps lies in the intense debate it provoked.

Key Terms: *African American feminist film studies, postcolonial feminist film studies, orientalism, hybrid identity, mimesis, mimicry, the imperial gaze, the oppositional gaze, phobogenic, the Black Other, trauma theory, negrophobia, subject-in-process, speaking nearby, post-third-worldist feminist film*

Suggestions for Further Reading, Viewing, and Discussion

1. Read hooks' "The Oppositional Gaze," Bobo's "Reading through the Text: the Black women as audience," and Claire Pajaczkowska and Lola Young's "Racism, Representation, Psychoanalysis." Compare and contrast their ideas. Whose ideas do you find most useful in thinking about the representation of African Americans in film?

2. Examine a contemporary film and/or a film from the cinematic past for its representation of African American female characters. Do these representations seem progressive or not? Explain.

3. Examine the representation of Black female characters in the work of an African American female and/or male director. See the filmography below for suggested films by African American women directors. Some prominent Black male directors include Spike Lee, Forest Whitaker, Carl Franklin, Lee Daniels, Antoine Fuqua, The Hughes Brothers, John Singleton, and F. Gary Gray.

4. Do you think Julie Dash accomplishes a progressive revision of the passing plot in *Illusions*? Why or why not? Read Nella Larsen's *Passing* and compare/contrast it to *Illusions*.

5. Watch Dash's *Daughters of the Dust* and/or *The Rosa Parks Story* and compare them to *Illusions*.

6. Read Gaines, "White Privilege and Looking Relations," Doane's "Dark Continents: epistemologies of racial and sexual difference in psychoanalysis and the cinema," Trinh and Chen's "'Speaking Nearby': a conversation with Trinh T. Minh-ha," and Shohat's "Framing Post-Third Worldist Culture: gender and nation in Middle Eastern/North African film and video." Compare and contrast their views.

7. Examine the other two films in Mehta's trilogy, *Earth* and *Water*, and compare/contrast them to *Fire*.

8. Examine the representation of Third World women in films by major female and/or male post-colonial directors. The filmography below suggests some prominent Third World women directors.

Filmography of African American and Third World Women Filmmakers

African American Women Directors

Kathleen Collins: *Losing Ground* (1982)

Julie Dash: *Daughters of the Dust* (1991); *The Rosa Parks Story* (2002)

Cheryl Dunye: *The Watermelon Woman* (1996); *My Baby's Daddy* (2004)

Sanaa Hamri: *Something New* (2006); *The Sisterhood of the Traveling Pants* (2008)

Leslie Harris: *Just Another Girl on the I.R.T.* (1996)

Kasi Lemmons: *Eve's Bayou* (1997); *Talk to Me* (2007)

Darnell Martin: *I Like It Like That* (1994); *Their Eyes Were Watching God* (TV, 1995)

Euzhan Palcy: *Sugar Cane Alley* (1983); *A Dry White Season* (1989)

Gina Prince-Bythewood: *Love and Basketball* (2000); *The Secret Life of Bees* (2008)

Third World and Third World Diasporic Directors

Suzana Amaral (Brazil): *Hour of the Star* (1986)

Maria Luisa Bemberg (Argentina): *Camila* (1984); *Miss Mary* (1986); *I Don't Want to Talk About It* (1993)

Gurinder Chadha (Kenyan Diasporic): *Bhaji on the Beach* (1993); *Bend It Like Beckham* (2002)

Joan Chen (China): *Xiu Xiu: The Sent-Down Girl* (1998)

Prema Karanth (India): *Phaniyamma* (1983)

Claudia Llosa (Peru): *Madeinusa* (2006); *The Milk of Sorrow* (2009)

Sarah Maldoror (Angola): *Sambizanga* (1973)

Deepa Mehta: *Earth* (1998): *Water* (2005)

Anne Mungai (Kenya): *Sarkati* (1992)

Mira Nair (Indian Diasporic): *Salaam Bombay!* (1988); *Monsoon Wedding* (2001); *The Namesake* (2006)

Maria Novaro (Mexican): *Danzon* (1991)

Pratibha Parmar (Kenyan Diasporic): *A Place of Rage* (1991) *Warrior Marks* (1993)

Lourdes Portillo (Mexico): *Las Madres: The Mothers of Plaza de Mayo* (1985); *The Devil Never Sleeps* (1994)

Aparna Sen (India): *Paroma* (1984); *Sati* (1989); *Mr. and Mrs. Iyer* (2002)

Moufida Tlatli (Tunisia): *The Silences of the Palace* (1994)

Trinh T. Minh-ha (Vietnamese): *Reassemblage* (1983); *Surname Viet Given Name Nam* (1989)

Chapter 7

The Woman Auteur

Auteurism has held a prominent position in feminist film theory as it has in film studies in general. The idea of the director as the auteur (author) of a film began in the 1950s and 1960s with French New Wave filmmakers, most notably with François Truffaut's polemical 1954 essay "Une certaine tendance du cinéma français" ("A Certain Tendency in French Cinema"). For French New Wave theorists the concept of the auteur was a way to establish the film director as the individual creative force behind a film and to see film not as a mere entertainment vehicle, but as the unique personal achievement of an individual artist. When American film critic Andrew Sarris took up the idea in his influential 1968 study of Hollywood directors, *The American Cinema*, he used it as a way to invest film with an air of respectability and prestige as an art form worthy of serious consideration. He also set out to establish a pantheon of notable directors who could be said to have placed their personal artistic stamp on their films even if they were working under the limitations imposed upon them by the studio system. To study film from an auteurist perspective involves looking at a director's body of work to ascertain narrative, thematic, and stylistic patterns that provide evidence of the director's personal artistic touch. This auteurist stamp might be found in plot conventions and formulas, recurring themes, shot construction, camera work, and other elements of film structure repeated throughout a director's films and said to reveal a distinctive style and overarching thematic interests. Once this signature auteurist stamp has been determined, it can be used as an evaluative tool that allows the films of an auteur to be marked as superior to those produced by directors considered only to be on the artisan level (Crofts 1998: 312).

Many critics have raised objections to this approach, arguing that it gives too much credit to the film director and ignores crucial aspects of the film text, such as its social, historical, ideological, generic, and production contexts. Stephen Crofts, for instance, characterizes auteurism as suffering from "theoretical bankruptcy" (1998: 311). Because film is a collaborative process and one deeply embedded in the social milieu that surrounds it, to designate the director as the single or even the dominant artistic force behind a film ignores the work of so many other professionals involved in the filmmaking process, like screenwriters, producers, cinematographers, editors, and actors. In fact, some critics, including myself, have argued that other figures in the filmmaking process should also be seen as auteurs. In my book, *The Actress: Hollywood acting and the female star* and here again in the chapter on the actress, I propose that prominent stars can have an influence on their films that should be seen as auteurist. Others have made similar claims for producers, cinematographers and in particular screenwriters. Many screenwriters feel that their contributions have been diminished by the auteurist notion that the director should be given full credit as the creative force behind a film. After all without a screenplay, how exactly would that director be able to exercise creative control?

The auteurist approach can also be criticized for promoting the "Great Man Theory of Film History," which limits one's understanding of cinematic development to seeing films exclusively as the product of the remarkable accomplishments of a series of individual directorial geniuses. Film history becomes the tale of great directors as transcendent figures divorced from their social and historical context and rising up one after another to create cinematic masterpieces out of thin air. Each film era has had its canon of auteurs, such as silent era pioneers Georges Méliès, D.W. Griffith, Charlie Chaplin, and Serge Eisenstein. Then, there were the Hollywood studio era auteurs like John Ford, Howard Hawks, Orson Welles, and Alfred Hitchcock, working to put their artistic stamp on films in spite of the restrictions of the studio system. There were also European directorial stars such as Jean Renoir, Ingmar Bergman, Luis Buñuel, and Federico Fellini. Even contemporary cinema has its auteurs in Martin Scorsese, Woody Allen, Robert Altman, and Quentin Tarantino. Note that this pantheon of great directors is also a pantheon of great men. Until quite recently, there have been no women included in the highest ranks of the major film auteurs. Even now, these ranks are overwhelmingly dominated by male directors.

An attempt to give auteurism a more solid foundation in film theory developed in the late 1960s and early 1970s as auteur-structuralism, which took the idea of constructing an auteur from elements of his or her films to unprecedented lengths. As exemplified by Peter Wollen's *Signs and Meanings in the Cinema* (1969), for instance, auteur-structuralism argues that a systematic analysis of the body of a director's work reveals a set of underlying stylistic and thematic characteristics, most often described as binary oppositions that if taken together constitute an "author-construct" (Crofts 1998: 315). Binary oppositions are opposites, such as civilization vs. wilderness or marriage vs. male comradeship. The oppositions found in an auteur's work come together to elucidate the underlying themes associated with his or her authorial signature. For the auteur-structuralist, an auteur is not a real person but an "author-construct" that serves as a repository for the structural qualities of a group of films, a vague force that is a function of the meanings embedded in or the viewer's interpretation of these texts. Problems with this approach are apparent. Clearly, there is a real director who has created these films and who has a distinct persona and artistic vision. It is difficult to see this auteur as entirely a construction of the films he or she has produced. Second, as Stephen Crofts points out, many of the binary oppositions found in a particular director's work are not necessarily unique to that director, but can be found in the films of other directors within the same genre, historical period, or national cinema (1998: 316). For instance, to say that John Ford's work in the Western is characterized by the binary opposition between wilderness and civilization ignores the fact that most Westerns contain this split, not just those directed by Ford.

More recent theorists of film authorship have returned to the idea of the director as a real person. They have begun to see the auteur neither as an individual creative genius, nor as entirely the product of his or her corpus of film texts, but rather as a figure both influenced by and influencing the production and consumption of these texts. The contemporary idea of the auteur sees the film director as both a product of and a force shaping the current cultural and social milieu and the state of the film industry. Contemporary auteurs have taken on commercial significance as superstar personalities and cult figures whose names are marketing labels used to promote their films. Biographical information about them circulated through public appearances, interviews, publicity, and promotion creates a public persona that influences the reception of their films (Lehman and Luhr 2008: 87–88). For instance, the name James Cameron, Steven Spielberg, or Quentin Tarantino attached to a movie has enormous cache and even takes on interpretive significance.

Because of the paucity of female directors considered to be of auteur quality, feminist film scholars have been critical of, yet at the same time attracted to auteur theory. The idea of auteurism has been seen as one reason why the work of female directors and women working in other aspects of the film industry, such as screenwriters, editors, costume designers, and actresses, has been ignored. The failure to include women filmmakers in the pantheon of great directors in part is the result of the overwhelming male domination of the film industry, where the top grossing Hollywood films are almost all directed by men, and women are greatly restricted in terms of employment as executive producers, producers, writers, editors and cinematographers. The only areas where women dominate are hair and make-up, wardrobe, and costuming (Gilligan 2003: 29–30, 35). Reasons proposed for this exclusion range from male prejudice against women in roles of authority, the tendency to connect the technical expertise involved in filmmaking with masculinity, the heavy manual labor involved in some aspects of the filming process, and Hollywood's boy's club atmosphere where men traditionally pitch their film ideas to other men in backroom meetings (Gilligan 2003: 35).

While the male-dominated nature of the film industry has led some feminist critics to advocate scrapping the whole concept of the film auteur and approaching film from an ideological, audience-oriented, or genre perspective, others have tried to make auteurism more feminist-friendly by rewriting film history to uncover the work of women filmmakers. To this end, just as literary critics have rediscovered and reevaluated the works of neglected female authors, so feminist film criticism has set out to rewrite film history to highlight women's involvement in all aspects of film. For instance, Gwendolyn Audrey Foster argues that it is not so much that there is a paucity of women who have been important figures in the film industry, but that male film historians have systematically ignored their accomplishments and focused only on women in front of the camera (1999: xiii). She calls upon feminists to undertake a retrieval and reevaluation process to uncover the creative achievements of women filmmakers. Some of this retrieval has already begun and involves rediscovering women pioneers of early silent cinema, such as Lois Weber and Alice Guy-Blaché, who actually directed the first narrative film. Foster also discusses the important work done in European cinema by female directors Germaine Dulac and Marie Epstein, and in Black independent cinema by Zora Neale Hurston, who made pioneering ethnographic documentaries about African American rural communities (1999: xiv). As Foster points out, this retrieval process is complicated by the fact that because women filmmakers were held in such low regard for so long many of their films have been lost or destroyed (1999: xiv–xv).

Although Foster points to the existence of many talented women in the early film industry whose work has been ignored by film historians, she argues that as Hollywood film gained more prestige and notoriety in the 1930s women's participation diminished significantly, and beginning in the 1940s female filmmakers sought outlets for their talents primarily in experimental films (1999: xvii), as was the case with Maya Deren. Since the 1940s, women's participation in avant-garde and experimental cinema has been consistently high with contributions by such major figures as Chantal Akerman, Shirley Clarke, Sally Potter, and Barbara Hammer, although again they have gotten much less attention than male directors. Even in the extremely male dominated Hollywood studio era, one can point to two major female auteurs: Dorothy Arzner and Ida Lupino. European female directors, such as Germaine Dulac, Marie Epstein, Agnes Varda, Margarethe von Trotta, and Agnieska Holland, have also made significant contributions throughout film history although again their work has gotten less attention than it deserves. Other important areas of study for feminist auteurist criticism involve examining the careers of contemporary female auteurs working within Hollywood (for instance, Kathryn Bigelow and Sophia Coppola), avant-garde and art films (e.g. Sally Potter and Su Friedrich), documentary filmmaking (e.g. Pratibha Parmar and Jennie Livingston), and Third World cinema (e.g. Aparna Sen and Maria Louisa Bemberg). This study of contemporary female filmmakers is complicated by the refusal of many women directors to accept the feminist label (Foster 1999: xvii), as we have seen with Chantal Akerman and Barbara Kopple and as we will see yet again with Margarethe von Trotta. Like these directors, many contemporary female filmmakers do not want to be seen as feminist, and some do not even want to be designated as women directors. Foster suggests this may be because they fear this designation will affect their acceptance in the industry's boy's club (1999: xvii), but it might also involve their lack of an understanding of feminism, as we will see in the case of the actress Susan Sarandon, and their feeling that to be labeled a woman or even worse a feminist will limit the types of films they might be seen as capable of making. For instance, Hollywood woman filmmakers have been restricted largely to making family melodramas, romantic comedies, and teen flicks, but the success of Kathryn Bigelow, unquestionably the most important contemporary Hollywood female auteur, as an action director may indicate that those limitations are lessening somewhat.

Feminist auteurist criticism not only has focused on the bodies of work produced by notable female directors, but also has raised a number of theoretical issues important to feminist film studies, the first of which deals with the very definition of women's cinema. What does female auteurship mean in feminist terms? Should feminist critics study every female filmmaker and consider her work part of women's cinema or should they limit themselves to those whose work can be clearly designated as feminist? And what exactly constitutes a feminist film anyway? As we have seen, some feminist critics argue that women directors should develop a new filmmaking practice that critiques dominant cinematic conventions. Rejecting mainstream filmmaking, the true feminist auteur, according to this perspective, must utilize avant-garde strategies or documentary modes of filmmaking to deconstruct the dominant patriarchal ideology expressed in Hollywood films. Others have proposed that women's cinema of all types should be studied, not just the work of those who pit themselves directly against the mainstream, and that even directors working within Hollywood can subvert dominant filmmaking strategies in subtle ways. In this regard, the work of Dorothy Arzner has taken on particular significance.

Dorothy Arzner was the only woman to establish herself as a major Hollywood director in the studio era. Her most notable films were all made within the short period between 1932 and 1940 after which she retired from filmmaking: *Merrily We Go to Hell* (1932), *Christopher Strong* (1933), *Craig's Wife* (1936), and *Dance, Girl, Dance* (1940). Known for eliciting outstanding performances from her actresses, she worked with such talented female stars of the period as Katherine Hepburn, Rosalind Russell, Sylvia Sidney, and Maureen O'Hara. Arzner was taken up by feminist critics in the 1970s as a subversive filmmaker who attacked Hollywood from within by making internally self-critical texts, films that seem on the surface to support the dominant ideology, but underneath contain an internal tension that ruptures the ideological coherence of their classical Hollywood form. Pam Cook in "Approaching the Work of Dorothy Arzner" and Claire Johnston in "Dorothy Arzner: critical strategies" (both originally published in 1975) hailed Arzner as a feminist auteur working within the Hollywood studio system who created in her films exactly the type of internal subversion that might serve as a model for the development of a contemporary Hollywood feminist filmmaking practice. Arzner challenged mainstream cinematic norms without disrupting the pleasure viewers obtain from Hollywood films. Cook and Johnston use Arzner not only to illustrate the importance of introducing the work of women directors to the study of film history, but also as the basis for theoretical formulations of the devices contemporary mainstream feminist filmmakers might use to create films that are internally subversive of dominant cinematic practices.

Examining Arzner's work, Cook uncovers a number of subversive qualities, including an episodic narrative structure composed of a series of tableaux that interrupt the smooth movement of the plot and encourage the viewer to question the film's portrayal of reality. Cook points to Arzner's use of "pregnant moments" that interrupt the narrative, freeze the action, and expose the illusionism behind it (1988: 52). Arzner also notably employed narrative reversals that take her plots in unexpected directions and the denaturalization of female stereotypes, such as the vamp/straight girl split that divides female characters into binary oppositions. Johnston adds to Cook's list of subversive strategies Arzner's organization of her films as female discourses that violate classical Hollywood's privileging of the male story. Using the terminology of Russian formalist literary theory, Johnston proposes that Arzner's subversive filmmaking practice succeeds in "making strange" male discourse. In other words, it makes the story being told seem unusual, contradictory, open to question, and not simply representative of what is natural or the ultimate truth (Johnston 1990a: 144). Finally, Johnston points to the endings of Arzner's films as systematically refusing the narrative closure and resolution so characteristic of classical Hollywood films. Any surface enactment of a happy ending is undercut and the Hollywood "myth of sexual complementariness" embodied in the formation of the perfect heterosexual couple is subverted (Johnston 1990a: 146). For Cook and Johnston, Arzner represents a perfect model of feminist auteurism within the mainstream. She created films that appear on the surface to be conventional Hollywood narratives, but underneath offer a critique of the very norms to which they seem to adhere. They are what French critics Jean-Lois Comolli and Jean Narboni termed

> films which seem at first sight to belong firmly within the ideology and to be completely under its sway, but which turn out to be so only in an ambiguous manner. ... The films we are talking about throw up obstacles in the way of the ideology, causing it to swerve and get off course. The cinematic framework lets us see it, but also shows it up and denounces it. ... An internal criticism is taking place which cracks the film apart at the seams. If one reads the film obliquely, looking for symptoms; if one looks beyond its apparent formal coherence, one can see that it is riddled

with cracks, it is splitting under an internal tension which is simply not there in an ideologically innocuous film. (1976: 27)

In her auteurist analysis of Arzner, Judith Mayne argues that Cook and Johnston ignore a crucial aspect of Arzner's work: her lesbianism. For Mayne, Arzner's lesbian identity is an important factor in shaping her subversive relationship to Hollywood filmmaking. Mayne points out that "the Arzner look," the way she dressed and posed in promotional photos, was clearly readable as lesbian and thus challenged 1930s Hollywood's closeting of gay industry professionals (1991: 110). According to Mayne, Arzner's lesbian sensibility led her to give relationships between women a special place in her films and to imbue those relationships with an underlying erotic charge that undermines the films' otherwise heterosexual romantic plots and breaks away from the patriarchal association of women with passivity (1991: 118, 127). The subversive qualities of Arzner's work thus include subtextual elements that open her films up to lesbian reading possibilities. Mayne's work on Arzner is significant not only because it brings to the surface the importance of Arzner's lesbianism to a complete understanding of her oeuvre, but also because it avoids the tendency in auteurist criticism toward hagiography, the overpraising of the auteur and emphasis only on the positive characteristics of her work. Mayne points out that Arzner's films are flawed by her use of racist stereotypes and clichés. Although her work may be progressive in terms of its treatment of gender issues, it is hardly forward-looking in its representation of race. While calling into question distinctions based on gender, Arzner's films unfortunately affirm those related to race (Mayne 1991: 125).

To see how theoretical and critical ideas about feminist auteurism can be applied to the work of female filmmakers in a more contemporary context, we will now turn to the films of a major European woman director who like Arzner is a mainstream feminist auteur, Margarethe von Trotta. Rather than focus on a single film, we will follow the tenets of auteurism and examine major films within von Trotta's entire body of work for the distinctive artistic stamp, both stylistic and thematic, that she imprinted on her films.

Films in Focus: Margarethe von Trotta

Like Dorothy Arzner who worked entirely within the Hollywood studio system, Margarethe von Trotta has always remained within the mainstream German film industry. She was a major figure in what came to be known as the New German Cinema of the 1960s–1980s and is a prominent director today. The mainstream popularity of her films has lead some German feminist critics to accuse her of compromising her feminist vision for popular success, yet like Arzner, von Trotta expresses beneath the surface conformity of her films an underlying feminist vision that subverts mainstream cinematic norms. Von Trotta began her career as an actress, working with such prominent directors as Rainer Warner Fassbinder and Volker Schlöndorff, whom she married in 1971. It was Schlöndorff who introduced von Trotta to directing. In 1975, he invited her to co-direct *Die Verlorene Ehre de Katharina Blum oder: Wie Gewalt entstehen und wohin sie führen kann* (American Title: *The Lost Honor of Katharina Blum*), a political thriller dealing with the over-reaction of the German government and tabloid press to 1970s terrorist organizations like the Baader-Meinhoff Group. The film became an enormous success in Germany and launched von Trotta's directing career.

The Lost Honor of Katharina Blum focuses on its female protagonist's persecution by the government and the press as a result of her romance with a man accused of being a terrorist. Von Trotta's focus on female characters would continue throughout her career and become a major aspect of her work. Her first independently directed film, *Das Zweite Erwachen der Christa Klages* (*The Second Awakening of Crista Klages*, 1978), also has a female protagonist (played by Tina Engel), who experiences life-transforming relationships with two other women: Ingrid (Silvia Reize), her life-long friend whom she helps leave a bad marriage, and Lena (Katharina Thalbach), a young bank clerk so inspired by Christa's determination to save her failing childcare center that she refuses to identify her to the police for robbing the bank. The range of von Trotta's portrayals of women and their relationships is impressive. *The Second Awakening* is the first of many films in which von Trotta portrays relationships between women as crucial to their personal growth as well as to their developing sense of social and political activism.

A recurring thematic concern in von Trotta's films is the relationship of the personal to the political. Her third film, *Schwestern oder Die Balance des Glücks* (*Sisters or the Balance of Happiness*, 1979) seems at first glance to deal with women's relationships on a purely personal level and to present them in a negative light. The film focuses on two sisters involved in a destructive symbiotic relationship, which many critics see as containing the dominance–submission patterns more commonly found in heterosexual marriage. Maria (Jutta Lampe) dominates her younger sister Anna (Gudrun Gabriel), and their relationship ultimately results in Anna's suicide. After Anna's death, Maria establishes a similar relationship in which she dominates a fellow female office worker. When this friendship falls apart, Maria is forced to come to terms with the destructive effects of her domination of others. What makes von Trotta's presentation of Maria's failed relationships with other women so complex and gives it an underlying subversive quality is that she does not condemn Maria or present her as a monstrous character; instead, she portrays her sympathetically and ends the film with her desperate attempts to understand the nature of her destructive relationships. Additionally, Maria's dominant personality can be read symbolically as a critique of the "technocratic system of production and efficiency" characteristic of industrial capitalism and its disastrous effect on interpersonal relations (Moeller 1986: 145).

Like *Sisters*, other von Trotta films on the surface present women's relationships in an unfavorable light, but the complexity of the characterizations of her female characters refuses such a simple surface reading. *Die bleierne Zeit*, (American title: *Marianne and Juliane*, 1981), *Heller Wahn* (*Sheer Madness*, 1983), and *Rosenstrasse* (2003) all present relationships between women that can be seen as destructive. *Marianne and Juliane*, which many critics see as von Trotta's most accomplished work, is yet another intense portrayal of an highly problematic sister relationship. With biographical roots in the lives of the notorious Baader-Meinhoff terrorist Gundrun Ensslin (Barbara Sukowa) and her sister Christiane (Jutta Lampe), a feminist journalist, *Marianne and Juliane* focuses on Juliane's attempts to come to terms with her sister's terrorist activities and resulting death in prison. Although Juliane's obsession with her sister has decidedly negative effects on her life, it also leads her to rethink the relationship between her political commitment and her role as a mother figure to Marianne's abandoned son. Again, the film can be read on the surface as about an intensely destructive sister relationship, but on a deeper level it moves from the portrayal of a personal attachment to its social and political significance. As many critics have pointed out, the troubled relationship between the two sisters can be read as a symbolic representation of the split within German leftist politics between the advocacy of moderate reform and the desire for radical change.

Sheer Madness, von Trotta's next film after *Marianne and Juliane*, presents yet another complex portrayal of an intense friendship between two women. The film's protagonist is a college professor who strikes up a relationship with a troubled artist. The attachment between the two women is extremely close, even erotically charged with repeated exchanges of longing gazes between them, but it is also presented with considerable ambiguity. It is unclear what

Figure 11 From left, Jutta Lempe as Juliane and Barbara Sukawa as Marianne in an intense prison scene from Margarethe von Trotta's *Marianne and Juliane.*

significance von Trotta hopes her viewer will take away from her portrayal of this troubled friendship. On one level, von Trotta uses the women's relationship to critique "the oppressiveness that is built into the social construction of heterosexuality, at the cost of the woman" (Quart 1988: 124). Ruth (Angela Winkler), the young artist, is in a disastrously bad marriage with Franz (Peter Striebeck), a man who is determined to reduce her to a state of complete dependence on him. Her friendship with Olga (Hanna Schygulla) seems to help her break out of that dependence, but their attachment does not seem to be entirely positive. As Barbara Koenig Quart points out, Olga is a strong woman who allows herself to be parasitically drained by everyone around her, including her ex-husband, her son and her male lover (1988: 125). Ruth is yet another person feeding off Olga's strength in a way that may benefit Ruth but is unhealthy and destructive for Olga. Like von Trotta's other films, *Sheer Madness* works on several levels. It can be read on the personal level as an examination of the complex nature of its female characters' relationship, which is shown to have both positive and negative components, but their friendship seems to have even larger implications. The film appears to have been inspired by debates circulating at the time concerning the role feminists should play in urging other women to give up their dependence on their husbands (Quart 1988: 126) and the possibly destructive effects this urging might have on women whose psyches have been severely damaged by this dependence.

Unlike von Trotta's earlier films, *Rosenstrasse* focuses not on a dyadic relationship between two female characters, but on a group of Aryan women who stood outside a detention center in peaceful protest until the Nazis finally released their Jewish husbands. Von Trotta combines this political story with a more personal one of the mother–daughter bond that forms between one of the women whose husband is being held in the center and a young Jewish girl whose mother is being detained there. Even this personal relationship is given a larger dimension; the film emphasizes the importance this early attachment had on the girl's development into adulthood, her relationship with her own daughter, and her acceptance of her daughter's marriage outside of the Jewish community. For von Trotta, personal connections always have larger social and political significance. Ellen Seiter even characterizes von Trotta's films as cinematic investigations of the feminist slogan, "The personal is political" (1986: 113), but I would argue that von Trotta's work is much too complex to be reduced to this rather overused catch phrase.

Von Trotta's major thematic concerns are two-fold. First, she sets out to examine the situation of women in contemporary society, and second, she places her examination within the context of German history and national identity. As Renate Hehr suggests, what interests von Trotta are the effects of political and social events on the everyday lives and relationships of the people who live through them (2000: 20). I would argue, however, that on another level, von Trotta uses the personal lives and relationships she presents to mirror and interrogate social and political situations. For instance, many of her portrayals of women's relationships symbolize what she sees as the divided self of modern Germany. Her darker repressed characters, like Anna in *Sisters* and Ruth in *Sheer Madness*, represent the repressed past, while the more efficient controlling types, like Maria in *Sisters* and Olga in *Sheer Madness*, symbolize modern German efficiency and the contemporary desire to move away from the dark Nazi past (Christiansen 1989: 211; Linville 1991: 7). As noted above, the relationship between the sisters in *Marianne and Juliane* represents the division between terrorism and reformism in modern German social thought, and the inter-generational relationship in *Rosenstrasse* evokes the legacy of the Nazi era and the horrors of the Holocaust.

Renate Hehr maintains that von Trotta's whole oeuvre is molded by feminist issues (2000: 89), yet Von Trotta has said (in a way very similar to many Hollywood women directors) that to designate her films as women's films would place them in a "thought ghetto" (quoted in Ward 1995: 59). Jennifer K. Ward claims that von Trotta refuses to self-identify as a feminist filmmaker because she fears it will prevent her films from gaining mainstream acceptance (1995: 54). It cannot be denied, however, that von Trotta's work is deeply imbued with feminist issues, including the need for free and available childcare, feminist magazine publishing, abortion rights, aid for single mothers, and equality in marriage. In addition, Von Trotta's feminism comes out very clearly in her portrayals of her female characters. She has said, "I just have more ideas about women. When I begin to write, I find I'm thinking about women" (quoted in Schutte 1985: 72). In fact, her films overwhelmingly focus on strong female protagonists brought to life through the impressive performances of noted actresses like Barbara Sukowa, Jutta Lampe, and Tina Engle. She is known as an actor's director, casting very versatile and expressive actresses who can relate emotionally and identify strongly with their characters. Then, she works closely with them to perfect their performances (Elsner-Sommer and Edelman 1999: 142). Her techniques consistently elicit from her actresses nuanced performances of great psychological depth that have consistently won international acting awards.

Von Trotta also allows her female characters to tell their own stories, something rarely done in mainstream films. Most of von Trotta's films are told from the female perspective, using introductory framing scenes and voice-over that clearly identify the female protagonist as the source of the narrative. As Quart suggests, von Trotta's films present themselves as discourses conducted by women for women (1988: 103). Hehr even proposes that a major element of von Trotta's cinematic language is her rejection of mainstream images of women and her search for a new way to present the female image on screen (2000: 86). In accordance with these ends, von Trotta refuses to idealize her female stars through camera placement, lighting, make-up, or costuming; instead, the women in her films assume a natural, de-glamorized appearance. Here, too, we see the influence of feminist ideas as von Trotta incorporates into her film aesthetics the image of women as actively engaged in a struggle to define their own lives and identities rather than serving merely as passive projections of male fantasies.

This quest for female self-definition often involves doppelgänger situations in which one women serves as the dark double or alter ego of the other. Most often, this shadow self is an externalization of different possibilities open to the female protagonist or a representation of the inner split that von Trotta sees as characteristic of the female psyche (Kaplan 1983: 107). Female characters in her films can represent the struggle between life-affirming and death-directed components of the psyche, between terrorism and reformist politics, or between freedom and dependence. Whatever the dichotomy, the film's protagonist must learn how to incorporate the impulses associated with her repressed double into her own psyche in order to achieve psychic health. This incorporation does not just occur on a personal level, but also involves interaction with a social or historical situation. German critics in particular have not always reacted favorably to von Trotta's handling of the social and historical dimensions of her films. Some of her fiercest detractors accuse her of presenting the socio-historical milieux of her films in ways that undercut her otherwise progressive themes. Critics have repeatedly attacked the historical accuracy of her films and her tendency to emphasize the effects of historical events on the personal lives of her characters. For instance, Byron Byg accuses von Trotta of stressing the idea that the personal is political "to the point of denying that the political is political" (1993: 267). Charlotte Delorme's article on *Marianne and Juliane* launches a scathing attack against von Trotta's treatment of historical facts. In what can only be called a fulmination against von Trotta's film, Delorme accuses the director and her co-screenwriter Christiane Ensslin of creating a completely inaccurate portrayal of the life of Christiane's sister Gudrun. Delorme claims the film represents an "intentional distortion of reality" (1985: 48) in order to take revenge against Gudrun, even after her death. Others have criticized the film for doing the exact opposite: refusing unequivocally to condemn Marianne's terrorism (Quart 1988: 116). Similarly, *Rosa Luxemburg* (1986), a biopic of the famous German Marxist activist, was criticized for inaccurately presenting the events of Luxemburg's life and downplaying her Jewishness, *The Promise* for distorting the situation in East Berlin in the post-war period, and *Rosenstrasse* for focusing on the courage of Aryan rather than Jewish women during the Holocaust.

It is perhaps inevitable that there would be considerable opposition to a filmmaker like von Trotta who has repeatedly used her films to fashion "an incisive critique of the moral corruption of German society" (DiCaprio 1984), connected historical events of the past to the problems of the present, and employed feminism as a critical tool to deconstruct and re-envision the existing social and political structure. Critics have attacked von Trotta not only for the supposed historical inaccuracy of her portrayals, but for adhering to the conventions of film realism, which are said to undermine her political message. Beginning her directorial career under the guidance of Volker Schlöndorff and heavily financed by his production company, Bioskop, of which she is part owner, von Trotta has been accused of employing a conventional realist film style in order to gain acceptance with mainstream audiences. Many German feminist critics have attacked her for working too closely within the system and creating characters too saturated in realist conventions to have any political value (Elsner-Sommer and Edelman 1999: 442). Even American feminist critics, like E. Ann Kaplan and Ann Seiter, have argued that von Trotta has "boxed [herself] in" by the "relentless realism" of her portrayals (Kaplan

1983: 112) and allowed the domestic melodramas of her plots to detract from her political and social critiques (Seiter 1986: 115).

Others have pointed to the unconventional stylistic aspects of von Trotta's filmmaking and have argued that she is a realist filmmaker who takes realism in a progressive direction. Like the work of Dorothy Arzner, von Trotta's films on the surface resemble conventional realist narratives, but below that surface realism, they are very different, and it is only by looking at this underlying difference that one sees the magnitude of her accomplishment. Like Arzner, von Trotta utilizes the structures of popular realist filmmaking to make her films "accessible, gripping, pleasure-giving," but she transforms this conventional realist style into a cinematic technique that takes her audience to "dark disturbing places that open our fundamental values to question" (Quart 1988: 93, 95). As Hehr points out, von Trotta creates multi-layered films that contain beneath their conventional surface content existential questions of personal identity, human interaction, social responsibility, and individual and collective guilt (2000: 8).

One of the most challenging aspects of von Trotta's style, and something that makes her again very similar to Arzner, is her use of open endings that challenge her audience and stimulate thought, rather than allowing viewers passively to accept the film's discourse as absolute truth. *The Second Awakening of Christa Klages* ends with an enigmatic exchange of glances between Christa and the bank clerk Lena after Lena has refused to identify Christa as the thief who robbed the bank where Lena works and took her hostage. This exchange can be read simply as indicating both women's personal awakenings, or in a "larger, more political feminist way" as symbolizing the "solidarity of women with women – as well as an opening of one part of the self to another, a conversation within" (Quart 1988: 102). Similarly, the ending of *Sisters* can be interpreted variously as indicating Maria's complete psychic disintegration as a result of her failure to come to terms with her sister's death, as her "final act of integration of self. ... [by] yielding up some of her own overbearingness, excessive responsibility and control; and by making contact with her own dreaminess, vulnerability, terror," or even symbolically as a reconciliation between the different sides of the German psyche (Quart 1988: 112). Considerable ambiguity is also found at the end of *Marianne and Juliane* when Juliane decides to take in Marianne's son Jan. Is this ending to be read as returning her to a traditional feminine role as nurturer, advocating a new form of motherhood, or symbolically representing the need for contemporary Germans to take responsibility for their country's future? Von Trotta's endings simply refuse to provide the resolution found in mainstream films. Like her oeuvre as a whole, her endings may on the surface seem to follow the tenets of conventional realism, but underneath they refuse to offer their audience the comfort of using cinema as an imaginary resolution to social problems (Hehr 2000: 21). They do not propose an "essential, singly defined truth"; instead, von Trotta's endings are "formally and thematically feminist and deconstructive", confronting their spectators with ambiguity and contradiction and placing them in a spectatorial position of "engaged indecision" (Linville 1991: 449, 452) and thoughtful reflection. These qualities would seem unquestionably to identify von Trotta as a feminist auteur.

Key Terms: *auteur, auteurism, Great Man Theory of Film History, auteur-structuralism, author-construct, binary oppositions, female auteur, feminist auteur, pregnant moments, internally subversive films, making strange*

Suggestions for Further Reading, Viewing, and Discussion

1. Do you see auteurism as a fruitful area of feminist film study? What does it add to feminist thinking about film? Should it be abandoned as a hopelessly masculinist concept?

2. What do you see as the proper object of study for the feminist auteurist critic? Should it be only women filmmakers who challenge mainstream conventions and whose films convey clear feminist messages?

3. Study the work of a major female filmmaker from an auteurist perspective. What are the major thematic and stylistic elements of her films? Do you see feminist elements in her work? Should she be seen as a auteur? Would you consider her a feminist auteur? The filmography below suggests some female directors (and three of their major films) who have amassed a body of films and can be considered auteurs.

4. Compare female auteurs from different periods in film history, types of filmmaking modes (e.g. documentary, avant-garde, Hollywood film), racial groups, and/or national cinemas. What does your study tell you about auteurism in these various different contexts?

5. View some of the films of Margarethe von Trotta. Do you agree that they exhibit feminist elements? Should she be considered a feminist auteur?

Filmography of Women Auteurs

Gillian Armstrong: *My Brilliant Career* (1979); *Little Women* (1994); *Charlotte Gray* (2001)

Dorothy Arzner: *Christopher Strong* (1933); *Craig's Wife* (1936); *Dance, Girl, Dance* (1940)

Kathryn Bigalow: *Blue Steel* (1989); *Strange Days* (1995); *The Hurt Locker* (2008)

Lizzie Borden: *Born in Flames* (1983); *Working Girls* (1986); *Love Crimes* (1992)

Jane Campion: *Sweetie* (1989); *The Piano* (1993); *The Portrait of a Lady* (1996)

Sophia Coppola: *The Virgin Suicides* (1999); *Lost in Translation* (2003); *Marie Antoinette* (2006)

Julie Dash: *Illusions* (1982); *Daughters of the Dust* (1991); *The Rosa Parks Story* (TV, 2002)

Claire Denis: *Nenette and Boni* (1996); *Beau travail* (1999); *White Material* (2009)

Marleen Gorris: *A Question of Silence* (1982); *Antonia's Line* (1995); *Mrs. Dalloway* (1997)

Amy Heckerling: *Fast Times at Ridgemont High* (1982); *Look Who's Talking* (1989); *Clueless* (1995)

Agnieszka Holland: *Europa, Europa* (1990); *Olivier, Olivier* (1992); *The Secret Garden* (1993)

Penny Marshall: *Big* (1988); *A League of Their Own* (1992); *Riding in Cars with Boys* (2001)

Sally Potter: *Thriller* (1979); *Orlando* (1992); *The Tango Lesson* (1997)

Aparna Sen: *Paroma* (1984); *Sati* (1989); *Mr. and Mrs. Ayer* (2002)

Agnes Varda: *Cleo from 5 to 7* (1962); *One Sings, the Other Doesn't* (1977); *Vagabond* (1985)

Lina Wertmüller: *The Seduction of Mimi* (1972); *Swept Away* (1974); *Seven Beauties* (1975)

Chapter 8

The Actress

Film scholarship has placed its emphasis on star studies rather than on the examination of film acting. As a result, the acting techniques of Hollywood stars have received far too little scholarly attention. Within the field of star studies, the focus has fallen overwhelmingly on ideological criticism of star images and the historical examination of the star system. The study of stars as actors, which is, after all, the major reason for their stardom, has been pushed to the side. Also, the common conception that stars actually cannot act but just play themselves on screen has interfered with the examination of their acting methods. This idea stems from the common association of star acting with personification, the mode of acting in which actors are seen as playing themselves in their various roles. The theory of personification insists that the "star is always himself or herself, only thinly disguised as a character." Actors are seen as not really acting, but just "being" on the screen, and their characters are considered merely "fictional extension[s] of the actors' true personalities" (Maltby 2003: 384). Barry King has called this type of acting "concerted cynosure," which involves the fusion of the roles actors play with their own personalities (2003: 46).

Because of this fusion, star acting is identified with non-acting or even worse with bad acting. It is contrasted unfavorably with the acting mode termed impersonation, which is said to involve the actor's personality disappearing into the role or the actor becoming or transforming him or herself into the character. Impersonation is associated in somewhat different theoretical terms with both Method and Broadway repertory acting and has gained considerable prestige from this association. In Method acting, the actor is said to become the character, whereas in Broadway repertory acting the actor pretends to be or imitates the character's actions and emotions, but in both acting styles, actors give up their own personalities to become someone else. Hence, their methodology is said to be impersonation. Personification, on the other hand, never involves this sacrifice of the actor's own personality. The star is always seen behind the role, and for this reason, someone employing this acting style is often condemned as a poor actor. Because star acting is so strongly associated with this mode of personification, the film apparatus is even said to make acting unnecessary and to require stage actors to undertake a "deskilling process" (Geraghty 2000: 192).

More recently, scholars have begun to question the validity of the distinction between personification and impersonation. For instance, Paul McDonald suggests that the two are not exclusive acting types at all, but are always combined in acting performances (1998: 32). As Barry King points out, impersonation has been cultivated in film acting because of its association with craft and technique (1991: 147). Alan Lovell even proposes that criticism of star acting as personification reflects anti-Hollywood sentiment rather than a legitimate critique of modes of acting. He questions the notion that playing oneself is necessarily bad acting, pointing out that accomplished people in all occupations concentrate their talents on a limited area of expertise which provides them with an avenue to success. He sees star actors who use typecasting as a means of establishing a stable "picture personality" as simply placing themselves in a venue where they feel their talents will benefit them, and he characterizes them as "the best actors by and large" (Lovell 2003: 263).

If star acting has been neglected as a subject of scholarly analysis, the work of the star-actress, and especially the contemporary star-actress, has been particularly ignored. This is not to say that the work of Hollywood actresses remains unexamined. Feminist film critics have made some interesting observations about female stars, but these stars have not been studied as actresses per se, but more as ingredients within patriarchy's ideological conception of an idealized femininity. Feminist approaches to the star-actress have been limited by her conception either as a representation of social stereotypes of women or as a fetishized object of the voyeuristic male gaze. In both instances, the star-actress is not seen as a skilled performer in her own right, but as "a construction, a product of culture, industrially manufactured, and prefabricated by men" (Gaines: 1990a: 1). Another reason for the neglect of the female star-actress is a long-standing tendency to denigrate the acting abilities of female stars in comparison to male stars. The classic expression of this idea is Josef von Sternberg's comment: "To study acting is one thing, but to study the actor and the female of the acting species is something else again. There would be no need to study them at all were it not that [films are] dominated by them, and it is necessary to become familiar with the material one is compelled to use" (quoted in Naremore 1988: 131).

Overwhelmingly, the work of female stars has been compared unfavorably to the accomplishments of their male counterparts. For instance, the acting abilities of female stars have traditionally been more naturalized than those of male stars, who are much more likely to be described as highly skilled and well-trained professionals whose success is the result of hard work and mastery of the craft of acting, rather than of their physical attractiveness and natural talent. Physical beauty has always been more important as a criteria for female stardom, but, as Virginia Wright Wexman points out, the work that an actress puts into her appearance has never been recognized as part of her acting skill (1993: 136). Instead, actresses are viewed merely as passive beauty icons who have risen to stardom due to their physical attractiveness or because they are willing to use their sexuality on "the casting couch" to get roles.

Star biographies are notorious for "emphasizing the training and work habits of men while focusing on the romantic adventures and pampered irresponsibility of the women" (Wexman 1993: 134). This emphasis on work, training and professionalism for male stars helps them to maintain their stardom even as they grow older, whereas female stars notoriously have great difficulty sustaining their careers once they reach the age of forty. One way ageing male stars extend their careers is by advancing from acting to directing and producing, but female stars rarely make this move, and when they do, they are seen as exceptional, like Jodie Foster, or difficult, like Barbara Streisand. Female stars have also often been portrayed as "Galatea figures," whose careers are launched and managed by powerful male directors or producers, while male stars are almost never portrayed in this way (Wexman 1993: 135). In addition, female stars' box office clout is traditionally lower than that of male stars. There are few female stars who can "open" (headline) a film based on their star status alone without a major male star opposite them. In addition, actresses over forty commonly lose almost all of their box office appeal and are no longer seen as candidates for high profile roles. Stars cannot get the choice parts that would allow them to ascend into the pantheon of major stardom until they have built a reputation in the industry. Thus, an actress would not be able to become a top box office draw until she hit her thirties, and given that an actress's career begins to decline when she turns forty, this leaves her with only a ten year window when she can enter the highest box office ranks, which are overwhelmingly dominated by male stars whose careers often thrive well into their old age (Kramer 2003: 202).

Another reason why female stars have been neglected as actresses may be that they are more closely identified with celebrity than with acting. In discussing star types, Christine Geraghty argues that female stars are much more likely to be perceived as celebrities rather than as professionals or performers because their private lives are more often the subject of celebrity gossip and their stardom is more commonly based on this gossip than is the case for male stars. In fact, some types of celebrity status distinct from acting, such as rock stardom or a modeling career, can serve as a means of entrée into Hollywood for female stars. It is especially common for popular singers to make the transition to star acting. One benefit of this situation for the female star is that she can maintain her star status through her "consistent extratextual interest as a celebrity," even when her films are only intermittently successful. Her celebrity affords her the star power needed to maintain her career even in the face of a string of bad performances (Geraghty 2000: 196–97). This celebrity status is especially important given that female stars have lower box office clout than male stars and often do not benefit as much from a reputation for acting ability. At least, they have their celebrity to fall back on.

Most studies of female stars look at them only as figures of commercialism and conspicuous consumption, especially in regard to fashion and beauty products. Much more than male stars, actresses are seen as "simplified frozen schema for commercial purposes" (Amossy 1986: 681). Partly, this comes from a strong cultural association between femininity and physical beauty. The need for physical perfection on screen is commonly seen as a result of film technology, especially the importance of the close-up and the larger-than-life quality of film projection, both of which tend to enlarge and accentuate an actor's smallest imperfection. Why the burden of this requirement has fallen so heavily on female stars, however, is not entirely clear. Part of the problem is that the standards of physical attractiveness required of male stars are only beginning to be investigated, so it is difficult to compare the importance of beauty for male and female actors. As noted earlier, the emphasis on female stars' physical attractiveness has traditionally been used to denigrate their talent and craft by attributing their fame to good looks, fashion, makeup, and more recently to plastic surgery, diet, and intensive exercise routines. Yet, as Virginia Wright Wexman points out, a number of major questions about the relation of female stardom to beauty have not been resolved. For instance, how important really is physical appearance to an actress's success when some of the most beautiful actresses never make it to the top level of stardom and others who are attractive but not sensationally so do? What is the effect of a star's physical attractiveness on the film audience? How much of stars' beauty is natural and how much is constructed, and how much do contemporary female stars rely on cosmetic surgery and other extreme beauty enhancing procedures and products to improve their physical appearance? Should beautification be considered a major aspect of the craft of the film actress? (Wexman 1993: 133).

Several studies have shown that studio publicity departments early determined that using female stars as walking advertisements for fashion and cosmetics was not only a good way to establish tie-ins with these industries, but also effective in creating a special bond between actresses and their female fans. Charles Eckert was the first to recognize a close mutual relationship between the studios and consumer culture, a bond which he sees as taking hold in the 1930s. Studio era films were used as "living display windows" for consumer products with the major models within these windows being female stars, whom Wexman calls "passive images of beauty and romantic desirability" within the film industry's "mystification of glamour" (1993: 145, 142). Jane Gaines and Charlotte Herzog have carefully traced the progression of Hollywood's long relationship with the fashion and beauty industries throughout the studio period. They point to the development of "clothes horse" stars, who were promoted by the fashions they wore both on-screen and off. Behind them were prominent male costume designers, such as Travis Benton for Marlene Dietrich, Orry for Grace Kelly and Bette

Davis, and Gilbert Adrian for Joan Crawford and Greta Garbo (Gaines 1990b: 198–99). Like directors and producers, these Svengali-like figures are often given credit for making an actress into a star by dressing her in their celebrated fashions. For instance, Lucy Fischer argues that Greta Garbo's star image in the 1920s was built on her presentation as an Art Deco fashion icon through costuming and set design. According to Fischer, Garbo came to represent the "coveted 'look' of the era," the look of "the 'new' or modern woman" (2003: 95, 112). Gaines and Herzog also point to the development of particular film sequences, known as the "social whirl" montage and the fashion-show-within-the-film, which became staples of woman's films of 1930s and 1940s and were constructed just to display current fashions on screen (1991: 78). Thus, within the studio period, a star's fashion wardrobe became a useful tool for solidifying her claims to stardom. It not only helped to give her an easily identifiable star image based on her sense of fashion, but also linked her off-screen star image with her screen personality.

This association of female stars with the fashion and beauty industry has certainly not diminished, although it has not been studied in regard to contemporary stardom to the extent that it has been for the studio era. For instance, Gwyneth Paltrow is a contemporary example of a "clothes horse" star, and throughout her career she has been lauded for her beauty, fashion sense, and glamour. While the association of the female star with beauty can lead to her worship as a screen goddess, there is a dark side to this association. Many female stars have been the victims of sexual and commercial exploitation due to Hollywood's obsession with female allure. The tragic lives of Marilyn Monroe and Judy Garland have been the subject of numerous star biographies, but serious scholarly analysis has yet to investigate fully the effects of commercial exploitation on female stars. This exploitation is exacerbated by the fact that contemporary stars now suffer from a new form of commercial commodification not found in the studio era: exploitation by the Internet porn industry. Internet porn sites place stars, and most often they are female stars, in a new context of commercial exploitation as sexual titillation for fans. Paul McDonald discusses two types of sites: celebrity nudes and fake celebrity nudes. The former shows stars in intimate scenes from their films, in porn films or nude photos they made before they became famous, or in paparazzi photos that catch them in various states of undress in private moments when they did not know they were being photographed. Fake celebrity nudes provide fans with "more intense voyeuristic fantasy" by using computer technology to alter star photos to place them in erotic contexts. McDonald proposes that these new forms of commercial exploitation, like older types of star publicity, sell what they claim to be revelations of the intimate caught-off-guard private moments of stars' lives as a way for the fan to get at the "hidden truth" behind the star's image. Fake celebrity nudes, however, have an even more sinister underlying purpose. They seek to mock and humiliate stars by placing them in erotic contexts that never really existed and that might cause them embarrassment. This is done to reduce the star's power and give fans a sense of control over the star's image (McDonald 2003: 35–37).

It is ironic that scholars have studied Hollywood actresses more fully in terms of their relationship to consumerism than to acting, but the closest critics have come to an analysis of female stars' acting is to devise typologies of female stars. These typologies put female stars into categories based on their screen image, role choice, or the social stereotypes prevalent at the time of their popularity, rather than their acting techniques. For instance, Richard Dyer places female stars into the categories of the pin-up, independent woman, exceptional woman, girl-next-door, and figure of sexual ambiguity (1979: 61). Similarly, Molly Haskell divides studio era female stars into superfemales and superwomen based on the roles they play. Because the superfemale is too intelligent and ambitious for traditional women's roles, she is led to demonic behavior (e.g. Bette Davis), whereas the superwoman adopts masculine characteristics in order to survive in a male-dominated society (e.g. Katherine Hepburn) (Dyer 1979: 61).

Dyer and Haskell query the exact social significance of these roles. Do they challenge the status quo by showing women's dissatisfaction with their allotted position in society or do they teach women that those who seek to move away from "proper" femininity will be punished? Haskell sees the influence of these images on female fans as largely positive, while Dyer is more uncertain of their overall effect. As Dyer points out, the superwoman who becomes in a sense a pseudo-male is perhaps not so much a product of women's discomfort with their limited social status as of a male rejection of femininity. The endings of films containing these socially critical star types usually contain what Dyer calls a "climb-down" for the female character as she is shown to be finally humiliated or punished (1979: 64). On the other hand, Haskell proposes that female fans tend to remember the personality of the star behind the role and ignore the character's "climb-down" ending (Dyer 1979: 56). The differences between Haskell and Dyer suggest one of the main problems with the typological approach. It tends to confuse the star with the character she plays. Dyer looks at the status of the character played by the star at the close of a film and sees this status as significant in terms of what fans make of the star's image, whereas Haskell discusses the star's image as based upon, yet also transcending, a given role. This conflation of star image and role makes it difficult to know exactly what to make of these star typologies that are based on characters stars play. Do they relate both to the star's overall image extracted from extratextual sources, like promotion and publicity, as well as to the roles the star plays, or are they simply a reflection of the star's screen personality extrapolated from her most notable film portrayals?

Other critics have examined common roles played by women and concluded that female stars often play some type of performer, such as an actress, dancer, or singer. Many possible reasons have been proposed for this casting choice. As Lucy Fischer points out, the role of performer places the actress's character in a glamorous, self-supporting occupation that puts emphasis on her beauty, sex appeal and romantic involvements rather than connecting her with the mundane world of work where she might be shown in competition with men. It also provides ample opportunity for close-ups to emphasize her physical attractiveness and highly emotional scenes to showcase the intensity of her acting (Fischer 1989: 145–47). As both Fischer and Wexman suggest, the association of the actress with theatricality, artifice, and deception also connects her with roles that diminish her recognition as an artist and a respected professional. She is portrayed as a role-player who is always hiding behind a theatrical mask, whose goal is to perform for and please men, and whose success is based on natural talent rather than hard work (Fischer 1989, 1999). Wexman argues further that casting female stars in roles as performers diminishes their association with power by identifying them with characters who are always guided by men, who suffer from self-destructive personalities, or who have lost their chance at love because of their career goals. When these same roles are enacted by aging female stars, they take on a subversive potential, threatening to demystify star glamour and expose its constructed nature (Wexman 1993: 145–46).

Wexman and Dyer both emphasize the relation between female stars' images and prevalent social types or mores. For instance, Wexman argues that female star images are strongly connected to social ideals of heterosexual romance and romantic love. Actresses are not only typecast in romantic roles, but these roles are complemented by close-up cinematography, an obsession with physical appearance, and an emphasis on the screen kiss, all of which work to create an "intimate rapport between actress and audience" that positions the female star as "an ideal of desirable emotional intimacy" (Wexman 1993: 239, note 10). Publicity also presents the actress as living in a world without material problems, where the work of acting is de-emphasized, and she is left to agonize over an endless stream of romantic relationships. According to Dyer, this presentation of female stars as romantic ideals positions their lives and the roles they play as models for viewer emulation. Female stars offer lessons in the inevitability of suffering and the need for endurance in romantic attachments, men's and women's proper roles in love relationships, and how to maintain a healthy marriage (Dyer 1979: 53). Wexman believes that in the final analysis female stars promote an ideal of heterosexual romance that advocates long-term monogamous romantic relationships. Even though female stars usually engage in many romantic attachments throughout their careers, they are presented as practicing serial monogamy, moving from one great love affair to another and always suffering from a failure to find, or from the tragedy of just having lost, their one true love (Wexman 1993: 24). As Wexman points out, this emphasis on romance in the biographies of female stars works to reduce their status as successful professional women and to place them in a subordinate position to men (1993: 134). In spite of all their acting accomplishments, their ultimate goal is repeatedly shown to be the acquisition of male affection, rather than the fulfillment of their own independent career ambitions.

Traditionally, acting success in film has been considered the "ultimate confirmation of stardom" (Gledhill 1991: xiii), and television actors have been regarded as rising only to the level of TV personalities. Because they lack the "rarity value" of film stars, television actors are said never to reach the pinnacle of true stardom (Ellis 1982: 314). The prevalence of female stars in made-for-television dramas, however, has called this division into question, and Joanne Lacey argues for a distinct category of female television stars, including, for instance, Valerie Bertinelli, Lindsay Wagner, Linda Carter, Melissa Gilbert, Meredith Baxter, Donna Mills, and Tori Spelling. Lacey proposes that these actresses transcend the level of television personalities. Because their star status is used specifically to promote their made-for-television films, they can guarantee high ratings, bring their star persona to bear on the characters they play, and amass large communities of female fans who follow both their careers and celebrity gossip about their personal lives. Made-for-television stardom has also been a traditional way for fallen or aging stars to resuscitate their careers. Yet made-for-TV stars do differ from film stars in that their careers are almost exclusively confined to television, their fans do not want them to move to the big screen, and they do not cultivate the image of great beauty and glamour associated with Hollywood female stardom. In fact, Lacey argues that the made-for-television star must possess a certain "plainness" to establish a connection with her fans and fit into made-for-TV dramas that are largely devoted to enacting "the trials of everyday life" (2003: 196–97).

Female stars not only can be typed by the medium in which they perform, but also by their style of performance. For instance, Christine Geraghty has made an interesting distinction between the acting styles employed by British and American female stars. She argues for two distinct female acting modes: heritage and glamour acting. The heritage style is associated with the British heritage films, which, as we have seen, fall into the categories of period dramas and literary adaptations. This style is employed most notably by prominent British actresses, such as Emma Thompson, Judi Dench, Kate Winslet, and Helena Bonham Carter, and is characterized by "restraint," rendering emotions through intellect rather than feelings, and a sense of "irony, which demonstrates the heroines' superior understanding" (Geraghty 2003: 108). Geraghty compares the level of prestige and aesthetic worth that accrues to actresses who employ this style to what Method acting has done for many male stars, giving them a reputation for acting prowess. As Geraghty suggests, the reason for the attribution of acting ability to female as opposed to male stars is actually very different. Male Method actors are seen as great artists because they are said to demonstrate emotional expressiveness, whereas heritage style actresses are granted prestige for showing emotional restraint.

Geraghty points to only one Hollywood actress who has cultivated the heritage style: Gwyneth Paltrow, whose penchant for both British films and British accents has led her in this direction. Yet Paltrow has not totally abandoned the dominant acting style common among Holywood actresses, which Geraghty characterizes as glamour acting. According to Geraghty, this acting technique emphasizes not intellect, aesthetic achievement, or restraint, but sensual appeal and physical presence and relies heavily on acting in close-up to show the star's perfect looks and model-like body (2003: 105–17). Glamour acting is the performance style associated most with "to-be-looked-at-ness," and it contributes greatly to the Hollywood actress's status as an object of desire and concomitantly detracts from her recognition as a skilled actress.

Although most typologies of female stars characterize them as serving to support dominant social values and mores either through their images, the roles they play, or both, occasionally a female star is said to break with the ideological status quo and offer herself as a figure of resistance. Dyer characterizes some stars as "alternative or subversive types," who embody positions in opposition to dominant ideological beliefs (1979: 59). Similarly, Pam Cook proposes that certain female stars throughout film history have resisted the conventional roles assigned them and come to represent models of an alternative identity for their female fans. Cook even claims that it is this subversive quality that actually accounts for an actress's "true star quality" (quoted in Geraghty 2000: 185). Feminist critics have debated extensively whether the roles played and images projected by Hollywood actresses actually challenge dominant ideological concepts in any major way or whether any challenge they offer is inevitably recuperated by the overarching power of patriarchal ideology. Even if female stars themselves may not be able to challenge the status quo, some feminist critics argue that female viewers can read them as such. As noted earlier, Andrea Weiss proposes that in order to reinforce their sense of lesbian identity lesbian viewers commonly read female Hollywood stars against the grain in ways that interpret their images as sexually ambiguous. She believes lesbian viewers of the 1930s did this with Greta Garbo and Marlene Dietrich. Using gossip about the star's lesbianism, they read these stars' androgynous, exotic, and ambiguously sexualized screen personas in ways that empowered lesbian viewers, resisted patriarchy, and affirmed lesbian identity (Weiss 1991: 297).

One tendency in the study of female stars is to investigate particular actresses as unique individual figures, rather than seeing them as part of an overall category, and this inclination has been pervasive throughout the history of star studies. Individual studies of prominent female stars have tended to look at them in isolation as unique instances rather than seeing them as representative figures. These studies have also tended to ignore the contemporary female star in favor of stars in the studio period and to laud these stars with a fan-like devotion as screen goddesses rather than seeing them as working professionals. This is not to say that studies of individual female stars have not shed considerable light on female stardom. Studies of prominent stars in the silent and studio period are particularly illuminating. In the silent period, focus has largely been placed on Lillian Gish and has involved the question of her status as a great actress. Scholars have argued against the notion that she was merely a "Galatea figure" created by director D.W. Griffith, proposing that she not only shaped her acting performances, but even created her own acting style by mixing naturalistic and ostensive acting techniques (see, for instance, Naremore 1988, Chapter 6). Wexman argues beyond this that Gish was not only a great actress in her own right, but a subversive figure who embodied the "victimized femininity" and "aura of feminine helplessness" that Griffith cultivated in her performances, but also challenged this characterization through her career success and reputation as the premier actress of the silent era (1993: 63, 134). Paul McDonald's work on Mary Pickford makes a similar argument. Like Gish, Pickford played "diminutive child-women," yet at the same time she was a shrewd businesswoman who quickly and effectively took control of her own career, negotiated lucrative contracts, exploited her child-like image, and shifted from one studio to another when it was to her advantage. Finally, she even co-founded United Artists Studio with Douglas Fairbanks, Charlie Chaplin, and D.W. Griffith. As McDonald suggests, although Pickford's career collapsed because she was unable to move into mature adult roles, she remains a female star of the silent period who had clout, business savvy, and the ability to move from acting to producing (2000: 38).

Studies of actresses in the studio period also address the issue of whether female stars had any real control of their careers. Studies of Marlene Dietrich's work in the early sound period exemplify this approach. Laura Mulvey saw Dietrich as essentially reduced in her screen roles to the position of a wax dummy manipulated by director Josef von Sternberg. According to Mulvey, Dietrich was merely an object of fetishistic scopophilia, totally subjected to the male gaze, and entirely supportive of patriarchal dominance (1989d: 22–23). Similarly, Gaylin Studlar envisioned Dietrich's screen image as "the cold feminine ideal of masochistic fantasy" embodied in a "powerfully sexual, androgynous ... punishing woman [who] is not sadistic, but exhibits the pseudo-sadism (punishing function) required within the purely masochistic narrative" (1990: 238–39, 235). Other critics, however, have argued that Dietrich was far from being totally under the power of von Sternberg and male desire, but actually had considerable control of her own screen image. For instance, Richard Dyer considers von Sternberg-Dietrich films symbolic enactments of the personal relationship between the director and his star, with the films' male characters serving as surrogates for von Sternberg and Dietrich representing the object of his voyeuristic scopophilia. Yet Dyer also argues that Dietrich did not passively accept this placement; instead, she resisted it in subtle ways (1979: 180). Following Dyer's lead, some critics have begun to portray Dietrich not as a simple pawn of patriarchy, but as a subversive figure more sophisticated than the material she was required to perform, gently satirizing her characters and the plots of her films, and seditiously critiquing patriarchy through her "masquerade of femininity" (Naremore 1988: 143). For these critics, she became a co-author of her performances with von Sternberg, indissolubly united with him in a relationship of collaboration rather than domination (Zucker 1990: 293–94). More recently, Dietrich has been proclaimed an ambiguously lesbian figure clandestinely affirming lesbian identity through her androgynous screen persona (Weiss 1991: 286–87). The progression of Dietrich criticism from her portrayal as the mindless creation of an omnipotent male director and a passive object of male voyeurism to a female star who covertly shaped their own career and image in anti-patriarchal directions is indicative of the movement in feminist film criticism to portray female stars not simply as passive Galatea figures controlled by a male-dominated industry, but as women with considerable influence and power within that industry.

In looking at actresses within the studio era, the counter-tendency is still there for scholars to see female stars as almost entirely products of the studio system or of dominant ideological conceptions of women's roles. For instance, both Cathy Klaprat and Martin Shingler portray the screen personality of Bette Davis, a star known for her heated disputes with studio executives, as completely shaped by studio publicity and role assignment. Klaprat and Shingler argue that the studio calculatedly shifted Davis's image first from a glamorous romantic leading lady to an independent, hard-boiled seductress and then to a highly accomplished and respected great actress. Similarly, James Naremore argues that Katherine Hepburn's early image was seen as too patrician and feminist for film audiences, so the studio systematically assigned her to roles that demonstrated her "retreat from assertiveness" and served to "dramatiz[e] her complete submission to patriarchal authority" (1988: 175–76). Whereas the studio construction of Davis's and Hepburn's images succeeded in making them huge stars, James Damico argues that studio fashioning led to Ingrid Bergman's bitter rejection by fans. Her studio-promoted persona of wholesome, pure, asexual saintliness and total devotion to her husband and family was completely shattered when her illegitimate pregnancy as a result of a scandalous extra-marital love affair with Italian film director Roberto Rossellini was revealed, and her fans viciously turned against her.

Critics have characterized other studio era actresses as products not so much of studio control but of ideological conceptions of proper womanhood. Proposing that star images resolve the unresolvable split between cultural definitions of the ordinary and the extraordinary, Richard Dyer's work has been crucial in initiating this type of ideological analysis. For instance, in *Heavenly Bodies* he portrays Marilyn Monroe's star persona as embodying the virgin/whore split in 1950s conceptions of womanhood and Lana Turner's glamorous image, girl-next-door background, and troubled personal life as enacting the ordinary/extraordinary dichotomy inherent in stardom. It is really Jane Fonda, a post-studio Hollywood actress, who serves as Dyer's poster girl for the ideologically constructed star. He sees her image as an unstable and shifting combination of conflicting elements connected to her troubled relationship with her father, the famous studio-era actor Henry Fonda; the exploitive nature of screen portrayals of her sexuality; her extra-cinematic association with political radicalism; and her reputation for acting talent. According to Dyer, Fonda's image changed with the times from progressive to reactionary (1979: 72–98). Tessa Perkins argues further that Fonda's persona not only changed in response to current issues, but became a matter of so much contention that it meant entirely different things to people with different political affiliations. According to Perkins, Fonda's image became a site of ideological struggle especially in the 1970s when the mainstream press attacked her as a radical feminist extremist, while the responses of actual feminist critics ranged from seeing her as a role model of feminist rebellion to regarding her as a bandwagon feminist whose life and roles did not entirely support her feminist reputation.

In *The Actress: Hollywood acting and the female star*, I initiated a fuller examination of the acting craft and ideological significance of contemporary actresses. I argue that it is important to consider how female stars fit into the male-dominated Hollywood industry and how they are shaped by and contest patriarchal ideology. We will keep these issues in mind as we look at the star image of Susan Sarandon and examine in particular her work in what is arguably the most feminist Hollywood film of the contemporary era, *Thelma & Louise* (Ridley Scott, 1991).

Films in Focus: Susan Sarandon and *Thelma & Louise*

Thelma & Louise is generally seen as the creative product of the combined efforts of its female screenwriter Callie Khouri and male director Ridley Scott. Khouri certainly deserves major credit for the film. As a novice screenwriter, she wrote the screenplay, her first, with the initial hope of directing it herself. When she began to shop her script around Hollywood, she met with a negative response from producers until Scott offered to produce and direct. Khouri has said that it was his interest that saved the project, although she also has suggested that, failing to direct herself, she would have preferred a female director. She agreed to Scott because she knew with his industry clout he would definitely get the film made. According to Khouri, the key to the contract agreement was Scott's promise that the script's ending would not be altered (Francke 1994: 132). Khouri's initial inspiration for the story came from her negative experiences as a young actress and video producer. She became frustrated with the limited roles offered to women: "It is such a rare thing to go to a movie and think, God, that was a really interesting female character. I feel that the roles generally available to women in Hollywood films are incredibly stereotypical: the girlfriend, the wife, the moll, the prostitute, the rape victim, the woman dying of cancer. I wanted to do something outside these terms" (quoted in Francke 1994: 130). Khouri decided that she "was fed up with the passive role of women. They were never driving the story because they were never driving the car" (quoted in Francke 1994: 127), so she created heroines who did both.

These heroines were brought to life by two actresses the importance of whose work on the film has largely been unexamined, especially the work of Susan Sarandon, who was really the film's star since Davis was much less well-known at the time. In order to assess Sarandon's contributions to the film, we will look not only at the feminist dimensions of the film, but also at how it fits into Sarandon's career, how her star persona and approach to acting contributed to the development of her character, the specific auteurist contributions she made to the film, and the feminist significance of her role and performance. *Thelma & Louise* was unquestionably a crucial film in the progression of Sarandon's career; it was the film that made her a major Hollywood star. Sarandon's progression to major film stardom was unusual in that most stars establish themselves with one breakout performance and then follow that up with a second success, which solidifies their star status. It took Sarandon over 20 years to establish herself as a major star because she never was able to follow up a big success with a second major film, she developed a reputation for being difficult to work with, and she was seen as far too eager to express her political views.

Figure 12 From left, Susan Sarandon as Louise and Geena Davis as Thelma in *Thelma & Louise*.

In interviews, Sarandon presents herself not only as someone who never managed or planned her career, but also as an iconoclast who broke all the rules of career wisdom and still miraculously managed to become a star. She said, "I am always incredibly shocked that I still have a career. I've done everything wrong, so there must be some kind of angel watching over me" (quoted in Johnston 2000). Actually, this characterization is not entirely accurate. She did a number of things "right" in promoting her career in spite of her rather cavalier attitude toward it. First of all, she aggressively pursued certain key, career-shaping roles and then worked hard to make them memorable. Although she has been in a remarkable number of bad films, she has also kept her career afloat by searching out career-defining parts in both commercially and artistically successful films, such as *Thelma & Louise*. The progress of Sarandon's career can be summarized as falling into three phases:

1. A lengthy early stage (1970–87) characterized by discovery, sporadic success, and identification with an earthy eroticism (major films: *The Rocky Horror Picture Show, Pretty Baby, Atlantic City, The Hunger,* and *The Witches of Eastwick*).

2. A stage of gradual development from minor to major stardom (1988–92) in which she was cast in roles that were still highly sexualized but were now also associated with intelligence and what can perhaps best be described as "an attitude," a brash "ballsy, don't-give-a-shit" manner

(Shapiro 2001: 54). (Major films: *Bull Durham, White Palace, Thelma & Louise*, which finally after twenty-two years in the industry made her a major star).

3. A final period of de-eroticized older women roles in which she has played a wide range of mother figures (1992-the present). (Major films: *Lorenzo's Oil, Little Women, The Client, Dead Man Walking, Stepmom, Anywhere But Here, The Bangor Sisters, The Lovely Bones,* and *A Solitary Man. Twilight, Alfie,* and *Shall We Dance* also fall within this period, but represent deliberate, and not entirely successful, at least in terms of box office success, attempts by the ageing actress to create a more mature version of her earlier sexualized-intelligent-heroine-with-an-attitude persona).

Thelma & Louise fits firmly into this career outline. It was a major box-office success and her star-solidifying film, but she failed to follow it up with a second big success. At the height of her stardom, she did *Lorenzo's Oil,* a film that initiated a long series of mother roles. Its grim portrayal of a child suffering from the ravages of Adrenoleukodystrophy (ADL) and his parents' prolonged struggle to find a cure for this horrific childhood disease makes it a harrowing viewing experience and one to which many filmgoers understandably chose not to subject themselves. Then, after finally getting her own big-budget Hollywood star vehicle, *The Client,* Sarandon took two glamourless mother roles in *Safe Passage* and *Little Women.* She would also follow-up her Oscar-winning performance in *Dead Man Walking* by taking three years off from acting to spend time with her family. Then, she went on to star in *Twilight* with the much older Paul Newman, Gene Hackman, and James Garner, a film that one critic dubbed a "geezer noir" that focused on all of its characters', including Sarandon's, advancing age (Turan, 1998: 1).

Thelma & Louise fits not only with Sarandon's career pattern, but also with her star image. Stars' images are constructed from several sources: promotional material (the deliberate creation of the star's public persona by the studio or the star's publicity agents), publicity (material that seems to have resulted from media interest in the star's films and personal life, rather than from deliberate studio promotion), the star's overall screen presentation throughout her career, and criticism/commentaries (ranging from film reviews to academic scholarship) (Dyer 1979: 69–72). The resulting image significantly influences how a star's performances and the characters she plays will be received. The star image Sarandon developed involves essentially two components, and both of them fit the role of Louise perfectly. The first is her combination of sexuality, intelligence, and "attitude," and the second is her reputation for rebelliousness. Yet Sarandon's early image was dominated by earthy sexuality and youthful incredulity, rather than intelligence or rebelliousness. In early films like *Joe*, *The Rocky Horror Picture Show*, *Pretty Baby*, and *Atlantic City*, her large eyes and rather blank open-mouthed stare give her characters a spacey, sex kittenish appearance that does not accord well with her later reputation for intelligence. It was her role in *Bull Durham* that transformed her from spacey sex kitten to the "hot but smart" woman who would become Susan Sarandon, the star, and would make her perfect for the role of Louise in *Thelma & Louise*.

Throughout her career, Sarandon had a reputation for unconventionality. When asked if she could relate to the rebel image the media had created for her, she proposed, "I think it's true. ... for better or worse, I don't have a good sense of what's 'normal'" (quoted in "The Anti-Star" 1995). This unconventionality was early associated with her sexuality. After the breakup of her first marriage to Chris Sarandon and before her long-term partnership with Tim Robbins, she was reputed to have led what she herself called a "pretty adventurous lifestyle" (quoted in Jerome 1994). She became romantically involved with a long list of actors and directors with whom she worked: directors Louis Malle and Franco Amurri (with whom she had a daughter outside of wedlock), actors David Bowie, Sean Penn, Christopher Walken, Kevin Kline, Don Johnson, and finally Tim Robbins. In 2009, she and Robbins split, reputedly because she became involved with the much younger manager of a ping-pong club which she owns in Manhattan. Repeatedly, she expressed a disdain for the institution of marriage: "I believe in love and commitment but not in marriage. Marriage may do something for lawyers and mothers but not for husbands and wives" (quoted in Shapiro 2001: 27). She told another interviewer: "I just naturally have a problem with institutionalized anything" (quoted in Hobson 1996).

Her unconventionality has also involved a highly sexualized screen image. Early in her career, sexuality became a major feature of her screen roles, and as her career developed, she became noted for the amount of nudity found in her films. Alan Lovell even proposes that she "has probably appeared nude more than any other actress of her age and generation" and adds, "This might appear odd for an actress who is keenly aware of the position of women in the movies and society" (1999: 105). Odd it might be, but Sarandon's penchant for screen nudity did much to sexualize her image. In 1981, her infamous topless scenes even won her the dubious distinction of being honored by *Playboy* for having the "Celebrity Breasts of the Summer" (Dreifus 1989: 64). The list of her sexually charged film roles is long: in *Pretty Baby*, her character seductively lies on a divan and strokes the nipples of her breasts with her moistened finger to make them more photogenic as she poses topless for a photographer. *Atlantic City* opens with what is commonly referred to as her infamous "lemon scene" in which Burt Lancaster's elderly character watches voyeuristically through an open window as she rubs her shoulders and breasts with a lemon, ostensibly to remove the fish smell on her skin from her job as a waitress in a casino restaurant. *White Palace* contains a vivid portrayal of Sarandon's character performing oral sex, and *Bull Durham* includes a steamy sex scene between Sarandon and Kevin Costner. In *The Hunger*, Sarandon engages in what has come to be regarded as a classic lesbian nude sex scene with Catherine Deneuve (although it is really only Sarandon's nude body that is shown).

In interviews, Sarandon downplayed her reputation as a diva of cinematic nudity and, in accord with her reputation for intelligence, waxed philosophically about the deeper significance of her sexually charged performances. She said, "I've never been incredibly comfortable just walking around naked, and I think that nipples upstage you anyway so no one's listening to anything you're saying for the first fifteen seconds, so why would you do it, right?" (quoted in Lipton 1998). She has also criticized sex scenes that are "not scripted ... [and] have no purpose" (quoted in Dreifus 1989: 64) and proposed, "I've never done nude scenes that are just generalized groping and heavy breathing while trying to hide behind the other person's body" (quoted in Goldman 1992). According to Sarandon, the best sex scenes that she has done do not really focus on eroticism, but on the romantic relationships involved. For instance, about *The Hunger* she said that "doing a love scene, whether it's with a man or a woman, in front of a room full of people, for three or four days is probably the most unnatural thing you could do. Forget about the gender of the person you're with. ... When you're doing a scene that's sexual, what's interesting is what leads up to it and what happens afterward. Everybody kinda' knows what's going on in between, and there's not that many variations on that that you can believe" (quoted in DiClementi 1999). She has even ridiculed the "lemon scene" in *Atlantic City*, saying, "Anyone who would rub lemons on her chest is completely insane" (quoted in Lipton 1998) and "God knows how that fish smell ever got to my breasts, but Okay. ... It's a European thing" (quoted in Lipton 1998). She also complained that, as a result of the scene's notoriety, she kept getting lemons sent to her in the mail by fans (Dreifus 1989: 64).

Although Sarandon has at times downplayed the glamorous sexual component of her stardom, she expressed genuine dismay when she had to play Sister Helen Prejean with an unflattering hair style and no makeup in *Dead Man Walking*. She said of the role, "I've gone all the way to the other end of the sexual spectrum. I hope I can come back" (quoted in Shapiro 2001: 184). The real Sister Helen, on whose memoir the film is based, told a reporter that she heard Sarandon cried when she first saw how she looked in the part ("Susan Sarandon" 1996). Sarandon later would admit that after *Dead Man Walking* she jumped at the opportunity to play an ageing movie star in *Twilight* because she "was looking for a role where [she] would wear make-up and f-me pumps, and have breasts again" (quoted in Johnston 2000). In spite of the strong sexual component to her image, Sarandon's stardom has never been totally based on her sexuality. There quickly developed within her image lexicon a duality between sexuality and intelligence. In interviews and personal appearances, she consistently presented herself as a mix of tough-minded independence, keen perception, and earthy sexiness. When asked by *Rolling Stone* magazine's interviewer how she wanted to be photographed, she said she would like a cardboard cutout of herself in "something slinky, something very sexy" with the real Sarandon holding the cutout and looking out from behind. She then elaborated on her reasoning: "I have no objection to being sexual – I hope you make me look great – but I'd also like to have people feel that I don't take myself incredibly seriously and that I have some sense of irony and am intelligent – however you can figure that out" (quoted in Wadler 1981: 39). Sarandon has perhaps been best characterized by Kevin Costner as "feminine but tough" (quoted in Dreifus 1989: 64), and she used these qualities to good effect to shape her role in *Thelma & Louise*.

It was *Thelma & Louise* that first established Sarandon, the older of the films dual heroines, as a mature sex symbol, and since then she has gone on to become a poster child of sorts for middle-aged female sexuality. She has claimed that she does not mind getting older (Shapiro 2001: 197) and that her ambition is the be "the world's oldest actress" (quoted in Smith 1993). Repeatedly, she has been on lists of Hollywood's sexiest women over forty and is said to be letting herself age naturally without resorting to cosmetic surgery. As a mature actress, Sarandon seems to have chosen roles in films like *The Banger Sisters*, *Cradle Will Rock*, *Illuminata*, and *Twilight* to solidify her image as the epitome of the sexy older woman. She said, "And I've recently been hearing from other actresses – some maybe seven to ten years younger than me – who say, I'm looking to you as the person who's going to say my career can continue into my fifties with interesting parts" (quoted in Fuller 1994: 147). Her recent dissolution of her long-time partnership with Robbins, who is 12 years her junior, in order reputedly to take up with a man who is 32 years younger than she, coupled with her earlier roles in older-woman-younger-man-romances, such as *Bull Durham*, *White Palace*, and *Earthly Possessions*, has only accentuated her image as a mature female sex symbol.

The sexual component of Sarandon's image, however, has never over-shadowed her reputation for intelligence, rebelliousness, and political activism. Although she has really done only a handful of overtly political roles, she has a reputation as "a political actress" largely because of her support for a wide variety of causes and her willingness to use her celebrity to promote them. Her wide spectrum of political activities includes participating in rallies, protests, and marches; speaking at political events; donating her time to charitable activities; spearheading organizations; lobbying congress; traveling for political organizations; narrating political documentaries; and using personal appearances and celebrity interviews to express her political views. Her activist involvement is extensive and includes, to name only some of the most notable of her causes, support for gun control, gay rights, abortion rights, food relief for underdeveloped countries, the protection of endangered wildlife, first amendment rights, funding for the National Endowment for the Arts, food for the homeless and aged, supplies for hurricane victims, support of non-traditional political candidates, AIDS funding, and opposition to corporate monopolies, U.S. policy in Nicaragua, and the war in Iraq. Sarandon has frequently explained why she feels justified in using her notoriety as a political forum: "As a celebrity who has access to the media, I think you have certain responsibilities. I have enormous respect for the decency of humankind and I believe that if people had information they would behave differently, you know, so I have access to information that a lot of people don't have and what am I going to do with that? So I'm kind of a reluctant flashlight" (quoted in Lipton 1998).

Sarandon's reputation for political activism certainly fits well with her role in *Thelma & Louise*, which was without question one of the most controversial films of the 1990s. It stirred heated debate in the press after it was associated with three volatile issues: feminism, violence, and male bashing. In interviews, Sarandon, Khouri and Davis all attempted to disassociate the film from feminism. According to Khouri, "*Thelma & Louise* is not about feminists, it's about outlaws," and Davis queried, "Why because [*Thelma & Louise*] stars women is this suddenly a feminist treatise, given the burden of representing all women?" (quoted in Holmlund 1994b: 82, n. 26). Yet Khouri seems definitely to have been motivated by feminist inclinations in writing the script. Her stated intentions to provide new, more active roles for her female characters clearly represent a feminist position. How new her characters really are and what exactly they stand for in terms of feminism is open to debate, and critics from both feminist and anti-feminist camps have reached no consensus about the film. When it was first released, it immediately rated a cover story in *Time* magazine, which focused on the "white hot debate [that] rages over whether *Thelma & Louise* celebrates liberated females, male bashers – or outlaws" (Schickel 1991). Some reviewers praised the film as a "butt-kicking feminist manifesto" that shows women fighting back against sexism (quoted in Holmlund 1994b: 147) and a brilliant depiction of the dire straits contemporary women feel themselves to be in, whereas others condemned it as an example of female escapism, a revenge fantasy, and a work that offers just enough "lite feminist fizz ... to be pleasant without seeming pretentious" (Klawans 1991: 863).

A number of critics objected strongly on feminist grounds to the film's representation of women. They felt it actually violated the things that feminism advocates, like "responsibility, equality, sensitivity, understanding – not revenge, retribution, or sadistic behavior" (Holmlund 1994b: 147–48). Others claimed that it resorted to the same voyeuristic display of glamorous female bodies that has always been characteristic of Hollywood films and that it attempted to empower women only by having them behave like men and act out a male fantasy of fast driving, hard drinking, loud music, and gun play (Dowell 1991; Carlson 1991). Finally, some saw the film as so pessimistic in its view of women's current social situation that it implied that little gains have really been won by feminism and conveyed a despairing message of patriarchy's invincibility (Carlson 1991: 57). While feminist critics registered their objections, anti-feminists criticized the film on other grounds, branding it feminist fascism that advocated transformative violence as the answer to women's problems, bashed men, and offered bad role models for female viewers. All of these criticisms were strenuously debated.

Khouri responded quickly and cleverly to charges of anti-male bias by arguing that the movie "isn't hostile to men, it's hostile to idiots" (quoted in Holmlund 1994b: 146). Elaborating further, she proposed: "You can't do a movie without villains. You have to have something for the heroines or anti-heroines to be up against, and I wasn't going to contrive some monstrous female, but even if this were the most men-bashing movie ever made – let all us women get guns and kill men – it wouldn't even begin to make up for the 99% of all movies where the women are there to be caricatured as bimbos or to be skinned and decapitated. If men feel uncomfortable in the audience it is because they are identifying with the wrong character" (quoted in Francke 1994: 129–30). In spite of Khouri's disclaimers, Thelma & Louise does portray men largely in terms of negative stereotypes, including the obnoxious, domineering husband (Darryl); non-committal, narcissistic boyfriend (Jimmy); irresponsible, sexually seductive bad boy (J.D.); woman-hating rapist (Harlan); infantile, harassing trucker; and paternalistic father figure (Detective Slocum). Marsha Kinder suggests, however, that the film is more an attack on images of men in "media culture" than on men themselves. She points out that its "parade of treacherous male characters" corresponds perfectly to well-known figures from popular movies ranging from the James Dean-ish outlaw figure to the foulmouthed trucker and the sensitive, paternal cop (Kinder 1991–92: 30). The overwhelming negativity of the film's portrayal of its male characters, like almost everything else about it, has been open to dispute. Not only has Khouri denied the film's anti-male stance, but some critics have staunchly defended its characterizations of men. Tom Prasch, for instance, argues that both Detective Slocum

(Harvey Keitel) and Jimmy (Michael Madson) are presented favorably and that J.D. (Brad Pitt) is an ambivalent figure (1991: 26). In fact, the seemingly endless debates about the film mark it as a perfect example of the openness to multiple reading possibilities that characterizes so many of the most popularly successful Hollywood films. As Harvey Greenberg suggests, Thelma & Louise contains an "exuberant polysemy." It not only addresses differing ideological agendas from feminist to anti-feminist and progressive to reactionary, but also "offers a wide range of possibility for contestation across the political spectrum over issues 'whose time has come' out of one contemporary circumstance or another" (1991–92: 20).

The controversy over Thelma & Louise cannot be entirely explained by the film's polysemy, however, as important as this characteristic may be in furthering the debates that surrounded the film. The initiation of the controversy and its prolonged nature seem also to reflect the film's clearly political nature – a political nature that fits well with the persona of its star, Susan Sarandon. As a female friendship film that focuses on the close relationship between its two female characters, Thelma & Louise does what few mainstream female friendship films have done. It moves its presentation of women's friendship out of the realm of personal development to offer an overtly political critique of women's position in contemporary society. It exalts the friendship between its heroines and places their close relationship squarely at the center of the narrative, but at the same time it violates female friendship film traditions by never overly sentimentalizing their relationship or overemphasizing moments of intimate self-disclosure (Simpson 1991).

In fact, Thelma & Louise seems to go out of its way to avoid sentimentalizing its female protagonists' friendship. Significant in this regard is Scott's decision to cut an important scene that strongly affects the development of Sarandon's character. In Khouri's script, Louise confesses to Thelma that she had been raped in Texas (Khouri 1990: 116). Scott's decision not to have Louise reveal the nature of her past trauma in the film provoked some critical disapproval. Lizzie Francke, for example, argued the deletion blurred Khouri's original vision of the two women's intimate relationship (1994: 132). Other critics suggested further that Louise's reticence to discuss her rape reduces the spectator's ability to empathize with her and to understand her murder of Thelma's rapist. According to Alice Cross, "Everything that happens in the movie is a consequence of that earlier experience, but because it is a hole, a blank, we are left detached where we ought to be most moved, angered, sympathetic" (1991: 33). Fitting the film squarely into the mold of sentimentalized female friendship portrayals, Cross and Francke wanted Thelma and Louise to engage in an emotional discussion of their shared abuse: "Without such a sharing of the past, the kiss that Louise gives Thelma before they plunge into oblivion means little. It is like so much in this film, just the same old story artfully disguised to look like something new" (Cross 1991: 34). Actually, in terms of the history of the female friendship film, the intimate sharing of confidences that Cross and Francke want is not at all new; instead, it is Scott's decision to have Louise refuse to talk about her rape that takes *Thelma & Louise* in a new direction. By not discussing her experiences as a rape victim, Louise refuses to engage in the kind of intimate self-disclosure that would render her a powerless victim of male abuse; instead, as Lynda Hart points out, Louise remains throughout the film a powerfully subversive figure. Hart proposes that having Louise confess her rape would allow for the patriarchal recuperation of her criminality: "Filling the empty space of her trauma might facilitate her reintegration into the symbolic order, but Louise is not disposed to collaborate with 'justice' ... " (1994: 70).

Using Sarah Kofman's distinction between the female criminal and the hysteric, Hart describes Louise as an unregenerate criminal, a figure Kofman sees as truly subversive of the patriarchal order. Like Kofman's conception of the unrepentant female criminal, Louise "knows her own secret" and refuses to share it because she is, or thinks she is, self-sufficient (Kofman 1985: 66). She will not submit to a psychoanalytic talking-cure as the hysteric does, and it is this unwillingness to speak, as much as what she does, that criminalizes her. Louise's criminality stems from her refusal to allow Detective Slocum, the male police officer who wants desperately to save her, to do so. Not only does Louise refuse to be "saved," but she takes the younger, less experienced Thelma with her. As Hart points out, Louise thoroughly mistrusts the existing social structure and has to teach Thelma to do the same. Thelma is at first naive enough to believe that telling the truth will clear them, but Louise shows her that "the symbolic order is a masculine imaginary in which their truths have no credibility" (Hart 1994: 71). In this way, she takes Thelma, and the film as well, into a much more socially critical realm than the intimate self-disclosure of sentimentalized female friendship films allows, and *Thelma & Louise* becomes as a result decidedly political. Marsha Kinder argues, to the contrary, that *Thelma & Louise* by refusing to "explore the repression of women in the context of larger issues of history and class conflict" fails to afford its viewers incisive political analysis (1991/1992: 30). Yet, as Elayne Rapping points out, although *Thelma & Louise* is not "an explicitly feminist movie, produced by politicos as an 'intervention,'" there still might be a reason for feminist critics to celebrate it. Rapping regards the film as an indication that feminist ideas have influenced the popular imagination to the extent that they are now part of "an oppositional way of thinking shared by a majority of women and lots of men." She adds: "The assault on this film must be read as part of a much larger political backlash against the real gains of feminism fueled by those for whom changes in gender power relations mean a serious loss of privilege and power. That they are so nervous proves to me that feminism has had a greater impact on this society than it sometimes seems in these politically dark days" (Rapping 1991: 30–31).

Indeed, *Thelma & Louise* does make a number of significant feminist political points. First of all, in accordance with Khouri's stated intentions, the film grants its female protagonists central roles in driving not only the car but also the plot. They are granted agency in the narrative, challenging the traditional cinematic association of activity with masculinity. They remain in charge of their own fate throughout, frustrating all attempts at male control up to the very end when they choose suicide over submission to male authority. While remaining resolutely heterosexual, they refuse to be defined entirely by their relationships with men; instead, they form at the film's conclusion a symbolic marriage of sisterhood. Significantly, this sisterly bond is not confined entirely to the private sphere of personal affection; instead, the women move out into the public world as outlaws attacking patriarchal laws and traditions, rejecting the traditional roles for women, and challenging men's control of public space. They bond for a cause beyond the level of personal attachment. Theirs is a union of two abused women who revolt against a society that has not adequately protected them from crimes of male violence.

The most overtly feminist political statement that the film makes is its attack on the legal system's response to the crime of rape. *Thelma & Louise* is not an incisive political analysis of the legal, psychological, and social questions related to the rape issue; instead, it is a popular culture expression of women's anger and frustration with the current situation in regard to this crime. As such, as both Carol Clover and Peter Lehman suggest, *Thelma & Louise* is a descendent of the low budget rape-revenge movies of the 1970s and 1980s, films like *Hannie Caulder* (Burt Kennedy, 1972), *I Spit on your Grave* (Meir Zarchi, 1978), and *Ms. 45* (Abel Ferrara, 1981) (Clover 1993: 84; Lehman 1993: 106). These earlier rape-revenge films were aimed at a male audience and intended as popular entertainment rather than as serious considerations of the rape issue. They offer their male audience the spectacle of watching a beautiful woman "wrecking havoc on the male body" (Lehman 1993: 107). Their formulaic plot structure begins with a brutal rape scene after which the rapists become victims themselves of the viciously vengeful woman whom they attacked. Their punishment is spectacularized in scenarios of excessive violence that Lehman believes offer the male spectator a "bizarrely pleasurable" viewing experience (1993: 107). According to Lehman, these rape-revenge films' address is not at all directed to female spectators, but to a male audience that takes pleasure in "a male masochistic fantasy so extreme that even brutal death can be part of the scenario" (1993: 113).

Thelma & Louise takes this generic configuration and transforms it to appeal to a female rather than a male audience. Instead of offering the protracted spectacle of a brutal rape, Thelma & Louise portrays in a decidedly non-voyeuristic fashion a very brief near-rape. The emphasis is placed on Thelma's response to the crime rather than on the rapist's pleasure. Lehman points out that low budget rape-revenge films portray their rapists as physically repulsive in order to allow the male viewer to distance himself from their criminality (1993: 108). Thelma & Louise allows for no such convenient distancing; instead, it presents Harlan (Timothy Carhart) as a handsome, charming rapist from whom the male viewer cannot so easily disassociate himself. Secondly, emphasis is not so overwhelmingly placed on the protractedly brutal punishment of the rapist. Harlan is shot efficiently and quickly once in the chest. The film's idea of female vengeance is related more to "the notion of corporate liability that makes every man pay," than to the concept of personal retribution (Clover 1993: 84). This idea of "corporate liability" allows no male audience member to escape responsibility for the continuance of a rape culture that refuses to prevent this heinous crime. Clover argues that the transformation of the rape-revenge drama from the bracket of the "B" movie to the bigger budget category usually creates a more "civilized version" of the story that loses sight of rape's effect on the raped woman herself and her need for retaliation (1993: 81). As a result, a big budget rape-revenge film like The Accused (Jonathan Kaplan, 1988) loses its feminist edge because it becomes a study of the workings of the legal system rather than of the crime of rape. Thelma & Louise avoids this pitfall and delivers a clear anti-rape message without losing sight of the individual victim.

Thelma & Louise's categorization as a feminist political film is very much tied to the nature of its conclusion. As we have seen, Khouri was adamant that Scott should not change her ending, and Sarandon claims that before she agreed to take the part she also insisted that her character had to die at the end (Shapiro 2001: 152). Khouri and Sarandon seem to have realized that the film's ending is crucial to its political critique. By choosing not to give up and in Thelma's words to "keep on goin'," the women remain subversive criminal figures through to the film's conclusion and beyond, never allowing themselves to be reintegrated into the existing social structure and forever unrepentant. Their friendship never becomes, as it does in so many female friendship films, merely a refuge that allows them to reintegrate into and better cope with the existing patriarchal order; instead, they remain throughout the film resistant to compromise with and recuperation by what they continue to view as an unreformed patriarchy.

Susan Sarandon's demand that the ending not be changed is just one of the many contributions she made to the film's feminism in terms of her acting choices and suggestions for scene changes. Sarandon is known as an actress who is not afraid to critique the work of her directors or to make suggestions for script alterations during shooting. If her account is accurate, her contributions to *Thelma & Louise* were extensive. She says simply, "Ridley [Scott] and I fought about things. We changed scenes," (quoted in Shapiro 2001: 153), and it appears that they changed quite a number of them. Sarandon was not the first choice for the part of Louise, which reputedly was originally offered to Meryl Streep and then Jodie Foster, both of whom turned it down (Lovell 1999: 92), and Sarandon says she took the role knowing that Thelma was the "more crowd-pleasing part." She also says that she feared it might "turn into some kind of male-revenge, Bronson kind of film" (quoted in Fuller 1994). In spite of not being the first choice for the role, Sarandon still made numerous demands of Scott, beginning, as noted above, with the ending: "The first thing I demanded from the director was that I die in the last scene. I didn't want the movie to end with me in Club Med. Once he assured me I was definitely on the death list, I accepted the part" (quoted in Shapiro 2001: 152).

She also made other suggestions: she proposed that in packing for the road trip Louise should show her meticulousness by putting her belongings in ziplock bags, the women had to get progressively dirtier as they moved down the road to their final doom, at some point her character should exchange her jewelry with an old man for his dirty hat, Louise should stop and have a pensive moment in the middle of the desert, and it would be inappropriate for her to have a love scene with her boyfriend Jimmy after she had just shot a man: "Originally in the script they were supposed to do a little marriage ceremony and sing songs and fuck, and I felt it was just so unrealistic. Not only would the film lose some of its tension, but also a woman who's just killed somebody because she's remembering having been raped — it's pretty hard to have sex under the circumstances and have it be great. Somehow that would cost us a lot of credibility" (quoted in Lovell 1999: 93–94). Sarandon also says she persuaded Scott not to make Geena Davis do a topless scene in the film. As Davis tells the story, "I thought this was a bad idea but I didn't say so. We broke for lunch and I ran over to Susan and said, 'What am I going to do? Ridley wants me to take my shirt off in this scene.' She said, 'Oh for heaven's sake, Ridley, Geena is not going to take her shirt off in this scene.' He said, 'Okay, okay'" (quoted in Shapiro 2001: 154). Sarandon also engineered a key alteration in the film's ending: "I also kissed her which nobody expected" (quoted in Lipton 1998). Sarandon says that there was some question about whether or not they were going to reshoot the scene to eliminate the kiss, which has, in fact, served as support for lesbian readings of the film (see, for instance, Griggers 1993): "They weren't sure about me kissing Geena at the end, because of the gay thing, but the sun was setting, we had to finish it in two takes, so I knew they'd have to go with it" (quoted in Chaudhuri 1994).

Sarandon's contributions to the film also involve her considerable acting talents. Over the years, she has outlined her views on acting more thoroughly than most actresses. She characterizes herself first and foremost as "an organic actress," someone who lacks formal training and works from a strong sense of intuition, which she describes as "finding out what I have in common with the character in terms of emotional life, motivation, background and going on from there" (quoted in Burrows 1977: 14). She says she got her training "on the job" and especially credits her work in the early 1970's television soap operas *A World Apart* and *Search for Tomorrow* as formative acting experiences. Although she lauds this early television training, Sarandon describes her approach to creating a scene as instinctive: "I just try to be there and be open and not push too much to have something happen that's not really happening. It helps when you have another actor who's giving you what you need. And then it's just praying that something will happen ... " (quoted in Smith 1993). Her interactions with Geena Davis in *Thelma & Louise* certainly have this instinctive, natural feel. Throughout her career, Sarandon has consistently characterized acting as "not really that complicated" (quoted in Chaudhuri 1994) and as a way "to have a good time" (quoted in Johnston 2000). She also says rather contradictorily that what really attracted her to acting is its challenge: "It's impossible to get it right, so acting becomes addictive. Every time I see one of my performances, there's always something I think I could have done clearer, better, faster. When a film is finished, you see, in hindsight, what it was really about. When you see it you think, 'Wow, I was on the right track with that, I wish I had been braver. I wish I had been committed 100% to that mistake'" (quoted in Grundmann and Lucia 1993: 100).

Sarandon does not subscribe to any established school of acting. Marc Shapiro says she early gained a reputation in the industry as a raw talent with a slightly unorthodox approach (2001: 71–72). For instance, Director Louis Malle said when he directed her in *Atlantic City*:

> One of the things I like about Susan is that she has no system. A lot of actors in this country go through schools where they learn a strictly disciplined, highly intellectual approach – such as the Method – where there's a lot of psychological interpretation. This can cause you to lose a lot of the stamina, the spontaneity, the surprise that is an essential part of acting. Susan reminds me of Jeanne Moreau, who hardly ever reads her lines, even on the night before a scene because she wants to be

completely open before the camera. Susan, too, comes to a role "fresh and innocent and flexible" (quoted in Flatley 1978: 66).

Because she lacks a systematic approach to her craft, Sarandon's acting has been categorized in widely divergent ways. Alan Lovell says her expressed views on acting place her squarely in the tradition of Stanislavskian naturalism. Indeed, as Lovell points out, in the Stanislavski tradition, Sarandon characterizes good acting as listening to the other actors and being open, spontaneous, and fresh, rather than coming to a performance with a set of prepared responses. She also gives her characterizations a strong sense of individuality by avoiding stock mannerisms and inventing responses that seem specific to the character (Lovell 1999: 93). She has said, "If you're not drawing from real life, then all you're doing is rehashing images you've seen in films. Even the image of yourself" (quoted in Seymour 1994).

Despite these aspects of naturalistic performance, Sarandon also possesses many of the qualities of the Hollywood star-actress – untrained, instinctual, larger-than-life, and essentially playing herself in each role. She repeatedly plays "characters not unlike herself in many respects – straight-talking, independent women who attain the self-knowledge which enables them to ask questions and take charge of their lives and their sexuality" (Grundmann & Lucia 1993). Even the progression of her film roles seems to parallel events in her life. Her initial sexualized image coincides with her early reputation as a free spirit who often became involved with her male co-stars and directors, her older woman-younger man romantic roles parallel her relationship with Tim Robbins, and her later assumption of maternal roles corresponds with her dedication to family life. Her comments about some of her roles also suggest that she feels most comfortable playing characters, like Louise, whom she regards as similar to her own off-screen personality.

Although Sarandon does not claim any affiliation with the Method school of acting, she has worked very effectively with actors, such as Christopher Walken and Sean Penn, who are noted for subscribing to its tenets. As Lovell points out, her acting is much too script-dependent to be characterized as Method (1999: 93); nevertheless, some of the statements she has made about her technique do draw on the Method approach. For instance, she has commented on her need to be "in the moment" when acting and advocates the use of improvisation to make "something unexpected" happen (quoted in Smith 1993). She also says that when doing a scene, "you want to personalize it. You have to make every scene very specific, you have to know what it is in the scene that triggers what, depending on what you're going after. Something very specific is triggered and you have to isolate that, and sometimes adding a word helps" (quoted in Smith 1993). She also finds it useful to respond emotionally to another actor by imagining that the actor's character is someone from her real life who "has some emotional resonance for you" (quoted in Smith 1993).

All of this indicates not that Sarandon belongs to one school of acting or another, but that she draws, as do so many contemporary actresses, from a number of schools, to form an eclectic style that adheres to no single approach. Although she has made brief forays into theater and made-for-television movies, Sarandon has established her career almost exclusively on the basis of her work in film. Her acting style is particularly suited to the screen because it is very controlled, precise, and unostentatious. As Tim Robbins explains, "She understands how to go to the heart of a character without resorting to flashy acting" (quoted in Shapiro 2001: 180). Like so many contemporary film actresses, Sarandon's acting is very focused on characterization. Her memorable depiction of Louise in *Thelma & Louise* is just one example of her ability to add substance to characters who seem on the surface to be stock and predictable. Louise could easily have been played as an uptight, damaged woman who leads her younger friend on a doomed flight from the police; instead, Sarandon created a character who is funny, vibrant, intelligent, and enormously sympathetic.

Sarandon is a very script-centered actress with her characterizations primarily based on an intelligent reading of the character as written, effective execution of dialogue, and "a deep understanding of the dramatic context" (Lovell 1999: 104). Lovell points out, for instance, that her performance in *Atlantic City* is particularly effective because Sarandon makes her character's insecurities and anxieties so vivid that she fits perfectly with the "overall anti-heroic perspective of the film" (1999: 98). Sarandon is also very adept at finding "strong and varied physical movements, gestures, and facial expressions to define the characters she plays" (Lovell 1999: 104). She has even described the actor's job as "to get the little specific things and put them into the [film's] structure" (quoted in Hobson 1996). Lovell compares two of her early performances in *Atlantic City* and *Bull Durham*. In the former film, she plays Sally Matthews, a familiar character type: an ambitious, but romantically naive young woman trying desperately to escape from her small town background. Yet Sarandon manages to make Sally interesting by using her voice, facial expressions, gestures, and body movements to convey in a "detailed and innovative way [how] she struggles to express and contain her feelings" (Lovell 1999: 96). In *Bull Durham*, Sarandon uses the way Annie Savoy sits, moves, stands, and gestures to create quite the opposite effect. Annie is a woman completely comfortable, easy, and confident in her sexuality. Sarandon uses physical cues to set up the emotional tone of Annie's character in the opening scenes and then maintains this tone throughout the film (Lovell 1999: 99).

In other films, Sarandon has employed physical cues not to set up her character's personality and maintain it throughout the film, but to signal character transformation. For instance, in the opening scenes of *The Witches of Eastwick*, she uses physical awkwardness to show her character's discomfort with her own body. Then, to convey her character's release from sexual repression when she meets Jack Nicholson's devil figure, Sarandon goes into what she herself has described as "a frenzy" (quoted in Smith 1993), exchanging sexually charged looks with Nicholson, assuming a provocative attitude, and seductively slinking about. Sarandon has also taken roles that proved to be quite physically demanding. She did her own stunts in early films such as *The Great Waldo Pepper*, in which she walked on an airplane wing and drove a car under a low flying prop-plane, and *The Other Side of Midnight*, in which she did a boating stunt that left her with whiplash and bruises (Burrows 1977). Her most physically demanding role was not in film, but on the stage. In the 1982 off-Broadway production of the rape-revenge drama *Extremities*, she had to fight off a brutal rapist for the whole first act. She stayed in the role for four months and one hundred performances although she suffered a fractured wrist, several jammed and broken fingers, chipped bones, frequent black eyes and bloody noses, as well as significant weight loss.

The physicality of Sarandon's performances allows her to impart to her characters an "expressive energy" that gives them an extraordinary dynamism (Lovell 1999: 104). This dynamism comes not just from her physical movements and gestures, but also from her dynamic rendering of dialogue. Sarandon, who has complained that contemporary actors have lost the ability to handle dialogue effectively, seems to give each of her characterizations a distinctive "vocal energy" (Lovell 1999: 100). As Lovell points out, she combines her natural tendency to speak quickly with a line delivery that through variations of rhythm and volume makes her words "shaped and pointed so that they have maximum effect." Lovell concludes that Sarandon's dynamic technique works best when she plays characters who are active, rather than reactive (1999: 105), yet I have argued that some of her most impressive acting, including her work in *Thelma & Louise*, involves the animation she imparts to characters who would otherwise be extremely passive and reactive (Hollinger 2006: 125). Lovell insists, for instance, that one of Sarandon's least interesting performances is the ageing film star Catherine Ames in *Twilight*. He argues that Catherine is "a passive 'iconic' figure" whom Sarandon cannot render dynamic because Catherine's film successes are all behind her (Lovell 1999: 105, note 9). It seems to me, however, that Sarandon is actually quite effective in the *Twilight* role because she refuses to play Catherine simply as a stereotyped femme fatale; instead, she humanizes her by showing how her twisted version of marital fidelity led to her involvement in several murders.

Catherine Ames in *Twilight* is not the only reactive character to whom Sarandon has brought an "expressive energy." Her characterization of Louise also falls into this category. Sarandon says that *Thelma & Louise* taught her that reactive acting need not be boring: "In that movie, mainly what I had to do was drive and listen. I had to concentrate on keeping the car in a certain relationship to the camera truck. Geena had all the lines. I was just concentrating on driving and occasionally replying. And somehow that would work. And I realized from that, you can do your best work when you're concentrating on something else" (quoted in Shapiro 2001: 155). As Lovell points out, the two female roles in *Thelma & Louise* were extremely demanding because they involve extended dialogue exchanges taking place primarily in the confined spaces of a moving vehicle or a hotel room, which offer restricted acting opportunities. Sarandon managed to intensify these exchanges by acting with her eyes, using them to register strongly in close-up (Lovell 1999: 101).

One of the most significant aspects of Sarandon's acting is its extraordinarily auteurist nature. Throughout her career, she has had an enormous creative influence on her films in a wide variety of ways including role choice, shaping roles through performance, influencing directorial decisions, and even assuming the role of producer herself. Gavin Smith calls Sarandon "a great actress who lacked great roles" (1993) and certainly her haphazard process of role selection and at times unfortunate role choice have placed her in some terrible films. Her tendency to reject safer projects for riskier choices, however, also has allowed her to play a wide range of different characters and to take roles in films that have a distinct relationship to the historical period in which they were made. Louise in *Thelma & Louise* is unquestionably just such a role. She fits perfectly with what Sarandon has described as her ideal role; she is a "well-rounded woman who gets to change in some way, has a sense of humor, and doesn't have to deny her intelligence or her sexuality" (quoted in Grundmann and Lucia 1993). As Lovell points out, Louise represents a combination of Sarandon's most successful previous roles: Sally Matthews in *Atlantic City*, Annie Savoy in *Bull Durham*, and Nora Baker in *White Palace* (1999: 92). A larger-than-life iconic figure of feminist rebellion, Louise is one of several roles that Sarandon has played in "watershed films. Movies that are controversial. They all hit very specific political and social changes that I've gone through. I think you choose projects to come into your life. And in doing so, in being true to yourself, it reflects what's going on for yourself and a lot of people" (quoted in Shapiro 2001: 234). A list of Sarandon films, including *Joe, The Rocky Horror Picture Show, Pretty Baby, White Palace, Lorenzo's Oil*, and *Dead Man Walking*, like *Thelma & Louise*, relate strongly to cultural issues prominent at the time of their release, and as a result, they all caused a considerable controversy.

Although Sarandon has said that her role choice is not determined by politics (Ellingson 2000), she has unquestionably been drawn, especially later in her career, to films with socio-political significance. She has said, "And if there's somebody that's trying to leave an abusive relationship, and they see Thelma & Louise, and they get out, I'm happy about that, you know? And if any of the movies that I do, make people have conversations after they leave the theater, then I think that's great" (quoted in DiClementi 1999). In particular, Sarandon has gravitated in her later career toward films that address social issues with distinctly feminist implications. Since Thelma & Louise, Sarandon has primarily played maternal roles, attempting, as she sees it, to reinvent the contemporary perception of motherhood (Shapiro 2001: 207): "I'll make a career to do every kind of mother there is. No one's tapped into this category because of the taboo. Most of the mothers we've seen on the screen have been one-dimensional, sappy, stand-by-your-man moms. Once you crossed that line, there was no turning back. You don't go to bed with someone as a mother" (quoted in Davis and Johnson 1999). Sarandon has discussed this stereotypical cinematic presentation of motherhood in distinctly feminist terms, arguing that it represents yet "another way of compartmentalizing women – you have your slut, your mother, your ice princess who's smart – but you can't be a mother who has a brain and also has fun" (quoted in Grundmann and Lucia 1993).

Not all critics have agreed that this wide variety of mother roles actually represents an innovation in the cinematic presentation of women, as Sarandon suggests it does. Elaine Rapping, for instance, regards Sarandon's mother series as a reaction to the subversiveness of Thelma & Louise, relegating Sarandon "to the sentimental sidelines" after she had made a film like Thelma & Louise that actually "let a grown woman loose on the screen." Rapping attacks Sarandon for playing "martyr-like mothers" in Lorenzo's Oil, Safe Passage, and Little Women and an "over-the-hill recovering alcoholic mother-substitute" in The Client. She points out that these roles are devoid of any hint of sexuality and each becomes "paler, more one-dimensional, and more maternally sacrificing and virtuous than the last." Rapping singles out Sarandon's role as Marmee in Little Women for particular disdain, proposing that "the smug, humorless political correctness of every smarmy line [Sarandon] uttered made [Rapping] cringe on behalf of progressive women everywhere" (1995: 36–37).

One might go even further and suggest that the feminist implications of Sarandon's image have been seriously compromised by the fact that early in her career she made numerous films in which she allowed herself to be objectified in scenes involving graphic sexuality and nudity and her recent film roles have deteriorated into a succession of mother figures, and most recently even a grandmother in The Lovely Bones. Nevertheless, I would still argue that

Sarandon's image has decidedly feminist dimensions and a progressive social significance. The combination of sexuality and intelligence that has been so prominent in her star persona is progressive in that it reconciles feminism with femininity, and *Thelma & Louise* is crucial to this reconciliation. The film's well-deserved reputation as a contemporary Hollywood feminist classic in itself would place Sarandon within the pantheon of feminist cinematic icons. Yet it would probably be a mistake to portray Sarandon as a paragon of feminist progressivity. What is so interesting about her celebrity is that it can combine such a high degree of progressivity and regressivity at the same time. The strong emphasis on sexuality in her image, on the one hand, promotes the exploitation of the female star as sexual spectacle. While films such as *Pretty Baby*, *Atlantic City*, *White Palace* and *Thelma & Louise* do make important statements about the connection between gender and class as sources of women's victimization, audiences will be more likely to remember the working-class characters that Sarandon portrays so effectively in these films for their representation of female sexuality rather than their social significance. Sarandon's activism is also impressive in terms of the depth and range of her conviction, but press releases too often have pictured her as extreme, radical, or far left. As a result, her activist work has too easily been dismissed as the ravings of a zealot rather than the thoughtful protests of a committed reformer. Perhaps the most distressing aspect of Sarandon's image is her ambivalent relationship to feminism, which she claims to reject, even though she strongly advocates many of its tenets.

In numerous statements, Sarandon has taken pains to disassociate herself from feminist ideas. In one interview she characterized a discussion of her feminism as "so boooring," and she went on to propose, "I don't have the faintest idea what feminism is now" (quoted in Pachero 1970: 35), suggesting that at some point in the past she may have understood it, but that feminism has moved far beyond most women's comprehension. When asked if she had read any feminist works, she stated unequivocally that she had not (Fuller 1994), and she has on several occasions demonstrated her very limited conception of what feminism actually is. For instance, she said, "I find that the label feminist is so self-defeating, because most people tend to think of feminists as strident, self-serving, and anti-male, and that's not what it should be about" (quoted in Fuller 1994). If she had read any of the feminist texts that she is so quick to disavow, she would know that it not only should not be about this, but that it *is* not about this. She has argued that she sees herself as a humanist rather than a feminist, offering the conventional argument that feminism fails to be all inclusive: "I consider myself a humanist – only because if you label yourself a feminist at this point in time, most people are so defensive that you can't accomplish anything. Surely if you're a humanist it encompasses everything that is feminist. People want to call me a feminist because I'm strong and I'm a woman who has some opinions. I certainly wouldn't go against it, but it's become a very divisive term – why not go for something broader? I don't disown the feminist movement, but I'm into something that encompasses the rights of men, the rights of children, the rights of gays. I think it's time for human rights" (quoted in Grundmann and Lucia 1993). Of course, if Sarandon knew more about feminism, she would know that it does work for the protection of all human rights, not just those of women.

Sarandon has also refused to accept characterizations of her films as feminist. This issue came up repeatedly with *Thelma & Louise*, which, as we have seen, many critics have characterized as a feminist manifesto. Sarandon adamantly fought that label, making comments that demonstrate conclusively that she indeed does not know what feminism means now, or really what it has ever meant. Sarandon suggested that *Thelma & Louise* is not a feminist film because it is "very entertaining" (quoted in Grundmann and Lucia 1993), is not "a movie that tells people what to think," and deals with two women who "are still concerned about the guys in their lives" (quoted in Fuller 1994). These statements suggest that she believes films that express feminist sentiments are necessarily unentertaining, tendentious, and hostile to men. She even went so far as to propose that *Thelma & Louise* would not have been as good if it had been directed by a feminist and to imply that a feminist filmmaker is a "lesser filmmaker" than someone who does not advocate feminist ideas: "Had this film been directed by a lesser filmmaker who hadn't given it such a heroic vista, had he been a feminist – which I assure you he [Ridley Scott] is not – maybe the film would not have been so entertaining and therefore would not have allowed people to go on that journey" (quoted in Grundmann and Lucia 1993).

Although she denies any feminist affiliation, Sarandon has made many comments that express feminist ideals. For instance, in the same interview in which she insists that talking about her feminism would be "so boooring," she goes on to criticize Hollywood for not creating fully developed female characters. She proposes that for women in films "[s]uffering in silence is the glorified virtue," sex appeal is related to the "ability to be penetrated," and women who make "selfish choices" are inevitably branded as evil (quoted in Pachero 1970). These comments reflect feminist concerns, and Sarandon has not only made them to the press, but on the sets of her films as well. She has complained repeatedly about the limitations of her roles on feminist grounds. As early as 1982 when shooting *Tempest*, she bitterly attacked screenwriter-director Paul Muzursky for failing to understand his female characters. She told an interviewer that when she was shown the final version of the script, "I just got sick. This woman was so uninteresting. All she wanted to do was get laid" (quoted in Shapiro 2001: 95). At a Women in Film Luncheon in 1990, she advised women who wanted power in Hollywood to develop their own channels of influence: "What is the point of seizing the desk, if you're going to have to keep quiet and stay within the confines of that structure, imitating their [men's] mistakes? Wouldn't it be better to have less power or our own independent power structures and be able to redefine how we work and how we accomplish things?" (quoted in Grundmann and Lucia 1993).

Sarandon has proposed that her film roles reflect the changing social position of women in contemporary society (Fuller 1994), and the same can be said in regard to her image as a whole. She represents the desire of many post-feminist women to combine femininity with feminism, while at the same time refusing to accept the much maligned label of feminist. Like Louise in *Thelma & Louise*, which will definitely come to be regarded as her most iconic role, Sarandon embodies the idea that women can be intelligent, independent, and sexy. Her screen persona distinctly repudiates Hollywood images of the independent woman as someone who adopts male characteristics or becomes evil and manipulative. Sarandon's image shows independent femininity as both challenging to men and in their best interests, and perhaps this is the crucial reason for the effectiveness of her characterization of Louise. Louise is a figure in accord with Sarandon's star image; she is a maverick who is also a sex symbol – a combination that is not found very often in contemporary female characters or in the stars who play them.

Key Terms: *personification, impersonation, Method acting, Broadway repertory acting, Glatea figures, stardom, celebrity, clothes horse star, superfemale, super-woman, television personalities, made-for-television stardom, heritage style of acting, glamour acting, subversive star types*

Suggestions for Further Reading, Viewing, and Discussion

1. Do some research into the development of the career of a Hollywood actress of the past or present using publicity, promotional material, reviews, and scholarly criticism (if you can find any), as well as film performances. Does the actress's star image, career, and approach to acting fit the prevalent theories of female stardom discussed in this chapter?

2. Compare the careers, star images, and approaches to acting of an actress of the Hollywood studio period to a contemporary actress. What do the similarities and differences that you find tell you about the positions of women in the Hollywood industry now and then? The filmography below lists some major actresses of the past whose careers might be interesting to examine as well as three of their most notable films.

3. Compare the careers, star images, and approaches to acting of a male and a female star from the same period in film history. What do the differences and similarities that you find tell you about the position of men and women in the film industry?

4. Compare the careers, star images, and approaches to acting of a Hollywood actress and a prominent actress from another country. What does the comparison tell you about the differences between the position of Hollywood actresses and actresses who work in other national cinemas?

5. Susan Sarandon has served as both a sex symbol and challenge to Hollywood images of women. Are there other actresses who have served this dual role? How do their careers exemplify this dualism? Can an actress be a sex symbol, yet also be a positive feminist figure?

6. Consider the debate over the progressivity of *Thelma & Louise*. Do you see the film as a progressive feminist text? Why or why not? Compare the film to other female friendship films of the 1980s and 1990s, such as *Mortal Thoughts*, *Beaches*, and *Steel Magnolias*.

7. This chapter argues that Susan Sarandon has been an auteurist actress who shaped in significant ways the films in which she starred. What other actors or actresses can be seen as auteurs? How have they transformed their films through role choice, character development, demands for script changes, and involvement in producing or directing?

8. What are your views on female nudity in films? Do you agree with Sarandon that it "upstages" the actress and prevents her from being taken seriously? Do you think the amount of sexuality and nudity found in an actress's films diminishes her feminist status?

Filmography of Major Actresses

Joan Crawford: *Mildred Pierce* (1945); *Johnny Guitar* (1954); *What Ever Happened to Baby Jane* (1962)

Doris Day: *Calamity Jane* (1953); *Love Me or Leave Me* (1955); *Pillow Talk* (1959)

Bette Davis: *Jezebel* (1938); *Now, Voyager* (1942); *All About Eve* (1950)

Marlene Dietrich: *The Blue Angel* (1930); *Morocco* (1930); *Shanghai Express* (1932)

Jane Fonda: *They Shoot Horses, Don't They* (1969); *Klute* (1971); *Julia* (1977)

Greta Garbo: *Queen Christina* (1933); *Camille* (1936); *Ninotchka* (1939)

Lilian Gish: *Broken Blossoms* (1919); *Way Down East* (1920); *The Wind* (1928)

Audrey Hepburn: *Sabrina* (1954); *Breakfast at Tiffany's* (1961); *My Fair Lady* (1964)

Katherine Hepburn: *Bringing Up Baby* (1938); *The Philadelphia Story* (1940); *Adam's Rib* (1949)

Marilyn Monroe: *Gentlemen Prefer Blondes* (1953); *Some Like It Hot* (1959); *The Misfits* (1961)

Mary Pickford: *The Poor Little Rich Girl* (1917); *Stella Maris* (1918); *Daddy-Long-Legs* (1919)

Elizabeth Taylor: *A Place in the Sun* (1951); *Cat on a Hot Tin Roof* (1958); *Who's Afraid of Virginia Woolf* (1966)

Lana Turner: *The Postman Always Rings Twice* (1946); *The Bad and the Beautiful* (1952); *Imitation of Life* (1956)

Bibliography

Alberge, Dalya. (1996) "Film Nonsense and Insensibility Almost Stopped Austen Epic," *The Times* (London), February 22: A5.

Altman, Rick. (1999) *Film/Genre*. London: BFI.

Amossy, Ruth. (1986) "Autobiographies of Movie Stars: presentation of self and its strategies," *Poetics Today* 7.4: 673–703.

Anderson, Carolyn. (1988) "Biographical Film" in Wes D. Gehring (ed.) *Handbook of American Film Genres*. New York: Greenwood. 331–51.

Arbuthnot, Lucie and Gail Seneca. (1990) "Pre-text and Text in *Gentlemen Prefer Blondes*" in Patricia Erens (ed.) *Issues in Feminist Film Criticism*. Bloomington: Indiana UP. 112–25. Originally published in (1982) *Film Reader* 5.

Austin, Thomas and Martin Barker. (eds) (2003) *Contemporary Hollywood Stardom*. London: Arnold.

Bachrach, Judy. (1994) "The Mom Bomb." *Allure*. (July): 118–20.

Barron, Alexandra Lynn. (2008) "*Fire*'s Queer Anti-Communalism," *Meridians: feminism, race, transnationalism* 8.2: 64–93.

Basinger, Jeanine. (1993) *A Woman's View: how Hollywood spoke to women 1930–1960*. New York: Knopf.

Benerji, Rima. (1999) "Still on Fire." *Manushi*, 113 (July), 18–21.

Bergan, Ronald. (1983) "Whatever Happened to the Biopic?" *Films and Filming* 346: 21–22.

Bergstrom, Janet. (1999a) "Chantal Akerman: Splitting" in Janet Bergstrom (ed.) *Endless Night: cinema and psychoanalysis, parallel histories*. Berkeley: University of California Press. 273–90.

——(1999b) "The Innovators 1970–80: keeping a distance" in *Sight and Sound* (November), np.

——(1977) "Jeanne Dielman, 23 Quai de Commerce, 1080 Bruxelles by Chantel Akerman" in *Camera Obscura* 2. 115–21.

Bhabba, Homi K. (1994) *The Location of Culture*. London and New York: Routledge.

Bingham, Dennis. (2010) *Whose Lives Are They Anyway?: the biopic as contemporary film genre*. New Brunswick: Rutgers UP.

Biskind, Peter. (1977) "Harlan County, USA: the miners. struggle," *Jump Cut* 14 (March): 3–4. Online. Available: <http://www.ejumpcut.org/archive/onlinessays/JC14folder/HarlanCty.html> (accessed July 12, 2010).

Blaetz, Robin. (2007) "Introduction: Women's Experimental Cinema: critical frameworks." *Women's Experimental Cinema: critical frameworks*. Durham, NC: Duke UP. 1–19.

Bobo, Jacqueline. (1995) *Black Women as Cultural Readers*. New York: Columbia UP.

——(1993) "Reading through the Text: the Black women as audience" in Manthia Diawara (ed.) *Black American Cinema*. New York and London: Routledge. 272–87.

Bobo, Jacqueline and Ellen Seiter. (1991) "Black Feminism and Media Criticism: *The Women of Brewster Place.*" *Screen* 32.3. 286–302.

Brakhage, Stan. (1991) *Film at Wit's End: eight avant-garde filmmakers.* Kingston, NY: McPherson & Co.

Briley, Ron. (2003) "Frida," *Film and History* 33.2: 75–77.

Brooks, Brian. (2006) Indiewire Interview: Barbara Kopple, Co-director of *Shut Up & Sing.* Online. Available: http://www.indiewire.com/article/indiewire_interview_barbara_kopple_co-director_of_shut_up_sing/ (accessed July 13, 2010).

Brownstein, Rachel M. (1998) "Out of the Drawing Room, Onto the Lawn" in Linda Troost and Sayre Greenfield (eds) *Jane Austen in Hollywood.* Lexington: University of Kentucky Press. 13–21.

Bruno, Guiliana. (1989) Untitled Contribution to "The Spectatrix" (special issue), *Camera Obscura* 20/21: 105.

Burrows, Roberta. (1977) "Susan Sarandon: the other side of midnight." *Interview* (May): 14.

Butler, Alison. (2002) *Women's Cinema: the contested screen.* London: Wallflower.

Byg, Barton. (1993) "German History and Cinematic Convention Harmonized in Margarethe von Trotta's *Marianne and Juliane*" in Sandra Friedan, Richard W. McCormick, and Vibeke R. Petersen (eds) *Gender and German Cinema: feminist interventions, Vol. 2.* Providence, R.I.: Berg Publishers. 259–271.

Carlson, Margaret. (1991) "Is This What Feminism Is All About?" *Time* 137 (June 24): 57.

Carson, Diane, Linda Ditmar, and Janice R. Welsch. (1999) *Multiple Voices in Feminist Film Criticism.* Minneapolis: University of Minneapolis Press.

Casey, Diana M. (1998) "Emma Thompson's Sense and Sensibility as a Gateway to Austen's Novel" in Linda Troost and Sayre Greenfield (eds) *Jane Austen in Hollywood.* Lexington: University of Kentucky Press. 140–47.

Casper, Drew. (2006) Audio Commentary. *Lust for Life.* Dir. Vincente Minnelli. Perf. Kirk Douglas, Anthony Quinn. 1958. DVD. Warner Home Video.

Chaudhuri, Anita. (1994) "Mother Complex." *Time Out.* (October 12–19): 18. Susan Sarandon Clippings File. Margeret Herrick Library of Motion Pictures Arts and Sciences, Beverly Hills, CA.

Chitterjee, Madhuri. (2007) "Women's Bodies, Women's Voices: exploring women's sexuality in Deepa Mehta's trilogy" in Jasbir Jain (ed.) *Films, Literature, and Culture: Deepa Mehta's element's trilogy.* Jaipur: Rawat Publications. 75–84.

Christiansen, Peter G. (1989) "Margarethe von Trotta's *Sisters* and the Grimm's Fairy Tales," *Rocky Mt. Review of Languages and Literature* 43.4: 211–22.

Chughtai, Ismat. (1999) "Lihaaf" ("The Quilt"). Trans. M. Asaduddin. *Manushi* 110: 36–40. Originally published 1942.

Clover, Carol. (1993) "High and Low: the transformation of the rape-revenge movie" in Pam Cook and Philip Dodd (eds) *Women and Film: a sight and sound reader.* Philadelphia: Temple UP. 76–85.

Collins, Amanda. (1998) "Jane Austen, Film and the Pitfalls of Postmodern Nostalgia" in Linda Troost and Sayre Greenfield (eds) *Jane Austen in Hollywood.* Lexington: University of Kentucky Press. 79–89.

Comolli, Jean-Louis and Jean Narboni. (1976) "Cinema/Ideology/Criticism" in Bill Nichols (ed.) *Movies and Methods, Vol. 1.* Berkeley: University of California Press. 22–30. Originally published in *Cahiers du cinema* in 1969.

Cook, Pam. (1988) "Approaching the Work of Dorothy Arzner" in Constance Penley (ed.) *Feminism and Film Theory.* New York: Routledge. 46–56.

Cook, Pam and Claire Johnston. (1990) "The Place of Woman in the Cinema of Raoul Walsh" in Patricia Erens (ed.) *Issues in Feminist Film Criticism.* Bloomington: Indiana UP.

19–27. Originally published in (1974) Phillip Hartley (ed.) *Raoul Walsh*. Colchester, England: Vineyard Press.

Cowie, Elizabeth. (1984) "Fantasia," *m/f* 9: 70–105.

Crofts, Stephen. (1998) "Authorship and Hollywood" in John Hill and Pamela Church Gibson (eds) *The Oxford Guide to Film Studies*. Oxford: Oxford UP. 84–98.

Cross, Alice. (1991) "The Bimbo and the Mystery Woman" in "Should We Go Along for the Ride? A Critical Symposium on *Thelma & Louise*." *Cineaste* 18.4 (December): 32–34.

Custen, George. (1992) *Bio/Pics: how Hollywood constructed public history*. New Brunswick, NJ: Rutgers UP.

Damico, James. (1991) "Ingrid from Lorraine to Strombol: analyzing the public's perception of a film star" in Jeremy G. Butler (ed.) *Star Texts: image and performance in film and television*. Detroit: Wayne State UP. 240–53.

Daughtry, J. Martin. (2009) "Shut Up & Sing," *Journal of the Society for American Music* 3.2: 269–72.

Davis, Tonya and Brian D. Johnson. (1999) "Reinventing Motherhood." *Maclean's* 112.45 (November 8): 80.

Davis, Zeimabu irene. (1991) "An Interview with Julie Dash," *Wide Angle* 13.3/4: 110–19.

de Lauretis, Teresa. (1994) *The Practice of Love: lesbian sexuality and perverse desire*. Bloomington: Indiana UP.

——(1991) "Film and the Visible" in Bad Object-Choices (ed.) *How Do I Look?: queer film and video*. Seattle: Bay Press. 259–62.

——(1984) *Alice Doesn't: feminism, semiotics, cinema*. London: Macmillan.

Delorme, Charlotte. (1985) "On the Film *Marianne and Juliane* by Margarethe von Trotta," *Journal of Film and Video* 37: 47–51.

Desmond, John M. and Peter Hawkes. (2005) *Adaptation: studying film and literature*. Boston: McGraw Hill.

"*Desert Hearts* Production Notes" (1985) housed in the Margaret Herrick Library of the Academy of Motion Pictures Arts and Sciences, Beverly Hills, CA.

Dickson, Rebecca. (1998) "Misrepresenting Jane Austen's Ladies: revising texts (and history) to sell films" in Linda Troost and Sayre Greenfield (eds) *Jane Austen in Hollywood*. Lexington: University of Kentucky Press. 44–57.

DiCaprio, Lisa. (1984) "*Marianne and Juliane/The German Sisters*: Baader-Meinhof fictionalized," *Jump Cut* 29: 56–59. <http://www.ejumpcut.org/archive/onlinessays/JC29folder/GermanSisters.html> (accessed June 28, 2011).

DiClementi, Deborah. (1999) "Feminist, Sex Symbol and Mom." *Lesbian News* 25.1: 30. *Academic Search Complete*, EBSCOhost (accessed October 17, 2010).

Doane, Mary Anne (1991) "Dark Continents: epistemologies of racial and sexual difference in psychoanalysis and the cinema" *Femmes Fatales: feminism, film theory, psychoanalysis*. New York: Routledge. 209–48.

——(1990) "Film and the Masquerade" in Patricia Erens (ed.) *Issues in Feminist Film Criticism*. Bloomington: Indiana UP. 41–57. Originally published in (1982) *Screen* 23.3–4: 74–87.

——(1989) Untitled Contribution to "The Spectatrix" (special issue), *Camera Obscura* 20/21: 142–43.

——(1987) *The Desire to Desire: the woman's film of the 1940s*. Bloomington: Indiana UP.

Dole, Carol M. (1998) "Austen, Class, and the American Market" in Linda Troost and Sayre Greenfield (eds) *Jane Austen in Hollywood*. Lexington: University of Kentucky Press. 58–78.

Dowell, Pat. (1991) "The Importance of Women" in "Should We Go Along for the Ride?: a critical symposium on *Thelma & Louise*." *Cineaste* 18.4 (December): 28–36.

Dreifus, Claudia. (1989) "Susan Sarandon: the playboy interview." *Playboy* 36.5: 63–80.

Dyer, Richard. (1986) *Heavenly Bodies: film stars and society*. New York: St. Martin's Press.

——(1984) "Stereotyping" in Richard Dyer (ed.) *Gays and Film*. New York: New York Zoetrope. 27–39.

——(1979) *Stars*. London: British Film Institute.

Eckert, Charles. (1991) "Shirley Temple and the House of Rockefeller" in Jeremy G. Butler (ed.) *Star Texts: image and performance in film and television*. Detroit: Wayne State UP. 184–202.

Ellingson, Annlee. (2000) "Making a Sweet Margarita." *Box Office Online* (January). Online. Available: <http://www.boxoffice.com/issues/janoo/Susan_Sarandon.html> (accessed October 20, 2010)

Ellis, John. (1982) *Visible Fictions: cinema: television: video*. London: Routledge.

Elsner-Sommer, Gretchen and Rob Edelman. (1999) "Margarethe von Trotta" in Amy L. Unterburger (ed.) *The St. James Filmmakers Encyclopedia: women on the other side of the camera*. Detroit: Visible Ink Press. 442.

Erens, Patricia (ed.) (1990) *Issues in Feminist Film Criticism*. Bloomington: Indiana UP.

Fabe, Marilyn. (1996) "Maya Deren's Fatal Attraction: a psychoanalytic reading of *Meshes of the Afternoon* with a psycho–biographical afterword," *Women's Studies* 25.2: 137–52.

Fanon, Franz. (2008) *Black Skin, White Masks*. New York: Grove Press. Originally published 1952.

Farwell, Marilyn R. (1990) "Heterosexual Plots and Lesbian Subtexts: toward a theory of lesbian narrative space" in Karla Jay and Joanne Glasgow (eds) *Lesbian Texts and Contexts: radical revisions*. New York: New York UP. 91–103.

Feld, Bruce. (1996) "Director Ang Lee Believes *S& S* May be His Best Film to Date," *Drama-Logue* December 21–January 3: 8.

Ferriss, Suzanne. (2008) "Fashioning Femininity in the Makeover Film,"in Suzanne Ferriss and Mallory Young (eds) *Chick Flicks: contemporary women at the movies*. New York: Routledge. 41–57.

——and Mallory Young (eds) (2008a) *Chick Flicks: contemporary women at the movies*. New York: Routledge.

——(2008b) "Introduction: chick flicks and chick culture" in Suzanne Ferriss and Mallory Young (eds) *Chick Flicks: contemporary women at the movies*. New York: Routledge. 1–25.

Fischer, Lucy. (2004) "*Marlene*: modernity, mortality, and the biopic" in Lucy Fischer. *Stars: the film reader*. New York: Routledge. 29–42.

——(1999) "Sirk and the Figure of the Actress: *All I Desire*," *Film Criticism* 23.2–3 (Winter/Spring): 136–49.

——(1988) "*Sunset Boulevard*: fading stars" in Janet Todd (ed.) *Women & Film*. New York: Holmes & Meier. 97–113.

——(1989) *Shot/Countershot: film tradition and women's cinema*. Princeton: Princeton UP.

Flatley, Guy. (1978) "Susan Sarandon Summer Stardom." *Cosmopolitan* (March): 66.

Foerster, Annette. (1990) "Chantal Akerman" in Annette Kuhn and Susannah Radstone (eds) *The Women's Companion to International Film*. Berkeley: University of California Press. 8–10.

Foster, Gwendolyn Audrey. (2003) "Introduction" in Gwendolyn Audrey Forster (ed.) *Identity and Meaning: the films of Chantal Akermann*. Carbondale, Illinois: Southern Illinois UP. 1–8.

——(1999) "Foreword" in Amy L. Unterburger (ed.) *The St. James Women Filmmakers Encyclopedia: women on the other side of the camera*. Detroit: Visible Ink. xiii–xviii."

Francke, Lizzie. (1994) *Script Girls: women screenwriters in Hollywood*. London: BFI. 129–30.

Fuller, Graham. (1994) "Susan Sarandon: the bigger picture revolution." *Interview* (October): 147.

Gaines, Jane. (1990a) "Costume and Narrative: how dress tells the woman's story" in Jane Gaines and Charlotte Herzog (eds) *Fabrications: costume and the female body*. London and New York: Routledge. 180–211.

——(1990b) "Introduction: fabricating the female body" in Jane Gaines and Charlotte Herzog (eds) *Fabrications: costume and the female body*. London and New York: Routledge, 1–27.

——(1990c) "White Privilege and Looking Relations" in Patricia Erens (ed.) *Issues in Feminist Film Criticism*. Bloomington: Indiana UP. 197–214. Originally published in (1986) *Cultural Critique* 4 (Fall).

——(1990d) "Women and Representation: can we enjoy alternate pleasures?" in Patricia Erens (ed.) *Issues in Feminist Film Criticism*. Bloomington: Indiana UP. 75–92. Originally published in (1984) *Jump Cut* 29.

Gaines, Jane and Charlotte Herzog (eds) (1990) *Fabrications: costume and the female body*. London and New York: Routledge.

Gallagher, Tag. (1985) "Tag Gallagher Responds to Tania Modleski's 'Time and Desire in the Woman's Film' (*Cinema Journal*, Spring 1984) and Linda Williams's '"Something Else Besides a Mother': *Stella Dallas* and the maternal melodrama (*Cinema Journal*, Fall 1984)." *Cinema Journal* 25.2: 65–66.

Gant-Britton, Lisbeth. (1995) "African Women and Visual Culture: a sample syllabus." *Camera Obscura* 36: 85–117.

Garrard, Mary and Gloria Steinem. (1998) "Now That You've Seen the Film, Meet the Real Artemisia Gentileschi … " Online. Available: <http://songweaver.com/art/artemisia.html> (accessed August 17, 2008).

Geller, Theresa L. (2006) "The Personal Cinema of Maya Deren: *Meshes of the Afternoon* and its critical reception in the history of the avant–garde," *Biography* 29.1: 140–57.

Geraghty, Christine. (2003) "Performing as a Lady and a Dame: reflections on acting and genre" in Thomas Austin and Martin Barker (eds) *Contemporary Hollywood Stardom*. London: Arnold. 105–17.

——(2000) "Re–examining Stardom: questions of texts, bodies, and performance" in Christine Gledhill and Linda Williams (eds) *Reinventing Film Studies*. London: Arnold. 183–201.

Gibson-Hudson, Gloria. (1994) "Aspects of Black Feminist Cultural Ideology in Films by Black Women Independent Artists" in Diane Carson, Linda Dittmar, and Janice R. Welsch (eds) *Multiple Voices in Feminist Film Criticism*. Minneapolis: Univeristy of Minnesota Press. 365–79.

Gilligan, Sarah. (2003) *Teaching Women and Film*. London: BFI.

Gledhill, Christine. (1999) "Pleasurable Negotiations" in Sue Thornham (ed.) *Feminist Film Theory*. New York: New York UP. 166–79. Originally Published (1988) in Deirdre Pribram (ed.) *Female Spectators: looking at film and television*. London and New York: Verso. 64–77.

——(1991) "Introduction" in Christine Gledhill (ed.) *Stardom: industry of desire*. New York: Routledge. xiii–xx.

——(ed.) (1987) *Home Is Where the Heart Is: studies in melodrama and the woman's film*. London: BFI.

——(1986) "Christine Gledhill on *Stella Dallas* and Feminist Film Theory." *Cinema Journal* 25.4: 44–48.

Goldman, Steve. (1992) "Careering Ahead." *The Sunday Times* sec. 6 (March 15): 10.

Gray, Beverley (1997) "*Sense and Sensibility*: a script revision," *Creative Screenwriting* 4.2: 72–82.

Greenberg, Harvey R. (1991–2) "Thelma and Louise's Exuberant Polysemy" in Ann Martin (ed.) "The Many Faces of *Thelma & Louise*." *Film Quarterly* 45.2 (Winter): 20.

Griggers, Cathy. (1993) "*Thelma & Louise* and the Cultural Generation of the New Butch-femme" in Ava Preacher Collins, Jim Collins, and Hilary Radner (eds) *Film Theory Goes to the Movies* New York: Routledge. 129–41.

Grundmann, Roy and Cynthia Lucia. (1993) "Acting, Activism, and Hollywood Politics." *Cineaste* 20.1 (July) EBSCOhost Academic Search Premiere GALILEO. <http://www.galileo.peachnet.edu> (accessed October 20, 2010).

Guzman, Isobel Molina. (2007) "Selma Hayek's Frida" in Myra Bendible (ed.) *From Bananas to Buttocks: the Latina body in popular film and culture*. Austen: University of Texas Press. 117–28.

Hansen, Miriam. (1986) "Pleasure, Ambivalence, Identification: Valentino and female spectatorship," *Cinema Journal* 25.4: 6–32.

Hart, Lynda. (1994) *Fatal Women: lesbian sexuality and the mark of aggression*. Princeton, NJ: Princeton UP.

Hartman, S.V. and Farah Jasmine Griffin. (1991) "'Are You as Colored as That Negro?': the politics of being seen in Julie Dash's *Illusions*," *Black American Literature Forum* 25.2: 361–73.

Haskell, Molly. (1999) "The Woman's Film" in Sue Thornham (ed.) *Feminist Film Theory*. New York: New York UP. 20–30. Originally published in (1974) *From Reverance to Rape: the treatment of women in the movies*. Chicago: University of Chicago Press. 153–88.

——(1974) *From Reverance to Rape: the treatment of women in the movies*. Chicago: University of Chicago Press.

Hehr, Renate. (2000) *Margarethe von Trotta: filmmaking as liberation*. Stuttgart and London: Edition Axel Menges.

Hobson, Louise B. (1996) "Reconcilable Differences" *Calgary Sun* (January 14). Online. <www.canoe.ca/jammoviesartistsS/sarandon.html> (accessed October 20, 2010).

Hollinger, Karen. (2006) *The Actress: Hollywood acting and the female star*. London and New York: Routledge.

——(2006) "Margarethe von Trotta and Films of Women's Friendship" in Esther Wipfler (ed.) *Freundschaft: Motive und Bedeutungen*. Munich: Scaneg Verlag. 217–257.

——(2008) "Afterword: once I got beyond the name chick flick" in Suzanne Ferriss and Mallory Young (eds) *Chick Flicks: contemporary women at the movies* (2008a) New York: Routledge. 221–232.

——(1998a) *In the Company of Women: contemporary female friendship films*. Minneapolis: University of Minnesota Press.

——(1998b) "Theorizing Mainstream Female Spectatorship: the case of the popular lesbian film" *Cinema Journal* 37.2: 3–17.

——(1987) "'The Look,' Narrativity, and The Female Spectator in *Vertigo*." *Journal of Film and Video* 39.4 (Fall 1987), 18–27.

Holmlund, Christine. (1994a) "Cruisin' for a Bruisin': Hollywood's deadly (lesbian) dolls." *Cinema Journal* 34.1 (Fall): 31–51.

——(1994b) "A Decade of Deadly Dolls" in Helen Birch (ed.) *Moving Targets: women, murder and representation*. Berkeley: University of California Press. 127–51.

——(1991) "When Is a Lesbian Not a Lesbian?: the lesbian continuum and the mainstream femme film." *Camera Obscura* 25–26 (January/May): 146–47.

hooks, bell. (1993) "The Oppositional Gaze: black female spectators" in Manthia Diawara (ed.) *Black American Cinema*. New York and London: Routledge. 288–302. Originally published in bell hooks (1992) *Black Looks: race and representation*. Boston: South End Press. 115–31.

——(1992) *Black Looks: Race and Representation*. Boston: South End Press.

Jain, Jasbir (2007a) "The Diasporic Eye and the Evolving I: Deepa Mehta's elements trilogy" in Jasbir Jain (ed.) *Films, Literature, and Culture: Deepa Mehta's element's trilogy*. Jaipur: Rawat Publications. 54–74.

——(2007b) *Films, Literature, and Culture: Deepa Mehta's element's trilogy*. Jaipur: Rawat Publications.

Jerome, Jim, (1994) "Susan Sarandon." *Ladies Home Journal* 111.8 (August) EBSCOhost Academic Search Premier. 39–53.

Jodha, Avinash. (2007) "Packaging India: the fabric of Deepa Mehta's cinematic art" in Jasbir Jain (ed.) *Films, Literature, and Culture: Deepa Mehta's element's trilogy*. Jaipur: Rawat Publications. 39–53.

John, Mary E. and Tejaswini Niranjana. (2000) "Introduction" in "The Controversy over *Fire*: a select dossier (part I)" *Inter-Asian Cultural Studies* 1.2: 371–72.

Johnston, Claire. (1990a) "Dorothy Arzner: critical strategies" in E. Ann Kaplan (ed.) *Feminism and Film*. Oxford: Oxford UP. 139–48. Originally published in Claire Johnston (ed.) (1975) *The Work of Dorothy Arzner: towards a feminist cinema*. London: BFI.

——(1990b) "Women's Cinema as Counter-Cinema" in E. Ann Kaplan (ed.) (2000) *Feminism and Film*. Oxford: Oxford UP. 22–33. Originally published in Claire Johnston (ed.) (1973) *Notes on Women's Cinema*. London: BFI. 24–31.

Johnston, Sheila. (2000) "It's Just a Chance to Use my Celebrity." *The Independent on Sunday*. (April 2): np. Susan Sarandon Clippings File, Margaret Herrick Library of the Academy of Motion Pictures Arts and Sciences, Beverly Hills, CA.

Kaplan, E. Ann. (2008) "A History of Gender Theory in Cinema Studies" in Krin Gibbard and William Luhr (eds) *Screening Genders*. New Brunswick: Rutgers UP. 15–28.

——(2005) *Trauma Culture*. New Brunswick: Rutgers UP.

——(2000a) (ed.) *Feminism and Film*. Oxford: Oxford UP.

——(2000b) "Is the Gaze Male?" in E. Ann Kaplan (ed.) *Feminism and Film*. Oxford: Oxford UP. 119–38. Originally published E. Ann Kaplan (1983) *Women and Film: both sides of the camera*. New York and London: Methuen. 23–35.

——(1997) *Looking for the Other*. New York and London: Routledge.

——(1990) "The Case of the Missing Mother: maternal issues in Vidor's *Stella Dallas*" in Patricia Erens (ed.) *Issues in Feminist Film Criticism*. Bloomington: Indiana UP. 126–36. Originally published in (1983) *Heresies* 16: 81–86.

——(1985) "Ann Kaplan Replies to Linda Williams's '"Something Else Besides a Mother': *Stella Dallas* and the maternal melodrama." *Cinema Journal* 24.2: 40–43.

——(1983) *Women and Film: both sides of the camera*. New York and London: Methuen.

——(1977) "Harlan County, USA: the documentary form," *Jump Cut* 15: 11–12.

Kaplan, Deborah. (1998) "Mass Marketing Jane Austen: men, women, and courtship in two film adaptations" in Linda Troost and Sayre Greenfield (eds) *Jane Austen in Hollywood*. Lexington: University of Kentucky Press. 177–87.

Kapur, Ratna. (2000) "Cultural Politics of *Fire*" in "The Controversy over *Fire*: a select dossier (part I)" *Inter-Asian Cultural Studies* 1.2: 379–381. Originally published in *Economic and Political Weekly* May 22, 1999.

Khouri, Callie. (1996) Thelma & Louise *and* Something to Talk About: *screenplays by Callie Khouri*. New York: Grove Press.

——(1990) *Thelma & Louise*: final shooting script. Housed in Margaret Herrick Library of the Academy of Motion Pictures Arts and Sciences, Beverly Hills, CA.

Kinder, Marsha. (1991/1992) "*Thelma & Louise* and *Messidor* as Feminist Road Movies" in Ann Martin (ed.) "The Many Faces of *Thelma & Louise*." *Film Quarterly* 45.2 (Winter): 30.

King, Barry. (1991) "Articulating Stardom" in Jeremy G. Butler (ed.) *Star Texts: image and performance in film and television*. Detroit: Wayne State UP. 125–54.

——(2003) "Embodying and Elastic Self: The Parametrics of Contemporary Stardom" in Thomas Austin and Martin Barker (eds.) *Contemporary Hollywood Stardom*. London: Arnold. 45–61.

Kino, Carol. (2002) "Does *Frida* Nail Frida's Life – or Her Art?" *Slate* October 29. Online. Available: *http://www.slate.com/id/2073286* (accessed September 15, 2010).

Kishwar, Machhu. (1998) "Naive Outpouring of a Self-Hating Indian: a review of Mehta's 'Fire,'" *Manushi* 109: 3–14.

Klady, Leonard. (1995) "Cents and Sensibility," *Variety* December 26: 8.

Klaprat, Cathy. (1985) "The Star as Market Strategy: Bette Davis in another light" in Tino Balio (ed.) *The American Film Industry*. Madison: University of Wisconsin Press. 351–76.

Klawans, Stuart. (1991) "Films." *The Nation* (June 24): 863.

Kleinhans, Chuck. (1977) "Barbara Kopple Interview." *Jump Cut* 14: 4–6.

Klotman, Phyllis Rauch. (1991a) "Biographical Sketch: Julie Dash" in Phyllis Rauch Klotman (ed.) *Screenplays of the African American Experience*. Bloomington: Indiana UP. 191–92.

——(1991b) "Introduction: *Illusions*"in Phyllis Rauch Klotman (ed.) *Screenplays of the African American Experience*. Bloomington: Indiana UP. 193–95.

Kofman, Sarah. (1985) *The Enigma of Woman: woman in Freud's writings*. Ithaca: Cornell UP.

Kramer, Peter. (2003) "'A Woman in a Male-Dominated World': Jodie Foster, stardom, and 90s Hollywood" in Thomas Austin and Martin Barker (eds) *Contemporary Hollywood Stardom*. London: Arnold. 199–214.

Kuhn, Annette. (2004) "The State of Film and Media Feminism," *Signs* 31.1: 1221–28.

——(1994) *Women's Pictures: feminism and cinema*. London: Verso.

Lacey, Joanne. (2003) "A Galaxy of Stars to Guarantee Ratings': made-for-television movies and the female star system" in Thomas Austin and Martin Barker (eds) *Contemporary Hollywood Stardom*. London: Arnold. 187–98.

Legiardi-Laura, Roland. (1992) "Barbara Kopple," *BOMB* 38 (Winter): 36–39.

Lehman, Peter. (1993) "'Don't Blame this on a Girl': female rape-revenge rilms" in Steven Cohan and Ina Rae Hark (eds) *Screening the Male: exploring masculinities in Hollywood cinema*. New York: Routledge. 103–17.

Lehman, Peter and John Luhr (eds) (2008) *Thinking about Movies: watching, questioning, enjoying*, 3rd edn. Malden, MA: Wiley-Blackwell.

Lesage, Julia. (1990) "The Political Aesthetics of the Feminist Documentary Film" in Patricia Erens (ed.) *Issues in Feminist Film Criticism*. Bloomington: Indiana UP. 222–37.

Lee, Nathan. (2006) "The Devil Wears Prada." *Film Comment* 42.4: 71–72.

Lent, Tina Olsin. (2007) "Life as Art/Art as Life: dramatizing the life and work of Frida Kahlo," *Journal of Popular Film and Television* 35.2: 68–76.

Levitan, Jacqueline. (2003) "An Introduction to Deepa Mehta: making films in Canada and India with extracts from an interview conducted by Kass Banning" in Jacqueline Levitan, Judith Plesis, and Valerie Raoul (eds) *Women Filmmakers Refocusing*. New York: Routledge. 273–83.

Levy, Lisa. (2002) "Storytelling: great love and great work in the biopic." *Radical Society* 29.2: 87–101.

Linville, Susan E. (1991) "Retrieving History: Margarethe von Trotta's *Marianne and Juliane*, PMLA 106:3: 446–58.

Lipton, James. (1998) Interview with Susan Sarandon. *Inside the Actors' Studio*, Bravo Television (November 15).

Longfellow, Brenda. (1989) "Love Letters to the Mother: the work of Chantal Akerman," *Canadian Journal of Political and Social Theory* 13.1–2: 72–90.

Looser, Devoney. (1998) "Feminist Implications of the Silver Screen Austen" in Linda Troost and Syre Greenfield (eds) *Jane Austen in Hollywood*. Lexington: University Press of Kentucky. 159–76.

Lovell, Alan. (2003) "I Went in Search of Deborah Kerr, Jodie Foster, and Julianne Moore but got Waylaid ... " in Thomas Austin and Martin Barker (eds) *Contemporary Hollywood Stardom*. London: Arnold. 259–70.

——(1999) "Susan Sarandon: in praise of older women" in Alan Lovell and Peter Kramer (eds) *Screen Acting*. New York: Routledge. 88–105.

Maltby, Richard. (2003) *Hollywood Cinema*, 2nd Ed. Malden, Mass. and London: Blackwell

Manlove, Clifford T. (2007) "Visual Drive. and Cinematic Narrative: reading gaze theory in Lacan, Hitchock, and Mulvey," *Cinema Journal* 46.3: 83–108.

Margolis, Harriet. (2003) "Janeite Culture: what does the name Jane Austen authorize?" in Gina Mcdonald and Andrew F. Mcdonald (eds) *Jane Austen on Screen*. Cambridge: Cambridge UP. 22–43.

Margulies, Ivone. (1996) *Nothing Happens: Chantal Akerman's hyperrealist everyday*. Durham, NC: Duke UP.

Martin, Angela. (1979) "Chantal Akerman's Films: a dossier," *Feminist Review* 3: 24–47.

May, John E. and Tejaswini Niranjana (eds) (2000a) "The Controversy over *Fire*: a select dossier (part I)" *inter-Asian Cultural Studies* 1.2: 371–81.

——(2000b) "The Controversy over *Fire*: a select dossier (part II)" *Inter-Asian Cultural Studies* 1.3: 519–20.

Mayne, Judith. (2004) "Marlene, Dolls and Fetishis," *Signs* 30.1, 1257–64.

——(1994a) *Directed by Dorothy Arzner*. Bloomington: Indiana UP.

——(1994b) "Feminist Film Theory and Criticism" in Diane Carson, Linda Dittmar, and Janice R. Welsch (eds) *Multiple Voices in Feminist Film Criticism*. Minneapolis: University of Minnesota Press. 48–64.

——(1991) "Lesbian Looks: Dorothy Arzner and female authorship" in Bad Object-Choices (ed.) *How Do I Look?: queer film and video*. Seattle: Bay Press. 103–35.

——(1990) *The Woman at the Keyhole: feminism and women's cinema*. Bloomington: Indiana UP.

McCabe, Janet. (2004) *Feminist Film Studies: writing the woman into cinema*. New York: Wallflower.

McCracken, Ellen. (2003) "Hybridity and Supra-Ethnicity in Plastic and Filmic Representation: Frida Kahlo's art and Julie Taymor's Frida" *Interdisciplinary Journal of Germanic Linguistic and Semiotic Analysis* 8.2: 243–59.

McDonald, Paul. (2003) "Stars in the Online Universe: promotion, nudity, reverence" in Thomas Austin and Martin Barker (eds) *Contemporary Hollywood Stardom*. London: Arnold. 29–44.

——(1998) "Film Acting" in J. Hill and P.C. Gibson (eds) *The Oxford Guide to Film Studies*. Oxford: Oxford UP. 30–35.

McGowan, Sharon. (2003) "Excerpts from a Master Class with Deepa Mehta" in Jacqueline Levitin, Judith Plessis, and Valerie Raoul (eds) *Women Filmmakers Refocusing*. New York: Routledge. 285–91.

McKechnie, Kara. (2001) "Mrs. Brown's Mourning and Mr. King's Madness: royal crisis on screen" in Deborah Cartmell, I.Q. Hunter, and Imelda Whelehan (eds) *Retrovisions: reinventing the past in fiction and film*. London: Pluto Press. 102–19.

Mellencamp, Patricia. (1990) *Indiscretions: avant-garde film, video, and feminism*. Bloomington: Indiana UP.

——(1994) "Making History: Julie Dash" *Frontiers: a journal of women's studies* 15.1: 76–101.

Merck, Mandy. (1993) "Desert Hearts" in Martha Geven, Pratibha Parmar and John Greyson (eds) *Queer Looks: perspectives on lesbian and gay film and video*. New York: Routledge. 377–93.

Miller, D.A. (2008/2009) "Vertigo," *Film Quarterly* 62.2: 12–18.

——(1991) "Anal Rope" in Diana Fuss (ed.) *Inside/out: lesbian theories, gay theories*. New York: Routledge. 119–41.

Modleski, Tania. (1999) "Cinema and the Dark Continent: race and gender in popular film" in Sue Thornham (ed.) *Feminist Film Theory*. New York: New York UP. 321–35. Originally published in (1991) *Feminism without Women: culture and criticism in a "postfeminist" age*. London and New York: Routledge. 115–34.

——(1988) *The Woman who Knew Too Much: Hitchcock and feminist theory*. New York: Methuen, 1988.

Moeller, H.-B. (1986) "The Films of Margarethe von Trotta: domination, violence, solidarity, and social criticism," *Women and German Yearbook* (2): 129–49.

Moore, Oscar. (1995) *"Sense and Sensibility," Screen International* July 7: 18.

Moorti, Sujata. (2000) "Inflamed Passions: *Fire*, the woman question, and the policy of cultural borders," *Genders* 32. Online. Available: <http://www.genders.org/g32/g32_moorti.html> (accessed June 29, 2010).

Mounsef, Donia. (2003) "Women Filmmakers and the Avant-Garde: from Dulac to Duras" in Jacqueline Levitin, Judith Plessis, and Valerie Raoul (eds) *Women Filmmakers Refocusing*. New York: Routledge. 38–51.

Mulvey, Laura. (1989a) "Afterthoughts on 'Visual Pleasure and Narrative Cinema' Inspired by King Vidor's *Duel in the Sun* (1946)" in Laura Mulvey, *Visual and Other Pleasures*. Bloomington: Indiana UP. 29–38. Originally published in (1981) *Framework* 15/16/17: 12–15.

——(1989b) "Film, Feminism and the Avant-garde" in Laura Mulvey, *Visual and Other Pleasures*. Bloomington: Indiana UP. 111–26.

——(1989c) "Notes on Sirk and Melodrama" in Laura Mulvey, *Visual and Other Pleasures*. Bloomington: Indiana UP. 39–48. Originally published in (1977–78) *Movie*.

——(1989d) "Visual Pleasure and Narrative Cinema" in Laura Mulvey, *Visual and Other Pleasures*. Bloomington: Indiana UP. 14–26. Originally published in (1975) *Screen* 16.3: 6–18.

Nae, Madhue Kiswar. (2000) "Outpourings of a Self-Hating Indian: Deepa Mehta's *Fire*" in John E. May and Tejaswini Niranjana (eds) "The Controversy over *Fire*: a select dossier (part II)" *Inter-Asian Cultural Studies* 1.3: 520–24. Originally published in *Manushi* 109 (1998).

Narboni, Jean. (1977) "Le quatrieme personne du singulier (*Je, tu, il, elle*)," *Cahiers du Cinema* 276 (May): 5–13.

Naremore, James. (1988) *Acting in the Cinema*. Berkeley and Los Angeles: University of California Press.

Neale, Steve. (2000) *Genre and Hollywood*. London: Routledge.

Negra, Diane. (2008) "Structural Integrity, Historical Reversion, and the Post-9/11 Chick Flick," *Feminist Media Studies* 8.1: 51–68.

——(2004) "'Quality Postfeminism?' Sex and the Single Girl on HBO," *Genders Online Journal* 39. Online. Available: <http://www.genders.org/p39/p39_negra.html> (accessed July 25, 2010).

Negra, Diane and Yvonne Tasker. (2005) "In Focus: postfeminism and media studies." *Cinema Journal* 44.2: 107–10.

Nichols, Bill (2001) *Introduction to Documentary*. Bloomington: Indiana UP.

Nochimson, Martha P. (2006) "The Devil Wears Prada" *Cineaste* 32.1: 48–50.

Pachero, Patrick. (1970) "Susan Sarandon: pretty woman." *After Dark* (June): 35.

Pajaczkowska, Claire and Lola Young. (2000) "Racism, Representation, Psychoanalysis" in E. Ann Kaplan (ed.) *Feminism and Film*. Oxford: Oxford UP. 356–74.

Paramesweren, Uma. (2007) "Problematizing Diasporic Motivation" in Jasbir Jain (ed.) *Films, Literature, and Culture: Deepa Mehta's element's trilogy*. Jaipur: Rawat Publications. 10–22.

Parrill, Sue. (2002) *Jane Austen on Film and Television: a critical study of the adaptations*. Jefferson, NC: McFarland & Co.

Patel, Geeta. (1998) "Trial by Fire: a local/global view," *GCN: Gay Community News* 24.2: 10–17.

Penley, Constance (ed.) (1988) *Feminism and Film Theory*. New York and London: Routledge.

Perkins, Tessa. (1991) "The Politics of Jane Fonda" in Christine Gledhill (ed.) *Stardom: Industry of Desire*. London: Routledge. 237–50.

Petro, Patrice and Carol Flinn. (1985) "Patrice Petro and Carol Flinn on Feminist Film Theory," *Cinema Journal* 25.1: 50–52.

Petrolle, Jean and Virginia Wright Wexman. (2005) "Introduction: experimental filmmaking and women's subjectivity" in Jean Petrolle and Virginia Wright Wexman (eds) *Women and Experimental Filmmaking*. Urbana: University of Illinois Press. 1–17.

Pollock, Griselda. (2001) "A Hungry Eye" in Ginette Vincendeau (ed.) *Film/Literature/Heritage: a sight and sound reader*. London: BFI. 32–37.

Pramaggiore, Maria. (1997) "Performance and Persona in the U.S. Avant-Garde: the case of Maya Deren," *Cinema Journal* 36.2: 17–40.

Prasch, Tom. (1991) "Women Outlaws: the sexual politics of *Thelma & Louise*." *The Ryder Magazine* July 17–30: 26.

Quart, Barbara Koenig (1988) *Women Directors: the emergence of a new cinema*. New York: Praeger.

Rabinovitz, Lauren. (1991) *Points of Resistance: women, power and politics in the New York avant-garde cinema, 1943–71*. Urbana: University of Illinois Press.

Rabinowitz, Paula. (1999) "Sentimental Contracts: dreams and documents of American labor" in Diane Waldman and Janet Walker (eds) *Feminism and Documentary*. Minneapolis: University of Minnesota Press. 43–63.

——(1990) "Seeing through the Gendered I: feminist film theory," *Feminist Studies* 16.1: 151–70.

Radner, Hilary. (2011) *Neo-Feminist Cinema: girly films, chick flicks, and consumer culture*. New York and London: Routledge.

Rajadhyaksha, Ashish. (1998) "Realism, Modernism, and Post-colonial Theory" in John Hill and Pamela Church Gibson (eds) *The Oxford Guide to Film Studies*. New York: Oxford UP. 413–25.

Ramanathan, Geetha. (2006) *Feminist Auteurs: reading women's films*. London: Wallflower.

Rapping, Elayne. (1995) "Movies and Motherhood." *Progressive* 59.7: 36–37.

——(1991) "Feminism Gets the Hollywood Treatment" in "Should We Go Along for the Ride? A Critical Symposium on *Thelma & Louise*." *Cineaste* 18.4 (December): 30–32.

Rich, B. Ruby. (1999) "The Crisis of Naming in Feminist Film Criticism" in Sue Thornham (ed.) *Feminist Film Theory*. New York: New York UP. 41–47. Originally published in (1978) *Jump Cut* 19: 9–12.

——(1998) "Designing Desire: Chantal Akerman" in B. Ruby Rich. *Chick Flicks: theories and memories of the feminist movement*. Durham: Duke UP. 169–73.

Rodowick, David N. (2000) "The Difficulty of Difference" in Kaplan (ed.) *Feminism and Film*. Oxford: OUP. 181–202.

——(1991) *The Difficulty of Difference*. New York and London: Routledge.

Rosen, M. (2004) "In Her Own Time," *Artforum International* 42.8: 122–27.

Rosen, Marjorie. (1973) *Popcorn Venus: women, movies and the American dream*. New York: Coward, McCann, and Geoghegen.

Rule, Jane. (1985) *Desert of the Heart*. Tallahassee, FL: The Nyad Press.

Ryan, Judylyn S. (2004) "Outing the Black Feminist Filmmaker in Julie Dash's *Illusions*" *Signs: Journal of Women in Culture and Society* 30.1: 1319–44.

Said, Edward. (1978) *Orientalism*. New York: Pantheon.

Samuelian, Kristen Flieger. (1998) "'Privacy Is Our Only Option': postfeminist intervention in *Sense and Sensibility*" in Linda Troost and Syre Greenfield (eds) *Jane Austen in Hollywood*. Lexington: University Press of Kentucky. 148–58.

Sarris, Andrew. (1968) *The American Cinema: directors and directions, 1929–68*. New York: Da Capo Press.

Satin, Leslie. (1993) "Movement and the Body in Maya Deren's *Meshes of the Afternoon*," *Women and Performance* 6.2: 41–56.

Saunders, Dave (2010) *Documentary*. London: Routledge.

Schickel, Richard. (1991) "Gender Bender." *Time*. 137.25 (June 24): 52.

Schutte, Wolfram. "An Editing Room of One's Own," *Art Forum International* 24 (November 1985): 66–72.

Seiter, Ellen. (1986) "The Political Is Personal: Margarethe von Trotta's 'Marianne and Juliane'" in Charlotte Brunsdon (ed.) *Films for Women*. London: British Film Institute. 109–16.

Sengupta, Jayita. (2007) "Gendered Subject(s) in Deepa Mehta's *Fire* and *Water*" in Jasbir Jain (ed.) *Films, Literature, and Culture: Deepa Mehta's element's trilogy*. Jaipur: Rawat Publications 100–17.

Sense and Sensibility Press Book. (nd.) Unpublished. Housed in the Margaret Herrick Library of the Academy of Motion Picture Arts and Sciences, Beverly Hills, CA.

Seymour, Gene. (1994) "She's Her Own Best Council." *LA Times* (July 17): np. Susan Sarandon Clippings File, Margaret Herrick Library of the Academy of Motion Pictures Arts and Sciences, Beverly Hills, CA.

Shapiro, Marc. (2001) *Susan Sarandon: actress-activist*. Amherst, NY: Prometheus Books.

Shingler, Martin. (1999) "Bette Davis: malevolence in motion" in Alan Lovell and Peter Kramer (ed.) *Screen Acting*. New York: Routledge. 46–58.

Shohat, Ella. (1997) "Framing Post-Third Worldist Culture: gender and nation in Middle Eastern/North African film and video," *Jouvert* 1.1. Online. Available: english.chass.ncsu.edu/jouvert/v1i1/shohat.htm (accessed May 31, 2011).

Simpson, Janice C. (1991) "Moving into the Driver's Seat." *Time*. (June 24): 5.

Siomopoulos, Anna. (1999) "'I Didn't Know Anyone Could Be So Unselfish': liberal empathy, the welfare state, and King Vidor's *Stella Dallas*." *Cinema Journal* 38.4: 3–23.

Sitney, P. Adams. (1979) *Visionary Film: the American avant-garde*. New York: Oxford UP.

Smith, Damon. (2007) "Spirit in the Dark: Barbara Kopple on filming the group that wouldn't shut up and sing," *Bright Lights Film Journal* 55. Online. Available: <http//www.brightlighsfilm.com/55/koppleiv.html> (accessed June 20, 2010).

Smith, Gavin. (1993) "Uncompromising Positions" *Film Comment*. 29.2 (March/August) EBSCOhost Academic Search Premier. GALILEO, <http://www.galileo.peachnet.edu> (accessed October 30, 2010).

Smith, Murray. (1998) "Modernism and the Avant-Gardes" in John Hill and Pamela Church Gibson (eds) *The Oxford Guide to Film Studies*. Oxford and New York: Oxford UP. 395–412.

——(1995) *Engaging Characters: fiction, emotion, and the cinema*. New York: Oxford UP.

Smith, Valerie. (1994) "Reading the Intersection of Race and Gender in Narratives of Passing," *Diacritics* 24. 2/3: 43–57.

Spivak, Gayatri. (1988) "Can the Subaltern Speak?" in Cary Nelson and Lawrence Grossberg (eds) *Marxism and the Interpretation of Culture*. Urbana: University of Illinois Press. 271–313.

Stacey, Jackie. (1995) "'If You Don't Play You Can't Win': *Desert Hearts* and the romance film" in Tamsin Wilton (ed.) *Immortal, Invisible: lesbians and the cinema*. New York: Routledge. 92–114.

——(1994) *Star Gazing: Hollywood cinema and female spectatorship*. New York and London: Routledge.

——(1990) "Desperately Seeking Difference" in Patricia Erens (ed.) *Issues in Feminist Film Criticism*. Bloomington: Indiana UP. 365–79. Originally published in (1987) Screen 28.1.

——(1989) "Desperately Seeking Difference" in Lorraine Gamman and Margaret Marshment (eds) *The Female Gaze: women as viewers of popular culture*. Seattle: The Real Comet Press. 112–29.

Stam, Robert. (2005) "Introduction" in Robert Stam and Alessandra Raengo (eds) *Literature and Film: a guide to the theory and practice of film adaptation*. Malden, MA: Blackwell. 1–52.

Straayer, Chris. (1996) "The Hypothetical Lesbian Heroine in Narrative Feature Film" in Chris Straayer. *Deviant Eyes, Deviant Bodies: sexual re–orientations in film and video*. New York: Columbia UP. 9–22.

——(1990) "The Hypothetical Lesbian Heroine," *Jump Cut* 35 (April): 50–58 (reprinted in Straayer's 1996 book *Deviant Eyes, Deviant Bodies: sexual re–orientations in film and video*).

Stubbs, Liz. (2002) "Barbara Kopple: through the lens fearlessly" in Liz Stubbs. *Documentary Filmmakers Speak*. New York: Allworth Press. 209–20.

Studlar, Gaylyn. (1988) *In the Realm of Pleasure: Von Sternberg, Deitrich, and the masochistic aesthetic*. Urbana: University of Illinois Press.

"Susan Sarandon" (1996) *People* (May 6): np. Susan Sarandon Clippings File, Margaret Herrick Library of the Academy of Motion Pictures Arts and Sciences, Beverly Hills, CA.

Taylor, Helen. (1989) *Scarlett's Women:* Gone with the Wind *and its female fans*. New Brunswick: Rutgers UP.

"The Anti-Star" (1995) *Buzz: the talk of Los Angeles* (February): 59–62.

Thompson, Emma. (1996) *The Sense and Sensibility Screenplay and Diaries: bringing Jane Austen's novel to film*. New York: Newmarket Press.

Thompson, James. (2003) "How to Do Things with Austen" in Suzanne R. Pucci and James Thompson (eds) *Jane Austen and Co.: remaking the past in contemporary culture*. Albany: State University of New York Press. 13–32.

Thornham, Sue (ed.) (1999) *Feminist Film Theory: a reader*. New York: New York UP.

——(1997) *Passionate Detachments: an introduction to feminist film theory*. London: Arnold.

Trinh, T. Minh-ha (1991) *When the Moon Waxes Red: representation, gender and cultural politics*. London and New York: Routledge.

——(1989) *Woman, Native, Other*. Bloomington: Indiana UP.

Trinh, T. Minh-ha and Nancy Chen. (1992) "'Speaking Nearby': a conversation with Trinh T. Minh-ha." *Visual Anthropology Review* 8.1: 82–91. Rept. in E. Ann Kaplan (ed.) *Feminism and Film*. Oxford: Oxford UP. 317–35.

Troost, Linda and Syre Greenfield (eds) (1998a) *Jane Austen in Hollywood*. Lexington: University Press of Kentucky.

——(1998b) "Introduction: watching ourselves watching" in Linda Troost and Sayre Greenfield (eds) *Jane Austen in Hollywood*. Lexington: University of Kentucky Press. 1–12.

Truffaut, François. (2004) "A Certain Tendency in French Cinema" in Philip Simpson, Andrew Utterson, and K.J. Shepherdson (eds) *Film Theory: critical concepts in media and cultural studies*. London and New York: Routledge. Originally published as "Une certaine tendance de cinema francais," *Cahiers du cinema* 31 (1954): 15–29.

Truffaut, François with Helen G. Scott. (1985) *Hitchcock* (revised edition). New York: Simon and Schuster.

Tunison, Michael. (1995) "A Sense of Balance," *Entertainment Today* December 14–21: 6.

Turan, Kenneth. (1998) "Nutcase Noir and Geezer Noir," *Los Angeles Times* March 6: 1.

Turim, Maureen. (2005) "The Violence of Desire in Avant–Garde Films" in Jean Petrolle and Virginia Wright Wexman (eds) *Women and Experimental Filmmaking*. Urbana: University of Illinois Press. 71–90.

——(2003) "Personal Pronouncements in *I … You … He … She* and *Portrait of a Young Girl of the 1960s in Brussels*" in Gwendolyn Audrey Foster (ed.) *Identity and Memory: the films of Chantal Akerman*. Carbondale: Southern Illinois UP. 9–26.

——(1990) "Gentlemen Consume Blondes" in Patricia Erens (ed.) *Issues in Feminist Film Criticism*. Bloomington: Indiana UP. 101–11. Originally published in (1979) *Wide Angle* 1.1: 52–59.

Turner, Lynn. (2003) "Braiding Polyphony: *Je, tu, il, elle and lui*," *Performance Research* 8.1: 93–100.

V.S. (2000) "A Lesbian Critique of *Fire*" in John, Mary E.and Tejaswini Niranjana (eds) "The Controversy over *Fire*: a select dossier (Part II)" *Inter-Asian Cultural Studies* 1.3: 519–20.

Wadler, Joyce. (1981) "Susan Sarandon: rough edges and no lingerie" *Rolling Stone.* (May 28): 39.

Waldman, Diane and Janet Walker (1999) "Introduction" in *Feminism and Documentary.* Minneapolis: University of Minnesota Press. 1–35.

Ward, Jennifer K. (1995) "Enacting the Different Voice: *Christa Klages* and feminist history" *Women in German Yearbook* 11: 49–66.

Weiss, Andrea. (1994) "A Queer Feeling When I Look at You: Hollywood stars and lesbian spectatorship in the 1930s" in Diane Carson, Linda Dittmar, and Janice R. Welsch. (eds) *Multiple Voices in Feminist Film Criticism.* Minneapolis: University of Minnesota Press. 330–42. Originally published (1991) "A Queer Feeling When I Look at You: Hollywood stars and lesbian spectatorship in the 1930s" in Christine Gledhell (ed.) *Stardom: industry of desire.* London: Routledge. 283–99.

West, Joan M. and Dennis West. (2003) "Frida," *Cineaste* 28.2: 39–41.

Wexman, Virginia Wright. (1993) *Creating the Couple: love, marriage, and hollywood performance.* Princeton: Princeton UP.

——(1986) "The Critic as Consumer: film study in the university, *Vertigo*, and the film canon," *Film Quarterly* 39.3: 32–41.

White, Patricia. (1999) *Uninvited: classical Hollywood cinema and lesbian representability.* Bloomington: Indiana UP.

——(1998) "Feminism and Film" in John Hill and Pamela Church Gibson (eds) *The Oxford Guide to Film Studies.* London: Oxford UP. 117–31.

White, Susan. (1991) "Allegory and Referentiality: *Vertigo* and feminist film criticism," *MLN: Modern Language Notes* 106.5: 910–32.

Williams, Linda (2004) "Why I Did Not Want to Write this Essay," *Signs* 30.1, 1264–71.

——(1999) "Film Bodies: gender, genre, and excess" in Sue Thornham (ed.) *Feminist Film Theory.* New York: New York UP. 267–81. Originally published in (1991) *Film Quarterly* 44.4: 2–13.

——(1998) "Melodrama Revisited" in Nick Browne (ed.) *Refiguring American Film Genres: theory and history.* Berkeley: Universtity of California Press. 42–88.

——(1993) "Mirrors without Memories: truth, history, and the new documentary," *Film Quarterly* 46.3: 9–21.

——(1986) "Linda Williams Replies." *Cinema Journal* 25.2: 67.

——(1984) "'Something Else Besides a Mother': *Stella Dallas* and the maternal melodrama," *Cinema Journal* 24.1: 2–27.

Wollen, Peter. (1969) *Signs and Meanings in the Cinema.* Bloomington: Indiana UP.

Wood, Robin (1983) "Fear of Spying," *American Film* 7.1: 28–35.

Young, Lola. (1996) *Fear of the Dark: race, gender, and sexuality in the cinema.* London and New York: Routledge.

Zucker, Carole. (1990) "'I am Deitrich and Deitrich is Me': an investigation of performance style in *Morocco* and *Shanghai Express*" in Carole Zucker (ed.) *Making Visible the Invisible: an anthology of essays on film fcting.* Metuchen, NJ: Scarecrow Press. 255–94.

Index